British Literature 1640–1789:
A Critical Reader

Blackwell Critical Readers

1 Romanticism: A Critical Reader
Edited by Duncan Wu

2 Victorian Women Poets: A Critical Reader
Edited by Angela Leighton

3 British Literature 1640–1789: A Critical Reader
Edited by Robert DeMaria, Jr.

British Literature 1640–1789:

A Critical Reader

Edited by
Robert DeMaria, Jr.

First published 1999

2 4 6 8 10 9 7 5 3 1

Blackwell Publishers Inc.
350 Main Street
Malden, Massachusetts 02148
USA

Blackwell Publishers Ltd
108 Cowley Road
Oxford OX4 1JF
UK

Library of Congress Cataloging-in-Publication Data

British literature 1640–1789 : a critical reader / edited by Robert
DeMaria, Jr.
   p. cm.
   Includes bibliographical references and index.
   ISBN 0-631-19739-7 (acid-free paper). — ISBN 0-631-19741-9 (pbk.
: acid-free paper)
   1. English literature—18th century–History and criticism.
2. English literature—Early modern, 1500–1700—History and
criticism.   I. DeMaria, Robert.
   PR442.B65   1999
   820.9′005—dc21   98–33639
                                                  CIP

British Library Cataloguing in Publication Data

A CIP catalogue record for this book is available
from the British Library.

Typeset in 10.5 on 12 pt Monotype Garamond
by SetSystem Ltd, Saffron Walden, Essex
Printed in Great Britain by T.J. International, Padstow, Cornwall

This book is printed on acid-free paper

Contents

A Note on the Form of Reference   vii

Notes on Contributors   viii

Acknowledgments   xi

Introduction   1

1 *Areopagitica*, Censorship, and the Early Modern Public Sphere   13
   DAVID NORBROOK

2 Milton and the Fit Reader   40
   SHARON ACHINSTEIN

3 The Balance of Power in Marvell's "Horatian Ode"   69
   THOMAS M. GREENE

4 *Oroonoko*'s Blackness   86
   CATHERINE GALLAGHER

5 Lordly Accents: Rochester's Satire   105
   CLAUDE RAWSON

6 Dryden's "Anne Killigrew": Towards a New Pindaric Political Ode   114
   HOWARD WEINBROT

7 Ironic Monologue and "Scandalous *Ambo-dexter* Conformity" in Defoe's *The Shortest Way with the Dissenters* 126
D. N. DeLuna

8 Strange Complicities: Atheism and Conspiracy in *A Tale of A Tub* 142
Roger D. Lund

9 *The Rape of the Lock* as Miniature Epic 169
Helen Deutsch

10 Anne Finch: Gender, Politics, and Myths of the Private Self 186
Carol Barash

11 The Spirit of Ending in Johnson and Hume 204
Adam Potkay

12 Mary Leapor Laughs at the Fathers: Reading "Crumble-Hall" 218
Donna Landry

13 *O Lachrymarum Fons*: Tears, Poetry, and Desire in Gray 233
George E. Haggerty

14 The Culture of Travesty: Sexuality and Masquerade in Eighteenth-Century England 251
Terry Castle

15 Theater and Counter-Theater in Burke's *Reflections on the Revolution in France* 271
Frans De Bruyn

16 Cowper's Hares 287
David Perkins

17 Colonizing the Breast: Sexuality and Maternity in Eighteenth-Century England 302
Ruth Perry

18 Unparodying and Forgery: The Augustan Chatterton 333
Claude Rawson

Select Bibliography 348

Index 367

A Note on the Form of Reference

Most works included in the select bibliography are cited in the text in the briefest possible form. Where a page or line number is unambiguous, that alone appears in parentheses. Frequently, however, an author's name or a name and date are necessary for clarity. A few works (mostly those that are part of multi-volume editions) are cited with short titles. Works not included in the select bibliography are first cited in notes in full and thereafter in the text in the briefest possible form. The bibliography is comprised of critical and historical works of some general interest to students of eighteenth-century British literature as well as of editions of eighteenth-century works.

Contributors

Sharon Achinstein is Associate Professor of English at the University of Maryland, College Park. She is the author of *Milton and the Revolutionary Reader* (1994), editor of the journal *Women's Studies, Literature, Gender, and the English Revolution* (1994), and has written essays on Milton and seventeenth-century literature, culture, and politics. She is currently completing a book entitled *The Dissenting Muse: 1660–1740*.

Carol Barash is Associate Professor of English at Seton Hall. She is the author of *English Women's Poetry, 1649–1714: Politics, Community, and Linguistic Authority* (1996) and editor of the forthcoming Oxford edition of the poems of Anne Finch.

Terry Castle is the author of a number of books, including *Masquerade and Civilization: The Carnivalesque in Eighteenth-Century English Culture and Fiction* (1986) and *The Female Thermometer: Eighteenth-Century Culture and the Invention of the Uncanny* (1995). Her most recent projects have included an edition of Ann Radcliffe's *The Mysteries of Udolpho* (1998) and an anthology of lesbian-themed writing from the Renaissance to the present.

Frans De Bruyn is Professor of English, University of Ottawa. He is the author of *The Literary Genres of Edmund Burke* (1996). He is currently engaged in two research projects: a study of the Dutch cultural response to the South Sea Bubble and a book on georgic form and agricultural writing in the eighteenth century.

D. N. DeLuna is a lecturer in the Johns Hopkins Writing Seminars. Her contribution to this volume forms part of a book she is currently completing entitled *Defoe and the Business of Satire*.

Helen Deutsch is Associate Professor of English at UCLA. In addition to *Resemblance and Disgrace: Alexander Pope and the Deformation of Culture* (1996), excerpted here, she has published translations of Latin poetry, and essays on topics in eighteenth-century culture and beyond, stretching backward to Propertius and forward to *Twin Peaks*. She is currently co-editing a volume with Felicity Nussbaum tentatively titled: *"Defect": Engendering the Modern Body*, and working on a book on Samuel Johnson and the mind-body problem.

Catherine Gallagher is Professor of English at UC Berkeley. Her published books include *Nobody's Story: The Vanishing Acts of Women Writers in the Marketplace 1670–1820* (1994) and *The Industrial Reformation of English Fiction: Social Discourse and Narrative Form, 1832–1867* (1985).

Thomas M. Greene is Frederick Clifford Ford Professor Emeritus of English and Comparative Literature at Yale University.

George E. Haggerty is Associate Professor of English at UC Riverside. He is the author of *Gothic Fictions/Gothic Form* (1989) and *Professions of Desire: Lesbian and Gay Studies in Literature* (1995).

Donna Landry is Professor of English at Wayne State University. She is the author of *The Muses of Resistance: Laboring-Class Women's Poetry in Britain 1739–1796* (1990) and the editor, with Gerald Maclean, of *Materialist Feminisms* (1993) and the *Gayatri Spivak Reader* (1996).

Roger D. Lund is Professor of English at Le Moyne College, Syracuse, NY. He is the author of numerous essays on eighteenth-century literature and the editor of *The Margins of Orthodoxy: Heterodox Writing and Cultural Response, 1660–1750* (1995) and *Critical Essays on Daniel Defoe* (1997).

David Norbrook is Professor of English at the University of Maryland, College Park. He is the author of *Poetry and Politics in the English Renaissance* (1984) and of *Writing the English Republic: Poetry, Rhetoric and Politics, 1627–1660* (1999).

David Perkins is Marquand Professor of English and American Literature Emeritus at Harvard University. He is the author of several books including *A History of Modern Poetry* in two volumes (1976 and 1987) and the anthology

English Romantic Writers (2nd edn, 1995). His contribution to this volume, "Cowper's Hares," is one of a suite of essays dealing with attitudes to animals expressed in British literature around Cowper's time.

Ruth Perry, Professor of Literature at MIT, is the author of *Women, Letters, and the Novel* and *The Celebrated Mary Astell*, the editor of George Ballard's 1752 *Memoirs of Several Ladies of Great Britain*, and co-editor and theorist of a volume of essays on nurturing creativity, *Mothering the Mind*. She is currently finishing a history of kinship and the family in relation to the novel in England 1750–1810 and collecting her essays on Jane Austen.

Adam Potkay, Associate Professor of English at the College of William and Mary, is the author of *The Fate of Eloquence in the Age of Hume* and the editor, with Sandra Burr, of *Black Atlantic Writers of the Eighteenth Century: Living the New Exodus in England and the Americas*. He also serves on the editorial boards of the journal *Eighteenth-Century Life*, and *British Issues and Ideas, 1660–1820*, a new series of reprinted books and pamphlets. The article reprinted in this volume is part of a book manuscript on Samuel Johnson and David Hume in the Enlightenment.

Claude Rawson is Maynard Mack Professor of English at Yale University and Chairman of the Yale Boswell Editions. His books include *Henry Fielding and the Augustan Ideal under Stress, Gulliver and the Gentle Reader, Order from Confusion Sprung, Satire and Sentiment: 1660–1830*, and (edited, with H. B. Nisbet), *The Cambridge History of Literary Criticism. Volume 4: The Eighteenth Century*.

Howard D. Weinbrot is Ricardo Quintana Professor of English and William Freeman Vilas Research Professor at the University of Wisconsin, Madison. He has written several books and numerous articles concerning eighteenth-century British authors and genres, especially satire, Alexander Pope, and Samuel Johnson. He is especially concerned with the relationships among Anglo-classical and Anglo-French historical and cultural contexts. He has received fellowships from the National Endowment for the Humanities, the Guggenheim Foundation, and the Institute for Advanced Study, Princeton.

Acknowledgments

In selecting these essays I had the benefit of advice from many colleagues in the field of eighteenth-century British Literature, including John Bender, Donna Heiland, and John Richetti. As usual, I am also grateful to Vassar College, not least of all for supplying my excellent research assistant for this volume, Jennifer Deane.

The editor and publishers wish to thank the following for permission to use copyright material:

Cambridge University Press for material from Donna Landry, *The Muses of Resistance* (1990) pp. 107–19; and Howard Weinbrot, *Britannia's Issue* (1993) pp. 359–72;

Catherine Gallagher for "*Oroonoko*'s Blackness" in *Aphra Behn's Studies*, ed. Janet Todd (1996), Cambridge University Press, pp. 235–58;

Harvard University Press for material from Helen Deutsch, *Resemblance and Disgrace: Alexander Pope and the Deformation of Culture* (1996) pp. 40–74. Copyright © 1996 by the President and Fellows of Harvard College;

The Huntington Library for D. N. DeLuna, "Ironic Monologue and 'Scandalous *Ambo-dexter* Conformity'" in Defoe's *The Shortest Way with the Dissenters*," *Huntington Library Quarterly* 57 (1994) pp. 315–35;

The Johns Hopkins University Press for George E. Haggerty, "O Lachrymarum Fons," *Eighteenth-Century Studies*, 30 (1996) pp. 81–5; Thomas M. Greene, "The Balance of Power in Marvell's 'Horatian Ode,'" *English*

Literary History 60 (1993) pp. 379–96; Roger Lund, "Strange Complicities: Atheism and Conspiracy in *A Tale of a Tub*," *Eighteenth Century Life* 13 (1939) pp. 34–58; Adam Potkay, "The Spirit of Ending in Johnson and Hume," *Eighteenth Century Life* 16 (1992) pp. 153–66; David Perkins, "Cowper's Hares," *Eighteenth Century Life* 20 (1996) pp. 57–69; and Ruth Perry, "Colonizing the Breast: Sexuality and Maternity in Eighteenth-Century England," *Eighteenth Century Life* 16 (1992) pp. 185–213;

Oxford University Press for material from Carol Barash, *English Women's Poetry, 1649–1714* (1996) pp. 271–87. Copyright © Carol Barash, 1996; and Frans De Bruyn, *The Literary Genres of Edmund Burke* (1996) pp. 165–99. Copyright © Frans De Bruyn, 1996;

Oxford University Press for material from Terry Castle, *The Female Thermometer* (1995) pp. 82–100. Copyright © 1995 by Terry Castle;

Princeton University Press for material from Sharon Achinstein, *Milton and the Revolutionary Reader* (1994) pp. 199–223. Copyright © 1994 by Princeton University Press;

Claude Rawson for material from *Satire and Sentiment: 1660–1830* (1994) Cambridge University Press, pp. 3–11; and "Schoolboy Glee: The Brilliance of Chatterton's Parodies and his Augustan Models," *Times Literary Supplement*, May 6, 1994, pp. 3–4;

University of Minnesota Press for David Norbrook, "*Areopagitica*, Censorship, and the Early Modern Public Sphere" in *The Administration of Aesthetics: Censorship, Political Criticism, and the Public Sphere*, ed. Richard Burt (1994) pp. 3–33.

Every effort has been made to trace the copyright holders, but if any have been inadvertently overlooked the publishers will be pleased to make the necessary arrangement at the first opportunity.

Introduction

Taken as a group, the eighteen essays collected here exhibit a striking interest in re-establishing the historical contexts of literary performances. Since all the essays were first published in their present forms within the last ten years and since they represent some of the finest work in the field, it seems fair to say that their interest in historicizing literary texts is representative of a trend in the criticism of eighteenth-century British literature, if not in all literary studies. Of course, I have chosen essays that I personally think best, and I had a preference for essays that discuss the principal works in *British Literature 1640–1789: An Anthology*. This is not, therefore, a scientifically or randomly chosen sample of the enormous amount of criticism written on eighteenth-century literature in the last ten years. Nevertheless, among the best and most influential books and articles, I think the prominence of the historicizing impulse is clear. But what does it mean to historicize a text and what happens to the text so placed, or replaced, in its historical context?

One result of the effort of historical contexualizing is that theoretical considerations are muted. Take the fine essay by D. N. DeLuna on what Claude Rawson has called Defoe's "final solution" essay, *The Shortest Way with the Dissenters*. Like many of the critics represented in this volume, especially the younger ones among them, DeLuna finds that his historical view of the text diminishes the validity of many of the theoretical considerations that have grown up among Defoe's interpreters over the last fifty years. DeLuna says bluntly, "when the most pertinent historical context for reading the pamphlet is identified and its verbal disguises revealed, the work proves considerably less provocative on the plane of critical theory." DeLuna acknowledges readings that emphasize the ambiguity of Defoe's text, the unreliability of its narrator or any of the other textual features that make the work interesting as a self-consuming artifact. However, she points out that Defoe's artistic devices in the essay were deployed for a historically recoverable purpose: "in *The Shortest Way*, through the innovative device of the ironic monologue, [Defoe] created a two-pronged satire that attacks not only the High Church support of the bill [banning occasional conformity] but also the practice of occasional conformity." In other words, the theoretically sophisticated ambiguity or agitation of the text can be explained in terms of Defoe's own complex opinion of occasional conformity (the practice of Church of England religious rites for the sake of qualifying for participation in state-run institutions). On the one hand, Defoe deplored the intolerance of the government in denying privileges to Dissenters like himself, and he hated to see the new regime tightening the loopholes through which Dissenters could avoid penalties for their faith; on the other hand, like his speaker in *The Shortest Way*, he despised the "Scandalous *Ambodexter* Conformity" practiced by those Dissenters who were unwilling to sacrifice privileges for the sake of their religious convictions. The question for more theoretically-oriented critics and for those whose main objective was to explicate Defoe's art, was whether or not Defoe sacrificed satiric art to his polemical objective, which was narrowly seen to be an attack on the bill against occasional conformity. Seeing Defoe's political views in more detail and with greater historical clarity, DeLuna asks the opposite question; she asks whether Defoe has sacrificed his polemical objectives to innovative artistic techniques. This rephrasing shows the emphasis in DeLuna's thinking, and this emphasis, I believe, is representative of the thinking in much of the best literary criticism of the last ten years.

Despite her change of emphasis and her depression of theoretical concerns, DeLuna is still interested in the textual details with which she is confronted as a reader. This is true of the other historicizing critics in this volume, and it is one of the features that distinguishes their work from an older kind of historicism that prevailed in literary criticism before the flood. In many of the articles in this volume there is a productive contest between theorizing and historicizing, and this is nowhere more true than in the pieces devoted to Milton and the British Civil War.

David's Norbrook's essay on *Areopagitica*, for example, begins by adjusting the theoretical spectacles through which he thinks it is appropriate to view Milton's great essay on the subject of licensing and the liberty of the press. By seeing the essay in the context of Milton's mixed and complex sentiments, both about freedom of speech and about the revolutionary government for which he worked, Norbrook shifts our vision of the work from an old-fashioned liberal, to a more recent, revisionist, Foucauldian perspective, and then to a Habermasian perspective. That is, he sees the work neither as a precursor to modern interpretations of the American first amendment (freedom of speech), nor as a founding moment in the discourse of an individualistic, capitalist discourse of authorship and publication. Such revisionist views make Milton a Foucauldian *avant la lettre*, but in fact, Norbrook finds, he may be more a Habermasian *avant la lettre*. Milton was not arguing for a privatized literary production; in fact, "an ethos of the public spirit" guided his work. Norbrook's reason for the shift is in his superior sense of context: "The liberal cult of *Areopagitica*, which takes sentences from the work out of context and tends to decontextualize the work as a whole, has long been under attack, but some of the recent revisionist views are also insufficiently contextualized."

Norbrook's superior contextualization depends upon his knowledge of Milton's intellectual and social milieu, as well as an appreciation of Milton's complex views about his own government. (How could we ever have believed that they would be any less complex than our own views of the governments we support?) Norbrook makes good use, for example, of Samuel Hartlib's criticisms of *Areopagitica*, which reveal some of the ways in which the piece is designed (and also in some ways fails) to achieve one of their common aims, "to glorify and embody a revival of public spirit." However, like Hartlib's criticism itself, Norbrook's reasoning about *Areopagitica* constantly returns to the text. Hartlib complained about Milton's highflown style, and Norbrook draws attention to Milton's language in this instance and finds, *pace* Hartlib, that in his style of speech Milton embodies a republican rhetoric, just as he embodies a republican politics: "Milton's display of rhetorical copia at once celebrates and exemplifies the 'flowry crop of knowledge and new light sprung up and yet springing up daily in ths City.'" In another instance, Norbrook explains how Milton's figures of speech lend shades of meaning to his position; he was not in favor of female suffrage, as were some of his colleagues, but he describes the household as a kind of public sphere or miniature polis, in which women are full citizens, and that is a step on the way to their civic empowerment. Examining another aspect of Milton's text, Norbrook finds the Athenian spirit of the work further embodied in the epigraph that Milton chose from Euripides' *The Suppliant Women*. He shows how these verses would be read in context as a defense of free speech and of democracy: "At a time when Parliament's cause was still officially monarchist ... Milton's allusion was cautious; it was nonetheless pointed, turning his own title page from an authoritarian piazza [decked with the imprimaturs of a state-run publishing establishment] to an embodiment of a classical forum." As this forum is essentially different from an authoritarian piazza, it is also different from a privatized patio or balcony on which the individual can sing to whomever may be willing to listen. This view of *Areopagitica* has the virtue of seeing

Milton's later role as licensor as something less than a radical departure from his famous early work. It was a retreat but not a departure because, although Milton countenanced the suppression of works calling for the overthrow of the parliamentary government of 1649, he appealed to *Areopagitica* in support of publishing works considered heretical. Founding and supporting the republic, with all that it would mean for free speech, was his primary goal. Norbrook's conclusions concern Milton's views and his intentions, but his way of arriving at them is enmeshed in the text, and, in the end, his method, throws new light on the aesthetic object as well as its intentions.

This same inter-involvement of text and context, aesthetic form and polemical intention, is apparent in Sharon Achinstein's book on Milton. In the chapter entitled "Milton and the Fit Reader," only part of which I reprint here, Achinstein begins where Norbrook leaves off – with the historical passage of a parliamentary licensing act, the Treason Act of May 14, 1649, which actually made authors liable to execution. This serves as part of the context for considering the old question of whether or not Milton was, as William Blake said, "of the Devil's party." This is a question that has attracted brilliant and extensive theoretical treatment, most notably perhaps by William Empson in *Milton's God* and by Stanley Fish in *Surprised by Sin*. Achinstein is highly conscious of these approaches, and, in the end, her conclusions are not radically different from Fish's. However, her approach to the question begins with a historical treatment of the Parliament of Hell allegory, a favorite device of Royalists anxious to avoid prosecution for treason under the Act of May 14, 1649. In *Paradise Lost*, particularly in Books I and II, Milton crosses this genre, and this makes Satan look like the Royalists' allegorical version of Cromwell. For example, Milton's presentation of the devilish Counsel resembles the worldview of the anti-tolerationist pamphlet *The Devil in his Dumps*, and there are numerous correspondences between other Parliament of Hell allegories and *Paradise Lost*. Taking account of this context, Achinstein concludes that, "in the first two books of *Paradise Lost*, Milton agreed with the royalist judgment on the leaders of the English Revolution; the leaders had become 'thyself not free, but to thyself enthralled,' as Abdiel had taunted Satan (*Paradise Lost* 6.181). But Milton disagreed with the Royalists about who was responsible for that fact. While the Royalists blamed Satan and praised God for his victory in 1660, Milton blamed the individual men who had failed so miserably in their pursuit of liberty."

Arriving at such a conclusion is not easy; it requires Milton's so-called "fit readers." These superior individuals must be skilled not only in hermeneutic techniques and Christian doctrine, as earlier commentators, like Fish, have said, but they must also know the history of contemporary politics. Like Fish, Achinstein sees Milton's text as a test, but she perceives more sharply the importance on the exam of recent political history: "One of the poem's essential meanings is to train fit readers in the context of contemporary politics.... Learning how to read is no easy project, and Milton scatters hard-to-read passages all over his text as a means to test his own readers' strenuousness, and to prepare them for the more difficult task of reading history."

Regardless of whether its final goals are political or aesthetic (we don't have to choose one to the exclusion of the other), the difficulties of Milton's text – its crossings with genres dominated by works with different political intentions and relatively simplistic, allegorical meanings – make it a fit introduction to a literary period in which satire, irony, and masquerade are predominant forms. Despite Milton's wish "to justify the ways of God to men," his text is full of problems, and only some men will solve them. In a way, Andrew Marvell is the first post-Miltonic poet; he deserves this title partly because he takes as one of his principal subjects the peculiar kind of irony that Milton generated by treating age-old poetic topics in a contemporary political context viewed from a particular, though complex, sort of exile. Marvell's poetry is not only often ironic; it is also about the trope of irony. Thomas Greene speaks about this in terms of Marvell's encounters with the "uncanny": "The Cromwell of the Horatian Ode embodies a darker version of the inscrutable in human affairs.... His inscrutability is the source of that uncanny quality which history has assumed with the advent of Cromwell; it teems with unreadable symbols. To this uncanny text of events Marvell brings his own deliberately dry and dispassionate art." The poetic problem and the political problem are inseparable as Marvell tries to address in cool Horatian form the uncanny events of Cromwell's reign, particularly the strangest, least assimilable event of all, the execution of Charles I. "Thus we might most profitably read the Horatian Ode as an attempt to bring to bear upon the demonic uncanny those devices of poetry which render the inchoate coherent and the illegible accessible." In what ways Marvell succeeds in this attempt and in what ways he leaves the contest in doubt are the subjects of Greene's fine judgments as a reader.

For obvious reasons, poetry concerned with national politics is suitable for historicizing critical treatment, but neither politics nor history have been limited, especially in the past decade, to matters of government. Milton could see the household as a miniature polis, but contemporary critics have expanded the relation and eliminated the disproportion between the domestic and the public sphere: sexual politics are politics, or even, the sexual is the political, we seem to say. Not surprisingly, then, numerous essays in this volume historicize the sexual politics in literary works of the period. In broad terms, the story they tell overall concerns the changing relations between Milton's miniature, household polis and the governmental, legal polis conducted mainly by men in the corridors of power. Mediating this relationship, of course, is the public sphere in which women could participate, not so much, perhaps, as coffee-house denizens but as an increasingly prominent part of the community of British readers. In *Resemblance and Disgrace*, for example, Helen Deutsch discusses the way that Pope turns the tables on Milton and other epic writers and miniaturizes the public world. He does so, of course, to place it in the female sphere and, to be literally historical for a moment, to court a female audience. His signal achievement in this way is in his translation of the *Iliad*, but he extends the effort and completes it in *The Rape of the Lock*. Helen Deutsch reads "Pope's *Iliad* against the *Rape* (and vice versa), situating both poems in relation to the potentially transformative perspective of an audience and a world of trivial things that Pope linked to the feminine.... Epic imitation and original mock-epic thus exist in a mutual play of transformation which makes of each poem, and its author, a beautiful monstrosity, an improper trifle of eternally shifting size and scale." Deutsch compares Pope's work of miniaturization with the increased interest in museums and collections in Europe in the eighteenth century and with the attitude or mentality of "curiosity" that they fed and nourished.

To see the greater world of epic strife and national glory in the lesser world of women is also part of Dryden's work in his famous "Ode to Anne Killigrew." In a very small but representative portion of his ambitious and wide-ranging book *Britannia's Issue*, Howard Weinbrot begins by dealing with the opinion that Dryden was discreetly mocking Anne Killigrew by writing such a grand ode about such a short and, finally, not grandly distinguished life. But Weinbrot finds the Ode working in a genre that "encourages symbolic linking of the subject to the gods, the sovereign, the nation, and the family. However valuable Anne is in her own right, she is yet more valuable as a hub of positive mythic and patriotic associations." Hence the grandeur of the Ode is justified. What we have here, Weinbrot perceives, is "the noble domestication of the noble ode." In Weinbrot's view, "Anne Killigrew is not merely a portrait painter; she is the modern female Noah whose art preserves God's monarch as surely as the Old Testament Noah preserved God's people." Moreover, Noah is associated, especially through his grandson Gomer, with the origin of the British race. Thus, Anne Killigrew is justly magnified, and the domestic sphere reflects the imperial realm without the irony that is inevitable in Pope's portrait of Belinda's mock heroics.

But how do women writing in this period imagine relations between their sphere and the public world of men? This is a question that students of the eighteenth century are much better prepared to answer now than they were twenty years ago. Indeed, the biggest difference between *British Literature 1640–1789: An Anthology* and its predecessors is the vastly increased presence of women writers. In this *Critical Reader* Catherine Gallagher, Carol Barash, and Donna Landry speak, respectively, about the literature and literary careers of Aphra Behn, Ann Finch, and Mary Leapor. In each case the politics of the life and works are intertwined, and the enterprise of publication is the simultaneously social and aesthetic activity that binds them. It is an interesting fact of recent cultural history that the increased interest in women writers coincides with the increased interest in the historical contexts of literature, and it would be a nice question for an historian of literary criticism to decide which interest (if either) preceded the other.

In "*Oroonoko*'s Blackness" Catherine Gallagher finds that the extraordinary blackness of Behn's most famous character is first of all, a trope for printing and through printing for the kind of luminous authorship she wished to achieve: "There is, then, a close connection between Behn's sustained authorial presence in this book, unprecedented in her works, and the black hero's lustre; as the story moves forward, a mutual polishing takes place in which narrator and hero buff off each other's obscurity. Although in the beginning Oroonoko had the misfortune 'to fall in an obscure world, that afforded only a female pen to celebrate his fame,' by the end the narrator presumes to hope 'the reputation of my pen is considerable enough to make his glorious name to survive to all ages.'" By means of authorship Behn remakes her social identity, and the particular way in which she remakes it has of course political meaning. The same blackness that stands for Behn's luminous authorship also stands in the book for kingship, Gallagher argues, and, paradoxically, for commodification. (Oronooko's blackness is a sign of his royalty and, from the Europeans' point of view, of his slavery.) All three concepts, however, are for Behn disembodied abstractions. Her hero literally disfigures himself in order to assume the intangible, mythic life of a divine-right monarch, and she achieves an ideal authorial existence. This social exchange, according to Gallagher, recapitulates the ideal social order of Robert Filmer's *Patriarcha* in which the king is divine and his subjects are commodities.

In the most important publication of her literary career another Jacobite female writer suppressed her earlier acknowledgments of Aphra Behn and turned away from the public sphere of politics. According to Carol Barash, "The publishing of *Miscellany Poems* in 1713 marks the single most important moment in Anne Finch's construction of herself as a poet of emotional rather than political and religious extremity." Barash fills in the historical reasons for Finch's change (the Finches' security in Winchelsea and their wish to disassociate themselves from more active Jacobites, who, with the impending death of Queen Anne, were stirring), but *"Miscellany Poems*, of course, mentions none of this, but subtly and repeatedly reworks a myth of female community initiated by Katherine Philips ... into a politically oppositional community of privately pro-Stuart women." With this inward turn, Barash asserts, "Finch creates the patterns that will dominate female lyric poetry for the next century and a half: a domestic world that opens out to and fuses with nature; female community as both a retreat from and a threat to the demands and assumptions of compulsory heterosexuality; linguistic difference – in the senses of both negativity and opposition – as an empowering but also potentially suicidal trope for the powers of a markedly female imagination."

However, political exile tells on literary expression in the form of irony, even when the genre in question is serious and celebratory. This was true even for so serious and lofty a poet as Milton, and it was true for many women writers. For me personally, the discovery of how much satirical poetry was written by women came as one of the most welcome discoveries of my efforts to make a new anthology of the period. Others have probably known this for some time. As Donna Landry points out, Mary Leapor's *Crumble-Hall* belongs to the tradition of English country-house poetry that runs from Aemilia Lanyer's *Cooke-ham* and Ben Jonson's "Penshurst," to Andrew Marvell's *Appleton House* and Pope's *Epistle to Burlington*, and beyond Leapor to Gray's "On Lord Holland's Seat" and Crabbe's *Silford Hall*. Like its predecessors, Leapor's poem celebrates the country house, but she explores different parts of it than earlier poets. She not only exemplifies the tendency of women's poetry to explore, in Barash's words, "a domestic world that opens out to and fuses with nature," she is also ironic and satirical. Leapor "forces us to re-read Pope's poem [and other predecessors in the genre] through the lens of her own, and to reread it in a different, more democratic and gender conscious way." Leapor trumps Pope's gentle mockery of Timon's materialistic approach to his studies and sends up both her economic and her literary masters with one bold stroke.

Since Mary Leapor lived only to the age of 26, toiled as a cook's maid in the kitchen of "Crumble-Hall," and possessed only a handful of books, it was surely difficult for her to guess how her life and works related to larger changes in the construction of gender and sexuality in British culture. Indeed, no one lost "in the puzzle of business" (to use Bacon's phrase) has the perspective to see very clearly the larger changes in which they are, willy-nilly, participating. The privilege of achieving that elevated perspective is left to posterity. Two of the most perceptive writers on the changing sexual polity of the eighteenth century are Terry Castle and Ruth Perry. In what may be the two best known essays that I have selected these writers respectively treat changes occurring in the middle and towards the end of the century. By focusing on the strange and unusually popular institution of the masquerade, Castle recovers the "lost world of eighteenth-century urban culture." She sees the "masquerade as a representative institution – a magic lantern, as it were, in which we may see illuminated the new erotic self-consciousness of the age." Its reflections in literature and in private life show much of what was so often concealed in earlier accounts of the period. Ruth Perry's "magic lantern" is not a social event but social constructions of "the maternal breast" which "served as the locus – both symbolic and real – of [a] new appropriation of women's bodies for motherhood and for the state." In the literature of the long eighteenth century Perry finds an advancing de-sexualization of women: "The rakish heroines of Restoration drama, the self-advertising amorous adventurers of the love-and-intrigue novels of Aphra Behn, Delarivière Manley, and Eliza Haywood, and the freewheeling protagonists of Daniel Defoe's *Moll Flanders* and *Roxana* stand on one side of this cultural divide, while on the other side are those latter-day paragons of virtue, Evelina, Sidney Bidulph, and Emmeline, as well as Samuel Richardson's heroines – Pamela, Clarissa, and Harriet Byron – each one arguably more sexually repressed and sexually repressive than the one before." This change in the literature represents for Perry the success of a "belief system whose tenets included the following: that women's essential nature was to be mothers; that men's rights in women's bodies extended to their reproductive functions and, indeed, that men's ascendancy over women was based on women's 'natural propensity' for motherhood; that maternal feeling was antithetic to sexual desire; and that men's heterosexual desire was an immature expression of the ultimate desire to procreate and to 'have' a family."

If "family values" predominated in public expressions of culture by the end of the century, the sexually transgressive culture of the masquerade was certainly not extinguished. In fact, in its coexistence with an aggressively promoted domesticity, it was beginning to take its modern forms. George E. Haggerty's article on Thomas Gray is a contribution to the growing body of work that focuses on hitherto unnoticed instances of same-sex desire in classic works of British literature. However, since Gray seems sometimes quite overt about his feelings, what Haggerty seeks to explain is not how Gray "kept his sexuality hidden, but rather how he could write it so large as to make it indistinguishable from values that were celebrated in the culture at large." Although "sexuality" had no currency as a term in the eighteenth-century, some aspects of what it describes were indicated in the very popular term "sensibility." Haggerty "queers" the term "sensibility." In the experience of "men of feeling," like Gray and his schoolmates, Horace Walpole and Richard West, says Haggerty, "we may trace the origins of (late twentieth-century) gay sensibility, with its open secrets, its spectacles of confession, its giddy masquerades, and its moments of deep and painful loss."

In a way, the culture of late eighteenth-century Britain was engaged in a debate over how to view such "giddy masquerades." Were they to be celebrated as expressions of freedom from confining social rules and roles? Or were they to be denounced as outbreaks of dangerous, transgressive behavior? Although he was writing on high state politics, and certainly not on sexual preference, Edmund Burke himself can be seen as contributing to the debate about masquerades, and this may show one of the innumerable ways in which the sexual and the political are inextricably involved. As Frans De Bruyn reads it, Burke's *Reflections on the Revolution in France* tries to put down "spurious, upstart attempts to refigure the Revolution as a lyric, comic celebration . . ." When *Reflections* is "resituated in the historical discourse of its time, its tone of magisterial authority gives way to one of strenuous striving and debate – a debate immersed in the contemporary, historically specific discourse symbolized by the Hanoverian calendar" of theatrical state events, such as the celebration of the Restoration, the Glorious Revolution, and the accession of George I. Burke sees Price and other members of private clubs, with their own calendars of state, newly rubricated on July 14, as posing an important threat to the standing order of society. They have developed a kind of "counter-theater," and for Burke their carnivalesque, saturnalian play of the crowd is no longer a release or safety valve for exuberant common feeling but a true threat to English society as he knew it.

Although there is a correspondence between the imagery in his critique of Dr. Price (and other celebrants of July 14) and the imagery of the critique of sexually transgressive cultural practices, Burke was not writing about sex. It is of course a mistake to believe that every cultural practice and every critique is about sex or politics or both, but cultural studies are now so prevalent that I find myself obliged to state the obvious fact that religious questions occupied the minds of many eighteenth-century writers. In some ways this aspect of the historical context has become the most foreign and difficult to recover of all others. The nuances of Christian doctrine over which eighteenth-century thinkers worried are increasingly difficult to perceive in a world where most forms of Christianity strain to be ecumenical, and agnosticism, if not atheism, is the default substitute for any sort of belief among intellectuals. Roger Lund shows how different and how much more complex the landscape of religious thought was at the time that Swift wrote *A Tale of a Tub*. He connects Swift with Irenaeus in earlier times and with Ralph Cudworth and Henry More in his own; like his forerunners, Swift is an encyclopedist of error, and he "accuses all his targets of atheism, through a kind of guilt by association." To perceive his conflation of various errors into the grand error of atheism we have to apply historical spectacles because succeeding intellectual history has, in effect, taken Swift's satire literally and substituted mere atheism for the full spectrum of religious errors and heresies that Swift descried.

Our tendency to round off our sense of the religious views of eighteenth-century writers – to put them in one or another of a very few camps – is the target of Adam Potkay's examination of Hume's essay "Of the Immortality of the Soul" and Johnson's *Rasselas*, the penultimate chapter of which is devoted to a discussion of the soul. Potkay says, "we might expect Johnson and Hume to espouse opposing points of view. Yet their opposition is, I dare say, more distinctly apparent to the casual than to the careful reader of their texts. For despite their pat differences, Johnson and Hume's *methods* of exposition – and hence, I will argue, their underlying intentions – actually converge. That is, a similarly conceived ambiguity animates the discussion of the soul in both *Rasselas* and "Of the Immortality of the Soul." Neither text declares itself wholeheartedly for or against the prospect of immortality, much as many readers would be pleased to have them do so." It sounds here as though Potkay is moving back in time and using aesthetic considerations to replace the old historicism. But his essay is animated throughout by the spirit of inquiry that inspires recent interest in historical contexts – a dissatisfaction with received answers and a wish to look at the facts for oneself. And, like the best of the recent historicists, Potkay recognizes that the text itself is one of the relevant facts of historical interpretation.

Perhaps the most startlingly eloquent interpreter of eighteenth-century texts is Claude Rawson. His two short pieces of criticism in this volume project his inimitable power of fashioning phrases that are peculiarly suited to describing the experience of reading the texts he treats. He too uses historical information, like the possibility that Rochester affected a slight stutter and information on the seizure of a parcel of dildoes by the London tax officials, but these are always merely scaffolding for the next assault on reaching a "true" reading of the text. When he speaks of a poem's "extraordinary thrust of jeering incandescence" or a its "hyperbolic fantastication" Rawson is reporting what he hears after tuning his ears to the accents of a speech that requires historical recovery to be heard in any detail at all. So attuned is Rawson to the sounds of eighteenth-century verse that he hears its inflections in Chatterton's verse where others, less attuned, have heard merely intimations of a dialect that only gained currency in the decades after the death of the "amazing whelp." Flying in the face of most modern interpreters, Rawson points out that "the most immediately arresting thing about Chatterton's work is, in fact, his power and fluency in modern English and in 'Augustan' literary modes."

The one essay in this volume that I have not yet mentioned is simply enititled "Cowper's Hares." It is by David Perkins, the senior statesman of this group of critics, some of whom are forty years his junior. Moreover, Perkins is not doing much here that he was not doing earlier in his career, either in method or in tone. But anyone can see how easily this essay sits in the company of seventeen others that are largely concerned with the "new" project of historicizing literary works. "The cultural history of [William] Cowper's time" is his subject here, and Perkins tells us about the features of hares that may have increased Cowper's well-known interest and, finally, his identification with them. Perkins then moves outward to discuss Cowper's views on the animal kingdom in general and the very interesting ways in which these views represent his feelings about himself as a social, sexual, and religious being. The essay explains something about Cowper's sexual "culture" and so deserves to be called a contribution to "cultural studies." It also teaches us to read Cowper's many short animal poems, as well as his epic *Task*. It is witty, urbane, informative writing, like the best work of the eighteenth or any other century.

I started this introduction by proposing a kind of antithesis between the demands of history and those of aesthetically oriented criticism. In consideration of the work I've chosen, I find the antithesis tends to break down. This volume of essays is clearly on the side of history, but the best historical work of literary criticism returns to aesthetic concerns lest its trove of facts become the "mouse-eaten records" of the historian in Sir Philip Sidney's *Apologie for Poetrie*. Twenty-five years ago, to suggest that criticism is a kind of poetry, as I've obviously just done, was to stress its value as hypothesis and its freedom from the so-called "facts" of literary history. To make the same suggestion today, I think, is only to say that criticism can be historical and still be interpretive, and even beautiful. To put this in terms of the eighteenth-century's favorite critical treatise, *Ars Poetica*, the best criticism instructs and pleases.

1

Areopagitica, Censorship, and the Early Modern Public Sphere

DAVID NORBROOK

Milton's *Areopagitica* is buried under the weight of its own celebrity: it has turned into a quarry of fine and somewhat empty phrases, legitimizing the belief that in modern liberal societies a near-universal freedom of speech has been attained. Recently, however, there has been a sharp reaction. The liberal cult of *Areopagitica* is criticized as mystifyingly idealist, positing a complete autonomy of the discursive subject in abstraction from material constraints on discourse. Recent work on *Areopagitica* has been strongly influenced by Michael Foucault's insistence that universal moral principles are always effects of power. Foucault takes a sharply revisionist line on the traditional values of a progressive politics. "One makes war to win, not because it is just": in this "Nietzschean" analysis, there can be no question of progress toward social justice, merely a random succession of forms of violence, each of which will legitimize itself in moralistic terms.[1] It is not surprising that Foucault should adopt a mordantly critical view of the belief in progress toward freedom of expression. If the ideal of a completely uncensored, unconstrained discourse is an illusion, then the emergence of the liberal campaigns against censorship can be seen as an ideological strategy to reinforce the idea of a pure, private, autonomous subject. As Foucault provocatively puts it, individual authorship emerged only when authors were subject to punishment. Censorship created the liberty that then protested against it: no mutilation, no Milton.[2] And in fact Milton supported some forms of censorship.[3] Despite the claims of autonomy, it is argued, what were really at issue were the demands of an increasingly individualistic, capitalist economic system. *Areopagitica* can be read as a founding moment of this discourse, with its recurrent parallels between ideas and merchandise and its vigorous defense of the rights of the author against external intervention.[4]

These revisionist readings of *Areopagitica*, however, have some serious limitations. The Foucauldians' iconoclasm, salutary as it can be, has often been manifested in a very one-sided way.[5] In reacting against the liberal model (which, however, is often caricatured), recent critics have come up with a rigidly deterministic model of the links between knowledge and power. The transition from the Stuart monarchy to the republic is seen not as the product of popular political agency but as determined from above by a state whose powers appear more massive and irresistible than those of the Hegelian *Geist*.[6] The phenomenon of political opposition is rendered a priori impossible by the dependence of knowledge on power. Foucauldian theory has thus fallen in with a very differently motivated form of revisionism, with the claim by certain political historians that prerevolutionary England was a world of patronage and clientage in which critical political thought was virtually unknown. Censorship, then, was not a serious problem because there was no serious pressure to trangress the limits of traditional thought, and in any case, censorship restrictions were far less draconian than Milton claims in *Areopagitica*[7] Milton's pamphlet thus emerges as the product of a personal grievance rather than part of a common political agency.

There is, I believe, a certain irony in the readings of *Areopagitica* that have resulted: *Areopagitica* itself challenges the very kinds of split between public and private, between power and knowledge, that are currently ascribed to it.[8] This is not to say that Milton is a Foucauldian *avant la lettre*. But perhaps, as Donald Guss has suggested, there is a certain validity in the anachronism of seeing him as a Habermasian *avant la lettre*. For Habermas has tried to develop a theory of the links between knowledge and power that would avoid the reductiveness of Foucauldian discourse, offering a model of power as cooperative as well as merely agonistic, criticizing the instrumental rationality of one mode of Enlightenment thought while still locating spaces for critical and reflective thought that is capable of some degree of autonomy. It is not my purpose here to offer a defense of Habermas's theories in general, which raise many problems; the status of his putative "ideal speech situation" has been much questioned. It is worth recalling, however, that the concept originated in a historical survey that specifically connected an ideal of unconstrained communication with concrete material and political contexts. I shall try to show that Habermas's model of the "bourgeois public sphere" opens up a more adequate historical contextualization of *Areopagitica* and that one reason for this is a certain interplay between Habermas's theories and Renaissance rhetorical and political theory.

It must be said at once that *The Structural Transformation of the Public Sphere* is not as it stands a reliable historical guide; it needs a great deal of qualification and supplementation with more recent work. On the other hand, its publication had a theoretical as well as a historical impact.

Habermas attempts to qualify the extremely dark picture of Enlightenment rationality presented by Adorno and Horkheimer in *Dialectic of Enlightenment*, tracing the emergence of a communicative rationality alongside a more narrowly instrumental rationality. His sense of the political issues at stake was sharpened by disquiet at the political ambience of another important critique of the Enlightenment, Heidegger's *Letter on Humanism*, which also appeared in 1947, and adroitly located the blame for the century's misfortunes on the "humanism" of the Enlightenment rather than on the Nazi reaction against its principles. Habermas was disturbed far earlier than poststructuralist theorists by the politics of the enormously influential *Letter*, by the way in which Heidegger had "stepped on stage after the War, like a phoenix from the ashes" in a "felicitously de-Nazified" form (Dews 1986: 159). *Structural Transformation* ends with an account of the commodification of twentieth-century discourse not so different from his predecessors', but it does attempt to provide a more nuanced narrative of the process.

In doing so, the book can be accused of giving an idealized history of the early modern bourgeoisie, who are presented as establishing a space for critical inquiry that would be unconstrained by traditional power interests, a mediating area between civil society and state.[9] While Habermas certainly notes the underlying economic constraints on the public sphere, his highly rationalistic portrait of the bourgeoisie fails to acknowledge the strong religious motivations behind the emergence of the public sphere in England. As a result, he oversimplifies its origins, dating them to the years 1694–5 on the basis of three criteria: parliamentary government, the collapse of licensing for the press, and the formation of the Bank of England. The first two of these conditions, however, had been temporarily fulfilled fifty years earlier, in the period of the English Revolution – a historical phenomenon of which Habermas makes no mention. Whatever its underlying economic determinants, the ideological motivation of these developments had been to a considerable degree religious rather than secular. Jonathan Scott has pointed out that the seventeenth century was "a century of disaster for European protestantism, which was reduced in its course to the fringes of the continent, and from 50 percent to under 20 percent of its total area" (1992: 8). The powerful pressure for parliamentary control of public affairs and for public discussion was fueled in the first instance by the fear that the English monarchy could not be trusted to resist that process, but was on the contrary likely to be complicit in it.[10] Those fears could on occasion outweigh traditional anxieties about "popularity." Milton's vindication of the freedom of the press needs in the first instance to be seen in the jumpily defensive context of this European ideological struggle, rather than of a serenely confident, "liberal humanist" belief in inevitable progress. By the end of the century there had been a certain secularization that allowed

Habermas to emphasize economic factors in the fully emergent public sphere. It may be questioned, however, whether that secularization ever entirely superseded the more directly religious motivations for the maintenance of a public sphere.

Despite these limitations, Habermas's public-sphere model does have the merit of making connections between areas that have often remained in different institutional compartments – the development of Parliament, political theory, literary history, and the study of the mass media. Such a global approach brings out phenomena that have been underplayed in revisionist historiography. The reaction against "grand narratives," though often presented as a modest refusal of authoritarian totalizing, may in fact prove obfuscatory, condemning such discrete analyses to remain isolated and atomized; only a more global approach that is responsive to political agency can make sense of their interrelations. If one takes a synchronic cross section through England in its unparliamentary moments, one ends up with something like the paradigm of the revisionists and some new historicists, a pre-Enlightenment world of bodily submission. If, however, like some recent historians one takes a close look at periods of parliamentary crisis, there emerges a very different picture of a society in conflict, in which agents are consciously collaborating to contest a loss of popular control of key decisions. There was a significant expansion in the political public sphere, especially from the 1620s onward, an emergent civil society whose means of communication – reports of parliamentary debates, newsletters, satires, and so on – circulated horizontally, cutting across the vertical power structures emanating from the court. The electorate significantly expanded, and elections became increasingly ideologically charged.[11] This process culminated in the political opening of the 1640s. By 1649 the journalist Daniel Border could write that in the reign of Queen Elizabeth, men were

> rather guided by the tradition of their Fathers, than by acting principles in reason and knowledge: But to the contrary in these our dayes, the meanest sort of people are not only able to write &c. but to argue and discourse on matters of highest concernment; and thereupon do desire, that such things which are most remarkable, may be truly committed to writing, and made publique.[12]

Recent research bears out Habermas's analysis of growing pressure for a political public sphere – what a contemporary described as a *"publick* and *communicative spirit."*[13] The steady revaluation of the traditional low estimate of "public opinion" can be traced in Milton's striking claim that "opinion ... is but knowledge in the making" (554).

While permitting a global perspective, Habermas's model does avoid a simple teleology: it can be adapted to account for the massively uneven development of the public sphere in the seventeenth century and beyond. It is not the case that after 1640, or after 1695, there suddenly was a securely established public sphere. On the contrary, there was a continuing political struggle to open up or to restrict its emergence. The newspaper press of the 1640s was gradually checked first by the republic and then by Cromwell before being dealt a coup de grâce by Charles II. The electorate expanded steadily up to the 1640s, underwent restrictions under Cromwell, and went through innumerable fluctations down to the Whig ascendancy and beyond. Triennial Parliaments were gained and then lost. As Habermas declares at the end of his book, the contest for a fully articulate public sphere is still continuing as we face what he terms a neofeudal era of media barons; and the British Charter 88 movement is currently campaigning for the fulfillment of some demands first made by the Levellers 340 years ago.

Habermas's model potentially permits a more nuanced narrative of modernity and the public sphere than those readings that find a sudden transmutation around the middle of the seventeenth century. And while it unduly downplays religious factors, it does open up secular elements in the development of the public sphere – and in Milton's discourse in *Areopagitica* – that deserve fuller attention. Habermas pointed the way toward complicating the stereotyped notions of Renaissance individualism and bourgeois humanism that are still found in many current narratives of early modern subjectivity.[14] There is a significant ambiguity in the term *bourgeois* or *Bürger*: it can be variously translated as "bouregois," an economic category concerned with the private negotiations of civil society, or as "citizen," a political category opening to the public sphere. Habermas draws attention to our need for a history of the citizen as well as of the bourgeois.

Certain sections of the bourgeoisie in the early modern period were intensely engaged with public issues. One reason was that they sought legitimation in an emulation of the classical political world. That history was already being written by 1962; significantly, two of its most prominent pioneers were exiles from Nazi Germany, Hans Baron and Hannah Arendt. Both took a somewhat more favorable view of humanism than their compatriot Martin Heidegger. Arendt strongly disagreed with the critique of agency and the will in Heidegger's *Letter on Humanism*,[15] but this did not make her a conventional liberal humanist: she was concerned also to contest the privatizing tendencies of modern liberalism, and she shared something of Heidegger's desire to turn to the ancient Greeks as a critique of modern trends, though with a significantly different political inflection. In his public sphere book, Habermas drew strongly on Arendt's *The Human Condition*, which appeared in 1958. Arendt strongly contested the separation between public and private, the "flight from the whole outer world," that had characterized much liberal thought. She went back to the classical polis, in which individual fulfillment was to be found not in the private but in the public sphere, in playing an active role in civic life. The word *privatus* retained its etymological sense of privation, of something lacking. Arendt urged a reconstruction of the classical valorization of the public life, which she later located in such unexpectedly collocated institutions as the early revolutionary soviet and the early American town meeting. For Arendt, one of the crucial features of the specifically political life was the fusion of speech and action. She points out that Aristotle defined man as a being capable of speech, and that the Latin translation as *animal rationale* elided the centrality of speech for the Greek polis. Discourse, then, was not a private realm cut off from power but precisely a means of engagement with the public world. The word *rhetor* effectively meant "politician" (27, 26 n.9). The criteria of rationality in the polis were not narrowly instrumental or cognitive; public life demanded a practical reason or prudence (*phronesis*), linking word and concept, power and knowledge in a quest for intersubjective agreement. Habermas drew on Arendt's analysis of classical political thought in formulating his own concept of praxis and of communicative as opposed to instrumental rationality.[16]

Arendt and Habermas anticipated a vein of scholarship that became more and more important in the 1970s and 1980s, tracing the complex effects of the revival of the values of the classical polis in early modern civic humanism.[17] The rise of the Roman empire and then of the church had marked a radical shift in relations between public and private. In the medieval world, with rule in the hands of a personal lord, public and private realms became inextricably mingled. The polis came under the hegemony of a super-*oikos*, the household of the emperor or monarch, and citizens became subjects, forced to revere their king as a father rather than debating with him as an equal. At the same time, a matter of much concern to Milton, the state and church vied with each other for monopolies of religious life, with "the Popes of *Rome* engrossing [note the economic term] what they pleas'd of Politicall rule into their owne hands" (501) and public revenues being siphoned into an unaccountable religious bureaucracy. That is one reason why, for Milton, "popery" is not to be tolerated: it "extirpats all ... civill supremacies" (565). But it is not just the state but the people who are thus disempowered; the people are now trying "to reassume the ill deputed care of the Religion into their own hands again" (554). In the secular sphere, too, the civic humanists of the Renaissance challenged that medieval blurring of public–private boundaries. Habermas gives a useful account of the ways in which the word *common*, in the medieval period connoting a social lowliness that was effectively the opposite of the public world of the court, became revalued into a positive sense of the public and universal (1989: 5). It was from the attempt to reclaim the public domain, the res publica, from private monopolies of power that *republican* as a noun emerged in the mid-seventeenth century. And *Areopagitica* can more fruitfully be seen against the background of Renaissance republicanism than of a later liberalism.

With the assault on private monopolies of power there went a comparable critique of monopolies of discourse, a call for universality of communication. This call for open communication was most vigorously made in the circle of the German émigré Samuel Hartlib, who welcomed the parliamentary reforms of the 1640s as an opportunity for establishing international communications in news and in theological and scientific knowledge.[18] The Hartlibians can be seen as exemplifying a shift toward instrumental rationality, calling for plain and simple communication and therefore somewhat suspicious of classical rhetoric. For some contemporaries, in fact, far from embodying a modern notion of language and truth, Milton was problematic precisely because he was not modern enough. Though Hartlib commissioned *Of Education* from Milton, some of his circle regarded it as somewhat too high-flown; and one of Hartlib's German correspondents complained that *Areopagitica* was "rather too satyrical throughout . . ." and because of his all too highflown style in many places quite obscure. Nevertheless, he hoped that the tract would be translated into German and given "good circulation in other lands where such tryanny reigns."[19]

It is in fact hard to make clear-cut distinctions in this period between a "modern" rationality, the classical discourse of civic *phronesis*, and the apocalyptic Protestant belief in progressive revelation. The Hartlibians shared with civic humanists the belief that rational inquiry depended on collective endeavor: to translate, not very satisfactorily, into Habermasian terms, instrumental rationality could best develop in a climate of communicative rationality. As John Hall, a great admirer of *Areopagitica*, wrote to Hartlib in 1647, the reform of learning could not depend on "the sparkles of a few private men"; echoing Milton's critique of a "fugitive and cloister'd virtue," Hall wrote that they must be "forc't from that solitude where in they wold be imersed."[20] Another member of the circle, Sir Cheney Culpeper, who was also interested in Milton's prose writings, attacked scholars who were "suffered to liue a monkishe life to the prejudice of the publike." Culpeper saw Hartlib's proposal to establish an "Office of Address" with a "Bureau of Communication" as part of a wider, apocalyptic process of bringing down monopolies: after the "monopoly of Power which the King claimes" there would fall "the monopoly of trade," "the monopoly of Equity . . . the monopoly of matters of conscience & scripture . . . all these & many more wee shall haue in chace & what one hownde misses another will happen in the sente of & thus will Babilon tumble, tumble,

tumble."[21] This process formed a part of a "democraticall growinge spirite" whose final outcome could not yet be foreseen.[22] Such assaults on monopolies did indeed open up a greater space for private interests;[23] Yet it is reductive to see the assault on monopolies of discourse simply as a rationale for laissez-faire capitalism. Culpeper's vision of an ongoing democratic revolution implied the importance of public as well as private spaces. As Pocock has demonstrated, there was a continual tension between the demands of commerce and those of virtue in republican theory; similar tensions can be found in the language of *Areopagitica*.[24]

If such proposals for a "modern" transformation of communications often adopted an apocalyptic idiom, they also drew on the idiom of classical republicanism. The more innovatively minded recognized that a revival of classical rhetoric and public discourse had to adjust to changed political and technological resources, the printing press made possible new modes of public rhetorical debate. The insistence on common participation in public affairs legitimized the expansion of the press, and newsbooks' titles often aligned them with classical forms of public speech: the courtly *Mercurius Aulicus* versus the parliamentarian *Mercurius Civicus*. This was the only period of English history when a newspaper entitled *Observations Historical, Political and Philosophical, upon Aristotles First Booke of Political Government* would have been considered marketable.[25] *Areopagitica* was an important factor in turning at least one young republican, John Hall, toward the newspaper medium, and Milton encouraged another journalist, Marchamont Nedham, to return to the parliamentarian cause. Nedham commented of his newspaper that "I entitle it [Mercurius] Politicus, because the present Gou[er]nm[ent] is verà πολιτέια [politeia] as it is opposed to the despotick forme" (French 1950, 2: 311). Nedham was not only the first great English journalist but also a significant theorist of republicanism. Milton has frequently been disparaged for associating with this vulgar popularizer, a charge that sits uneasily with concomitant attacks on his elitism.[26]

Areopagitica formed part of that common project of reclaiming public space: the tract, Milton insists, was "not the disburdning of a particular fancie" but was voicing a "common grievance," the "generall murmur" (539). Here and elsewhere, Milton used the word *public* and its compounds about twice as much as *private*; books, he proclaimed, were "the living labours of publick men" (493). Francis Barker claims that the Order of Parliament that Milton commends in *Areopagitica* provided for "the protection of copyright vested, for the first time, in the author" (1984: 49);[27] but while such a reading fits in with the thesis that Milton privatized literary production, there is no evidence that Milton or the Order he mentions effected such a transfer. In fact, the system by which copyright rested with the publisher rather than the author did not prevent authors from having a say in the content and revision of their works (L. Patterson 1968: 65 ff) and Milton certainly took such an interest; but in the 1640s he was as much concerned with the collective as with the private aspect of literary production. He had witnessed in Italy the contrast between the restrictive system of aristocratic patronage and the more open press of the Venetian republic (Lindenbaum 1991). If the latter system allowed the author more autonomy, it was nonetheless associated with an ethos of public spirit, and it was that ethos that the Hartlib circle were concerned to instill in England. John Hall repeatedly proclaimed his determination to be "subservient to the Commonwealth of letters";[28] it was in that spirit that Milton turned away from his private literary studies to his prose writings.

What Milton objects to about prepublication licensing is precisely that it claws back what ought to be a public space for a particular interest, that of the presbyterian "at home in his privat chair" (540). Similarly, the Leveller William Walwyn urged Parliament to oppose licensing because "It is not to be supposed that You who have so long spent Your time in recovering the common liberties of *England*, should in conclusion turne the common into particular" (Milton, *Complete Prose Works*, 2: 86). Milton insists that writing ought to be a collaborative process – a writer "likely consults and conferrs with his judicious friends" (543). This process is one reason why good texts are seldom fixed and finished: a writer who is "copious of fancie" will want to keep revising (532). Intellectuals should "joyn, and unite into one generall and brotherly search after Truth" (554) and welcome anyone willing to "bring his helpfull hand to the slow-moving Reformation which we labour under" (565). Here it is presumably the slowness of progress that makes the reformation seem a labor, though there is perhaps a buried reference to the birth of new ideas; here and elsewhere writing is seen as work, an "act" (532). Milton declares that *Areopagitica* itself has been part of this collaborative process: he is voicing complaints that he had heard in Italy and was shocked to find being uttered "so generally" in England when he returned. He was "loaded ... with entreaties and perswasions" to write his treatise (539). The worst effect of licensing is that it turns the intellectual community into egotists who are "over timorous" (556, 558) and fear "the shaking of every leaf" (539). Milton conjures up this effect in his brilliant vignette of Italian title pages: "Sometimes *Imprimaturs* are seen together dialogue-wise in the Piatza of one Title page, complementing and ducking each to other with their shav'n reverences" (504). Milton conflates the public space of the title page with that of the Italian cities where the defeat of the republican communality of the Roman forum and later of the piazza are registered in the common complicity in servility of the groveling instruments of the hierarchy, acting "dialogue-wise" because the genuine dialogue of republican culture has been reduced to empty stage dialogue. Elsewhere Milton compares the imprimatur to the papal prison, the "castle St. *Angelo*" (537). Milton warns that such values have been transferred to England in his references to licenses being obtained from "the West end of *Pauls*" (504). St. Paul's was a crucial site for the emergent public sphere in England: the district around the churchyard was a center for printers and booksellers, while the interior of the church had functioned as a kind of forum where news was exchanged, and the sermons at Paul's Cross had sometimes been politically controversial. Laud had expelled the strollers from the church to a neoclassical portico where political gossip would be overshadowed by regal statues, and had muzzled the sermons: these moves, in conjunction with ecclesiastical, "patriarchal" (533) control over licensing, seemed to threaten to reduce English spaces likewise to such deferential theatricality. The presbyterians would reintroduce a climate of fear, making people "afraid of every conventicle" (541, cf. 547).

Milton dramatizes the reverse process, of writing with a "ventrous edge" (534), a "fearlesse and communicative candor" (*Complete Prose Works*, 2: 226), by defying the licensers in publishing without an imprimatur or printer's name and by the boldness of his approach to Parliament. He emphasizes that, like Isocrates and Dion Prusaeus, he is in "a private condition" (486), but he does so in order to bring out the contrast with his desire to "advance the publick good." He dramatizes the process by which he overcomes his initial "feare" of public discourse and claims an equal right to members of Parliament themselves to discuss public issues. His aim is to animate "private persons" with a new respect for Parliament in its receptiveness to "publick advice" (488); its openness contrasts with the "cabin[et] Counsellours" who tried to confine decision making within a narrow and exclusive space. Parliament is become more responsive to the demands of its people, opening up a public sphere that "obeyes the voice of reason from what quarter soever it be heard speaking" (490). Milton emphasizes that the most enlightened states accept advice from overseas as well as from their own nation; figures like Comenius had been drawn to England from the Continent because of Parliament's apparent enthusiasm for reform, and later in *Areopagitica* Milton lays new emphasis on this internationalism (552). Just as the House of Commons comes to see itself as representing a general rather than a particular interest, so Milton's private voice becomes common. In an escalating communicative interchange, Parliament was beginning to print its proceedings, while as Milton had admiringly noted, it was more and more open to petitions even from "the meanest artizans and labourers, at other times also women" (*Complete Prose Works*, 1: 926). In praising "the magnanimity of a triennial Parlament" (488) Milton explicitly links a general moral virtue with a specific political form: Parliament had gained control over its regularity of summoning from the king and was hence more open to the public's demands. Conversely, the people's creativity had been facilitated by the material conditions created by Parliament. The role of Parliament throughout the tract deserves attention: as the central nexus between communication and power in a society without a court (the king goes conspicuously unmentioned), it is best able to govern when it is most responsive to communicative processes diffused throughout society. In a complex dialectic, Milton says that it is impossible that "ye [Parliment]" should "first make your selves, that made us so, lesse the lovers, lesse the founders of our true liberty" (559).[29] The people's intellectual achievements are "the issue of your owne vertu propagated in us" (559): Parliament instills a *virtù* in the people that is at once moral and Machiavellian.

The jaw-breaking title of *Areopagitica* makes more sense when the licensing controversy is set in this wider context of reclaiming public space. "Things concerned with the Areopagus": the reader's attention is directed away from legal minutiae and toward the constitution of ancient Athens. That concern can be seen as an instance of Milton's elitist pedantry: Sue Curry Jansen has given the name "Areopagite" to the self-satisfied literary intellectual.[30] But what is at issue in Milton's Greek allusions is something a lot more politically sensitive than scoring points in cultural literacy: for his first readers, an admittedly limited audience of humanists, his allusions had a high political charge. The title and allusions effectively make the text an early manifesto of English republicanism.

To understand the potential explosiveness of Milton's allusions to the rhetoric of the Greek polis, we need to try to forget the encrustations of later liberal cults of Athenian democracy and remember just how raw and new an enthusiam for Athens would have been at this time. Most political discourse centered on conflicting versions of a time-hallowed "ancient constitution"; it is hard today to recall how provocative Milton was being in attacking the ancient English feudal constitution as "the barbarick pride of a *Hunnish* and *Norwegian* statelines" (489). In *Areopagitica* the English monarchy dwindles to a dead voice from the tomb of Henry VII (567), just as the figure of the king is conspicuously absent from Milton's reworking of the story of Solomon's temple (555). Instead, Milton, like James Harrington, turns to the classical polis as embodying an ancient prudence superior to the degenerate political forms of feudalism. One reason for condemning licensing is that it is a modern invention, not part of the ancient "prudence" (522) that republicans wished to emulate, and hence unworthy of the "prudent spirit" of Parliament (490). The demand for unlicensed printing proves to be a transitional demand: to embody fully the principles behind that demand, to reform "the rule of life both economicall and politicall" (550), would involve a radical restructuring of the English state, a "generall reforming" (566). The reception of *Areopagitica* indicates that it fueled demands for changes going far beyond the immediate issue of licensing.[31]

Areopagitica is a prime illustration of Thomas Hobbes's fears that a cult of Greek and Roman liberty was beginning to emerge in England.[32] Having translated Thucydides' history as a warning against democracy, Hobbes attacked the great orator Pericles, the hero of Athenian democracy, on the ground that "the tongue of man is a trumpet of warre, and sedition" (*De Cive*, 88).[33] The Athenian ethos is conveyed not only in the title but also in the quotation from Euripides' *The Suppliant Women* on the title page.[34] The full connotations of the speech act involved in this citation cannot be explored here, but it can be pointed out that the passage Milton cited was itself metacommunicative, discussing the differing speech acts characteristic of different political forms. A herald arrives from the kingdom of Thebes and asks, "What man is master in this land?" Theseus replies that he has got off to a bad start in asking for a master: the city is free and not ruled by one person, and the poor have an equal share. The herald responds to this challenge by forgetting all about the message he came to deliver and shifting to the political implications of the medium, the forms of discourse characteristic of a democracy. Athens is controlled by the mob, who are incapable of judging arguments properly and are therefore swayed this way and that by rhetoricians. If poor men work hard they will have no time to learn about public affairs.

This exchange was heavily freighted with political implications in its original context. Edith Hall writes that Greek drama was militantly ideological, displaying "breathtaking anachronism" in projecting the values of Athenian democracy onto the distant eras it portrayed. The tragedies helped to portray a "discourse of Barbarism," constructing an image of the other of Athenian democracy. The Athenian polis was seen as "the highest rung on the ladder of human evolution," and monarchical states were presented as primitive and barbaric. In Athenian tragedy Thebes sometimes functioned as Athens' other, a barbarian residue; but this antithesis often functioned as a submerged allusion to the more immediate rivalry with Sparta, whose more aristocratic regime was attacked by democrats but covertly favored by conservatives.[35] The Theban herald adopts the stock arguments of pro-Spartan, antidemocratic thinkers – arguments that were also of course adopted by conservative Athenians like Plato, whose sympathies went toward Sparta. In 1644 such arguments were currently being marshaled against the parliamentarians by the royalists who similarly pilloried their enemies as uncouth barbarians favoring mob rule. Milton attacked those who saw "the common people" as "a giddy, vitious and ungrounded people" (536). The Athenian discourse of barbarism made a particularly powerful riposte to such arguments, and Milton quotes on his title page from Theseus' reply to the herald, in which he denounces absolute rule and praises democracy where the poor and the rich must be subject to the same, written laws. He gives a historical analysis of democracy, seeing it as part of a progress from primitive absolutism toward a written constitution. And it is in this context that Theseus offers the defense of free speech that Milton places on his title page. Milton's version is:

> This is true Liberty when free born men
> Having to advise the public may speak free,
> Which he who can, and will, deserv's high praise,
> Who neither can nor will, may hold his peace;
> What can be juster in a State then this?

This exchange is not just about freedom of speech as some separable political issue: it can be read as a straightforward opposition, not just between monarchy and republicanism, but between monarchy and democracy. This fact was registered in Renaissance editions, one of which glossed Theseus' speech as a "praise of democracy."[36]

At a time when Parliament's cause was still officially monarchist and the republican MP Henry Marten had been expelled for questioning that stance, Milton's allusion was cautious; it was nonetheless pointed, turning his own title page from an authoritarian piazza to an embodiment of a classical forum. His "Frontispice" was "dangerous" (525).[37] His more particular concern, freedom of expression and publication, itself raised more general political issues; as has been seen, the exchange between Theseus and the herald implies that moral values need to be considered in relation to specific political structures and their characteristic speech acts. Blair Worden has questioned whether the seventeenth century had any universalizing concept of freedom of publication as a right, rather than a privilege handed down from above (1988: 45–7). But Greek discourse offered a number of terms for such a right with implications broad enough to be easily extended to the new medium of print. As I. F. Stone has pointed out, the right to speak out boldly on any issue was effectively identical with the civic identity of the free Athenian, and there were at least four different words for freedom of speech, of which perhaps the strongest was *parrhesia*.[38] This is a favorite word in Euripides: as Jocasta says in the *Phoenissae*, "this is slavery, not to speak one's thoughts."[39] The word occurs twice in the *Electra*, the play with which Milton in "Captain or Colonel" imagined charming the royalists. Its fortunes had declined with the decline of Greek democracy: the more conservative Romans had often translated *parrhesia* as *licentia* or *contumacia*. Such pejorative associations tended to cling to the word: the Elizabethan rhetorician Henry Peacham warns that "rude boldnesse" must be tempered by "humble submission."[40] The edition of Euripides owned by Milton reflected that negative attitude toward Athenian democratic values; its commentary on the Theseus-herald exchange declared that grave authors like Xenophon and Aristotle had condemned such *parrhesia* or *licentia plebis*.[41] Milton, by contrast, celebrates such boldness, and *Areopagitica* urges its readers to translate the values of the polis into the England of the 1640s. The pamphlet's subtitle draws attention to the changes made possible by shifts in medium: though presented as a "speech," it is of course so only in a formal, generic sense; yet Milton also reminds us that English traditions deny the ordinary citizen access to the nation's assembly, a right that any Athenian freeman enjoyed. In one sense Milton then appeals over Parliament's head to a wider public sphere; in another sense he also foregrounds his exclusion from a Parliament that represented its people only in a very indirect sense. Before long, the Levellers were to press for more direct forms of representation. Milton was to quote twice from this same speech in his defense of the regicide, the *First Defence of the English People*.[42]

The *Areopagitica* title page, however, bears a contradictory message. Milton modifies Euripides to stress that participation in politics is a matter of free choice and that not all will choose to participate.[43] And his title evokes the Areopagus, a residual element of aristocratic power that was ousted in a democratic revolution. Milton compared himself to Isocrates, who had called for the Areopagus to be restored to its old authority. Such anomalies have led some critics to read the title ironically,[44] while Annabel Patterson suggests that they point to a hermeneutics of ambiguity and indeterminacy (1984: 111–19). Indeterminacy, however, is not quite the term; we are left in no doubt about the wickedness of the royalists, let alone of the Catholics, and those who were on the receiving end of the policies Milton was to support in Ireland will not have found them very indeterminate. It is within a particular framework of a reformed Protestant constitution that Milton does admit openness. Like Machiavelli, Milton believes that an element of disunity may be beneficial rather than destructive for an expanding commonwealth. In an oxymoron that would have seemed even more staggering then than it does now, he praises God for shaking kingdoms with "healthfull commotions to a generall reforming" (566).[45] And among those commotions Milton implicitly includes tensions between democratic and aristocratic elements. In choosing democratic Athens rather than conservative Rome as his model, and then emphasizing one of the Athenians' more conservative institutions, Milton sets up a complex counterbalancing of political forces. In 1644 the aristocratic element was represented by the House of Lords, and throughout the tract Milton insistently uses the coordinate form "Lord and Commons" as part of a larger rhetorical pattern of doublets, building up a picture of unity in controlled variety. His insistence on the House's role, while doubtless partly designed to reassure anxious readers, was not necessarily as conservative in implication as it may seem: some leading members of the independent party were to be found in the Lords, formulating an aristocratic variety of republicanism (Adamson 1990). Milton's urging that the state be magnanimous, that it offer "liberall and frequent audience" to the sects (567), appeals to a semiaristocratic sense of condescension. After the revolution, however, it was the elected Council of State that came to seem the obvious equivalent of Areopagus, and Milton's friend Marchamont Nedham and many other republicans made the analogy.[46] Down to 1660, Milton was to hold to the general principle of counterbalancing a full democracy with a contrary element.

It was not necessarily that Milton always feared popular radicalism: he feared that some or most of the people were not radical enough, that they would be swayed by an easy sympathy for the rituals of monarchy. By the end of the 1640s he was lamenting that the British lacked experience in republican culture. His variety of republicanism was vanguardist: the radical elite would gradually wean the people off their devotion to traditional forms. And it was also militant: rhetoric is consistently associated with preparation for battle. The tract was published at a time when the war had gone very badly and the presbyterians were calling for a settlement that would probably leave in place a state church and suppress the sects. Since the presbyterians seemed to be strengthening their power in Parliament, renewal of the licensing laws was likely to mean a consolidation of their hold on power, and possibly the dissemination of royalist propaganda (570). In the first instance, the protests against licensing at this time had the highly particular aim of trying to counter the moves to suppress the sects and negotiate with the king from a position of relative military weakness. Milton throws his weight behind those who were campaigning for the formation of the New Model Army. The Areopagus was named after the god of war. The revolution was to involve virtually continuous military campaigning, first at home and then abroad, for the defense and then the expansion of the republic; Milton supported these campaigns, and he had given military education a prominent place in *Of Education*. His powerful evocation of the military as well as intellectual activities of a city under siege recalls the extraordinary collective agency when elaborate defenses were built up by London's citizens – including oysterwomen who marched to work under an emblem of the goddess of war (Pearl 1961). The vivid reference to royalist newssheets circulating with the ink still wet is a reminder to Parliament that wartime conditions need vigilance. Milton evokes Livy's story of the heroic struggles of the young Roman republic, with the royalists cast in the role of the barbaric Carthaginians (557). Given the polemical thrust behind his attack on presbyterian licensing, Milton's later role as a licenser was less radically inconsistent than it may seem, though it undoubtedly did represent a retreat.[47] Like many republicans, he thought that a historic opportunity had been provided for the foundation of a republic in 1649: if the chance was lost it might not recur; he therefore countenanced the suppression of tracts and newspapers agitating for its overthrow. He does, however, seem to have considered the republic to be at least partly fulfilling the ideals of *Areopagitica*, and continued to appeal to the pamphlet in supporting the licensing of works considered heretical.[48]

The martial language of *Areopagitica* has been seen by some recent commentators as exposing a more general link between Enlightenment values and violent repression, between the will to knowledge and the will to power: in *Areopagitica*, that connection is the more apparent because Enlightenment rationality has not yet fully disguised its own violence.[49] Such a reading would square with Foucault's only extensive engagement with seventeenth-century England, a lecture in which he presented a radically antihumanist discourse as emerging from the pressure of political crisis. Writers like Coke and Lilburne, Foucault claims, threw out illusions like justice and truth and saw history as a "state of war between two hostile races," which they wanted to bring to a final millennial act of revenge.[50] It requires considerable distortion, however, to turn Lilburne into a Nietzschean *avant la lettre*: his justification of godly warfare did not derive from an epistemological relativism. And however strongly Milton may have insisted that prophets had to be armed, what is remarkable in the context is the force of his argument against militaristic values, against allowing the practical means of revolution to destroy the ends. The images of the defensive city under siege are counterposed to celebrations of open, receptive bodies (e.g., 537, 547, 548). In the terms of Pericles' funeral oration, Milton presents London as a new Athens, able to nourish the arts even in times of war, and derides the "muselesse and unbookish" Spartans whose "surlinesse" minded "nought but the feats of Warre" (496). And yet the urgency of the war effort remains vivid in his language, conjuring up almost surreal images:

> The shop of warre hath not there more anvils and hammers waking, to fashion out the plates and instruments of armed Justice in defence of beleaguer'd Truth, then there be pens and heads there, sitting by their studious lamps, musing, searching, revolving new notions and ideas. (554)

Here manual and intellectual labor are working in harmony rather than opposition, but the force of the figurative language, where the mechanical instruments whether of making arms or of writing take over from the men doing the work, gives an unusual twist to this analogy. Milton's famous emendation of "wayfaring Christian" to "warfaring Christian" (515) indicates his desire to startle his readers with striking juxtapositions. Perhaps the most startling for contemporary readers would have been this: "The Temple of *Janus* with his two *controversial* faces might now not unsignificantly be set open" (561). While the closing of Janus' gates signified for royalists the unity and peace of Stuart rule, Milton finds such closed unity stifling and endorses the opening of the gates: the wars of truth are not a final goal but are better than the frozen January of a tyrannical peace (545). Unity is still to be sought, but it lies in the future rather than the present; in the meantime, discourse must indeed be Janus-faced.

Milton works through the tension between aristocratic and populist elements, and between war and peace, in the turbulent style and structure of his tract. His frequently noted commercial figures, which compare truths to commodities, serve to deflate a traditional elitism that sets mental against manual labor; yet his equally assertive foregrounding of literary culture works against a purely utilitarian model of democratic discourse: in this prose poetry with its constant interplay of vernacular and latinate diction, commerce and virtue are set in a complex tension.[51] In lavishing on the traditionally despised medium of the pamphlet the imagistic and allusive resources normally thought appropriate to court poetry or masques, the pamphlet embodies a challenge to fit readers to redirect their cultural energies to the struggle for liberty. The text is a public manifesto of a republican rhetoric and poetics as well as a republican politics, revealing the nation's quest for liberty "by the very sound of this which I shall utter" (487). Milton consciously reworks the poetics of royalist poets for whom unity was the central virtue of monarchies and disunity the vice of republics; like Machiavelli, Milton turns such arguments against the royalists, celebrating the greater dynamism of disunity while insisting that mechanisms can be found to save it from becoming anarchy. Milton inaugurates a long tradition of contrasting English rhetorical oppenness with French neoclassical formality when he writes that "*Julius Agricola* . . . preferr'd the naturall wits of Britain, before the labour'd studies of the French" (552).[52] Milton revises conventional valuations of the body politic figure to find an image for the difficult unity he aims at in the state, a unity very different from the sterile conformity urged in the traditional monarchist figure of the body politic: a flushed countenance is a sign not of sickness but of resourceful adaptation to change (557). Milton uses the term *sublimest* to describe such mental processes; and in pushing figures beyond the conventional limits of representation he may well have been thinking of Longinus's treatise on the sublime, which his admirer John Hall was soon to translate. The constantly shifting, sublime body of the text images the reconstituted body of a reformed state. Truth, for Milton, needs a body in order to speak, and yet that body resists full representation, and to represent it fully is already to bind it by tuning truth's voice according to the time (563).[53] Milton sets his visionary sight against the deluded sight of everyday perception:

> We boast our light; but if we look not wisely on the Sun it self, it smites us into darknes. . . . The light which we have gain'd, was giv'n us, not to be ever staring on, but by it to discover onward things more remote from our knowledge. (550)

Milton thus anticipates the dialectic of outer and inner lights that he was to work out more fully in *Paradise Lost*. The ultimate guarantor of the validity of Milton's text would then be the degree to which it inspired a continual revaluation of the reformative process that it inaugurates.[54]

Milton's tract proposes, then, a quest for truth that is more rhetorical than simply logical: truth exceeds "the pace of method and discours" (521), and as many critics have pointed out, Milton enacts this process of excess in his virtuoso linguistic displays. This does not mean that his text is infinitely open-ended, or that rhetoric completely subverts rationality: the tract's apocalyptic discourse is firmly committed to the erroneousness of Catholic doctrine and to the ultimate revelation of Protestant truth. Its openness remains confined to a relatively narrow spectrum of advanced Protestant opinion, at a particular moment when new revelations are in progress. Nevertheless, Milton's rhetorical strategy highlights the points of tension between knowledge and power, between truth and its institutional and linguistic embodiments. His presentation of the active citizens of London as "reading, trying all things, assenting to the force of reason and convincement" (554) conveys this tension between Truth as absolute and Truth as process. Milton's position is not at this point simply antinomianism, with personal truth transcending any institutional embodiment: he accepts the need for a state church and insists that progress in the quest for truth has been made possible by the "State prudence" of Parliament (570, cf. 490, 557). Milton's display of rhetorical *copia* at once celebrates and examplifies the "flowry crop of knowledge and new light sprung up and yet springing daily in this City" (558). The truth emerges in dialogue, not simply in individual inspiration; some forms of power can make knowledge possible, and Parliament's pursuit of liberty is the "immediat cause" of the elevation of men's spirits (559). There is thus a convergence between the timeless truths of Christianity and the time-bound prudence of the classical polis. There remains, however, a strong tension: the evil of licensing is precisely that it encourages a "temporizing and extemporizing" attitude (531), a subordination of long-term inquiry to short-term interests, of knowledge to power. Authorized books, writes Milton after Bacon, *"are but the language of the times"* (534). In his analysis of the corruption of knowledge under empire and papacy, a more open and communicative rationality becomes subordinated to a narrowly instrumental rationality. *Areopagitica* conveys the intellectual and political ferment that emerges when those millennial processes begin to be reversed.

Far from merely calling for a retreat into the privacy of negative liberty, then, *Areopagitica* at once glorifies and embodies a revival of public spirit. And yet the civic humanist reclaiming of public space certainly did imply a redefinition of the private, and it remains to consider some of the implications of that redefinition. Though Habermas has hardly been true to his principle of dialogue with relation to feminism, his analysis does draw attention to problems of significance to feminist critique.[55] In the classical polis, women were normally denied access to the public sphere and confined to the household.[56] Insofar as the public sphere marked a return to the polis, it can be argued, it narrowed the scope for female agency. When Milton declared that "the whole breed of men" came forth from the household, he was translating Bucer's less explicitly gendered *cives* (*Complete Prose Works*, 2: 476). Just as the tragedians of the Athenian polis looked back with horror to an older order where women were allowed to corrupt the realm, so Milton was fiercely hostile to the influence of Charles's queen. Habermas points out that the emergent public sphere was a male preserve and that there are signs that some women resisted it for that reason (1989: 33).[57] In *Areopagitica* there is a strong emphasis on the "manhood" (487) or brotherhood (554–5) of reformers, recalling Carole Pateman's (1988) analysis of the seventeenth-century social contract as inherently fraternal and hence excluding women. There is an unease about female agency on the figurative level: licensing is a Juno who tries to suppress the birth of Hercules, an image of republican *virtù* (505).

And yet there was room for tension in Milton's attitude to gender roles. The private world of the household was after all a condition for public endeavor: Milton speaks of "the household estate, out of which must flourish forth the vigor and spirit of all publick enterprizes" (*Complete Prose Works*, 2: 247). Moreover, Habermas points out that the revival of the classical public-private split was asymmetrical, that the private sphere was not simply demoted but invested with a new affective significance as a sphere of intimate communication that would provide a base for the male's entry into the public sphere. As marriage took on this new ideological role it became involved in contradictions: as agent of society and emancipation from society, a site of patriarchal authority and of human closeness, liberation for the male and constraint for the female (1989: 43ff). Those contradictions are of course obtrusive in Milton's divorce tracts. For Milton, speaking is just as crucial to the private as to the public sphere; he seeks "an intimate and speaking help ... a fit conversing soul" as opposed to "a mute and spiritless mate" (*Complete Prose Works*, 2: 251). The *oikos* becomes a miniature polis. Puritans tended to give a strongly ideological character to the household as a kind of alternative public sphere, a counterweight to the corrupt institutions of church and state. And yet Milton insists that the head of the household should have a prepolitical, God-given authority and presents marital conversation as a relief, "delight-full intermissions" (2: 597). The woman's role is at once to provide dialogue and to listen to a monologue; she must become a vehicle for agency without herself achieving it. This is a textbook example of what Habermas describes as systematically distorted communication.

There is, then, a considerable irony in the fact that *Areopagitica*, that great paean to undistorted communication in the public sphere, should have arisen out of a crisis of communication in the private sphere. Nevertheless, there are unevennesses in Milton's implicit and explicit positions. The figurative strategies of *Areopagitica* point at the inadequacy of existing modes of representation, both linguistic and political, and it is striking that in his climactic image of the national body as sublime, that body shifts gender in midsentence (558). Milton recognized the crucial effects of new technology: the invention of the printing press opened up public access in a way that potentially cut across not only class but also gender. Three of Milton's poems of the 1640s emphasize the public role of women, and two – or at least one – commemorate women who were involved in the public sphere.[58] Women were taking an increasing interest in public affairs, to the extent of putting new pressure on traditional voting rights. Although most parliamentarians regarded the prospect of votes for women with horror, this position was not universally adopted: John Seldon, who is highly praised in *Areopagitica*, strongly insisted on women's fitness for high office.[59] Milton himself did not go so far, but he did praise Parliament for accepting petitions by women, a phenomenon that occasioned much controversy; and in arguing against restrictions on prophecy he was opening the way for the female writers and prophets who were to become such a controversial feature of the 1640s and 1650s. Milton made a remarkable identification with such figures when he included another quotation from Euripides on the title page of *Tetrachordon*, the tract immediately following *Areopagitica:*

> If you put new ideas before the eyes of fools
> They'll think you foolish and worthless into the bargain;
> And if you are thought superior to those who have
> Some reputation for learning, you will become hated.[60]

The speaker here is Medea, who denounces those who criticize her for bringing up her children with unorthodox ideas.

Milton sets up in his readers at the very least a double take: Euripides was after all reputed to be particularly hostile to women, and Medea is certainly no model heroine; yet her eloquence in defense of her rights does exemplify the kind of boldness of speech Milton is celebrating. He expected the title page to shock complacent readers, as we know from the sonnet he subsequently wrote in which he envisaged a reader picking up the book and puzzling over the title. The irony of the sonnet is that the strategy fails: the ignorant readers, who are presumed to be presbyterians, stumble over the harshly unnaturalized Greek word. Milton's communicative strategy in his pamphlets is a complex one: he addresses an audience sympathetic to the classical polis over the heads of more conventional figures. On one level, this is certainly an elitist strategy, deliberately evading more direct communication. Yet its social gesture is complex: the sixteenth-century scholars Milton admired had argued that Greek was closer to the structure of English than Latin, more easily adaptable to the common understanding: evoking the Greek language and Greek political structures had a doubly populist aspect.[61] Milton defies conventional communicative structures that he regards as repressive in order to galvanize his readers into imagining new structures. I have tried to suggest that the text is not infinitely open, that it does have some very specific – and not entirely liberal – strategies to propose. Yet by engaging as strongly as it does in the materiality of discourse, by a politically self-conscious form of reflexivity, it points beyond its immediate contexts rather than merely tuning its voice "according to the time."

NOTES

This essay owes a particular debt to I. F. Stone, who at a Folger Institute Seminar on seventeenth-century political thought raised the need to bring Greek ideas to bear on English discourse and also demonstrated that perhaps the public sphere has not entirely diminished to academic "interpretive communities." I am also grateful to Richard Burt, Edith Hall, Lorna Hutson, Peter Lindenbaum, and Diane Purkiss for discussion of specific issues, and to William Kolbrener for showing me the draft of a forthcoming article.

Citations of *Areopagitica* are from Milton, *Complete Prose*, vol. 2 and are indicated in this essay by a page number only.

1 For Foucault's claim, in a debate with Noam Chomsky, that there could be "no objection" (except from a bankrupt and sentimental humanism) to a proletarian revolution involving "a violent, dictatorial, and even bloody power," see Fons Elders, *Reflexive Waters: The Basic Concerns of Mankind* (London: Souvenir, 1977), 182. This exchange dates from Foucault's Maoist phase and cannot be taken as a final guide to his political agendas; the contrast with Chomsky's libertarian socialism, however, is interesting.

2 See, for example, Abbe Blum in Nyquist and Ferguson 1987: 82.

3 This point is, however, often made by recent critics with an air of novelty, as if it had been covered up by a liberal humanist conspiracy; in fact it has been extensively commented on from David Masson's great nineteenth-century *Life* down to the Yale edition, as Michael Wilding points out in an important reading (1986: 38 n.63). The dismissive term "liberal humanist" elides political complexities in the text's reception: the term hardly applies either to some of the communist sympathizers who extolled *Areopagitica* on its anniversary in 1944 or to George Orwell, who strongly criticized their willingness to suppress the facts about Spanish anarchism. See George Orwell, "The Prevention of Literature," in *Collected Essays, Journalism and Letters of George Orwell*, ed. Sonia Orwell and Ian Angus, 4 vols (London: Secker and Warburg, 1968), 4: 59ff and George Orwell and Reginald Reynolds, eds, *British Pamphleteers, vol. 1: From the Sixteenth Century to the French Revolution* (London: Wingate, 1948), 68–9.

4 The most extreme postmodern reading draws on the work of the French *nouveaux philosophes* to demonstrate that in Milton's prose "the Third Reich speaks *avant la lettre*" and that "terrifying modern institutions" like "liquidation centres or gulags … rest on principles which are at least broached in texts like *Areopagitica*" (Rapaport 1983: 168ff).

5 For a proposal to connect Foucault's analysis of the early modern period with that of historians of political thought such as J. G. A. Pocock, see Graham Burchell, "Peculiar Interests: Civil Society and Governing 'The System of Natural Liberty,'" in *The Foucault Effect: Studies in Governmentality*, ed. Graham Burchell, Colin Gordon, and Peter Miller (London: Harvester Wheatsheaf, 1991), 119–50. As Burchell notes (123), Pocock offers a history of citizens, Foucault a history of subjects.

6 Francis Barker sees *Areopagitica* as "the text of a new power," its values the "*effect* of a powerful new dominion" (1984: 48, emphasis added).

7 For revisionist accounts, see Sheila Lambert 1987 and 1989. See also Blair Worden 1988. I am grateful to Professor D. F. McKenzie for giving me copies of his unpublished Lyell lectures, which question conventional accounts of censorship and publication in the period. Both Lambert and McKenzie emphasize the role of the market as being at least as important as politics in limiting the circulation of books; but as theorists of "market censorship" have

reminded us, markets are not necessarily unpolitical; and they would not have been regarded as such in the seventeenth century.

8   This is one reason why several readings have sought the text's unconscious meanings, which can more easily be made to yield the "liberal humanist" position it is expected to hold. For a critique of such readings, see William Kolbrener 1993.

9   Neil Saccamano (1991) suggests links between the limitations of Habermas's historical analyses and the more general theory of the ideal speech situation. On the other hand, Foucauldian discourse can be accused of mechanistic rigidity in writing the possibility of critical discursive spaces out of history: in a revealingly static and reductive metaphor, Barker describes civil society as the "recto" of the state's "public verso" (1984: 48).

10 On religious factors see also David Zaret, "Religion, Science and Printing in the Public Sphere in Seventeenth-Century England," in Craig Calhoun, ed. *Habermas and the Public Sphere* (Cambridge, MA. and London: MIT Press, 1992), 212–35.

11 For an introduction to recent work in this area see Richard Cust and Ann Hughes 1989.

12 The *Perfect Weekly Account*, January 17–24, 1649, 357–58; quoted by Anthony Cotton 1971: 327.

13 Thomas Fuller, *Ephemeris Parliamentaria* (London, 1654), Preface. I owe this reference to Joad Raymond.

14 On Habermas's debt to Renaissance humanism, see Victoria Kahn, "Habermas, Machiavelli, and the Humanist Critique of Ideology," *PMLA* 105 (1990): 464 –76.

15 Elisabeth Young-Bruehl, *Hannah Arendt: For Love of the World* (New Haven, CT, and London: Yale University Press, 1982), 362ff; for Heidegger's chilly response to Arendt's *The Human Condition*, see 307.

16 There is no space here to explore the considerable differences between Arendt's and Habermas's concepts of practical reason; see Jürgen Habermas, "Hannah Arendt: On the Concept of Power," in *Philosophico-Political Profiles*, trans. Frederick G. Lawrence (London: Heinemann, 1983), 171–87, and Daniel Lubman, "On Habermas on Arendt on Power," *Philosophy and Social Criticism* 1 (1979): 79–98. Kahn makes a comparison between Machiavelli and Habermas somewhat comparable to Lubman's between Arendt and Habermas: in each case, Habermas's ideal of consensus is seen as politically as well as philosophically limited.

17 The seminal work in this area is of course J. G. A. Pocock, *The Machiavellian Moment*; see also Gisela Bock et al. 1991.

18 See the magisterial account by Charles Webster 1975.

19 Leo Miller, "A German Critique of Milton's *Areopagitica* in 1647," *Notes and Queries* 234 (1989): 29–30 ("fast all zu satyrisch, auch wegen seines all zu affectaten styli an vielen orten ohne ursach gar obscur"). *Areopagitica* is not named in the letter, but Miller suggests that it is the only plausible candidate; it is just possible, however, that the reference could be to one of the divorce

tracts. I am grateful to Dr. Timothy Raylor for providing me with a copy of this letter. Dr. Raylor has pointed out that Milton's relations with Hartlib were closer than has sometimes been suggested: see his "New Light on Milton and Hartlib." Milton's *First Defence* was widely circulated, and censored, in Germany.

20 Sheffield University Library, Hartlib Papers 9/10/2A, 9/10/1A-B, letter to Hartlib March 29, 1647. The Hartlib Papers are quoted from transcripts prepared by the Hartlib Papers Project, University of Sheffield, by permission of the project directors and the university librarian. Contractions here and elsewhere have been silently expanded.

21 Letters to Hartlib, January 28, 1645, 13/70A; March 4, 1646, 13/136A.

22 Letter to Hartlib, March 11, 1646, 13/70A.

23 See J. A. W. Gunn 1969.

24 On Milton's ambiguous attitudes to commerce, see Wilding 1986: 25 and Christopher Kendrick 1986: 41ff and passim, and on their interaction with his conceptions of authorship, see Sandra Sherman 1993.

25 The news was carried in the latter pages of each issue, and the controversial political commentary was clearly the main object of interest. The author, John Streater, an ex-soldier who printed Harrington's *Oceana*, shows a strong awareness of the links made in the Greek polis between language and political action. Freedom of speech ensures the dominance of public over private interests: just as "the whole is before the parts" so "the publick should be before the private" (no. 9, June 13–20, 1654, 66). Though there is no evidence that Streater had read Milton, he certainly represents the kind of artisanal audience with a passionate interest in recreating the Greek polis that Milton was trying at once to reach and to create; criticisms of Milton's elitism risk patronizing the radical political culture of the day.

26 Thus in a sharply revisionist essay Abbe Blum asserts that Nedham was really a closet royalist and that Milton was complicit with him in exchange for Nedham's showering Milton with praise; unfortunately, she relies on dated sources and assumptions for her account of Nedham (Blum in Nyquist and Ferguson 1987: 91–2, 96, and contrast Cotton 1971 ch. 9, and Joad Raymond 1993: ch. 8).

27 Blum questions whether Milton argues for authorial copyright (93 n.11). Ambiguity arises from Milton's phrasing: he endorses that part of the 1643 ordinance that "preserves justly every mans Copy to himselfe" (491). The ordinance itself, however, definitely reaffirms traditional arrangements. I am indebted to Professor D. F. McKenzie for discussion of this point.

28 Hall to Hartlib, February 8, 1647(?), 60/14/20A.

29 Cf. Milton's declaration in a subsequent tract, *Tetrachordon*, that more works would be forthcoming as "my public debt to your public labours" (*Complete Prose Works*, 2: 579).

30 Sue Curry Jansen, *Censorship: The Knot That Binds Power and Knowledge* (New York and Oxford: Oxford University Press, 1988), 71ff.

31 It has often been claimed that *Areopagitica* had very little contemporary

influence: see, for example, Nigel Smith 1990: 118. Though the point cannot be argued here, I believe that for a significant minority it had a considerable influence. For example, Noah Biggs's tract *Mataeotechnia Medicinae Praxeos* (London, 1651) draws heavily on some of the most celebrated passages in *Areopagitica* to call for the reform of medicine. On Biggs and his possible links with the Boyle and Hartlib circles, see Webster 1975: 191, 263–4.

32 *Behemoth; or, The Long Parliament*, ed. Ferdinand Tönnies (London: Simpkin, Marshall, 1889), 3.

33 In his antiepiscopal tracts Milton twice refers to Pericles, "a powerfull and eloquent man in a Democratie, [who] had no more at any time than a Temporary, and elective sway, which was in the will of the people when to abrogate" (*Complete Prose Works*, 1: 640; on the funeral oration, see 1: 701).

34 For discussion, see Annabel Patterson 1984: 115–16. While I agree with some of Blum's reservations about Patterson's analysis, her own reading of the title page as demonstrating Milton's narrowly individualistic self-aggrandizement fails to take any account of the Euripides quotation that makes up the largest single component.

35 Edith Hall, *Inventing the Barbarian: Greek Self-definition through Tragedy* (Oxford: Clarendon, 1989), 190ff. On Thebes as the other of Athens, see Froma I. Zeitlin, "Thebes: Theater of Self and Society," in *Greek Tragedy and Political Theory*, ed. J. Peter Euben (Berkeley, Los Angeles, and London: University of California Press, 1986), 101–41, especially 116ff.

36 *Euripidis tragoediae*, ed. Guilielmus Xylandrus (Basel, 1558), 424: "Democratiae uituperatio." Theseus' retort has the marginal comment "Turannidis uituperatio, – laus Democratiae."

37 Cf. *An Apology for Smectymnuus* (*Complete Prose Works*, 1: 876), where Milton attacks his antagonist's title pages for preempting open discussion.

38 I. F. Stone, *The Trial of Socrates* (New York: Little, Brown, 1988), 215–24; Stone notes the link with *Areopagitica* on 224.

39 Euripides, *Phoenissae*, 1. 392. *Parrhesia* also occurs in five other surviving plays by Euripides. It does not occur at all in Thucydides; Isocrates, Milton's model for *Areopagitica*, used it twenty-four times.

40 Diane Parkin-Speer, "Freedom of Speech in Sixteenth-Century English Rhetorics," *Sixteenth Century Journal* 12 (1981): 64–72 (67–8).

41 *Euripidis tragoediae: cum Latina Gulielmi Canteri interpretatione*, ed. Paulus Stephanus, 2 vols (Geneva, 1602; Bodleian Don. d 27–28), 2: 116 (notes on *Supplices*: there are successive runs of pagination). Such topics as *parrhesia* were cross-referenced: a note on the word in the *Ion*, 672, refers the reader to the debate between Theseus and the herald. *Parrhesia* was translated as *libertas loquendi* or *dicendi*. On Milton's close reading and annotation of his copy, see Maurice Kelley and Samuel D. Atkins, "Milton's Annotations of Euripides," *Journal of English and Germanic Philology* 60 (1961): 680–7.

42 Milton quoted twice from the scene in his *First Defence of the English People* (*Complete Prose Works*, 4.1: 440, 455). The exchange is also cited by another republican, Peter English, in *The Survey of Policy* (London, 1654), 57. On the

Areopagus and Euripides in regicidal contexts, see also *Complete Prose Works*, 3: 205, 589.

43   David Davies and Paul Dowling, "'Shrewd Bookes, with Dangerous Frontispices': *Areopagitica's* Motto," *Milton Quarterly* 20 (1986): 33–7; but see John K. Hale, "*Areopagitica's* Euripidean Motto," *Milton Quarterly* 25 (1991): 25–7.

44   See Wittreich 1972; for a different ironic reading, from the school of Allan Bloom, see Paul M. Dowling 1985.

45   Cf. Loewenstein (1990: 49ff).

46   On the Areopagus as the aristocratic element in government, see Nedham 1969: 105, and Sidney 1751: 133.

47   Blum explains the inconsistency in terms of "Milton's desire both to repudiate and embrace a discourse of power associated with a principle of authorial autonomy" (1987: 74); rather than trying to locate such a uniform unconscious "desire" in Milton, I would see him as being far more uneasy about a presbyterian-dominated regime than about a republic established by the independents.

48   Leo Miller, "New Milton Texts and Data from the Aitzema Mission, 1652," *Notes and Queries* 235 (1990): 279–81. Though the republic's censorship regulations were particularly draconian, as in other periods the application of the regulations was inconsistent: see Michael John Seymour, "Pro-Government Propaganda in Interregnum England 1649–1660," unpublished Ph.D. thesis, Cambridge, 1977, 410–16.

49   See Barker 1990.

50   Michel Foucault, "War in the Filigree of Peace: Course Summary," trans. Ian Mcleod, *Oxford Literary Review* 4 (1980): 15–19; cf. Barker 1990.

51   Tom Paulin compares the "city of refuge" passage to Whitman in *Minotaur: Poetry and the Nation State* (London and Boston: Faber & Faber, 1992), 30–1.

52   On the politics of the Longinian tradition, see Michael Meehan 1986.

53   On sublimity, cf. Nigel Smith 1970: 109–10, and Norbrook 1990: 155–6.

54   Stanley Fish gives an excellent account of the ways in which the text summons its readers to continual self-criticism (1987: 234–54). While Fish recognizes, contra Barker, that Milton's individualism has political implications (253–4), he underestimates the extent to which Milton sees material institutions as potentially enabling, rather than simply resisting, change. He thus inscribes in the text the dualism he makes in his analysis of the modern academy, with the "literary" processes of reading cut off from the "political" world outside the academy (248–52).

55   For a nuanced critique, see Nancy Fraser, *Unruly Practices: Power, Discourse and Gender in Contemporary Social Theory* (Minneapolis: University of Minnesota Press, 1989), 113–43.

56   This generalization, made by Arendt and accepted by Habermas (1989: 52), is increasingly coming under challenge; one area in which women did have a public identity was in certain religious rituals, forming an interesting parallel with seventeenth-century women's quest for a voice through prophecy. (I owe this point to Margaret Williamson.)

57 John Streater attacks dainty ladies who are unwilling to undertake household work (*Observations* no. 5 [May 2–9, 1654], 36).

58 Sonnets IX, XIV (to the wife of the printer and book collector George Thomason), and possibly X (to Lady Margaret Ley). See Anna K. Nardo 1979: 43ff; Nardo accepts E. A. J. Honigmann's suggestion that the Ley sonnet was written to preface her edition of her father's writings. For a fascinating study of the possibilities offered by print culture for female agency – at least for those in the anomalous legal position of widows – see Maureen Bell 1989.

59 Selden's *Ianus Anglorum* provides the epigraph for Charlotte Carmichael Stopes, *British Freewomen* (1907).

60 Euripides, *Medea* 298–301, trans. Rex Warner, in *The Complete Greek Tragedies: Euripides 1*, ed. David Grene and Richard Lattimore (Chicago and London: University of Chicago Press, 1955), 69.

61 *The Three Orations of Demosthenes*, trans. Thomas Wilson (London, 1570), sigs. *i'ff. See also J. B. Trapp, "The Conformity of Greek and the Vernacular," in *Classical Influences on European Culture*, AD 500–1500, ed. R. R. Bolgar (Cambridge: Cambridge University Press, 1971), 239–44.

2

Milton and the Fit Reader

SHARON ACHINSTEIN

Paradise Lost and the Parliament of Hell

Paradise Lost is no squib nor a polemical barb in some pamphlet war; it is, rather, an extraordinary epic poem, encompassing far more than simply a topical political intention. Andrew Marvell summed it up best by listing the ingredients of *Paradise Lost* as an almost unimaginable heap: "*Messiah* Crown'd, God's Reconcil'd Decree, / Heav'n, Hell, Earth, Chaos, All" ("On *Paradise Lost*," 3–4). In that frail "All" hangs the entire tale. However, in its mission to justify the ways of God to men, and also to find a "fit audience ... though few," Milton's poem is consistent with the ethical concerns voiced in his prose. Soon after his Interregnum books were indexed, Milton's great poem appeared, with the approval of the licenser Thomas Tomkins, and was duly entered into the Stationers' Registers in 1667. Milton did not put his name on the title page of several of these 1667 editions, only his J. M., and he may have found some anonymity in that; he also sold the rights to the publishers so that any risks of scandal would involve the publisher rather than the author; he did name himself, however, on the title page of the 1674 edition (Parker 1968, 1: 602). Was Milton one of those adaptable loyalists, like Marchamont Nedham, or even Dryden, who was to be forgiven for the sins of his Interregnum politics?[1]

Did Milton purge his magnificent poem of all political intention? It appears not, especially since in the first two books of his epic, Milton repeated certain words and situations that were constantly appearing in pamphlets of the Parliament of hell genre.[2] In *Paradise Lost*, the Devil is the "author" of "woe"; devils appear as fallen angels or saints; they embark on a mission to retrieve former glory through deceit: "our own loss how repair,

/ How overcome this dire Calamity" (1: 188–9); they take their revenge in
the form of political seduction: "Seduce them to our Party"; they contrive
to make "that thir God / May prove thir foe ... This would surpass /
Common revenge" (2: 367–71); they use persuasion and false rhetoric as
their tools, with Belial using "words cloth'd in reason's garb" (2: 226) and
Beelzebub speaking as the Devil's mouthpiece; they appeal to the multitude,
"the popular vote" (2: 313); the hellish crowd is "the hasty multitude" (1:
730) or a "captive multitude" (2: 323), over which skilled orators exert
power. The poem even seems to share the very words of *Bradshaw's Ghost*
(1659), for example, a pamphlet in which Bradshaw insists, "To drive black
Pluto's Coach I'd rather dain, / Than to be Wagoner to *Charles'* wain" (1),
just as Satan in *Paradise Lost* refuses, "To bow and sue for grace / With
suppliant knee, and deify his power" (1: 111), insisting, "Better to reign in
Hell, than serve in Heaven" (1: 263). In *Bradshaw's Ghost*, Bradshaw boasted,
"for where / So e're I am, Hell properly is there" (2), just as Mephistopheles
in Marlowe's *Doctor Faustus* remarked, "but where we are is hell. / And
where hell is, There must we ever be" (2.1.122–3).[3] In these lines, we also
hear Satan in *Paradise Lost* who has "The Hell within him, for within him
Hell / He brings, and round about Him" (4: 20–1). In the case of *Bradshaw's
Ghost*, there is a precise analogy to current English history, as the "hell"
described in that pamphlet is the chaos that resulted from the Interregnum
period. In Milton's case, any analogy between the demons of *Paradise Lost*
and the Interregnum political figures is imprecise, yet the language is similar.[4]
The Miltonic representations of hell build force within the context of the
other like references to particular political figures in the pamphlet literature
of the English Revolution. To me, these similarities suggest that the author's
involvement with this genre may be quite deep indeed.

There are several possible explanations for this resemblance. Though
Milton does not allegorize particular figures in the manner conventional to
Parliament of hell pamphlets, nevertheless, by drawing upon the same
tropes, Milton might still raise fears about current popish or radical plots,
and thus signal his continuing commitment to the Protestant cause. In
picturing Satan in his *Paradise Lost*, Milton loads him with images from
antipopery propaganda. And it is true, Milton remained a fierce enemy of all
popery throughout his life. It would have been important for Milton, an
advocate of religious toleration, to oppose Catholicism with virulence,
especially in the Restoration, where defenders of religious toleration were
accused of also defending Catholicism. However, Satan more closely resembles the parliamentary figures lampooned in the Parliament of hell genre of
the Interregnum than he does the conventional papist.

Milton's use of this royalist convention could lead us to draw a surprising
conclusion, that *Paradise Lost* expressed not only a general anti-Catholic

sentiment, but specifically voiced an anti-Cromwellian, and even a royalist, message. Given the pervasiveness of the Parliament of hell conventions in the revolutionary period, we might infer that Milton's own readers would compare his Satan to the Royalists' accounts of the rebels during the English Revolution. There is much to compare. In *Paradise Lost*, Satan begins his second war campaign with a rally to his troops, using republican rhetoric (5: 772–907) which recalled that of the Interregnum leaders: "what if better counsels might erect / Our minds and teach us to cast off this Yoke?" (5: 785–6). Abdiel's response, that Satan "hast'n to appease / Th'incensed Father, and th'incensed Son, / While Pardon may be found in time besought" (5: 846–8), is perhaps that of the post-Restoration parliamentarian, who hoped for mercy and an "act of oblivion" to be dispensed by the returning king. Could Milton have welcomed the second Charles, like Marvell, who in disavowing the "Good Old Cause," reported, "I think the Cause was too good to have been fought for"? (*The Rehearsal Transpros'd*, 135). Milton has been associated with Royalism before; this evidence of his condemnation of the revolution could be used to deliver a fatal blow to the recent Marxist-inspired image of Milton as a left-leaning radical even to the end of his days. If Milton adopted the royalist genre, then perhaps we ought to reconsider Milton's political allegiances in the Restoration.

Yet Milton just never gave in and supported Charles II. Just a little more than a month before the king returned, Milton brought out a second and enlarged edition of his *Readie and Easie Way*; "What I have spoken," he revealed in its introduction, "is the language of the good old cause" (Woolrych, 135). Though he might have come to disapprove of the Interregnum government's means, he never wavered in his commitment to the fundamental principles of "spiritual or civil libertie," as he described them in *The Readie and Easie Way*. His opposition to arbitrary power as a kind of self-enslavement keeps popping up in the poem, and so at many times his beliefs conflicted with the Restoration Royalists' scheme.

Or could Milton have presented this episode to throw Royalists off his scent? By evoking the royalist tradition in the first pages of his book, Milton could be steering potentially hostile readers toward a judgment that he had indeed changed his mind about the Interregnum, while covertly remaining loyal to the Good Old Cause. Any reader who picked up *Paradise Lost* in 1667 looking for political intent could have seen those fallen angels in hell in the first books as the convention dictated: as a condemnation of Cromwell and his crew. By opening with this recognizable genre, perhaps Milton evaded the Restoration censors. In his account of *Paradise Lost*, Christopher Hill suggests that vigilant readers will penetrate beyond the "deliberate mystification" of his poetry to get at Milton's true meaning, as, for example, in Milton's epithet "sons of Belial," which Hill argues "everyone would understand" to refer to Cavalier and new-Cavalier "bullies" (1977: 406–9). Yet if all we need is a "key," as Hill recommends, if Milton encodes his poem with things "everyone would understand," then we might imagine the censor's job to be quite easy. If this were the case, we would have no *Paradise Lost* in the seventeenth century.

Paradise Lost, of course, is a censored text, but not in the way that Hill sees it. *Paradise Lost* is not merely a stump for Milton's revolutionary political ideas, now unpopular in the current political climate, ideas that under specific circumstances could not be voiced overtly. The very circumstances of Milton's work – the restoration of monarchy, the new literary milieu, the tempering of religious enthusiasm – are all integral to Milton's poem. We cannot merely remove such aspects in order to find the "real" meaning of the poem – for these constitute the meaning of the poem. I see *Paradise Lost* as a work that expresses anxieties about the status of indirect, allegorical, and censored writing, conditions specific to the Restoration literary milieu but ones that, as Milton sadly came to realize, were inherent in public writing.

I argue here that in *Paradise Lost*, Milton not only thwarted the expectations that might be raised by the Parliament of hell trope; he also rejected a simple ratio of literary representation to history and cleared the way for his revolutionary reader to perform interpretive acts in the future. Milton evoked this genre in order to convey his loyalty to the spirit of the revolution, though not to its agents. Milton shared with the Royalists a degree of contempt for actors on the Interregnum political stage. But he did not go so far as to condemn the revolution. With his representation of the devils in hell, Milton showed that a single set of signs could bear numerous interpretations; that political allegory – and allegory in general – required special skills in reading; and that, finally, the failure of the English Revolution was not a matter of God's decree, but of human weakness. Consequently, I focus on Milton's search for a "fit audience" in light of the demands of the mode of allegory on its readership. In *Paradise Lost*, Milton summons readers to become more keenly aware of their susceptibility to political deception. Milton aimed to promote readerly skills as a means for English citizens to regain the individual freedoms that had slipped through the revolutionary leaders' fingers.

Milton and the Parliament of Hell: Political Intention in *Paradise Lost*

Mixing bejeweled imagery of Oriental splendor with the mundane tropes of republican rhetoric, Milton creates an entirely original Satan in his first two books of his poem. But Milton begins *Paradise Lost* with a conventional

Parliament of hell scene, as Satan greets his host and convenes his stygian council. Just as the Devil, who, represented in numerous pamphlets in the Restoration, plotted to regain England from his hellish headquarters, Milton's devils in *Paradise Lost* vowed to "reascend" and "repossess thir native seat" (1: 633–4; 2: 75–6). Moloch's plan of "open War" (2: 51) mirrors the parliamentary strength, its New Model Army. Satan's throne, "of Royal State, which far / Outshone the wealth of *Ormus* or of *Ind,* / Or where the gorgeous East with richest hand / Show'rs on her Kings *Barbaric* Pearl and Gold" in *Paradise Lost* (2: 1–4) resembles that of the illegitimate parliamentary leaders in the royalist pamphlet *Mercurius Elencticus* (1649): "They have murdered the King; Banished or Imprisoned his Consort, Children, seized upon his Palace, set his Crown on their heads; wear his Apparel, and Furniture; and then they cry out – see in what splendor we sit."[5] Much like Hugh Peters in *The Famous Tragedie of King Charles I* (1649), whom the dramatic character Cromwell praises for his "insinuating persuasive art" (1), Milton's Belial touts a "persuasive accent," making "the worse appear / The better reason, to perplex and dash / Maturest Counsels" (2: 118, 113–15).[6]

Worst of all, Satan in *Paradise Lost* has become a tyrant. In hell, the obedient fallen angels "towards him they bend / With awful reverence prone; and as a God / Extol him equal to the highest in Heav'n" (2: 477–9). Fawning and idolatrous, these minions have surrendered their liberty to their diabolical master. In the royalist Parliament of hell genre also, the devil's sway over his underlings was envisioned as a tyranny. In *A Trance; or, News from Hell* (1649), one underling gleefully reports to Lucifer her lord: "We have reduced that Kingdom to a new conformity with this of your Majesties'" (6). This royalist picture matches Milton's estimation of Satan's power over his fleet: "Devil with Devil damn'd / Firm concord holds" (2: 496–7). Full obedience to Satan is also presented in *The Parliaments Petition to the Divell* (1648), in which Parliament swears "that we (to serve you) have laid aside all service of God, all Loyalty towards our King, and all Christian love and charity towards men, we have robbed God of as much of his glory as we possibly could"; later, Parliament grants, "we are your creatures," wholly merging with their creator and owner, Satan (3, 7).

In *Paradise Lost*, Satan's tyranny consists partly in not allowing free debate. For the debate in hell is not really a free exchange of ideas; Satan wrote a script in which Beelzebub would propose his plan, and then Satan himself "prevented all reply" (2: 467). This is not a true dialogue, such as that in which truth and "Falsehood grapple; who ever knew Truth put to the worse, in a free and open encounter" (*Areopagitica, Complete Prose Works* 2: 561). Rather, Satan coerced his audience by his sole voice's power: "But they / Dreaded not more th'adventure than his voice / Forbidding; and at once with him they rose" (2: 473–5). The debate in hell is one example of falsified public speech, a context in which Truth may not "open herself faster" (*Areopagitica*, 521).

Yet the Royalists found the Devil's reign politically unsatisfactory only in that it placed the wrong man on top. According to the royalist renditions of the Parliament of hell, once God reinstated Charles II in his proper spot at the top of the pyramid, all Satan's evil effects would be reinverted. In the Restoration Parliament of hell genre, this is so. In *The Trial of Traytors; or, The Rump in the Round* (1660), for example, the Rump Parliament is represented as a coven of Devil's minions who futilely attempt to stop "time's wheel" from revolving, to stop the Restoration of monarchy. Too late. The figures in the illustration – half beast, sporting heads of animals like goats, cats, and foxes and cloven hoofs – all wear the dress of Puritans, stand upright, and are labeled with the names of Parliament-men and other Interregnum figures, including Judge Cook (ram), Hugh Peters (buck), Arthur Haselrig (fox), and Henry Vane (wolf). The "Rump's Scout," parodying the name of the parliamentary newsbook, is represented as the Devil himself, with his wings, curled tail, horns, and staff prodding his men on. The author of the piece reveals that,

> These Traitors all who had the World at will,
> Have now their *Scout* continues with them still;
> He pokes them forward with a Fork of steel,
> Urging Sir *Arthur* [Haselrig] for to stop the Wheel
> A while, but stay Time's Wheel is turned round,
> All's for the KING, but traitors in the Pound.[7]

In this Restoration Royalist's opinion, the return of the king was God's way of reasserting control over satanic forces; there was something inevitable, and surely providential, about the proper reinstating of cosmic hierarchy.

Yet in Milton's eyes, the hierarchy itself was part of the problem; in thinking that earthly politics mirrored celestial politics, Royalists were making a mistake. As Joan Bennett has persuasively argued, Satan's logic of analogy between his own realm and God's – and, by implication, the earthly arena and the divine – is completely flawed (1989: 50). But a further argument against Satan's rule is that his hierarchy did not allow for the exercise of free reason. In spite of Satan's rhetoric of "mutual league," the outcome of Satan's regime was conformity. For Milton, forcing conformity is sin: "How goodly, and how to be wished, were such an obedient unanimity as this, what a fine conformity would it starch us all into!" (*Areopagitica*, 545), Milton writes of censorship. Conformity not only bridled the human spirit, but it went against conscience, a view Milton expresses in his poem "On the New Forcers of Conscience under the Long Parliament," where he railed against the tyranny of the Presbyterians:

> Dare ye for this adjure the Civil Sword
> To force our Consciences that Christ set free,
> And ride us with a classic Hierarchy . . . ?

Those newly in power may be tyrants just like those whom they have evicted, as Milton asserts as he ends his poem: "*New Presbyter* is but *Old Priest* writ Large" (*Complete Poetry*, 144). In *Paradise Lost*, tyranny in hell and on earth may be the same. Milton disavows the kind of tyranny Satan imposes – not because it is Satan's – but because it is tyranny. Milton raises the question of legitimate or coerced persuasion as a kind of satanic tyranny in his example of Abdiel, who refused to adhere to Satan's program. In fact, the kind of tyranny Satan projects is like any other kind of tyranny, including that of Charles I and even that of the parliamentary leaders.

In finding Interregnum leaders were satanic, Milton puts himself in the same camp as the Royalists. Royalists had also blamed individual figures for ambition: meeting in hell in the pamphlet *Bradshaw's Ghost* (1659), Charles asks John Bradshaw, What is the good old cause? "As for the thing called the *Good Old Cause*," Bradshaw answers, "it is no other than the *Quarrel* at first begun with *you*, and now newnamed, nicknamed, or indeed rather *rebaptised*, but it was not long reverenced either for its *age*, or *goodness*, but like an old Almanack laid aside as useless, and this was it that broke my heart, the air of a *Common-wealth*, with the profit arising thereby, might have lengthened my life, but to see *Mars* triumphant, and yet *ourselves* cashiered, would it not even vex a *Saint*?" (11). But Milton's resemblance to the royalist critique of the Interregnum leaders stops there. For Milton, the Interregnum leaders exerted tyranny over free conscience, and that was their sin. Even as early as the *Second Defense* (1654), Milton expressed apprehensions about the ambitions of the leaders of the new government. When he praised Cromwell for refusing the crown, he also warned him that to have taken it would make it seem "as if, when you had subjugated some tribe of idolators with the help of the true God, you were to worship the gods you had conquered"; Milton also cheered Fairfax for having overcome "ambition ... and the thirst for glory which conquers all the most eminent men" (*Complete Prose Works* 4: 672). But Milton's worst fears did come true; the leaders of the revolution did prefer their own ambitions to the country's interest. Milton, it has been argued, began to lose faith in the English rulers as early as February 1649.

We are treading on the dangerous terrain of analyzing *Paradise Lost* for topical political intention. Of course, *Paradise Lost* is no political pamphlet.

But in his masterpiece of poetry, Milton expresses ethical concerns that arise out of his political moment, though they are not restricted to it. In a different manner, but not perhaps with a different intent, Milton also voices ethical aims in his prose writings; as we have seen in *Areopagitica*, Milton works to promote a reasoning, virtuous subject. In his *History of Britain*, Milton explicitly states his sour views about Parliament, and it is to these we shall turn in exploring the meanings of Milton's "Parliament of Hell" scenes in *Paradise Lost*. Because of its thorny publication history, it is not clear whether the views Milton expresses in the *History of Britain* are those of 1649, a warning to the Interregnum Parliament leaders, or of 1660, as an intervention in Restoration politics. The *History* itself was published in 1670, yet the section in which Milton comments directly on his political milieu, the *Character of the Long Parliament*, also called the "Digression," was not released until well after his death, withheld from print until 1681, and at that late date it was made to serve Tory political interests in the Exclusion crisis.[8] Only in 1932 did the full text of Milton's Digression appear. It is not clear why the Digression was omitted from publication in 1670, whether it was Milton's decision or that of Roger L'Estrange, the censor. Perhaps Milton struck the passage because it was terribly dark. Masson thinks the excision was Milton's decision, since the passage had become "irrelevant" (1859–94, 6: 811). But the Digression is relevant to us, for in it Milton gives not only his opinions about the Long Parliament – even if he withdrew them later – but also, and most importantly here, an image of a revolutionary reader.

Vociferously in the Digression, Milton voices dissatisfaction with Parliament. In his complaints, he sounds like the satirical Royalists who used the Parliament of hell genre to demolish the Parliamentarians during the Interregnum. Milton refers to the committeemen as "Children of the Devil" (*Complete Prose Works* 5: 449). He reviles them and the Presbyterian divines for having "set up a spirtual [*sic*] tyrannie by a secular power to the advancing of thir owne authorit[ie]" (447). Rather than reforming the Commonwealth, the end for which they were raised to power, they acted "unfaithfully, unjustly, unmercifully, and where not corruptly, stupidly" (449). What is more, the people blindly followed them. "Thus they who but of late were extolld as great deliverers, and had a people wholy at thir devotion," Milton wails, "by so discharging thir trust as wee see, did not onely weak'n and unfitt themselves to be dispencers of what libertie they pretended [*sic*], but unfitted also the people, now growne worse & more disordinate, to receave or to digest any libertie at all" (449). Like the Royalists who mocked the giddy multitude, the people were rendered "unfit" for liberty by their traitorous leaders in Milton's view: "For libertie hath a sharp and double edge fitt onelie to be handl'd by just and virtuous men, to

bad and dissolute it become[s] a mischief unweildie in thir own hands"
(449). In like manner, Milton had chided the people of England for
swallowing the king's book whole: "that people that should seek a King . . .
would shew themselves to be by nature slaves, and arrant beasts; not fitt for
that liberty which they cri'd out and bellow'd for, but fitter to be led back
again into thir old servitude, like a sort of clamouring & fighting brutes,
broke loos from thir copy-holds, that know not how to use or possess the
liberty which they fought for" (*Eikonoklastes, Complete Prose Works* 3: 581).
Milton concurs, then, with the royalist author of *A Trance; or, News from Hell*
(1649): "And never did the common people more truly act the part, and
discover the genius of a common people more lively, whose nature is still
thirsting after novelties and Utopian reformations, though they fool themselves thereby into a baser kind of slavery" (9).

Milton may agree with the Royalists in finding that the behavior of the
common people in the Interregnum was wholly despicable, but he comes to
a different conclusion about what is to be done in consequence. The royalist
solution was to reinstate the king and restore the lower sorts to their lower
places. In his *History of Britain*, however, Milton may have reviled his beloved
English and their leaders, but he would not wish them to be placed under a
leader's thumb. Rather, Milton thought that the common people must be
prepared for freedom in the future better than they were in 1649. What was
needed was a "fitter" people, able to withstand corrupt leaders. A fitter
people would be hard to find in Britain, whose citizens succeeded at the
arts of war rather than at those of peace: "For Britain (to speake a truth not
oft spok'n) as it is a land fruitful enough of men stout and couragious in
warr, so is it naturallie not over fertil of men able to govern justlie &
prudently in peace; trusting onelie on thir Mother-witt, as most doo, &
consider not that civilitie, prudence, love of the public more then of money
or vaine honour are to this soile in a manner outlandish; grow not here but
in minds well implanted with solid & elaborate breeding" (*Complete Prose
Works* 5: 451). Milton urges that leaders, like farmers and husbandmen,
implant "solid & elaborate breeding" in the people in the future. Writing
poetry was a like task, as he remarked in the prologue to the second book
of his *Reason of Church Government*: the aim of poetry was "to inbreed and
cherish in a great people the seeds of virtue and public civility" (*Complete
Prose Works* 1: 816).

The antidote to the miserable state of unfitness of the English people
lay in their pursuit of that "strenuous liberty" Milton alludes to in
Areopagitica, a liberty that is to be obtained through proper education, and
their reading. He remarks in the Digression that virtue may be culled from
the past by reading stories: "for stories teach us that libertie out of season
in a corrupt and degenerate age brought Rome it self into further slaverie"

(*Complete Prose Works* 5: 449). In his *History*, Milton believes that the public and its leaders could withstand these temptations if they knew more history. Milton urges his public to become educated in "civilitie, prudence," and "love of the public." For the English do not know history, "bred up, as few of them were, in the knowledge of Antient and illustrious deeds" (451). Because of their lack of this kind of training, like their forbears, the Britons, "what in the eyes of man cou[ld] be expected but what befel those antient inhabita[nts] whome they so much resembl'd, confusion in the end" (451).

In writing the *History of Britain*, Milton wants to make sure that, should another opportunity present itself, the people of England will not be so ill-equipped to meet it. His own writing will help to prevent that unfortunate outcome, for the failure of the Long Parliament was its "ill husbanding of those faire opportunities" (*Complete Prose Works* 5: 443). The story of the fate of the Britons after the demise of Roman rule offers an enlightening analogy: "Considering especially that the late civil broils had cast us into a condition not much unlike to what the *Britans* then were in, when the imperial jurisdiction departing hence left them to the sway of thir own Councils" (129). Milton knows he makes an unappealing comparison, but it is one that offers lessons in England's current weaknesses. Milton writes in his opening paragraph to the third book:

> Which times by comparing seriously with these later, and that confused Anarchy with this intereign, we may be able from two such remarkable turns of State, producing like events among us, to raise a knowledg of our selves both great and weighty, by judging hence what kind of men the *Britans* generally are in matters of so high enterprise, how by nature, industry, or custom fitted to attempt or undergoe matters of so main consequence: for if it be a high point of wisdom in every private man, much more is it in a Nation to know it self; rather than puft up with vulgar flatteries and encomiums, for want of self knowledge, to enterprise rashly and come off miserably in great undertakings. (129–30)

In this extremely rich and promising paragraph, Milton urges self-knowledge on the part of the entire nation as a first step in political liberty. Milton's political vision is premised on a personal vision of the individual self-scrutinizing soul, "a high point of wisdom in every private man," which is to be the model for an entire nation. If individuals are prideful, "puft up with vulgar flatteries and encomiums, for want of self knowledge," so much more are they a danger to the people over whom they are stewards. Milton presented another case of failed self-knowledge that led to a divine punishment in his account of David's taking the census in *Christian Doctrine*. There, Milton recollects language very like that of the passage from the *History of*

Britain: "as a result of his power King David's spirit was so haughty and puffed up" (*Complete Prose Works* 6: 333). The lesson in *Christian Doctrine* of this failure in self-knowledge was that David suffered punishment for his sins, but also that "God always produces something good and just out of these" (333). In his *History of Britain*, Milton hopes to help English citizens gain knowledge from their sins, offering a remedy to his troubled times of renewal and giving the entire English people a task to complete. When Milton draws a connection between the nation and an individual reader of texts, he recommends that reading itself is a means to a political end, of which self-knowledge is to be the base. Thus Milton asks his readers to pay especially close attention to history, which "may deserve attention more than common, and repay it with like benefit to them who can judiciously read" (*Complete Prose Works* 5: 129). By appealing to those who can "judiciously read," Milton understands his political analogy to include an ethical mission, one in which he presses for citizens of his nation to become readers, educating themselves in spiritual matters and history. Such ethical training may resolve the question of responsibility for the failure of the English Revolution.

The royalist allegory of the Parliament of hell put the responsibility for the Restoration squarely in God's hands. Milton, on the other hand, blamed humans. By casting such blame, Milton finds that God's justice allows for free will: "So we must conclude that God made no absolute decrees about anything which he left in the power of men, for men have freedom of action" (*Complete Prose Works* 6: 155). By encouraging humans to learn how to read as a first step toward ethical and political improvement, Milton vouches for the exercise of the will. By this logic, just as Adam and Eve's Fall in *Paradise Lost* was not proof that God foreordained it, the English Revolution was not divinely fated to fail. Rather, its current leaders, like their prototypes, Adam and Eve, freely fell by making bad political choices, by reading history badly or not at all.

Since humans, and not God, had failed England, what remained then was for humans to make themselves capable of succeeding in the future when another opportunity for liberation reared up. In the mean time, Milton believed, preparation was needed, to make "the people fittest to choose and the chosen fittest to govern" (*Complete Prose Works* 4: 615), through an education in "moulding the minds of men to virtue (whence arises true and internal liberty), in governing the State effectively, and preserving it for the longest possible space of time" (615).[9] These goals, while patently republican in their political vision of an "immortal commonwealth," as Harrington would put it, also are ethical, as Milton expresses a continued optimism about human capacity for change and growth. Harrington, by contrast, never gave the people a chance, sneering in 1656:

A people, when they are reduced unto misery and despair, become their own politicians, as certain beasts when they are sick become their own physicians and are carried by a natural instinct unto the desire of such herbs as are their proper cure; but the people, for the greater part, are beneath the beasts in the use of them. Thus the people of Rome, though in their misery they had recourse, by instinct as it were, unto the two main fundamentals of a commonwealth, participation of magistracy and the agrarian, did but taste and spit at them, not (which is necessary in physic) drink down the potion and in that their healths.... But if you do not take the due dose of your medicines (as there be slight tastes which a man may have of philosophy that incline unto atheism), it may chance to be a poison; there being a like taste of the politics that inclines to confusion, as appears in the institution of the Roman tribunes, by which magistracy, and no more, the people were so far from attaining unto peace that they, in getting but so much, got but heads for eternal feud. (*Oceana*, 277)

Milton, in opposing this shabby portrait of the people, believes that individuals may be made fit to govern themselves effectively; he believes they may be made so by acquiring habits of reading. It is true that Milton had pictured the mob as "a herd confus'd / A miscellaneous rabble, who extol / Things vulgar, & well weigh'd scarce worth the praise" (*Paradise Regained* 3: 49–51). But their leaders had been even worse. The people may be yet molded: "to guide Nations in the way of Truth / By saving Doctrine, and from error lead / To know" (*Paradise Regained* 2: 473–5). Over the passage of time, Michael explains in *Paradise Lost*, humans will be brought "Up to a better Cov'nant, disciplin'd / From shadowie Types to Truth, from Flesh to Spirit" (12: 302–3), finally able to convert their "works of Law to works of Faith" (12: 306). Satan will not be destroyed until the Second Coming, but his ability to affect men will diminish before that time: "nor so is overcome / *Satan* ... but his works / In thee and in thy Seed" (12: 390–5).

Thus in the first two books of *Paradise Lost*, Milton agreed with the royalist judgment on the leaders of the English Revolution; the leaders had become "thyself not free, but to thyself enthralled," as Abdiel had taunted Satan (6: 181). But Milton disagreed with the Royalists about who was responsible for that fact. While the Royalists blamed Satan and praised God for his victory in 1660, Milton blamed the individual men who had failed so miserably in their pursuit of liberty. In *Paradise Lost*, Milton corrected the current notion that Providence had designed the Restoration from the start.[10] As he wrote on Providence in *Christian Doctrine*, "even in sin, then, we see God's providence at work, not only in permitting it or withdrawing its grace, but often in inciting sinners to commit sin, hardening their hearts and blinding them" (*Complete Prose Works* 6: 331). Evil does not come from

God, "but he directs a will which is already evil" (332; Guns don't kill people; people kill people). Milton's example showing God's leaving the human will free to sin is David's evil action of taking the census. In that case, Milton explains, God "was the instigator of the deed itself, but David alone was responsible for all the wickedness and pride which it involved" (333). The lesson in *Christian Doctrine* of this failure in self-knowledge was that David suffered punishment for his sins. The general lesson is this: "God always produces something good and just out of these and creates, as it were, light out of darkness" (333).[11] How would humans in Milton's own time attain the understanding of the light that comes out of darkness, the good that comes out of evil, when their own leaders, from David on down, had failed to understand this?

"Darkness Visible": Milton and the Reader of Allegory

They would do so by reading. "Light out of darkness"; "From shadowie Types to Truth": Milton writes of the spiritual education of humans as if writing about reading allegory. Milton presents these inscrutable images to portray his process of educating readers to become virtuous, to become revolutionary readers. Learning how to read is no easy project, and Milton scatters hard-to-read passages all over his text as a means to test his own readers' strenuousness, and to prepare them for the more difficult task of reading history. Over and over in representing hell in *Paradise Lost*, for example, Milton presents scenes that challenge his readers to work, not only in the mirroring of the Parliament of hell genre, but also in those passages in which we find the motif of darkness visible, a literal paradox. When Satan is compared to the eclipse (1: 595–600), he is "Dark'n'd so, yet shone" (1: 600). Before Satan leaves the strange, indistinct geography of hell, he must pass through Chaos, but before that, he must exit the gates that are guarded by two figures who present the clearest instance of allegory in the poem; but its very clarity throws all the other semi-allegories in dark relief.

Sin is a figure identified with the eclipse. Her hellhounds, repeatedly returning into the kennel of her womb, follow her as they follow "the Night-Hag, when call'd / In secret, riding through the Air she comes / Lur'd with the smell of infant blood, to dance / With *Lapland* Witches, while the laboring Moon / Eclipses at thir charms" (2: 662–6). The eclipse metaphor appeared frequently as a royalist political allegory. It is significant that the eclipse image frequently served in a circuit of meanings during the English Revolution, specifically to do with the activity of interpreting political rhetoric. The author of *Mercurius Bellicus*, for example, used the eclipse metaphor to protest printing conditions: "Nothing but *Lyes* may bee now *Printed*: Truth hath received a *totall Eclipse*: else sure, the last *Lyurnall* had never had so strict a charge, to *conceale* the *Coppy* of the *Kings* last *Letter* . . . they will Print nothing that shall tend to the least *disturbance* of their own *Peace*, or *quiet*."[12] Truth, like the sun, is masked by Parliament's avid press corps, the diurnals, which this author derisively nicknames "Lyurnalls." If truth was often equated with King Charles, it was also likened as often to the sun in the civil war pamphlets. The Royalist Sir George Wharton, in his *Mercurio-Coelico-Mastix* (1644), opposed his accuser John Booker's almanac: "your opacious, dark, and unweildy stars at Westminster, who reject to be enlightened with the lively and wholesome rays of the Sun (I mean our Gracious King Charles)" (13). In a similar spirit, *The Downfall of Cerberus* (1660) cheered the return of monarchy and the demise of the Interregnum press. The three-headed "Cerberus" was explicitly taunted as the triumvirate of parliamentary mercuries, *Britannicus, Pragmaticus*, and *Politicus*: "'tis like thou'lt be / In *Pluto's* Parliament a *Mercury*, / From whence perhaps thy friends may look to hear / From thee, what news, and the nocturnals there." Rather than a "diurnal," these writers will produce business of the night, of darkness, "nocturnals."

Yet, as Joan S. Bennett has shown in her excellent analysis *Reviving Liberty*, Milton makes ample use of the image of an eclipse, or of the shadowed sun, fashioning a metaphoric structure in *Paradise Lost* to play against a very familiar royalist image. Though Bennett's account stops at the Restoration, the recurrence of this allegory even after 1660 takes on a significance like that of the Parliament of hell, vindicating the royalist perspective of a cosmic, natural hierarchy. Restoration Royalists used this eclipse image in their panegyrics to the returning monarch to justify a divine right theory of monarchy, as a theory that was not just a theory, but a natural reality. Among other poems greeting Charles II to the throne of England were Cowley's "Ode on the Blessed Restoration," Dryden's "Astrea Redux," Davenant's "Upon His Sacred Majesties Most Happy Return," and Waller's "To the King, Upon His Majesties Happy Return": all use the image to refer to Charles's recovery of his throne. Thomas Higgins, in "A Panegyrick to the King" (1660), writes: "As the sun, though he break out but late, / Darkness dispells, and drives all Clouds away. / A gloomy Morn turn to a glorious day" (Joseph Frank 1968: 456).

Milton's contribution, the antipanegyric to Satan, virtually echoes this Restoration royalist figure, both before and after his success (2: 486–95).[13] But Milton uses the eclipse image to turn it on its head. After Satan's victory, we have:

> At last as from a Cloud his fulgent head
> And shape Star-bright appear'd, or brighter, clad

> With what permissive glory since his fall
> Was left to him, or false glitter: All amaz'd
> At that so sudden blaze . . .

(10: 449–53)

According to Bennett, Milton uses the sun imagery to mark instances of false rulers (Satan in *Paradise Lost* and Charles I in *Eikonoklastes*) who fail to shine with the light given them, in contrast to the true ruler who keeps a proper balance of power and maintains God's law and spirit, and thus shines as a vehicle of those qualities. In his use of this image throughout the poem, then, Milton undermines the doctrine of the divine right of kings (37–9). Yet in the passage above, Milton makes clear that the shadows that fall upon Satan's head come from the true light of God, who has dispensed "permissive glory." The passive mood, "with what permissive glory since his fall / Was left to him," makes clear that Satan shines from no light of his own, but purely from reflected light, which the reader views glancing off his fallen form. Milton forces the reader to coincide with his point of view: who, after all, finds Satan's glory "permissive" or "left," but Milton? By calling into question the purity of the image of Satan as the returning ruler in eclipse, by parodying the Restoration panegyric, Milton asks readers to call into question the whole scheme of representation.

The eclipse was one sign of the problems of reading allegorically. Milton used the allegory of Charles or Satan as the sun not merely to evoke and to reject pervasive royalist imagery, but also to mark the difficulties of proper interpretation within an allegorical scheme of representation. In *Paradise Lost*, even for monarchs, the eclipse is something that "Perplexes"; the word *perplex* itself follows a chain of association denoting acts of failed or incomplete interpretation. For Milton, *perplexity* is a mark of interpretive challenge to make readers fit, as the first step to enlightenment. We recall Belial, who can make "the worse appear / The better reason, to *perplex* and dash / Maturest Counsels" (2: 113–15, italics mine). Milton's own readers must push beyond Belial's words to discover their inner worthlessness. One of Milton's first readers, Andrew Marvell, also used the term *perplex* to denote the beginning of his readerly task. Marvell linked his poem to Milton's when he revealed the difficulty of the task of reading. As Marvell grew "less severe" in his reading, he grasped the success of Milton's "Project." Marvell describes his own readerly conduct rather in the same manner as does the royalist James Howell, writing that his "Knowing Reader" should read more than once to obtain the valuable truth hidden inside his text; in response to *Paradise Lost*, Marvell was first "misdoubting his Intent," but "growing less severe" as he read. When Marvell started to "fear" that project's success, he admitted,

> Yet as I read, soon growing less severe,
> I lik'd his Project, the success did fear;
> Through that wide Field how he his way should find
> O'er which lame Faith leads Understanding blind;
> Lest he perplex'd the things he would explain,
> And what was easy he should render vain.
>   ("On *Paradise Lost*," Milton 1957: 209–10, 11–16)

Marvell applauds Milton for not making things too difficult. Marvell's use of the word *perplex* in his dedicatory poem might then reflect his understanding of the process of reading as a rocky path toward understanding. Significantly, the word *perplex* features in the passage on which the censor allegedly choked. Marvell's term *perplex* directly links his own response and the passage in Milton's *Paradise Lost* that supposedly ran into trouble with the censor, and Marvell may be said to exonerate Milton from a dangerous kind of perplexity.

In Milton's poem too, *perplexity* is both a physical and a mental condition, one involving the difficulties of finding one's way in a confusing field of signs. As a physical condition, it is associated with a difficult journey: Satan's tour of earth is "pensive and slow," because the thick "undergrowth / Of shrubs and tangling bushes had perplext / All path of Man or Beast that pass'd that way" (4: 175–7). *Perplexed*, Satan finds his way obstructed by the rich foliage in Eden. Journeying in *Paradise Lost* is not something those in Eden generally want to do; the only human journey – the expulsion of Adam and Eve – is an unwanted one. However, of all the creatures in Eden, only Satan actually wants to *go* somewhere. For the beasts and the humans, this undergrowth is not an impediment, but "fram'd" – as are all things made by God – "to man's delightful use" (4: 691–2). Satan's "wand'ring quest" (2: 830) through Chaos and beyond, "alone, and without guide, half lost" (2: 975), signifies not only his moral condition, but also his interpretive fallen state.

In the poem, *perplexity* in general is a satanic mode, both as a physical and a mental act, similar to Spenserian error but also to Milton's own concept of failed virtue.[14] After Satan's announcement to his hellish assembly, for instance, the angels bide time until their leader's return, "wand'ring, each his several way / Pursues, as inclination or sad choice / Leads him perplext, where he may likeliest find / Truce to his restless thoughts" (2: 522–6). The fallen angels hope to ease the psychological torment of "restless thoughts" by physical wandering; we find them later "in wand'ring mazes lost" (2: 561), mazes that are not material, do not resemble the Renaissance genre of romance and errantry, but that are intellectual, "vain wisdom all, and false Philosophie" (2: 565). Their perplexity consists in the devils' failings in – or in their being prevented from – apprehending the simple truth of God's eminence. This satanic perplexity contrasts to Adam and Eve's manner, both before and after the Fall. The angels have free will in hell, but the direction of their wandering is a "sad choice"; it contrasts with the better choice of Adam, who, responding to Raphael's lesson, becomes "clear'd of doubt." Having been "freed from intricacies" by his lesson before the Fall, Adam is "taught to live / The easiest way, nor with perplexing thoughts / To interrupt the sweet of Life" (8: 179, 182–4). The angels, in contrast, choose the physical directions that get them morally lost, erroneously searching for inner peace by exterior voyage.

After the Fall, Adam too loses this "easiest way" to the "sweet of Life." In the final book of *Paradise Lost*, however, Adam's condition may resemble in many ways that of the fallen angels in book 2, except that he rises above perplexity:

> now first I find
> Mine eyes true op'ning, and my heart much eas'd,
> Erstwhile perplext with thoughts what would become
> Of mee and all Mankind; but now I see
> His day, in whom all Nations shall be blest
>
> (12: 273–7)

The lessons of Adam in book 8 are different for the fallen man in book 12; that experienced man lives with perplexities he must himself solve.[15] In the passage from book 12, Adam relates a narrative, a before-and-after story. Yet unlike Satan's before-and-after, Adam recognizes the changes within himself.

Perplexity thus stands as a starting point for Milton's revolutionary reader. Michael Wilding has suggested that the Fall of the humans may be seen as a fall into a world of politics, that, "when both have eaten the apple, their plight is described in political terms. As a result of the fall they have become political beings. Political–Satanic–language enters," and thus, "part of the knowledge achieved by eating the fruit of the tree, then, is a political knowledge" (1987: 229–30). Wilding makes a mistake in equating political language with Satan or the Fall, however, by implying that there is another, preferable, kind of language. My point here is that Milton insists that humans have no access to this language, even if it existed. This is as much to say that books are inherently bad, an argument Milton opposed in *Areopagitica* when he wrote, "wholesome meats to a vitiated stomack differ little or nothing from unwholesome, and best books to a naughty mind are not unappliable to occasions of evill" (*Complete Prose Works* 2: 512). The effects of books – evil or good – depend on the reader's state to begin with. The lesson there was, "to the pure all things are pure" (512). In the case of postlapsarian language, there can be no inherently "satanic" language either:

Milton appears to agree with Hobbes that language does not form a natural connection to the signified. Fallen, political language is the only language to be had, Milton seems to say, and Adam and Eve had better get used to it. It is neither inherently "satanic" nor "angelic"; as the last two books of *Paradise Lost* show, Adam has as much difficulty conversing with the Angel as he might have with the Devil.

After the Fall, though, reading takes on a new role, because there is another kind of representation to deal with. There is first of all history, which offers the human pair new perspectives and occasions upon which to test their ability to discern truth. Understanding history and politics after the Fall are equivocal tasks, because there are multiple ways of seeing and of speaking. But these tasks are vital to Milton's intention voiced in his *History*: history teaches humans the lessons they so often fail to learn in life. Adam has to learn to interpret the equivocal signs so that he sees properly. His heart may be repentant after the Fall, but his eyes are yet clouded. In the final books of *Paradise Lost*, Adam undergoes a training in hermeneutics under the tutelage of Michael. David Loewenstein has eloquently mapped Adam's education in *Milton and the Drama of History*, in which Adam learns that history will be "an essentially tragic process full of confusion and violence" (100); further, this is a vision Adam can perceive only by resisting false appearances. Loewenstein focuses on the content of this history, its dark, almost deterministic patchwork of repeated failures and its ambiguous relation to typological, progressive history. But after the Fall, there is something aside from the simple lessons of history; there is the fact of mediation for humans to cope with. Adam's current clear sight is the result of a vision of history that has been properly mediated, in this case, by Michael's narrative.[16]

After the Fall, however, Adam and Eve are separated from God, and their understandings are shaded by that distance.[17] The heavens recede to a great height; the human pair must be removed from their birthplace. In the process is Adam's learning how to read, a process that, it has been argued, is the subject of the epic (Radzinowicz 1968: 31–51). Reading is explicitly and inherently a mediated process. After the Fall, Adam no longer stands in a direct relation with God. He fears the disunion, and it prompts his first query to Michael:

> This most afflicts me, that departing hence,
> As from his face I shall be hid, depriv'd
> His blessed count'nance; here I could frequent,
> With worship, place by place where he voutsaf'd
> Presence Divine
>
> (11: 315–19)

Michael explains that though it appears there is a gap between Adam and the divine, God will be with him. When he reassures Adam, however, his language is vague: "Yet doubt not but in Valley and in Plain / God is as here, and will be found alike / Present" (11: 349–50): the "is as here" presents a muddle: is God or is God not here? Michael insists that God may be felt by marks of his presence, though he may no longer be perceived directly:

> and of his presence many a sign
> Still following thee, still compassing thee round
> With goodness and paternal Love, his Face
> Express, and of his steps the track Divine.
> (11: 351–54)

Adam will have to learn how to read those signs. We hear an echo of Milton's abject state, "In darkness, and with dangers compast round, / And solitude" (7: 27–8).

Even before his history lesson, however, Adam has already felt abject on his own, and this condition requires some kind of practical response: reading. In his first deed of repentance, Adam feels the presence of God, but this presence is only surmised, and it involves interpretation: "Methought I saw him placable and mild, / Bending his ear; persuasion in me grew / That I was heard with favor" (11: 151–3). Adam's solution is based upon conjecture; "Methought" is an opinion, a "persuasion," not an unmediated fact. His first fallen act thus involves interpreting his station relative to God, which is now a state of abjectness. Unlike Satan, however, he fully accepts it. Adam's second interpretive action follows immediately on the first, and it involves reading the world around him. There is something new, animals hunting one another, in a glorious dance of airy predator and prey; and there is the figure of the eclipse:

> Nature first gave Signs, imprest
> On Bird, Beast, Air, Air suddenly eclips'd
> After short blush of Morn; nigh in her sight
> The Bird of *Jove*, stoopt from his aery tow'r,
> Two Birds of grayest plume before him drove:
> (11: 182–6)

Viewing nature's new way, Adam interprets, only gropingly:

> O *Eve*, some furder change awaits us nigh,
> Which Heav'n by these mute signs in Nature shows

Forerunners of his purpose, or to warn
Us haply too secure of our discharge
From penalty . . .

(11: 193–7)

His second lesson in reading is reading death. Though he does not know what these signs are, he knows they are bad. He is sure that they mean something. After the Fall, there are immediate changes in his perceptual powers: "doubt / And carnal fear that day dimm'd *Adam's* eye" (11: 211–12).

But Adam also inhabits an unfamiliar world, and needs knowledge for new purposes. In his new world, he must do more than sing praises to God or chat with Eve. For Adam, there is now the knowledge of politics, of society, and of sin to contend with. This knowledge, further, is mediated through Michael's historical representations. Such clear sight, however, is not so readily available to the rest of humanity. Adam, presumably, will go out of Eden equipped with the ability to apply his lessons. How will Milton's own readers be so well supplied?

In *Paradise Lost*, Milton takes on Michael's mission, performing for his reader the intermediary acts that will justify the ways of God to men. Just as Adam's knowledge is received through the intercession of Michael, the reader's knowledge is received through Milton. But first, those readers must be made fit. How are they to be made so? Michael supplies the answer. Attending for the grace of the Lord's Second Coming, Adam in the meantime must be "disciplin'd / From shadowy Types to Truth, from Flesh to Spirit, / From imposition of strict Laws, to free / Acceptance of large Grace" (12: 302–5) (Madsen 1968; Schwartz 1988). Until that time, there is an earthly rent in the representational order. In his lesson in reading, Adam has begun to learn how to work through this disjunction, but it will take many more steps along the way. The problem is one and the same as the angel's "lik'ning spiritual to corporeal forms, / As may express them best" (5: 573–4): that of understanding how meaning might from "corporeal to incorporeal turn" (5: 413). It is the task of reading allegory. To return to the image of the eclipse, then, and to its "perplexity," we find Milton making an early signal by this image in the first book of *Paradise Lost*, that representational imagery, whether it is the holy image of the divine or the polemical use of allegory, is to be treated with suspicion.

The first book is spattered with epic similes and classical allusions, and critics have associated these with Milton's rejection of the classical epic. But these similes also perform a task of separating the reader from immediate experience of the events transpiring in hell. These call for the readers to make interpretations, to be prompted to apply readerly skills and power.

Milton sometimes gives a poor guide for the reader's understanding, offering only qualification upon qualification through these difficult similes. When Satan alights on dry land, for example, Milton does not present a clear picture: "if it were Land that ever burn'd / With solid, as the Lake with liquid fire / And such appear'd in hue; as when the force / Of subterranean wind transports a hill" (1: 228–31). We can know this landscape only by comparison, but it is by comparison to things we have never seen.[18] It appears that Milton, and not just the sociable angel, must liken "spiritual to corporeal forms, / As may express them best" (5: 573–4) in his representation of Satan in hell.

Similitude and conditionality both are forms of negation. And negation is the prime means by which Milton expresses the features of hell. Satan walks with "uneasy steps / Over the burning Marl, not like those steps / On Heaven's Azure" (1: 295–7). Satan's hell is most unlike Lucifer's heaven, but only through a negative analogy can one know hell. When Satan's legions come awake, "Nor did they not perceive the evil plight / In which they were, or the fierce pains not feel" (1: 335–6). Negative upon negative: Milton's language asserts that they did perceive their plight and feel their pain – or did they?

Simile offers another form of negation, because it asserts what exists in the form of what does not. Readers see the hellish figures summoned by Satan only indistinctly:

> As when the potent Rod
> Of *Amram's* Son in *Egypt's* evil day
> Wav'd round the Coast, up call'd a pitchy cloud
> Of *locusts*, warping on the Eastern Wind,
> That o'er the Realm of impious *Pharaoh* hung
> Like Night, and darken'd all the Land of *Nile*
> So numberless were those bad Angels seen.
>   (1: 338–44)

Satan wields his wand like Moses, now lord of the flies. Readers must make their way through this terrain by groping. Satan's crew hearkens to its leader as from the mists of sleep (1: 332–4), much like the reader of these scenes who sees only as through a glass, darkly. The crowd throngs "numberless" (1: 780), like "Faery Elves, / Whose midnight Revels, by a Forest side / Or Fountain some belated Peasant sees, / Or dreams he sees, while over-head the Moon / Sits Arbitress" (1: 781–5). The reader's position is marked as that of the "belated Peasant" – perhaps the rustic shepherd of pastoral, perhaps Spenser's Colin Clout – but also as the poet, the ever-belated Milton. The way to understand hell is tenebrous indeed: does that peasant "see," or merely "dream he sees"? With the hellish throng turning a stygian day into night by masking the sun, we have an image of "darkness visible," very much like that of the sun in eclipse.

Milton refused to allegorize in his representation of Satan and in the account of the war of the angels in *Paradise Lost*, and Michael Murrin has suggested that "this choice signals the end" of a literary tradition of allegory in epic (1980: 153). Milton's biblical poetics and his preference for typology were partly responsible for his choice, Murrin argues, but the poet's "iconoclastic theology" was what finally determined his literary mode. "Linguistically," Murrin writes, "iconoclasm cut Milton off from the traditional language of analogy. . . . The tradition of neither biblical nor secular allegory was available to Milton. He was a literalist in his scriptural interpretation" (167, 169). The only instance of allegory – the brief Sin and Death scene – is strictly satanic, continues Murrin; allegory is itself rendered a satanic mode (cf. Ferry 1963). Though others have disputed Murrin's claims, explaining that with *Paradise Lost* we have not the end of a particular allegorical tradition, but rather an epistemological complication of it, it is generally agreed that, whether in the Spenserian high mode or in Bunyan's "mechanick Puritan mode," allegory as a literary kind died out in the seventeenth century. Stephen Fallon attributes this to a "decline in the status of universals" (1987: 338, 350). I suggest that there is another factor to take into account: the crisis in hermeneutics that was the result of the writing of the English Revolution. *Paradise Lost* engages with contemporary allegorical representations of Satan in hell as a response to this crisis, and as a rejection of the royalist interpretation of cosmic hierarchy.

What Happens at Night: Making Darkness Visible

What does Milton do to offset the political investment in allegory? He interprets perversely, like Abdiel in his opposition to Satan. God rewards Abdiel: "To stand approv'd in sight of God, though Worlds / Judg'd thee perverse" (6: 35–6), and Milton offers the example of Abdiel as a mark that individuals may take actions against the forces of tyranny by performing seemingly perverse acts, which, when properly interpreted, are glorious. Abdiel's actions may be judged "perverse" by the world (6: 29–37), but they are the virtuous ones. Reading allegories may also be reading perversely. Until the Second Coming, all reading is somewhat perverse. Until that day, "so shall the World go on, / To good men malignant, to bad men benign" (12: 537–8). Since humans, and not God, had failed the revolution, humans needed better preparation before they could reform the world, and part of their preparation was in learning how to read.

In *Paradise Lost*, Milton uses the motif of darkness as a figure for this condition of hermeneutic struggle, inverting the common sense in which darkness connotes a spiritual condition of abjection from God. Like Abdiel's perversity, blindness itself can be a virtue. The sun in *Paradise Lost* is not always preferable to the moon. Indeed, much happens under cover of darkness, starting with the creation of Milton's poem. As we know, Milton's muse assaults him at night. Urania, "who deigns / Her nightly visitation unimplor'd, / And dictates to me slumb'ring" (9: 21–3; cf. 7: 29) is the patroness of astronomy and queen of the night. But the muse is also "Light" itself, whom Milton claims, "Nightly I visit" (3: 32). Thus when Milton invokes "The meaning, not the Name" of his muse (7: 5), he presents a linguistic obfuscation, a mimetic paradox, light in the midst of darkness.

Adam and Eve, even before the Fall, have to explain the presence of darkness in their world as a necessary absence of light. In book 4, before Adam and Eve first consummate their marriage and share in God's creation, they have a little discussion about what happens at night. In this conversation, Adam reveals that he knows something about the universe, well before his celestial instruction. Eve asks, "But wherefore all night long shine these, for whom / This glorious sight, when sleep hath shut all eyes?" (4: 657–8); to which Adam answers:

> Those have thir course to finish, round the Earth,
> By morrow Ev'ning, and from Land to Land
> In order, though to Nations yet unborn,
> Minist'ring light prepar'd, they set and rise;
>
> (4: 661–4)

The stars first express a cosmic order, a cycle of nature in which the whole earth is held. But further, they express a spiritual order as well:

> Lest total darkness should by Night regain
> Her old possession, and extinguish life
> In Nature and all things, which these soft fires
> Not only enlighten, but with kindly heat
> Of various influence foment and warm,
> Temper or nourish, or in part shed down
> Thir stellar virtue on all kinds that grow
> On Earth, made hereby apter to receive
> Perfection from the Sun's more potent Ray.
>
> (4: 665–73)

The stars keep night at bay, but they also prepare the human world for the light of the sun. Adam suggests that the sun is too powerful at times, and needs its way muted before the sensitive apprehension of humans. Adam stresses the limitations of human perception, knowing the frailty of human abilities: those on earth, too, need to be made "apter to receive" the sun's light. What happens at night, when the moon holds sway, is a planning, a "fomenting" and "nourishing."

Adam's account matches Milton's explanation of his own writing process, as Milton, too, uses nighttime to advantage. Adam continues, in one of the loveliest passages in the poem:

> These then, though not unbeheld in deep of night,
> Shine not in vain, nor think, though men were none,
> That Heav'n would want spectators, God want praise;
> Millions of spiritual Creatures walk the Earth
> Unseen, both when we wake, and when we sleep:
> All these with ceaseless praise his works behold
> Both day and night: how often from the steep
> Of echoing Hill or Thicket have we heard
> Celestial voices to the midnight air,
> Sole, or responsive each to other's note
> Singing thir great Creator: oft in bands
> While they keep watch, or nightly rounding walk,
> With Heav'nly touch of instrumental sounds
> In full harmonic number join'd, thir songs
> Divide the night, and lift our thoughts to Heaven.
> (4: 674–88)

The stars have work to do. They "shine not in vain," and at night give the light by which the "millions of spiritual Creatures" may praise God. The stars illuminate the world for those who "keep watch," the faithful many who sing unheard songs. Milton echoes the Puritan language of preacher Francis Woodcock, who explained his mission as God's "people's Watchmen, and his own Remembrancers," an allusion to Isaiah's watchmen on the walls of Jerusalem.[19] Adam's unfallen description of what happens at night sounds like a benign version of Milton's description of his own condition. Rather than sweet succor, though, Milton finds the stars give him only intermittent comfort:

> though fall'n on evil days,
> On evil days though fall'n, and evil tongues;
> In darkness, and with dangers compast round,
> And solitude; yet not alone, while thou
> Visit'st my slumbers Nightly, or when Morn

Purples the East: still govern thou my Song,
Urania, and fit audience find, though few.
(7: 25–31)

Like those unseen millions of "Spiritual Creatures," singing while Adam sleeps, "Sole, or responsive each to other's note" (4: 81), Milton is not alone, but is joined by his muse. His nightly visions encourage him to "shine on" in his writing, "as the wakeful Bird / Sings darkling, and in shadiest Covert hid / Tunes her nocturnal Note" (3: 38–40). With the failure of the English Revolution, with "*Bacchus* and his Revellers" (7: 33) carousing until dawn, in *Paradise Lost* Milton urges his fellow countrymen not to give up faith in their cause; he seeks a "fit audience ... though few" to prepare and keep watch in the meantime.

With this concept of stellar virtue, Milton expresses his own spiritual hopes, and he also explains his literary impulses. In the nighttime of the earthly kingdom launched in the Restoration, these faithful few, keeping watch, await the true light of day, the true Kingdom of God. For Milton, the task ahead was to keep up the faith, either "Sole, or responsive each to other's note." In my reading, Milton never gave up on the people of England, and these passages in Eden explain the value of night, offering us a method for understanding how Milton thought the faithful ought to spend their time in the meanwhile. The period of darkness affords time to nourish "all kinds that grow" to become "apter to receive / Perfection from the Sun's more potent Ray" (4: 671–3) a time of heuristic growth. What follows this passage is the first lovemaking in Eden, an episode that seals the bond between husband and wife, and through which Milton links humanity to the order of God's Creation. Creation thus follows darkness, just as Milton's poem emerges after nightfall.

While they wait for a better future, however, there is night, the cover of darkness, in which both Satan and the poet take wing. Under that cover, however, the distinctions between good and evil are veiled. When Beelzebub speaks, for instance, the crowd is fixed, "still as Night / Or Summer's Noon-tide air" (2: 308–9): either apogee will do.[20] Back in hell, Mammon fails to see the difference between the condition of true light and the light they might recreate in hell:

This deep world
Of darkness do we dread? How oft amidst
Thick clouds and dark doth Heav'n's all-ruling Sire
Choose to reside, his Glory unobscur'd,
And with the Majesty of darkness round
Covers his Throne; from whence deep thunders roar
Must'ring thir rage, and Heav'n resembles Hell?

As he our darkness, cannot we his Light
Imitate when we please?

(2: 262–70)

When Mammon claims the devils can make a heaven out of hell, he reads the figure of the sun behind the clouds as a token of the commensurability of the two realms. But in this reading, he expresses a flawed theory of imitation: he believes since hell bears a physical resemblance to heaven at times, as when clouds cover the sun, hell may thus become a heaven to its inhabitants. Erroneously thinking that the qualities of light and darkness are reversible, Mammon interprets the figure of the sun and clouds as encouragement that those in darkness may yet recover light. But Milton and his readers know that this can never be. The state of hell is evil in its imitation of God's true state in heaven. In thinking the fallen angels can "imitate" God, they are reading incorrectly, incorrectly transcribing the text of heaven in another text, the text of hell. Milton offers his own text as an authentic rewriting of heaven's text, though one that is aware of its status as thoroughly mediated.

Milton suggests there is a discrepancy between interpretations made in hell or on earth and those made in heaven. True intepretation comes from without, as God's word is rewritten in a man's heart. Abdiel in his "testimony of Truth" (6: 33) rebukes Satan for his reading of matters, first on doctrinal grounds, and then on experiential ones: "by experience taught we know how good, / And of our good, and of our dignity / How provident he is" (5: 826–8). Abdiel is commended by God, for withstanding the hellish ridicule: "though Worlds / judg'd thee perverse" (6: 35–6), in God's perspective he is on the right path. Authentic signification is difficult to distinguish in the lower realms, and may indeed appear "perverse." Milton thus resists the satanic practice of allegory, in which there is a one-to-one relation between the political order, the cosmic order, and the representational order. In so doing, Milton resists the Royalists' appeal to an audience to read history along the fixed lines of those correspondences. Milton acknowledges the mediation required to understand the figures of history.[21] *Paradise Lost* is principally concerned with proper interpretation, given the human condition of contingency, both in spiritual and in political terms.

Milton's repeated strategy of provoking allegorical interpretations while refusing to supply unequivocal "keys" to the allegory is meant as a lesson, a challenge, and more importantly, as a warning to his revolutionary readers. He presses the stress points of a popular contemporary political allegory, and baffles readers' expectations of a clear meaning. Doing so, Milton, in the first two books of *Paradise Lost*, sets before the reader a subtext of the multiple political possibilities of literary genres, and the rest of the poem leads readers down a path toward spiritual enlightenment that involves learning how to read. Milton used what Annabel Patterson has called "the concept of functional, intentional ambiguity" (1984: 158), not to encode a particular meaning, as if the fit reader could find the "key" to unlock Milton's cabinet. Rather, Milton exposes the dangers of such allegories for the unwary reader. This is not to say that Milton "gave up" on his public, or even on history, in playing indeterminately upon this allegory, or that he retreated into an unpolitical "Paradise within." The lessons of *Paradise Lost*, on the contrary, are activist and engaged. Milton urged his readers to become a fit audience, revolutionary readers, and they were to do this by reading between the lines, by becoming adept at detecting and resisting propaganda: not because rhetoric and propaganda were inherently evil or satanic; nor because a plain style was better (in fact, there was no such thing as a plain style, except in Eden and in heaven: the one irrevocably in the past, and the other presently always mediated through fallen language). Members of Milton's fit audience sit and wait in the darkness, but they read by candlelight in the meantime.

NOTES

This essay is excerpted from a chapter of Achinstein's book *Milton and the Revolutionary Reader* (Princeton: Princeton University Press, 1994). Citations of Milton's poetry are from Hughes' edition (Milton 1987).

1   After all, Milton, Marvell, and Dryden, as employees of the Protectorate, all walked in the procession at Oliver Cromwell's funeral in September 1658 (Hill 1978: 1).
2   Achinstein discusses this genre in detail earlier in her chapter; see my introduction, p. 4 above.
3   This is also an echo of Achilles in *Odyssey* 11.460; Christopher Marlowe, *Doctor Faustus*, in Russell A. Fraser and Norman Rabkin, eds., *Drama of the English Renaissance: The Tudor Period* (New York: Macmillan, 1976).
4   Of current scholars, Michael Wilding (1987: ch. 8) makes the closest concrete connection between the devils in *Paradise Lost* and midcentury political figures, though Wilding argues that Milton was critical of the Interregnum parliament, which, reflecting the tyranny of Satan, exemplified the dangers of democracy.
5   *Mercurius Elencticus*, no. 6 (May 28–June 4, 1649), 42.
6   Barbara Lewalski (1985: 84–97) discusses Milton's treatment of Satan's deliberative rhetoric as a "genre of the damned." Michael Wilding (1987: 229) urges that we see the first two books in *Paradise Lost* as an example of the dangers of politics, where Milton is warning the reader that beautiful rhetoric can waylay democratic processes.

7   The same illustration was used in *The Dragon's Forces totally Routed* (1660).

8   Nicholas von Maltzahn dates the Digression in February 1649 (1991: 31); Hill takes these ominous statements as a sign of Milton's losing hope in 1654 (1977: 193); Austin Woolrych dates the Digression in 1660, finding that Milton retained optimism until 1659 (1986: 236–41). For the controversy over the dating of the Digression, see von Maltzahn 1991: 22–48.

9   In my argument here I concur with Mary Ann Radzinowicz's superlative account of Milton's late politics in *Toward "Samson Agonistes"* (1978: 145–9), though, as I will go on to show, my sense of Milton's educational program involves readers not just learning political truths but acquiring interpretive activities.

10 Thus I disagree with Don M. Wolfe who found that Milton believed the Restoration was God's punishment to the people of England (1941: 342).

11 On the debate over whether Milton wrote *Christian Doctrine*, see William B. Hunter 1992, who argues that he did not; and, arguing that he did, Barbara Lewalski 1992: 143–54; and John T. Shawcross 1992: 155–62.

12 *Mercurius Bellicus*, no. 2 (November 22–29, 1647), 10.

13 Lois Potter also examines the sun and clouds imagery in such civil war royalist writing, though she does not draw the connection to *Paradise Lost's* use of this figure (1989: 65–71).

14 Gordon Teskey argues that Miltonic error is represented dialectically, through negation, in contrast to Spenserian error, which is represented diagetically, through narrative (1986: 9). In the concept of "perplexity" in *Paradise Lost*, however, I see creatures not only making the wrong choices, but lacking any clear sense of what to choose between: this is more similar to Spenserian error than Teskey's dichotomy would allow.

15 Many critics have seen the lesson in the final books as one in fortitude: George Williamson stresses the didactic content of the final books, where Adam is given information to keep up his hopes, learning by exemplary teaching, acquiring wisdom and love rather than rational knowledge (1965: 284–307); patience is also the lesson in Barbara K. Lewalski 1963; Gerald J. Schiffhorst (1984) reads patience and optimism in the last two books; Lawrence A. Sasek defends the last books by stressing the lesson of "Christian fortitude" (1962: 196). But others have detected a discreet revolutionary tone in these books, as, for example, David Loewenstein 1990, *Milton and the Drama of History*. Another option is for readers to "act now": Radzinowicz 1968; and Wilding 1987: 229.

16 Arnold Stein sees in the last books Adam taking his "final intellectual step" (1965: 598); I would say it is his first intellectual step in the world that resembles Milton's own. I agree instead with Robert L. Enzminger: "Accustomed to the purely referential language he has employed in Eden, Adam is not yet equipped to turn to effective use the ambiguities of diction and syntax Milton trusts his readers to appreciate through most of the epic. Adam must come, guided by Michael, to approximate the reader's sophistication" (1978: 208), though I disagree that the language in Eden was "purely referential."

Rather, the uses of language seem to me to be different in Eden and after the Fall, with the application of the lessons of history.

17 As Maureen Quilligan has pointed out, Eve was always already in a mediate position, receiving truth only indirectly, even before the Fall (1983: 224, 226).

18 Stanley Fish's brilliant and indispensable *Surprised by Sin* analyzes these and other impossible metaphors (22–37).

19 Francis Woodcock, *Christ's Warning-Piece* (1644), A3.

20 Albert R. Cirillo addresses Milton's use of the structure of the "Platonic Great Year": in the poem, noon and midnight, sunlight and eclipse are not irresolvable opposites; rather, in God's viewpoint, they are resolved in the Crucifixion, "the symbol of the noon of eternal life" (1962: 230).

21 Maureen Quilligan has argued that, because of her inherently mediated status, "Eve's initial interpretive situation is closer to the fallen reader's corrected reading than any other perspective in the poem (1983: 242).

3

The Balance of Power in Marvell's "Horatian Ode"

Thomas M. Greene

The attention of most students of Marvell's "Horatian Ode upon Cromwel's Return from Ireland" has been directed toward questions of fairly concrete historical specificity – questions about the poet's real opinion of Cromwell, his views on the overthrow of royalty, and his greater or lesser ambivalence, according to the reader, regarding one man's violent seizure of power in England. This attention is not surprising, in view of the poem's ostensible subject, but the lack of critical unanimity suggests the conclusion recently formulated by Frank Kermode and Keith Walker – that the poem is "baffling to anybody who wants simply to know where the poet stood with Cromwell in 1650" (1990: viii). Baffling apparently it will remain, despite the most earnest hermeneutic footwork. The essay that follows will draw upon the insights to be found in its predecessors and like them it will necessarily pay attention to certain specific historical events, but it will assume Marvell's own bafflement by that particular historical text the ode attempts to read. It will begin with the assumption that the fragment of history meditated by the ode is represented not only as inherently mysterious but arcane. The true subject of the poem seems to me to be the intrusion of the uncanny into history. In various forms this is of course a property of experience in more than one of Marvell's poems, and I want to approach the "Horatian Ode" by means of an excursus devoted to the poet's fullest development of this property in another, very different poem. Thus the ode will be read with or against the closing episodes of "Upon Appleton House," where the presence of the uncanny will come as a surprise to no one.

This presence is most notable in the remarkable section of that poem devoted to the wood at Nun Appleton (stanzas 61–78), where the speaker's promenade through his employer's property eventually leads him. This is that place in Marvell's poetry where things invite most subtly and yet most urgently an interpretation for which the text offers the term "mystick." The tone is so delicate that all exegesis must violate it, but its tantalizing impressions need nonetheless to be teased out. The whole movement of the poem until the final episode leads away from the architectural to the "magic wood" (Colie 1970: 235–6) or the "magic grove" (Marcus 1986: 258) where everything speaks in a prophetic language the poet miraculously understands. Here the poet becomes "a numinous human figure," who communicates effortlessly with birds and plants.[1]

> Already I begin to call
> In their most learned Original:
> And where I Language want, my Signs
> The Bird upon the Bough divines.
>   (569–72)[2]

This haunting episode reflects a sensitivity to things as hieroglyphs, a quality of attention to natural objects out of which the mind interprets or creates meanings. The leaves as perceptible objects are presented as signifiers to be read, leaves in a sacred book replete with lore the poem affirms but fails to communicate. The wood is a place of beneficent sacrifice, where the hewel fells an oak without pain or protest, and a place of supernatural insight.

> Out of these scatter'd Sibyls Leaves
> Strange Prophecies my Phancy weaves:
> And in one History consumes,
> Like Mexique Paintings, all the Plumes.
> What Rome, Greece, Palestine, ere said
> I in this light Mosaick read.
> Thrice happy he who, not mistook,
> Hath read in Natures mystick Book.[3]
>   (577–84)

The whole poem in its play of increasingly extravagant vision seems to move toward this Mosaic light, this prophetic perspective which poses esoteric mysteries apparently soluble only by the heightened understanding of the speaker. He has penetrated what he first perceives as a Night (504) formed by the grove's dense trunks, and then reaches that light which he tells us illumines mysteries. According to his account, he not only penetrates but finally assumes the arcane as simultaneous prelate and victim nailed to the earth by briars that complete his initiation.

The wood at Nun Appleton becomes a kind of Utopia of meanings to the "easy philosopher" who passes among them; everything is replete with a significance which trembles on the brink of revelation but never passes into definition. But the copia of meaning may be deceptive; it is never even perfectly clear that the contents of the mystic book ever amount to more than the whimsical notions of the philosopher's fancy. The Mosaic light, the prophetic illumination, may prove to be a dilettante's mosaic, no more permanent than the leaves trembling in the breeze which are as volatile as the leaves of the Cumaean sybil. The antique learning may only be antic. The reader moves with the "careless" philosopher through a scene whose every sight and sound signal a potential profundity which the text genially affirms but fails to communicate. The repeated motif of sacrifice *might* lie at the core of the proliferating hints, but no single interpretation of the motif organizes its recurrences. The foliage of signifiers surrounds the intruder, binds him, crucifies him, but finally leaves him free to leave, *not* transformed, not visibly illumined with a metamorphic vision. This plenitude of potential signifiers which keep their secrets is what marks the scene as uncanny but not, I submit, "magical," since it ultimately effects no transfer of arcane energy of the kind magic claims to induce. The visitor is no "Magus," as he has been claimed to be, because he brings nothing about; he remains only a supremely sensitive observer of a semiotic imbalance, the uncanny imbalance of multitudinous uninterpreted signs. He registers and perhaps multiplies the fabulous wealth of his semiotic Land of Cockaigne.

The Utopian fantasy is finally transcended, exposed as fantasy, only in the final section which returns to the garden of the house and to the master's daughter Maria. The transitional stanzas between the wood and garden (79–82) begin to invest the poet's solitude with a laxity which will then contrast with the rigor attributed to the girl as she walks in the garden as governess to the world. The hyperbole of compliment invites skepticism, but in fact Marvell seems nowhere so serious as in the celebration of that human civilizing presence which he chooses to incarnate in Maria. Here indeed one might speak correctly of magic, but of a sort that is properly understood to stem from a perceptive and responsive human consciousness.

> 'Tis She that to these Gardens gave
> That wondrous Beauty which they have;
> She streightness on the Woods bestows;
> To Her the Meadow sweetness owes;
> Nothing could make the River be
> So Chrystal-pure but only She;
> She yet more Pure, Sweet, Streight, and Fair,
> Then Gardens, Woods, Meads, Rivers are.
> Therefore what first She on them spent,
> They gratefully again present.
> (689–98)

What is celebrated here is a projective human power which organizes and defines its context, assigns qualities, and thus meanings, to the random objects about it: "See how loose Nature, in respect / To her, it self doth recollect" (657–8). The garden with Maria in it is not uncanny, because her presence effects that semiotic balance which the wood failed to achieve. The wood speaks with fanciful languages whose import remains elusive. Maria, we discover, is a mistress of usable languages.

> She counts her Beauty to converse
> In all the Languages as hers;
> Nor yet in those her self imployes
> But for the Wisdome, not the Noyse;
> Nor yet that Wisdome would affect,
> But as 'tis Heavens Dialect.
>
> (707–12)

Wallace Stevens is not far off, and the Maria episode can appropriately be read in Stevensian terms.

> It was her voice that made
> The sky acutest at its vanishing.
> She measured to the hour its solitude.
> She was the single artificer of the world
> In which she sang.[4]

The apparent pseudo-magic of hyperbole in "Upon Appleton House" can be regarded, should in fact be regarded, as the legitimate "magic" of human perception and re-creation, "arranging, deepening, enchanting" the world around it. This power of imagery is not a fantasy; it is that true power we do potentially possess (although vulnerable to distortion and pathology), the power eminently visible in this text.

In Marvell, as in Stevens, this power seems to derive from a circle of projection and assimilation. What Maria "spends" on her surroundings "they gratefully again present," just as Stevens's jar placed in Tennessee allows the speaker to appropriate the landscape it centers and dominates (76). Through a creative phenomenology, consciousness projects anthropomorphisms – perceptions, names, metaphors, interpretations – on things, anthropomorphisms which assign them meanings and so permit the reader to "take them in," to apprehend and internalize things newly understood. This opening of a projective–assimilative circle is what poems do, and not least "Upon Appleton House." Like the ordering of the slovenly wilderness in Stevens's Tennessee, Marvell's garden projects a "decent order" on a world otherwise "negligently overthrown" (763, 766). It is the process celebrated by "The

Garden," where the activities of projection and reception become inextrica- ble. The mind, the ocean where all things find their resemblance, creates by projecting an oxymoronic green thought, a unified conflation of image and idea, upon the green shade which is both context and fabrication. The soul perched within the garden boughs receives the various light in order to "wave" the light in its plumes and thus humanize it. One discerns a nascent conception of human creative vision as a dual movement outward and inward, a "spending" of images and symbols that permits a simultaneous appropriation of the world thus ordered. This dual movement which reduces itself to one single act would account for an authentic magic, a fundamental, human magic raised many degrees by the artist, which "corrects" that imbalance of signs signaled by the uncanny and achieves a temporary equilibrium. Such a primary magic would not be an instrument of desire or fear, but a means of cognitive and intuitive enrichment.

The term "magical" is nothing if not slippery and I fear that it invites misunderstanding. It is commonly used almost more frequently as a meta- phor (a "magical experience") than as a proper term, or it is used in a rhetorical gray area where its force remains uncertain ("magical thinking"). I would like to use it here with whatever technical precision is possible, and to this end it may be useful to cite a formulation of its supposed workings by a professional ethnographer. Claude Lévi-Strauss repeatedly discusses pre-literate magic, shamanistic magic, as an attempt to right a semiotic imbalance which he sees as inherent in the intellectual condition of mankind.

> In a universe which it strives to understand but whose dynamics it cannot fully control, normal thought continually seeks the meaning of things which refuse to reveal their significance. So-called pathological thought [attributed here by Lévi-Strauss to the shaman], on the other hand, overflows with emotional interpretations and overtones, in order to supplement an otherwise deficient reality.... Through collective participation in shamanistic curing, a balance is established between these two complementary situations.[5]

In a later text, discussing the analysis of magic by Marcel Mauss, Lévi- Strauss returns to the same imbalance:

> In his effort to understand the world, man always disposes of a surplus of meaning (which he distributes among things according to the laws of symbolic thought which it is the task of ethnologists and linguists to study). This distribution of a supplementary ration ... is absolutely necessary in order that ultimately the available signifiers and the perceived signifieds remain in that relation of complementarity which is the very condition of the exercise of symbolic thought.[6]

Lévi-Strauss goes on to associate what he calls the floating signifier with poetry, myth, and aesthetic creation. The weakness of his analysis lies in a post-Saussurean emphasis on more or less static semiotic relationships, an emphasis which slights the transfer of energy supposedly inherent in all magic. But the conception of a semiotic imbalance, which we have already met in the wood at Appleton House, is indeed fruitful, and one can properly follow Lévi-Strauss in understanding poetry to mitigate the imbalance if one stresses the dynamism released by the projective circle which "names," metaphorizes, anthropomorphizes. Poetic naming enlarges the number of signifieds available for apprehending our world. Plato's Diotima tells Socrates that poetry calls "something into existence that was not there before" (*Symposium*, 205b). Poetry can be understood to carry to exceptional lengths the productivity of a creative circle which we all to some degree project. The uncanny plenitude of uninterpreted symbols in Marvell's wood would then become an exaggerated example of a human condition which it is the business of magic, shamanistic or aesthetic, to mitigate. The literalism of shamanistic magic can be regarded as a misplaced imitation of that fundamental, universally human magic which men and women need to live sanely. The stanzas devoted to the transformative presence of Maria, speaking as she does "Heaven's Dialect," might be read as an allegory of the transformations of poetic power. The circular activity of the mind resembles the activity of the drop of dew in the poem of that name which

> recollecting its own Light,
> Does, in its pure and circling thoughts, express
> The greater Heaven in an Heaven less.
>
> (24–6)

The light can be recollected, regathered in the drop, precisely because it circles. The Maria episode of "Upon Appleton House," in its adumbration of this projective assimilation, this primary means of achieving meaning, would then function as a response to the uncanny Utopia of semiotic superabundance in the wood. Under the guise of genial flattery, it would assert the possibility of a creative complementarity, concluding a poem concerned with the various relations of art and nature, signs and referents, with a definitive, fundamental, and dynamic relation.

II

The Cromwell of the "Horatian Ode" embodies a darker version of the inscrutable in human affairs, and in his case the portents that accompany his mystifying career are signs of apocalyptic violence. Cromwell is "climactéric" (104), ominous, fatal to his enemies and even to "his own side." His awesome and blazing apparition is not amenable to judgment: "'Tis Madness to resist or blame / The force of angry Heaven's flame" (25–6). The problem posed by this turbulent and revolutionary epiphany cannot be solved by the conventional exercise of ethical reason; he is beyond ethical categories. The problem is rather how to keep one's life and one's poise in the face of a phenomenon which resists explanation, resists not only eulogy but the kind of interpretation derived from "the great work of time" which Cromwell has ruined. This is a career which cries out for rationalization but offers it no purchase; its meaning is super-human, explosive, revolutionary, but absent. Its portents are everywhere but they defy unravelling. In this perspective, the man Cromwell offers a demonic counterpart to the mystery of the wood at Nun Appleton. His inscrutability is the source of that uncanny quality which history has assumed with the advent of Cromwell; it teems with unreadable symbols. To this uncanny text of events Marvell brings his own deliberately dry and dispassionate art.

The "Horatian Ode" is framed with shadows. It begins with an emergence from them:

> The forward Youth that would appear
> Must now forsake his Muses dear,
>   Nor in the Shadows sing
>   His Numbers languishing.
>
> (1–4)

and it ends with Cromwell penetrating them, not without risk:

>   And for the last effect
>   Still keep thy Sword erect;
> Besides the force it has to fright
> The Spirits of the shady Night,
>   The same Arts that did gain
>   A Pow'r must it maintain.
>
> (115–20)

The metaphorical shadows are not presumably quite the same in both cases, but the sinister and haunted obscurity of the future into which Cromwell is disappearing in the closing lines obliges us to alter slightly our understanding of the shade from which the forward youth of the opening is to "appear." A subsequent passage will compare Cromwell's emergence to this hypothetical youth's by means of the adverb "so" ("So restless Cromwel could not cease..." [9]), and the shadows obscuring the youth will be implicitly likened to the clouds where Cromwell was "nursed" and from which he is represented as "breaking" like "three fork'd Lightning" (13–14). This retrospective deepening of the shadows around the forward youth only contributes to the slight hermeneutic uncertainties of the first stanza. Are the shadows nothing more than the obscurity of a reputation? Is it admirable to be ambitious, "forward," at a moment of political crisis and tragedy? Is the obligation conveyed by the verb "must" ethical or prudential? To what degree is the youth to be identified with the twenty-nine year old Marvell? Is Marvell's choice of a military theme the equivalent of the youth's abandonment of his languishing numbers, which sound like love poetry?

These questions are not clarified by the second stanza.

> 'Tis time to leave the Books in dust,
> And oyl th' unused Armours rust,
>   Removing from the Wall
>   The Corslet of the Hall.
>
>   (5–8)

If the parallel between the youth and the poet is pressed, then the corselet might arguably be read as a metaphor of the poem we are reading. It is worth remarking that readying the armor, and not least the corselet, is a defensive preparation; the youth is not enjoined to take up a pike or sword, although in the subtext by Lucan, Roman citizens are depicted as snatching javelins and swords as well as shields (*Pharsalia* 1: 239–43). The sword will itself become defensive at the close; it will become a talisman holding off the potentially hostile spirits of the dead, just as Odysseus uses his sword in Homer's underworld to hold off the peaceable spirits crowding about him. Marvell doubtless had no way of knowing the ancient Irish use of the word *lorica*, Latin for breastplate, the generic term for the apotropaic spells produced by Old Irish culture. This was a term derived from the Pauline injunction (*Ephesians* 6: 14) to put on the breastplate of righteousness, "loricam iustitiae." Marvell probably had no way of knowing this word, but his text allows us to ask whether it should not be regarded as *his* corselet, a protective garment under which we try to make him out as he appears and disappears in the ambiguities of his qualified tribute.

Protection is indeed a relevant need in view of the intrusion of mystical violence into history. It breaks upon events like "the three fork'd Lightning," "burning through the Air," rending "Pallaces and Temples" (13, 21–2). Protection is all the more relevant because lightning can, as we have seen, "[break] the Clouds where it was nurst," just as Cromwell "Did thorough his own Side / His fiery way divide" (15–16). Partisans of the fulgurous hero may be exposed to the greatest dangers, since history has transcended conventional forms and assumed the apocalyptic mode. A representative swerve among many into the uncanny follows the one moment of historical description, the famous and moving evocation of King Charles's execution placed at the center of the poem. Marvell's account of that event, presented explicitly as a tragedy, provides the only non-metaphoric images given us, but it yields to a remote historical allusion which will transform the event into a portent.

> This was that memorable Hour
> Which first assur'd the forced Pow'r.
> So when they did design
> The Capitols first Line,
> A bleeding Head where they begun,
> Did fright the Architects to run;
> And yet in that the State
> Foresaw its happy Fate.
>
> (65–72)

These lines refer to an anecdote mentioned by several Roman authors, including Livy, Varro, and Pliny. Livy's account, the fullest, describes a "strange event, which seemed to foretell the grandeur of our empire."

> A man's head with the features intact was discovered by the workmen who were digging the foundations of the temple [of Jupiter Capitolium]. This meant without any doubt that on this spot would stand the imperial citadel of the capital city of the world. Nothing could be plainer – and such was the interpretation put upon the discovery not only by the Roman soothsayers but also by those who were specially brought from Etruria for consultation.[7]

Scholars have noted that Marvell adds the architects' fright and the qualifier "bleeding." He also suppresses the principal element in the original story, the intact flesh of the head. He injects a macabre note which was missing in the sources; essentially he replaces firm flesh with blood and joy with terror. The phrasing which introduces his version of the story links it with Charles's execution, thus presenting Livy's portent as a commentary upon or even an illumination of that event's true meaning. The shedding of Charles's blood, ostensibly a tragedy, becomes a portent of the republic's happy future. This is an example of the uncanny. The crime of regicide becomes a *meurtre créateur* like the killing of Remus; in a mysterious way, the sacrificial blood is necessary to found a state. The execution, evoked with careful detail, becomes itself an augury, an apocalyptic sign which has to be interpreted paradoxically ("And yet . . ."). Cromwell the man, however fleshly, becomes an awesome portent, as lightning was once thought to be a portent, or as military victories were regarded as portents, not least by Cromwell himself. This human augury "appears" on the scene by "urg[ing] his active Star" (12), manipulating astrological influence for his own purposes. If he has "cast the Kingdome old / Into another Mold" (35–6), the new mold introduces an arcane dimension into history which leaves beholders awed, frightened, but grudgingly respectful. It is true that Cromwell is praised for personal traits of practical effectiveness; he is said to display "industrious valour" (33) and again, in an effective phrase, to be one "That does both act and know" (76). But the poem's dominant interpretation of recent history subordinates these traits to the flame of angry heaven. This introduction of a transcendent and esoteric power into British politics emerges as the poem's underlying subject. It is perpetuated by that final apotropaic image of the sword held erect to ward off potentially hostile spirits.

The presence of the uncanny raises the problem of *control*. The mysterious character of Cromwell's apparition upon the politico/military stage constitutes a problem for his nominal superiors, the members of Parliament; the same apparition in the ode constitutes a problem for the poet. If the latter is acknowledged only indirectly, the former becomes explicit when Marvell's impressionistic survey of past events reaches the present time, the moment of composition, as Cromwell's return from the masterful and cruel subjection of Ireland raises questions about the real center of power in the nascent republic. The text deals with these questions by praising the man of fate optimistically for his relative deference to Parliament: "Nor yet grown stiffer with Command, / But still in the Republick's hand" (81–2). The "yet" and the "still" here are ominous, as though the Commander's future impatience with Parliament could already be discerned. How long may we hope that the republic's hand will subdue him? Colonel Pride's purge had already occurred when the poem was written. The disturbing simile which is ostensibly intended to reassure only deepens one's disquiet.

> So when the Falcon high
> Falls heavy from the Sky,
> She, having kill'd, no more does search,
> But on the next green Bow to pearch;
> Where, when he first does lure,
> The Falckner has her sure.
>
> (91–6)

Nothing in fact seems less sure than the future affirmed by that wan last word, its very weakness focusing the drama of precarious control over a wild rapacious thing whose docility remains in doubt. Parliament as the falconer stands waiting for the bird of prey, "heavy" because sated with meat, to return to the lure on the wrist. The bird has not yet done so, and we are left with that drama of uncertain and fateful expectation. The fact of satiety, apparently, weighs as a hopeful factor; she has *already* killed enough. The image carries with it a certain helplessness on the falconer's part. He can only whistle and wait; what he cannot do is reason with a force of deaf, unreasonable nature.

The poet's stance bears some analogies with this falconer's. To produce a coherent poem, the poet needs to control in some measure the uncontrollable force incarnated by Cromwell. Can it be subdued by poetry any more than by the republic? Perhaps only an arcane operation, a spell or a rite, would suffice to bring that force back to the hand. From the flattest (and most ambiguous?) lines of the poem, the reader learns that "if we would speak true, / Much to the Man is due" (27–8), that Man, as the wandering sentence finally concludes, who "ruin[ed] the great Work of Time" (34). Much indeed is due, but precisely what? Can the poem fathom the mystery of events sufficiently to tell us?

> 'Tis madness to resist or blame
> The force of angry Heavens flame.
> . . . .
> Though Justice against Fate complain,
> And plead the antient Rights in vain:
>   But those do hold or break
>   As Men are strong or weak.
>   (25–6, 37–40)

Perhaps a strong poem will be able to transcend a destruction of rights which is unflinchingly represented as sacrilegious.

One prominent uncanny element in the Cromwellian apocalypse is this inexplicable suggestion of providential desecration which is ambiguously justified by the portent of success. And if the whole career is marked by providential sacrilege, there can be no doubt that the supreme crime against the sacred is the murder of the king. When Marvell writes that Charles did not call "the Gods ... to vindicate his helpless Right" (61–2), he does *not* mean, as John M. Wallace would have him mean, that Charles wisely surrendered his divine right by his silence on the block (1968: 81–4). Marvell means rather that Charles would have had no more success, had he attempted to assert his right, than, in the allegorical debate depicted above, Justice had had against Fate in pleading the ancient and still valid "rights." Charles's silence is consistent with his dignity and distinction, surrounded with the vulgarity of Roundhead noise: "While round the armed Bands / Did clap their bloody hands" (55–6). There is no mitigation of this crime within the terms familiar to the poet and his audience. There is only an appeal to "another mold" which is tolerable because inevitable. The Horatian form of the ode, including the quiet formality, the brevity of the lines, the refusal of the incantatory, can be read as counter-apocalyptic. The poem resists that incantatory temptation as though it were crafted to remain aloof from the melodramatic and lurid mysteries it reflects upon. But this rhetorical reticence cannot disguise the fact of a subject which is radically, metaphysically ungovernable. The poetic problem cannot really be distinguished from the political problem.

The reader's problem, in any case, clearly cannot be reduced to the calculus of the poem's moral attitude toward its amoral subject. The problem might rather be said to lie in the interplay of metaphor with phenomenon. Is the poetic language primarily protective, according to the hypothesis already suggested? Does this poet want to *disappear* rather than to appear, like the forward youth, behind carefully crafted pseudo-compliments ("[The Irish] can affirm his Praises best . . ." [77])? Perhaps the mind of the speaker may not after all prove to be so very different from the "party-colour'd" or particolored mind of the Pict, shrinking underneath his symbolic plaid, "Happy if in the tufted brake / The English Hunter him mistake" (109–10). The Scot clearly *doesn't* want to appear, and an analogy might be drawn between his self-concealment in the shadowy brake and the reticence of a text that doesn't want to give itself away too facilely. But that harsh verdict doesn't really account for a text which has after all appeared as a formidable member of the small collection of major public poems our language affords.

III

The idea of the uncanny will lead some readers' thoughts to Freud's monograph on the "Unheimlich," and it may be worth noting that in that paper Freud curiously mentions "a severed head" as well as other dismembered bodily parts as having "something peculiarly uncanny about them." But more significant is Freud's analysis of the semiotics of the general phenomenon:

> An uncanny effect is often and easily produced by effacing the distinction between imagination and reality, such as when something that we have hitherto regarded as imaginary appears before us as reality, or when a symbol takes over the full functions and significance of a thing it symbolizes, and so on. It is this element which contributes not a little to the uncanny effect attaching to magical practices.[8]

Freud's intuition that the uncanny effect stems from a confusion of symbol and referent is sound and sheds light on the "Horatian Ode." One can locate that uncanny blurring in a single word, the pivotal "So" which links Charles's execution with the incident on the Capitoline. Just as the execution assured the "forced power," *so* the bleeding head frightened the architects "And yet in that the State / Foresaw its happy fate" (71–2). Does this mean that the execution was a necessary sacrifice to assure the English state's future? The degree of causality is left vague, but the removal of Charles *can* be interpreted as one of Freud's "magical practices," just as the Capitoline head begins to take over "the full functions and significance" of the thing it symbolizes. The magical identification of sign and referent has virtually become an ethnographic commonplace, although it was not yet one in 1919, the date of Freud's monograph. Nonetheless it is important to maintain the distinction between an uncanny *effect*, which stems from a symbolic excess, and a magical *practice*, which lays claim to an efficacity which would mitigate the excess.

Freud's reference to magical practices is useful here if it reminds us that this humanly contrived magic, as distinct from the providential uncanny, was an integral element in those institutions Cromwell was instrumental in abrogating. That earthly magic immemorially believed to protect a king is symbolized in the "Horatian Ode" by the imperial laurel supposed to be proof against lightning, but now incapable of saving Charles.

> Then burning through the Air he went,
> And Pallaces and Temples rent:
> And Caesars head at last
> Did through his Laurels blast.
>
> (21–4)

The great work of time now ruined depended on ritual, which properly defined always contains a core of magic. The rite of coronation with its core of royal anointment was eminently magical, and it is to this core that Shakespeare's Richard II first appeals after learning that his authority has been challenged (3.2. 54–62). The doctrine of royal divine right can legitimately be glossed by Frazer's two volumes on kingship and magic and by the ethnographic synthesis of A. M. Hocart.[9] The early medieval belief that healing energy emanated from the bodies of monarchs was perpetuated in touching for the king's evil, a practice which the Stuarts did not hesitate to take over from the Tudors as the Tudors had from the Plantagenets. Charles as portrayed in the ode has seen this charismatic energy pass from him to a figure from the whirlwind ("Nature ... must make room / Where greater Spirits come" [41–4]), but the deep sense of sacrilege that infuses his execution stems nonetheless from the ritual untouchability of both his bodies.

The ode, then, bears witness to the substitution of a transcendent, uncanny force of Fate for an established ritual magic. Ritual magic lies within human control. By reifying the sign, by identifying sign and thing, this magic makes a primordial attempt to impose control, an attempt as old as culture. But the equally primordial uncanny, which invests things with an aura of inscrutable meaning, escapes human control. Thus in Marvell's ode, the ultimate significance of the royal sacrifice, if it is one, has to be divined. The execution as ritual is blurred. And the final image of the sword with force to fight as a talisman against nocturnal spirits reaches back to an atavistic sorcery. The ode is a palimpsest of magical signs. It chronicles the return and the shattering dominion of portentous history (already present *passim* in Livy) over ritual history.

The palimpsest indeed is even denser than this account would suggest if one considers the force of poetry as itself a type of precarious magic. The magic of "naming," metaphorizing, projecting a defining image upon the inscrutable, succeeds, as I have argued above, in reducing that superiority of portents to understandings, signifiers to signifieds, which troubles Cromwell's England as, according to Lévi-Strauss, it perennially troubles to some degree the life of the human mind. Thus we might most profitably read the "Horatian Ode" as an attempt to bring to bear upon the demonic uncanny those devices of poetry which render the inchoate coherent and the illegible accessible. The poem would then become a struggle between a blind force incapable of projection, on the one hand, and on the other the projected analogies which would, if successful, permit the poet and reader to confront an ominous epiphany and come to terms with it, "receive" it as a phenomenon tolerable to the intelligence. The poem would adjust the semiotic imbalances which are so bewildering as to be intolerable, just as Lévi-Strauss's shaman uses his tribal mythology to perform an analogous adjustment. The result of the contest would not be pre-ordained, since the devices available to the poet are metaphysically insecure, unlike those attributed to the professional magician. That is to say, the metaphor, the apostrophe, the anthropomorphism, are provisional constructs which have no firm ontological grounding; they only provide temporary and fleeting instruments of control. Poetic striving is necessarily dependent upon images and tropes which are either improvised or else inherited from history and thus weighted and tarnished. In this striving lies the central interest of the poem, and its outcome, as in Marvell's ode, is never assured in advance.

The elegance of the poem lies in the sparseness of its rhetorical means.

What Field of all the Civil Wars,
Where his were not the deepest Scars?
(45–6)

This might mean that Cromwell emerged from his battles more badly scarred than any of his fellow-soldiers. But this on the face of it is improbable, both as fact and as interpretation. The lines mean more plausibly that Cromwell inflicted deeper scars on his enemies than anyone else. This is a tribute of sorts, but not the highest tribute; it leaves a glimpse of England peopled by men gashed by the future Protector. It leaves open the possibility that the scar abides not only in the flesh. It even permits a wilder image of the fields themselves bearing the ugly marks of this one soldier's aggression. The lines "name" Cromwell as one who leaves scars behind him, in his zealous momentum. The praise for the scar-giver, if that is what it is, is precisely tempered; it tells a kind of truth which corresponds to the valor of its subject, but also to his lack of moderation. It projects a *definition* upon the human wonder which does not falsify or vulgarize him, a definition which allows the reader, so to speak, to take him in. It registers economically, reticently, the degree of praise he deserves, and in so doing allows us as readers to receive him as he is represented. The poem stops short of the definitive gesture which might destroy it, as the flight to Carisbrooke destroyed Charles.[10] It evades those nets which landed the gulled king, making his desperate gamble for a final resolution, in a "narrow case" (47–52) and led him to the block.

If one considers the forces which the poem attempts to render assimilable, it must be admitted that its tropes – the lightning, the Capitoline head, the falconer, the exemplary names of Caesar and Hannibal, the hunter of Caledonian deer, the erect sword piercing the shady night – these and their companion tropes do not succeed in imposing a stable order on the forces which have ruined the great work of time. The tropes collectively do not produce an order which would legitimate a given moral choice. An element of bewilderment remains, and a residue of divided loyalties. The metaphors move in and out from various directions, highlighting various facets of the elusive truth. The ode never achieves a complete *prise de possession*. More significantly, the one overarching, crucial occasion, the execution, never loses its fatal ambiguity as tragic drama and auspicious augury. It could be argued that the speaker as a human subject fails to acquire coherence, and the projective circle fails to provide an account of events that proves to be fully assimilable.

But this last argument would miss, I think, what coherence the ode does achieve, and with it the speaker who does truly appear in all his lucid alertness. The ode does not dispel the speaker's division but acts it out with candor. It might be said to take possession of its own uncertainties. If the text contains a true metaphor of itself, this metaphor is not a protective corselet, nor is the speaker to be identified with the forward youth pushing for notoriety. The apter metaphor would lie in a detail characterizing Charles during the last minutes of his life.

> He nothing common did or mean
> Upon that memorable Scene:
>   But with his keener Eye
>   The Axes edge did try.
> Nor call'd the Gods with vulgar spight
> To vindicate his helpless Right,
>   But bow'd his comely Head,
>   Down as upon a Bed.
>
>   (57–64)

The king's eye is said to be keener than the edge of the axe, as though there were a contest between them. This *is* in fact the contest which organizes the ode, the contest between cool perception and crude violence. The text seeks to attain that distinction of poise displayed by the king which is the one unambiguous virtue it can offer, a poise which could measure the danger of violence without the loss of discipline. It is this poise which avoids the vulgarity of melodrama and allows one to bow his head with grace. But the poise does not affect the force of the blow when it comes. Because the falling axe is subject to many interpretations, because like all history it leaves us with a deficiency of final meaning, the eye has to be keen that takes its measure. History produces an inadequate ritual, uncanny in its indeterminacy, and the observer keeps trying its edge, testing it with tropes, hoping to assign it magically a significance that will satisfy the needs of the mind.

NOTES

1   The phrase just quoted is Colie's. It is Marcus who refers to the speaker as a "divine Magus" (1986: 257).
2   All quotations from Marvell are taken from the first volume of *The Poems and Letters of Andrew Marvell*.
3   *OED*: "mystic." 1a. "Spiritually allegorical or symbolical; of the nature of, or characteristic of, a sacred mystery; pertaining to the mysteries of the faith" (first recorded usage 1382). 2. "Pertaining to the ancient religious mysteries or to other occult rites or practices; occult, esoteric" (first recorded usage 1615).
4   Wallace Stevens, "The Idea of Order at Key West," *The Collected Poems of Wallace Stevens* (New York: Knopf, 1964), 129.

5   Claude Lévi-Strauss, "The Sorcerer and his Magic," in *Structural Anthropology*, trans. Claire Jacobson and Brooke Grundfest Schoepf (New York: Basic Books, 1963), 181. Lévi-Strauss would later repudiate the equivalence asserted here of shaman and neurotic, and would reformulate his ideas in the next text to be quoted.

6   Claude Lévi-Strauss, "Introduction à l'oeuvre de Marcel Mauss," in Marcel Mauss, *Sociologie et anthropologie* (Paris: Presses Universitaires de France, 1968), xlix. My translation.

7   Livy, *The Early History of Rome*, 1.55.6, trans. Aubrey de Sélincourt (New York: Penguin, 1980), 95.

8   Sigmund Freud, *Studies in Parapsychology*, ed. Philip Rieff (New York: Collier, 1977), 49–50.

9   Sir James Frazer, *The Magic Art and the Evolution of Kings*, 2 vols (vols 1 and 2 of *The Golden Bough*) (New York: Macmillan, 1935); A. M. Hocart, *Kingship* (London: Oxford University Press, 1927).

10 Charles left his comfortable palace arrest at Hampton Court in order to flee to the fortress of Carisbrooke on the Isle of Wight, where he mistakenly believed the governor supported his cause. This flight was used as a pretext for his execution. Many believed, and Marvell clearly among them, that Cromwell conspired to mislead the king into making this disastrous move.

4

Oroonoko's Blackness

CATHERINE GALLAGHER

The hero of Aphra Behn's *Oroonoko; or the Royal Slave* is not just black, but *very, very* black. His blackness is, moreover, luminous, beautiful, wonderful. *Oroonoko* emphatically breaks the traditional western metaphoric links between black skin and moral degeneracy, a connection that Behn herself had assumed in an earlier story. I want to explore this extraordinary blackness. It has, I believe, three layers of significance: it celebrates a certain textual effect produced by print, which *Oroonoko* allies with heroic authorship; it emblematizes the hero's kingship; and it is a metonymic sign of his commodification. These three layers – textuality, kingship and commodification – are bonded together by their paradoxical recognition and denial that blackness means racial difference. That is, each level seems to contain and displace an acknowledgment of the racial significance of blackness. I hope to show that, at each level, the racial meaning is displaced by the author's fascination with disembodiment and her attraction to dispossession.

On several occasions during her career as a playwright, Behn had complained about the difficulty of communicating with her audience through the gross medium of actors on stage. In contrast, she had extolled the wonders of print for what she considered its relative thinness of obstructive mediation. In her tales, too, we can see evidence that print's seeming disembodiment, its mobility and even its potential anonymity gave it a magical quality. The reproduction and sale of the *identical text* in numerous copies provided proof of her ideas' transcendent non-materiality, their escape from the physical accidents of place and time,[1] and therefore of their substantive likeness to the immaterial and immortal mind they represented.

Of course, such a notion of a transcendent text, elevated above all materiality, preceded print; but print paradoxically gave material evidence for a text surpassing all copies. The potential for seemingly infinite reproduction obviated the possibility of equating the text with any, or for that matter, all of its instantiations. Behn apparently imagined that, through such wide dissemination, her ideas can be anywhere and yet nowhere in particular. Like other seventeenth-century writers,[2] she seems fascinated with not only the appearance of the anonymous hand but also the gap between the physical act of writing and the immaterial result. She confesses, for example, the haste of the book's composition in the dedication to *Oroonoko* – "I writ it in a few hours ... I never rested my pen a moment" (Behn 1986: 25) – even as she contrasts the ephemeral, bodily labor to the eternal, static, spiritual product: "[poets] draw the nobler part, the soul and mind; the pictures of the pen shall out-last [the drawing] of the pencil, and even worlds themselves." Here the author reminds us that writing is not really a graphic art. The black ink that outshines the "pencil" marks of the visual artist signifies the incorporeal and eternal, not only because it "draws[s] the nobler parts," but also because the text perpetuated in print seems to rise above its own graphics. The blackness of ink, therefore, seems to indicate a state beyond its own visibility.

That Oroonoko's blackness is associated for Behn with this inky abstraction is an inference I draw from several pieces of evidence. First, Behn had, in an earlier story, linked black skin with anonymous writing. In "The Unfortunate Bride; Or, The Blind Lady a Beauty," Behn's narrator – herself a rather shady character – claims that much of her information comes indirectly from a black woman, Mooria, who not only longs to be the object of the hero's love but also steals his letters to his mistress and forges new ones to drive the lovers apart. The story makes the lady's blackness a metaphor for her "dark designs" and for her means of accomplishing them: stealing the writings of others and rewriting them "in a disguised hand." The black lady, in other words, is an inky creature who separates people from their written representations and plunges them into obscurity. She is more designing than the narrator and more adept than any other character at achieving her designs by textual misrepresentation.

Although there are several such women in Behn's stories, who manipulate the action by disguising their "hands," Mooria is the only one who *embodies* this form of power. The darkness of her skin is associated with invisibility and magical powers of transformation; that is, her skin color is a metaphor for the disembodying and hence anonymous potential of writing. The very ink that allows graphic representation and hence the dissociation of bodies and language, seems to cover the body of Mooria herself, making the same association between black bodies and writing that was figured in the novelty inkwells wrought in the shape of African heads in a somewhat later period.

Since Mooria's skin seems an emblem of the disembodying power of writing, for which the blackness of ink is a related sign, we might also see in her a figure for the "anonymous hand" par excellence: print, the medium of the story's dissemination. Print intensified anonymity simply by increasing standardization, making the graphemes relatively interchangeable regardless of their origin, and by wide dissemination, which broke the link common in scribal culture between texts and specific places where they could be read. The more identical copies of a text there were, the less it seemed to occupy any particular location, and hence the less it seemed any body's physical emanation. The figure of the black woman, then, combines the blackness of racial difference, the obscurity of the narrative "I" in this particular story, and the potential erasure of the writer, which might in turn call to mind the "anonymous hand" of publication.

In the character Mooria, therefore, Behn had already used dark skin to signify a certain impersonal textual effect. Bearing this in mind, we can go on to look at the internal evidence linking Oroonoko's blackness to the wonder of print. But the first thing that might strike us as we move from a consideration of "The Unfortunate Bride" to an analysis of *Oroonoko* is that the later story associates the blackness of the character not with authorial obscurity but with authorial transcendence.

In this regard, *Oroonoko* seems the polar opposite of "The Unfortunate Bride." The narrator not only claims her authorial identity and her personal experience of the events, but also gives herself an important role in the story and hence a sustained presence.[3] She identifies herself as Aphra Behn, a writer already known to the public as a playwright, one whose established reputation should guarantee the story's veracity. She even discusses her next play, stressing that it, like *Oroonoko*, is at least to some extent based on her life experience.

This stress on the work as an expression of the author's authentic identity has a parallel in the metaphoric use of blackness. Whereas in "The Unfortunate Bride" the narrator's anonymity seemed intensified by the "dusky" obscurity of Mooria, in *Oroonoko*, the gleaming blackness of the eponymous hero corresponds to the narrator's heightened presence. If Mooria's color emphasized her invisibility and that of the narrator, Oroonoko's radiates a light that illuminates the narrator's identity. He is blacker than the black lady, indeed he is blacker than anybody, but that does not make him "dusky." Instead, it makes him brilliant: "His face was not of that brown, rusty black which most of that nation are, but a perfect ebony or polished jet" (80–1). He is not a *brown* black, but a black black. Behn's distinction between brown blacks and black blacks departs from the usual conventions of representing sub-Saharan native people, who, according to Winthrop Jordan, were normally all described as absolutely black: "blacke as coles," as one voyager to Guinea put it a century earlier.[4] By making complete blackness a distinguishing characteristic of the noble Oroonoko, Behn attached a positive aesthetic value to the color: the brown blacks are dull, but the shiny black black reflects light.[5] Even when dressed in slave's clothes, Oroonoko's gleaming blackness "shone through all" (108). The lustrous quality of the hero's blackness, which is "so beyond all report," requires the eye-witness reporting of a known author; Aphra Behn, therefore, must emerge from her obscurity and explain the circumstances of her witnessing.

As a character, she is, indeed, paralleled with Oroonoko.[6] Like him, she arrives a stranger in Surinam, but is immediately recognized as superior to the local inhabitants; like him, she appears a shining marvel when she travels to the Indian village; and like his, her words are always truthful. As narrator, she repeatedly identifies herself as the well-known author, Aphra Behn, in order to vouch for the otherwise incredible brightness of Oroonoko. There is, then, a close connection between Behn's sustained authorial presence in this book, unprecedented in her works, and the black hero's lustre; as the story moves forward, a mutual polishing takes place in which narrator and hero buff off each other's obscurity. Although in the beginning Oroonoko had the misfortune "to fall in an obscure world, that afforded only a female pen to celebrate his fame" (108), by the end the narrator presumes to hope "the reputation of my pen is considerable enough to make his glorious name to survive to all ages" (141).

Hence through an intensification of blackness, hero and narrator emerge into the light. This process can be read as a celebration of the bright, transcendent possibilities inherent in print. Oroonoko resembles the mystical body of the text;[7] his blackness is a luminous emanation of authorship, which gleams forth from multiple inscriptions.

Such an interpretation of this "admirably turned" (80) ebony figure is quite consonant with one of Oroonoko's most-remarked features: the fact that he is densely over-written. Indeed, the narrator seems quite self-consciously to present her hero's story as a layering of narrative conventions. The early part of Oroonoko's story depends on references to the theater and on the self-conscious employment of courtly intrigue conventions to familiarize and authenticate the action. And the brief idyll of the middle section is similarly realized through reference to a literary model; when Oroonoko and his wife Imoinda are reunited, Oroonoko's English protector and putative master, looking on, "was infinitely pleased with this novel" (112).[8] One could continue to multiply the evidence, for the last half of Oroonoko's history is particularly thickly encrusted with tragic references and is highly wrought in the histrionic codes of heroic drama.[9]

This dense literary artificiality has exasperated some modern readers of

Oroonoko and has been the chief evidence in the twentieth century for the story's inauthenticity.[10] The stress on Oroonoko's conformity to literary conventions, however, was probably intended to make him seem believably noble. The narrator proves the hero's greatness by showing how closely he adhered to heroic models. The sense that Oroonoko was made up of myriad literary conventions would have made him familiar and hence credible to contemporary readers, for real heroic action was necessarily imitative.[11] The resolute intertextuality of the narrative, then, was not a failure of imagination, but rather a proof that the author deserved fame because she had a property, a legitimately heroic story, which was recognizable as such only because it conformed to other such representations.

We can read Oroonoko's gleaming blackness, then, as a celebration of inscription without turning it into a self-reflective modern text. However, a danger lurks in such a reading. If Oroonoko's blackness becomes mainly an allegory of textuality, even with such historical and formal qualifications as have been introduced, we will lose sight of the phenomenal wonder that empowers the text in the first place. Unless we acknowledge that Oroonoko's blackness refers to racial difference and indeed is dependent on a stock response of racial prejudice in the reader, we cannot explain what was supposed to be so wonderful about him and so meritorious in the author. The reader is frequently invited to marvel at the fact that Oroonoko, *although black*, behaves just like a perfectly conventional European tragic hero. Hence the first full description of Oroonoko relies for its sense of the marvellous on the very racial prejudice it seems to be in the process of dispelling:

> His nose was rising and Roman, instead of African and flat. His mouth, the finest shaped that could be seen; far from those great turned lips, which are so natural to the rest of the Negroes. The whole proportion and air of his face was so noble, and exactly formed, that, bating his colour, there could be nothing in nature more beautiful, agreeable and handsome. . . . Nor did the perfections of his mind come short of those of his person; for his discourse was admirable upon almost any subject; and whoever had heard him speak, would have been convinced of their errors, that all fine wit is confined to the white men, especially to those of Christendom; and would have confessed that Oroonoko was as capable even of reigning well, and of governing as wisely, had as great a soul, as politic maxims, and was as sensible of power, as any prince civilized in the most refined schools of humanity and learning, or the most illustrious courts. (80)

Oroonoko is a wonder because blackness and heroism are normally thought to be mutually exclusive qualities; indeed, the passage asserts that they normally *are* mutually exclusive. It is only in his differences from other Africans that Oroonoko achieves heroism, but it is in his blackness that his heroism partakes of the marvellous. His is a "beauty so transcending all those of his gloomy race, that he struck an awe and reverence, even in those that knew not his quality; as he did in me, who beheld him with surprise and wonder" (79). Thus his color, as a sign of racial difference, is the very thing reminding us that all of his features are different from those "which are so natural to the rest of the Negroes."

Oroonoko's blackness must therefore be seen at once as authentically and unnaturally African. It is the exotic trait that makes his story worth writing, the feature that makes him unprecedented as hero and hence a wonder. However, it is also the feature that necessitates such an energetic marshalling of heroic literary precedents. His blackness is presented as something the hero and writer must overcome, something that "naturally" threatens to become the condition of his obscurity. Simultaneously, it is presented as that which makes him worthy of fame. The author's virtue lies in so densely packing Oroonoko with heroic reference as to prove him wonderful; that is, to make his very blackness shine. Hers is an especially great achievement because in English stories blackness doesn't normally shine. Blackness as racial difference, therefore, at once helps explain why Oroonoko's color gleams with "unnatural" intertextuality and reveals how such gleaming redounds to the glory of the author.

Oroonoko's blackness is consequently to be read as a "natural" physical indication of racial difference, even inferiority, textually transubstantiated into a wonderful sign of heroic distinction. It is thus highly appropriate that descriptions of Oroonoko's and his wife Imoinda's heroic bodies should emphasize their artificiality; they are not so much bodies of flesh and blood as pieces of polished handiwork. "The most famous statuary could not form the figure of a man more admirably turned from head to foot" is the sentence that precedes the description of Oroonoko's color as "not of that brown, rusty black which most of that nation are, but a perfect ebony, or polished jet," with "the white of [the eyes] being like snow, as were his teeth" (80–1). Readers are being called on here to put the actual African bodies they might have seen (the *brown* black ones) out of their imaginations and substitute for them statues of ebony and ivory. Indeed, when Oroonoko alights at Surinam dressed in his "dazzling habits" to be gazed at in his journey by the whites and the merely "brown" blacks, he resembles nothing so much as a magus statue. The common brown Africans eventually greet him as "King" and even, in a scene that fuses Christ child and magus, fall to worshipping him as divine when he finally arrives at his destination.

Imoinda's body is also artifactual, but in a slightly different way. At first she is described merely as a female version of Oroonoko, but the allusions are appropriately classicized to accommodate a female divinity: "To describe her truly, one need say only, she was female to the noble male; the beautiful black Venus, to our Young Mars" (81). Like his, her features are to be imagined as European, and the description of the pair of lovers might well have evoked images of Ben Jonson's *Masks of Blackness*, or of the actors and actresses in black face and lavish costumes who played the "kings" and "queens" of Africa and India in the Lord Mayors' Pageants.[12] Such figures would have been quite appropriate to the court intrigue section of the novel. However, after Imoinda has been sold into slavery, had her name changed to Clemene, as Oroonoko has his changed to Caesar, and emerges into our view through the eyes of the white colonists, her body undergoes a fabulous transformation:

> Though from her being carved in fine flowers and birds all over her body, we took her to be of quality before, yet, when we knew Clemene was Imoinda, we could not enough admire her.
>   I had forgot to tell you, that those who are nobly born of that country, are so delicately cut and raced all over the fore-part of the trunk of their bodies, that it looks as if it were japanned; the works being raised like high point round the edges of the flowers. (112)

This abrupt scoring of Imoinda's body, so strongly and clumsily marked in the text ("I forgot to tell you") coincides with the narrator's re-vision of her as at once slave and romantic heroine, "Clemene" and Imoinda. Appropriately, Imoinda's body is not just transformed textually, through metaphor, but is supposed to have been transformed materially into an artificial decorative object of exotic origin; she is "japanned," like a highly varnished and intricate piece of oriental carving. And yet she isn't quite statuary in this description because the plasticity and pliancy of actual flesh, as well as its susceptibility to wounding, scarring and discoloration are invoked by the description. Finally, the reference to "high point" makes Imoinda's flesh into its own laced clothing.[13] Her body becomes a fabric representing other things; it is, if I may be allowed one pun, all texture.

The descriptions thus stress the exotic artificiality of both Oroonoko and Imoinda, but the artifactual nature of Imoinda presents sublimation, the process of becoming art, as an ordeal through which a body passes. That is, the reader's experience of flesh is not altogether banished from Imoinda's description, as it is from Oroonoko's. Even more obtrusively than Oroonoko's, Imoinda's is a body of representation. However, we are required, in this revision of her half way through the story, to imagine her skin as the material out of which the representations are made. Oroonoko, on the other hand, is a completed representation; the African body is useful to his description only as contrast. Imoinda reminds us that such refinement uses up bodies. Consequently, her image directs us to a consideration of the full relationship between Oroonoko and the commonplace "brown" Africans in the novel.

The overwrought artificiality of Oroonoko, symbolized by the gleaming blackness of his body, not only sets him apart from his countrymen but also suggests the two ways in which he absorbs and represents them: through kingship and commodification. On an abstract level, one could point to a structural homology between Oroonoko's unnatural blackness and kingship as it was conceived from the late Middle Ages through the seventeenth century.[14] Just as Oroonoko can be seen as the mystical body of the text, that which outlives myriad graphic instantiations to become the repository of overlapping forms of heroism; and just as his heroism, like the book's textuality, both depends on and is poised against the blackness of print and the blackness of racial difference (both, in turn, concepts abstracted from physical objects); so kingship was perceived as a mystical body standing above and incorporating all bodies in the realm but also outliving them and thus proving the realm's continuity through time.

In Ernst Kantorowicz's well-known account of this concept, the mystical body of the king both depends on physical bodies and is contrasted to them.[15] Since all the realm's bodies are imagined to be incorporated in one, with the king as the head, all are imagined to be, in some sense, the bodies of the king; and yet in no physical body, not even his own, is true kingship completely contained, for the king's physical body, subject to decay and death, merely represents the immortal kingship that temporarily inhabits it. How the king's physical body represented kingship was a subject of some debate, especially in the years preceding and following the regicide, which Parliament justified by claiming in effect that *it* was the mystical body of the king, and Charles I's body was that of an enemy to the "real" sovereign. Such a radical splitting off of the actual and mystical bodies, however, was abnormal, and the explicit ideology of a high Tory like Behn would have held that the king's actual body, as long as it breathed, was the sacred and unique incarnation of the realm's mystical incorporation. Nevertheless, the king's two bodies were conceptually separable, and in *Oroonoko* they emphatically come apart so that the body of kingship itself, like the text, achieves a kind of incorporeality.

The narrator often refers to Oroonoko's kingship as if it were comparable to normal European models. In the initial description quoted earlier, for example, her stress on his heroism culminates in the greatest wonder of all, which her European readers would have found most difficult to believe: "That Oroonoko was as capable even of reigning well, and of governing as wisely ... as any prince civilized in the most refined schools of humanity and learning, or the most illustrious courts." It is not surprising that such an ideal of princely capability would be figured in a bloodless statue of a body, one contrasted to living bodies and made imperishable through metaphors, for Behn represents in this figure not just a king, but kingship. As a specimen of a mere African king, we are given Oroonoko's grandfather, who is "a man of a hundred and odd years old" (79), but who, far from having any marks of immortality about him, is senile and sexually impotent. Moreover, and most tellingly, the actual king's body is indistinguishable from the bodies of his subjects; to get his first glimpse of Imoinda, he dresses himself as the "slave and attendant" of a "man of quality" (84), and is wholly successful in this disguise. In contrast, Oroonoko, as we've seen, had a "beauty so transcending all those of his gloomy race, that he struck an awe and reverence, even in those that knew not his quality" (79). This king's body, then, is to be imagined as one of that mass of brown black bodies that Oroonoko's unnatural blackness is defined against.

Even though the king's actual and mystical bodies seem thus separated in Oroonoko's home kingdom, Oroonoko's blackness is nonetheless defined against the mass of African bodies as an abstracted essence of them, as if his blackness were the sum and intensification of their less perfect darkness. The mystical body of kingship continues to represent even that against which it is defined, the physical bodies that constitute the realm, and the physical bodies are incorporated into the mystical body. Oroonoko's representation conforms to the imaginative pattern informing centuries of monarchist thought, pageantry, state organization, criminal law, family relations, and so forth; it was the common cultural property of the time.

Such a pattern of thinking, however, does not fully account for the representation of kingship in *Oroonoko*, for it does not explain why the salient physical attribute of the African bodies that is abstracted, refined, and intensified in Oroonoko's body should be their darkness. Of all the attributes of their bodies, why this one? In making her hero darker than his subjects, Behn departed radically from the traditional portrayal of the noble African or Moor,[16] who was often painted white. Of course, I've already partly answered this question in discussing textuality and racial difference, but neither of those issues comprehends Oroonoko's princeliness, his relationship to his subjects. Why should the sign of his kingship be a body from which everything that is African is explicitly banished except a hue that can only abstractly be described as "black"?

The answer lies in the fact that Oroonoko's subjects, unlike those of a modern European king, are also his commodities. The narrator painstakingly explains that the word "black" distinguishes the bodies of people who can be bought and sold from those of people who cannot. To a twentieth-century reader, the history of slavery makes this linkage obvious, but in the seventeenth century, before racial ideologies of slavery were developed, and in the midst of the racialization of the institution itself, it bore reiterating.[17]

The word "blacks" first appears in *Oroonoko* in contrast not to "whites" but to natives of Surinam, who are "a reddish yellow" (76). These last, we are told, are not used as slaves because, through their fishing, hunting and industry, they supply the colony with such necessities that they must be lived with in "perfect tranquillity, and good understanding" (77).[18] Hence "Negroes, black-slaves altogether," are imported. "Black" as it is used here differentiates the body of the African from that of the Native American; it signifies that one has been made a commodity, and the other has not. Because this "blackness" is the mark of commodification, we are then told, everything else about these bodies becomes indistinguishable:

> Those who want slaves, make a bargain with a master, or captain of a ship, and contract to pay him so much apiece, a matter of twenty pound a head . . . So that when there arrives a ship laden with slaves, they who have so contracted, go aboard, and receive their number by lot; and perhaps in one lot that may be for ten, there may happen to be three or four men; the rest women and children. (78)

The twenty pounds paid, then, is for a "black" person, regardless of any other physical characteristic. Gender, age, strength, size, beauty were all indifferent. Nor will any other color suffice, as the case of the Frenchman, seized along with Oroonoko, but emancipated because of his color, makes clear. "Black" is a word that is used to describe a skin tone differing from all others that allows a body to have an abstract exchange value independent of any of its other physical qualities.

"Black," then, is connected to bodies but is also an abstraction from them signifying exchangeable value. It is not so much descriptive of the skin as of the difference between African skin and all other skin that has arbitrarily come to take on the meaning of exchange value per se. Hence the narrator immediately becomes chary of using it as a "literal" term describing bodies. "Coramantien," we are told, is "a country[19] of blacks *so called*" (78, emphasis mine), that is, a country of people one could call black and thus exchange for twenty pounds apiece. But this designation "black," as we've already seen, is explicitly denied by the narrator to describe the literal color of the African body, which in its physicality is merely brown. "Black" identifies the commodity value of the slave body, its exchangeability for twenty pounds, as opposed to its physicality.

Thus the terrifying condition of slavery, having an African body that could be called "black," is transfigured in this novel, into a gleaming vision of disembodied value in the figure of Oroonoko's kingly blackness. Oroonoko's utterly unnatural body is the only one in which the word signifying exchangeability, "black," and the actual color of the body coincide. Only in his body is value realized as blackness. The intrinsic, non-negotiable kingship of Oroonoko is thus paradoxically figured in the same blackness that designates the principle of exchange itself.

The superimposition of kingship and exchange, odd as it might at first appear, was not in itself uncommon. Money, after all, was similarly a representation of exchange value underwritten by the idea of the English state's sovereignty, the mystical body of kingship. Although the relationship between the sovereign power and money was substantially revised in the course of the seventeenth century, and the last decade saw a strong parliamentary attempt to discount the "extrinsic" value that money received from its association with sovereignty, the very agitation of the issue would have given the relationship a pronounced ideological importance.[20] What is odd about *Oroonoko*'s way of depicting this relationship is its insistence on the exchangeability of the subjects themselves for money. Exchange value and kingship are both realized in *Oroonoko* at the vanishing point of the African bodies, the moments when the king sells his subjects.

The kingship represented in Oroonoko, then, cannot be explained simply by noting that the king's mystical body underlay commerce; it is, rather, related to developments in the ideology of absolutism that reimagined the king's sovereignty as an absolute *property* right in the bodies of his subjects. It is to this notion of sovereignty that I will now turn.

The idea of property as an absolute right to dispose of something in any way one saw fit – to use it, destroy it, alienate it through exchange, etc. – was still not fully developed in English law in the seventeenth century. Nevertheless, such an idea of property underlay the vast expansion of trade during that century, and the desire of subjects to have greater dominion over their property came into conflict with what some saw as increasing claims of the crown for dominion. Conversely, some advocates of monarchical "absolutism" argued that the secure property rights of Englishmen would prevent the king from becoming a despot, but even here the complete freedom of a subject to dispose of his own and the power of the monarch are counterpoised. To dissociate absolute individual property claims from the claims of absolute monarchy, however, would be mistaken, for the two were sometimes powerfully conjoined.[21] Indeed, never was the ideological connection closer than during the Exclusion Crisis of 1679–81, when the most famous work of Robert Filmer, *Patriarcha*, originally written in the 1640s, was published and widely cited to defend James's right to the throne. *Patriarcha* bases kingship itself on a God-given, patriarchal ownership of the bodies of the subjects. No matter how severely qualified by the customs and laws of modern nations, Filmer argued, the king's divine right derived ultimately from his private property right in these bodies, his right to dispose of them in any way he saw fit.

Any legitimate limitation on this right, he argued further, was to be construed as self-imposed by the king.

As John Locke pointed out in the first of his *Two Treatises of Government*, Filmer's defence of absolutism essentially turned subjects into slaves:[22]

> This *Fatherly Authority* then, or *Right of Fatherhood*, in our Author's sense is a Divine unalterable Right of Sovereignty, whereby a Father or a Prince hath an Absolute, Arbitrary, Unlimited, and Unlimitable Power, over the Lives, Liberties, and Estates of his Children and Subjects; so that he may take or alienate their Estates, sell, castrate, or use their Persons as he pleases, they being all his Slaves, and he Lord or Proprietor of every Thing, and his unbounded Will their Law. (Locke 1960: 9–10)

It was Filmer, according to Locke, who thus pressed a claim of unlimited private property and Locke who refuted that claim in order to promote "the older and more traditional constitutionalist or consent theory of government" (Tully 1979: 119).[23] Filmer made not only all property ultimately the property of the king but also all proprietors, arguing that they held their very lives as well as their livelihoods by a royal gift.

Without implying that Aphra Behn had actually read *Patriarcha* or that Filmer's formulations per se directly influenced her thinking, I would suggest that *Oroonoko*'s royalism, imagined as it is through the institution of slavery, is Filmeresque.[24] I would also venture, however, that because the tale depicts kingship as the absolute ownership of others, the essence of which is the right to exchange or destroy them, it is constantly rendering problematic the very thing it takes for granted: that someone can be owned, even by himself.

The narrator never claims that the subjects of the kingdom of Coramantien are slaves of their king, but the distinction between subject and slave is often blurred. The slaves Oroonoko trades in are supposed to be prisoners of war, in conformity with traditional European ideas of how slaves might legitimately be acquired. Because Oroonoko conquered them and could have put them to death, their lives are forfeit to him, and hence he can spare them and make them the property of others. Slavery, then, is legitimate because it is incidental to war. But Coramantien is also presented as a place where war is the only enterprise and slaves the only commodity,

> for that nation is very warlike and brave, and having a continual campaign, being always in hostility with one neighbouring prince or other, they had the fortune to take a great many captives; for all they took in battle, were sold as slaves, at least, those common men who could not ransom themselves. (78–9)

In this account, war seems incidental to the slave trade rather than vice versa. Moreover, as the story progresses, we are told often of attendants, mistresses, friends, and even wives who are sold as slaves. Although it is a dishonor for a subject to be sold into slavery, the king has a right to make such a sale, and we are told that every husband has the right either to take the life of his wife or to sell her. The kingdom is imagined to work on patriarchal principles closely resembling those that Filmer describes, with the members of each family living only by the father's sufferance, and the king, as the father of all, holding the same absolute power to dispose of all his subjects: "for they pay a most absolute resignation to the monarch" (83). The real status of a subject, therefore, is that he may at any moment be converted into a commodity.

Indeed, the proof of the monarch's power is precisely in such acts of alienation, for merely to keep and use a slave, as one would any other servant or subordinate, is not to assert fully one's right of ownership. Hence, it is by virtue of having previously sold the slaves that Oroonoko encounters in Surinam that he is recognized as their king:

> they all came forth to behold him, and found he was that prince who had, at several times, sold most of them to these parts; and, from a veneration they pay to great men, ... they all cast themselves at his feet, crying out in their language, "Live, O King! Long live, O King!" And kissing his feet, paid him even divine homage. (109)

Kingship, the right of ownership, and the act of exchange entail each other so closely in *Oroonoko* that they are virtually identical. It is consistent with this logic that kingship should be painted black, the color of exchange. It also follows that the representative of kingship, more perfectly and conspicuously identified by this color than anyone, should ultimately be himself taken for a commodity in the very trade he practiced.

If Oroonoko's abduction and sale seem inevitable, however, the logic of this version of absolutism must be deemed highly paradoxical. If absolute kingship is ownership, and absolute ownership is exchange, then the enduring, stable possession of a person, even of oneself, becomes a near impossibility. Sovereignty keeps sliding into self-alienation, and keeping someone entails the renunciation of property claims. Perhaps the most complex variation on this theme is the drama surrounding the possession of Imoinda, for in *Oroonoko* as in *The Luckey Chance*, the paradoxes of absolute property in persons become most starkly apparent precisely where, in the culture at large, the property relation would be deemed most "natural": in the relation of husband and wife. Imoinda's possession is problematic from the outset. Plighted to Oroonoko, she is appropriated by his grandfather, the king, but the old man cannot consummate the relationship by "possessing" her sexually. Aware of the king's impotence, Oroonoko continues to consider her his and succeeds in possessing her clandestinely, whereupon the lovers are discovered, and Oroonoko must flee.

Up to this point, the story is an utterly conventional intrigue plot, but here the slave market intervenes, giving the old man an unusual means of proving that Imoinda is actually his: he sells her. The act eventually, after Oroonoko's enslavement, reunites the lovers, but their second marriage, which takes place when they are both "slaves in name only," exacerbates the problems of possession. For Imoinda and Oroonoko slavery means nothing but potential commodification; they are not forced to labor, and their activities are almost completely unrestricted. However, as long as they remain in Surinam, they are officially another man's property and hence vulnerable to sale. As soon as Imoinda becomes pregnant, this state of affairs becomes intolerable to Oroonoko, for the prospect of fathering a child while officially a slave, while his patriarchal right is legally violable, makes him suddenly aware that Imoinda's body is a medium for his self-alienation. By possessing her sexually he produces another property, a child, whom he cannot legally call his own. The reappropriation through revolt of Imoinda and all the Africans he formerly sold into slavery then seems exigent, and when this plan fails, Oroonoko's only means of keeping Imoinda and his child from the market is to "free" them both from life altogether. Thus the integrity of Oroonoko's kingship is accomplished by the final "carving" of Imoinda's body:

> The lovely, young and adored victim lays herself down, before the sacrificer, while he, with a hand resolved, and a heart breaking within, gave the fatal stroke, first, cutting her throat, and then severing her, yet smiling, face from that delicate body, pregnant as it was with the fruits of tenderest love. (136)

This quite literal defacing of Imoinda, the lifting of her still-smiling face, as if it were a mask or portrait, off her body is presented as the "brave and just" (135) liberation of her self from the body that was perpetually exchangeable. Oroonoko, the king of exchange, only keeps her and returns her to herself through this ultimate form of alienation.

Imoinda's severed face is not the first such mask we've seen in the book signifying integrity or self-possession, for the problem of owning in the tale extends even to one's relationship with oneself. The great Indian warriors, for example, prove their fitness for leadership by defacing themselves.[25] The narrator described the contest for generalship this way:

> He, who is first ... cuts off his nose, and throws it contemptibly on the ground, and the other does something to himself that he thinks surpasses him,

and perhaps deprives himself of lips and an eye. So they slash on till one gives
out, and many have died in this debate. And 'tis by a passive valour they show
and prove their activity, a sort of courage too brutal to be applauded by our
black hero; nevertheless, he expressed his esteem of them. (124)

This bizarre chopping away of bits of one's body becomes, by the end of
the story, the heroic alternative to the alienation of marketplace exchange,
which appears to require whole bodies. Thus, although the Indians' self-
mutilation seems "too brutal" at first to Oroonoko, he copies it in the
sacrificial transfigurations that are supposed to give him back his kingly
sovereignty. After being cornered by his pursuers, Oroonoko turns on them:

> "Look ye, ye faithless crew," said he, "'tis not life I seek, nor am I afraid of
> dying," and at that word, cut a piece of flesh from his own throat, and threw
> it at them, "yet still I would live if I could, till I had perfected my revenge.
> But, oh! it cannot be; I feel life gliding from my eyes and heart; and if I make
> not haste, I shall yet fall victim to the shameful whip." At that, he ripped up
> his own belly, and took his bowels and pulled them out . . . (138)

Later, in the actual execution scene, Oroonoko seeks the dismemberment
of his entire body, which appears all the more bloodless, inhuman, and
indestructible with each partition:

> And the executioner came, and first cut off his members, and threw them into
> the fire. After that, with an ill-favoured knife, they cut his ears, and his nose,
> and burned them; he still smoked [a pipe of tobacco], as if nothing had
> touched him. Then they hacked off one of his arms, and still he bore up, and
> held his pipe. But at the cutting off the other arm, his head sunk, and his pipe
> dropped, and he gave up the ghost, without a groan, or a reproach. . . . They
> cut Caesar in quarters, and sent them to several of the chief plantations. . . .
> (140)

Although this horror was aimed at "terrifying and grieving" the slaves "with
frightful spectacles of a mangled king" (140), it also creates the spectacle of
the body of kingship, which appears most powerfully in such vanishing acts,
when bodies seem at once reduced to mere things and transcended
altogether. Now deprived of that which first constituted it – the ownership
and exchange of others – Oroonoko's kingship becomes his godlike willing
of the piecemeal alienation of himself. In this contradictory manner, he
proves that he still owns it. Although the moment of death is noted ("his
pipe dropped, and he gave up the ghost"), this anticlimactic act seems just
another stage in the separation of his parts. Oroonoko undergoes an
extraordinary self-division, only to become all the more singularly immortal,

for "he" is now unlocatable. The mystical body of kingship and the actual body of Oroonoko again become identical by the fragmentation and scattering of the latter. Just as the brown bodies reached their vanishing point in Oroonoko's black body of kingly and monetary representation, so his own body of representation reaches its vanishing point in this dispersion.

At this point in the text, the narrator makes her most striking appropriation in the form of a disclaimer: "Thus died this great man, worthy of a better fate, and a more sublime wit than mine to write his praise. Yet, I hope, the reputation of my pen is considerable enough to make his glorious name to survive to all ages, with that of the brave, the beautiful and the constant Imoinda" (141). Oroonoko's "worth" demands more sublimity than she can summon, yet her own authorial reputation, itself a mystical body existing in and between texts, will be the support of "his glorious name." Ending the text with the word "Imoinda" reminds us of Behn's special fitness to tell this love story, her femaleness, and yet the effect of authorship here transcends all such physical accidents even as it takes them into account. If Oroonoko scatters his members to maintain his integrity, Behn performs a similar act of disowning the story (insisting that it is really Oroonoko's and Imoinda's) to open a rhetorical space in which she can remind us of her authorship and the obligation it imposes. In her dedication of the book to Richard Maitland, she similarly at once claims and disclaims her product: "'Tis purely the merit of my Slave that must render [the book] worthy of the Honour it begs; and the Author of that of subscribing herself, My Lord, Your Lordship's most oblig'd and obedient Servant, A. Behn" (Behn 1987: 3).

In this odd mixture of appropriation and disowning ("'Tis purely the merit of *my Slave* that must render" the book worthy of Maitland), the author trades in the "parts" she claims are not exactly hers, and thus she avoids identifying herself with her commodity. Despite the insistent presence of the first-person narrator in *Oroonoko*, then, the phenomenon of authorship per se comes into view here as the principle of the exchange of representations. Behn merely transfers "the nobler part" from one great man, Oroonoko, to another, Richard Maitland. Unlike Oroonoko's sovereign self or "the beautiful and constant Imoinda," such representations are endlessly negotiable precisely because they are not really owned, and hence they make their vendor invulnerable.

Notes

1 See Elizabeth L. Eisenstein's remarks on the preservative powers of print (1983: 78–88). She explains that wide dissemination became the means of making the text imperishable. "The notion that valuable data could be preserved best by being made public, rather than by being kept secret, ran counter to tradition," she claims, and was still controversial in the eighteenth century. Behn, however, seems to have been quite secure in the belief that publication would make her words immortal.

2 It was not until the Restoration that writers began exploring the implications of the fact that authors communicated with their readers through print. Regardless of the fact that the technology was two hundred years old by 1660, Dryden seems to have been the first author to notice its impact. "Dryden is among the first English writers to understand, at least implicitly, the conditions imposed on a literature that is primarily printed and read ... where books and writing are the main instruments of transmission," claims James Engell (1989: 22).

3 This is not unusual in stories about the wonders of the New World, where narrators routinely felt obliged to claim that they were eyewitnesses of the events they relate. Most of the evidence, though, does point to Behn's presence in Surinam in the early to mid 1660s. For presentation of this evidence, see Katherine Rogers 1988: 1–3.

4 *White Over Black: American Attitudes Toward the Negro, 1550–1800* (Chapel Hill, NC: University of North Carolina Press, 1968), 5.

5 In a footnote, Jordan names several later writers who celebrate "the Negro's jet blackness" (10, n. 23), but Behn's is the earliest instance by over thirty years.

6 For analysis of the narrator-hero relationship, see Brownley 1977: 174–81; Margaret Ferguson 1991: 165–6; Pearson 1991: 184–90; Jane Spencer 1986: 47–52; and Starr 1990: 362–8.

7 For a discussion of the parallels between kingship and textuality in the early modern period, see David Lee Miller, *The Poem's Two Bodies: The Poetics of The Faerie Queene* (Princeton: Princeton University Press, 1988).

8 "Novel" here can mean both "novelty" and "romantic tale."

9 In 1696 Thomas Southerne turned the story into just such a play, which, in various versions, was a staple of the eighteenth-century repertory.

10 See, for example, Ernest Bernbaum 1913.

11 On *Oroonoko*'s relation to heroic drama, see Laura Brown 1987: 48–51.

12 For a description of the black-face characters in the Lord Mayor's Pageants, see Anthony Gerard Barthelemy 1987: ch. 3. For other possible references in Imoinda's iconography, see Margaret W. Ferguson 1991: 181, n. 49.

13 The Reverend Richard Hakluyt, indeed, calls this kind of African body carving a form of "branched damaske" and says that it takes the place of clothing. Hakluyt, *Principle Navigations, Voyages, Traffiques and Discoveries*, 4: 62. For other discussions of the insistent physicality of Imoinda and its hint of a conflict

between the narrator and this black heroine, see Ballaster 1992: 290–3; and Ferguson 1991: 170–1.

14 I am not arguing here that Oroonoko is supposed to be any particular king or all of the Stuarts collectively. My argument, rather is that Oroonoko, although he may indeed bring to mind certain Stuarts, is the symbol of an entity that is itself symbolic, Kingship, and that he represents a seventeenth-century revision of that entity. For arguments that detect likenesses with the Stuart kings, see Guffey 1975: 3–41; and Brown 1987: 57–9.

15 I give in this paragraph a schematic summary of the intricate and complicated arguments described by Kantorowicz in *The King's Two Bodies* (Princeton: Princeton University Press, 1957).

16 See Barthelemy's discussion of the contrast between the heroic white Moor and the villainous black Moor in George Peel's *The Battle of Alcazar* (1589) (1987: 75–81).

17 For various accounts of why and how Africans came to be the enslaveable race, see Winthrop Jordan, *White Over Black*, esp. 91–101; Barbara Fields, "Ideology and Race in American History," in *Region, Race, and Reconstruction*, ed. J. Morgan Kousser and James M. McPherson (New York, 1982); David Brion Davis, *The Problem of Slavery in Western Culture* (Ithaca: Cornell University Press, 1966), 178; and William D. Phillips, Jnr., *Slavery From Roman Times to the Early Transatlantic Slave Trade* (Minneapolis: University of Minnesota Press, 1985), 184.

18 The narrator is not always perfectly consistent on this point. On at least one occasion she speaks of their "Indian slaves," but she seems to use the term loosely in that case as a synonym for "lowly servant." She never describes the commodification of Indians.

19 In fact, "Coramantien" was not a country at all but a port on the Gold Coast where the English had a trading station. According to Katherine Rogers, though, planters in America generally referred to Gold Coast Africans as "Coramantiens" (1988: 6).

20 For a discussion of the larger political implications of the debate over money at the end of the seventeenth century, see Appleby 1978: 236–41. She argues that "Locke's denial of the extrinsic value of coin carried with it a limitation of government in economic affairs" (237). She also quotes John Briscoe's 1696 attack on the state's power to fix the value of money, an attack phrased in language peculiarly relevant to *Oroonoko*: "[as] it is a mark of slavery, so is it the means of poverty in a State, where the Magistrate assumes a Power to set what price he pleases on the Publick Coin: It is a sign of Slavery, because the Subject in such Case lives merely at the Mercy of the Prince, is Rich, or Poor, has a Competency, or is a Beggar, is a Free-Man, or in Fetters at his Pleasure" (237).

21 The once widely held view that the Whigs represented the interests and ideology of trade while the Tories stood for an older aristocratic order that shunned commerce is no longer tenable. The most concise statements revealing the errors and simplifications of this position are J. G. A. Pocock's "The Mobility of Property and the Rise of Eighteenth-Century Sociology" and "Authority and Property: The Question of Liberal Origins" (Pocock 1985).

These show the strong connections between absolutist ideology in the seventeenth century and the spread of a notion of property as that which can be exchanged. To be sure, a certain kind of Tory ideology grew up in the 1690s and early eighteenth century, which vociferously opposed this idea of property, but Pocock, again, has shown that the Toryism of Harley and St. John descends from theorists like Locke as opposed to absolutists. There is, then, no ideological contradiction between Behn's Restoration Court Toryism and her presentation of Oroonoko as a heroic warrior *and* slave-trader. The general intellectual history is complicated by the fact that slavery was sometimes identified as a characteristic of pre-commercial societies; slavery in *Oroonoko*, however, is not presented as a semi-feudal but as a fully commercial institution. That is, exchange, rather than mere ownership, is its essence.

22   Indeed, it gave them a status lower than that of slaves under English law, for even slaves were deemed to have something like a natural right to life, and in many of the English colonies (including Surinam) they could own property themselves.

23   For other contributions to the debate about sovereignty and the rise of absolute property, see Ryan 1984: 14–48; Pocock 1985; and Alymer 1980: 87–97.

24   Behn's articulation of kingship and property in subjects is similar to Filmer's although not necessarily derived from his. It isn't clear how widely influential *Patriarcha* was in the 1680s; but it certainly stands as a prominent landmark in the ideological terrain of the decade, which allows us to locate the general vicinity of Behn's tale. For a contrasting view of Oroonoko as the Lockean bourgeois subject, see Weston 1984: 59–71. For a discussion of a possible link between *Oroonoko* and a Hobbesian view of the world, see Starr 1990.

25   For another discussion of mutilation and self-mutilation in *Oroonoko*, see Ballaster 1992: 292.

5

Lordly Accents: Rochester's Satire

CLAUDE RAWSON

According to John Aubrey, Marvell, "who was a good judge of witt," said Rochester "was the best English satyrist and had the right veine." We don't think of him as a satirist *comme les autres*, writing formal verse satires and epistles and Horatian imitations, though his "Allusion to Horace" is said to have taught the genre to better-known practitioners, and the remarkable epistle "From Artemiza to Chloe" is now enjoying a vogue, partly fuelled by feminist preoccupations. Our view of satire is still largely Pope-centered, and, although Rochester had a substantial influence on both Swift and Pope, their feelings about him seem to have been lukewarm. And he is really very unlike. He was of "the Mob of Gentlemen who wrote with Ease" (*Imitations of Horace*, Ep. 2. 1. 108), a Popeian put-down meaning "holiday writers." The "Ease" was not quite the quality which Pope meant when he praised Petronius for uniting "the *Scholar's Learning*, with the *Courtier's Ease*" (*An Essay on Criticism*, 668), and which he mythologized into that witty urbanity, neither Roman nor strictly courtly, which is sometimes, to the dismay of latter-day pedagogues, called "Augustan."

That Rochester was both a lord and a courtier, as Pope was not, is one of the paradoxes which surround the English Augustan style and its curious patrician pretensions. He came closer perhaps than Pope's description did to the Petronius who is remembered as the raffishly elegant sophisticate of Nero's court portrayed by Tacitus, and as the author of the exuberantly obscene *Satyricon* (if they were indeed the same person). Rochester's "ease" was of a sort which, in wit as in other things, spilled over into excess. It thus differed from the Popeian version, which suggests containment and measure, but its way of being excessive included a sense of command. The dramatist Lee called him "Lord of Wit" in a sycophantic dedication, but he also gave, after Rochester's death, one of the best accounts of what this might seriously mean: "his Genius was so luxuriant, that he was forc'd to tame it with a Hesitation in his Speech to keep it in view." If this sounds a bit like a calculated stammer raised to the level of art, the fact is appropriate: Rochester's poetry, like Pope's in its different way, is never far removed from the social ploy. But what is more importantly implied, I think, is a unique form of *sprezzatura* which readily expresses itself in passionate or high-spirited accents. It may accommodate coarseness and even obscenity, as Fielding's manner sometimes could but Pope's could not (or not without loss of "ease," which is perhaps one test of the lordly):

> You Ladyes all of Merry England
> Who have been to kisse the Dutchess's hand
> Pray did you lately observe in the Show
> A Noble Italian call'd Signior Dildo?
> (Rochester 1984: "Signior Dildo," 1–4)

It is a low-pitched example, from a poem which has been praised for having "the characteristic uncertainty of accent of the street ballad." There's justice in this. A command of low styles, and a taste for them, have often been paraded as badges of patrician freedom, a specialized expression, perhaps, of the cultural antinomy mythologized, with a fervid gravity Rochester might have scorned, in Yeats' "Dream of the noble and the beggarman," both poets excluding the intermediate figure of the cit or merchant at his greasy till. But "uncertainty" hardly describes the masterly hint of metrical dislocation, the colloquial stumble which is part of the poem's thrusting plasticity, and which seems a prosodic manifestation of the "hesitation" Lee was talking about. The hard finish of the lines comes over with none of the bland orderliness of Waller or Denham, and is equally unlike the strong coupleteering summations of Dryden or Pope. Demotic vitality is mimicked with a buoyancy which is really quite *un*hesitant, just as elsewhere some gnarled muscularities in the "strong lines" idiom are transfigured by a species of headlong grace. The stanzas of "Signior Dildo," the driving phantasmagoric couplets of "A Ramble in Saint James's Parke," the bravura quatrains of "The Disabled Debauchee," bring home, as much as any stylistic evidence can, how unlikely Rochester is to have composed the yokel couplets of *Sodom*, capable though he was of every obscenity in that feeble play. Pope thought Rochester's versification "bad," a remark approximately on a par with his reported statement to Voltaire that Milton had not written in rhyme "because he could not."

"One Man reads *Milton*, forty *Rochester*," wrote Defoe. This had little to do with the prosody of either: "One wrote *the Lewd*, and t'other *the Sublime*."[1]

As Fielding's Squire Booby made clear when he found Shamela in the act of reading, "*Rochester*'s Poems" was more or less synonymous with "dirty book." Rochester is not "pornographic." He is obscene but not, like *Fanny Hill*, arousing: he would, I think, have shared Fielding's distaste for those "whose Devotion to the Fair Sex … wants to be raised by the Help of Pictures." This was not a matter of prudery, but of patrician cool. Fielding's jibe included Richardson's love-scenes along with *Venus in the Cloister*, a book also owned by Shamela. Rochester uses every bad word in the language, and reports more deeds than will be familiar to most readers of this book, but never enticingly, or intimately, or graphically. It's partly a matter of distance, of the unruly knowingly kept at arm's length, and not unconnected with "excess." Those much-quoted mandrakes "Whose lewd Topps Fuckt the very Skies" ("A Ramble in Saint James's Parke," 20), or the Duchess who "Has Swallow'd more Pricks, then the Ocean has sand" ("Signior Dildo," 38) are phantasmagoric enormities, as of a Rabelaisian gigantism worked over by a Gothick imagination. It's overheated if you like, but as a brilliant virtuosity of fantastication, like some of the wilder flights of Swift's *Tale of a Tub*, not as any sort of sensuous daydream. There could hardly be much in it for the auto-eroticist.

Hyperbolic fantastication, like any other form of excessive utterance, is usually more preoccupied with itself than with its ostensible subject. It flourishes on a built-in assumption that the reader will discount a good deal, providing its own ironic guard. The limitation in turn acts as an enabling or releasing force, since the self-unrealizing that attends the more colossal sexual imaginings offers a dispensation from reticences which are normally activated when we mean to be taken "seriously." Obscenity grows gigantic as arousal is neutralized, as well as vice versa. Something similar may happen with invective, whose great masters (Rabelais, Swift, Céline) are fantasists of an enormity which signals that the calls to hatred or to massacre don't really mean what they say, but don't not mean it either. Invective often borrows the rhetoric of sexual obscenity, in Rochester as in Rabelais, with both forms of incitement held in check by the play of aggressive utterance:

> Bawdy in thoughts, precise in Words,
> Ill natur'd though a Whore,
> Her Belly is a Bagg of Turds,
> And her Cunt a Common shore.
> ("On Mistress Willis," 17–20)

The style of these lines more particularly suggests a late-Swiftian exuberance of imprecation, in the drumming manner of *Traulus* or the *Legion Club*. There's also a grandiloquent triumphalism that is almost celebrative, cheekier and more light-hearted, as well as more rejecting, than Yeats' "foul rag-and-bone shop of the heart," but with something of the same excitability bordering on eloquence. In a related poem,

> By all *Loves* soft, yet mighty *Pow'rs*,
>   It is a thing unfit,
> That *Men* shou'd Fuck in time of *Flow'rs*,
>   Or when the *Smock's* beshit
> ("By all *Loves* soft, yet mighty *Pow'rs*," 1–4)

the squalors of the female pudenda are projected with a festive insolence which is in itself unSwiftian, but which, when coupled with Swiftian "intensities," may produce a Yeatsian mix. The lines again express an opposite feeling to that of Yeats' "Love has pitched his mansion in / The place of excrement," but they are closer to a Yeatsian mood than those more traditional patristic or Swiftian reminders that procreation takes place *inter urinas et faeces* which Yeats is resublimating.

Rochester's lines have a scabrous splendor, enhanced no doubt by the linguistic accident that "flowers" meant menstrual discharge, as in French *fleurs*, from which the English term derives. (The etymology suggests "flow" or "flux," from Old French *flueurs*, Latin *fluor*, but colloquial usage assimilates the term to its more familiar homonym, of which it is sometimes understood as a metaphorical extension). It would be characteristic of Rochester to exploit the pun again, adding a festive insolence, so that the painful and the spectacular unite, as in those blood-stained sunsets and sunrises of Baudelaire, Laforgue or Apollinaire. Like those French poets, Rochester was a good mocker, though his style of mockery differed from theirs. His repudiations have a gaiety, a "sudden glory" in jeering which gives the Hobbesian phrase an unexpected surplus aptness: "I'le write upon a double Clowt / And dipp my Pen in Flowers" (*On Mistress Willis*, 7–8). There are no Baudelairian luxuries, whether of grandeur or repudiation. The poet of "To the Post Boy," who wrote that "the Readyest way to Hell" was "by Rochester" (15–16), who "for five years together ... was continually Drunk," who experienced some extreme states of both debauchery and devotion, and died at 33, obviously had much in common with the *poètes maudits* of a later time. He would have rejected the phrase as too solemn, just as in his lordly way he would have rejected the lordly guilt-ridden grandeurs of Byron's Lara or Cain (though he hoped on his death-bed that God would not drive him "like Cain from before His presence").

Nor would he have had much truck with the alternative solemnities, "carefree" or debonair, of the later bohemian variety. Though often broke and "faine to borrow mony," he would have despised the insolent garreteers of the 1670s and the 1890s alike: in this, as in much else, he was "Augustan" to the core. His jokeyness on painful subjects, and his harping on impotence, might seem to align him with a Laforguian–Prufrockian sub-species of Romantic Agonist. But he is self-mocking without being "self-ironic" in the Laforguian way, and his stanza on impotence addressed to a lady in flowers has a genial insolence which sounds more like Macheath than like Prufrock:

> If thou wou'dst have me true, be wise,
>   And take to cleanly sinning;
> None but fresh *Lovers Pricks* can rise,
>   At *Phillis* in foul linnen.
> ("By all *Loves* soft, yet mighty *Pow'rs*, 13–16)

The fact that we don't associate Macheath with the copulatory indignity or with such brutal language makes the resemblance especially arresting. Impotence is an insistent theme of Rochester's, cheekily flaunted in what amounts to a machismo of sexual debility. These lines are a specialized specimen, indicating that he's a jaded (rather than a "fresh") lover, not absolutely "disabled." Displays of sexual weariness are easily presented as admissions or even boasts of sexual excess, a recurrent feature of the Rochesterian, though not of the Laforguian, mode. The Disabled Debauchee speaks "of *Honourable Scars*, / Which my too forward *Valour* did procure" (21–2). Rochester said in "To the Post Boy" that he had "swived more whores more ways than Sodoms walls / Ere knew" (5–6), an exhaustiveness of possible postures complemented in "The Disabled Debauchee" and elsewhere by a penchant for permutating not only the positions but the sex of his paramours:

> And the best Kiss, was the deciding *Lot*,
> Whether the *Boy* fuck'd you, or I the *Boy*.
>   (39–40)

The Freudians sometimes go on about homosexuality as a latent force in compulsive Don Juanism. Since everything in this domain can be said to be latent when it isn't patent, we might feel that the ride we're being taken on is something of a circular tour. Rochester's "case" is in fact one of the patent ones, and his bisexuality is declared without fuss. What one senses about the main examples, however, is not the experience in itself but the concern to register a kind of exhaustiveness of sexual pursuit, a *jusqu'auboutisme* of erotic transaction. This pedantry of the senses finds its mental complement in the refinements of guilt and a strong urge towards spiritual system-making. (The inordinate devotion of some learned students of erotica to their bibliographical, editorial, and biographical labors also suggests a predisposition to the perfectionisms of pedantry in a more literal sense.) Like other amateurs of systematic debauchery, Rochester was drawn not only to states of introspection, but to large-scale theorizing. When abetted by Burnet, Rochester's theorizing turned to the theological. That of Sade, another libertine aristocrat, was anti-theological and probably not so very different in its native impulse. If such intellectual system-making seems surprising in confirmed sensualists, we should perhaps remember that "sensualism" is itself an ism. No isms are more doctrinaire or persistent than isms of excess, which readily pursue metaphysical exhaustiveness as much as physical exhaustion.

As often as not, "impotence" is presented in Rochester as an imagined state, on a par with other erotic possibilities. In "The Disabled Debauchee" the speaker is frankly imagining future incapacities, not describing present ones. The pleasures of memory he anticipates take the form of a comprehensive survey of the modes of modern sinning, so that the poem's present offers some of the mental satisfactions of a catalogue, to which can be added some voyeuristic joys and some refinements of pandarism, plus a future replay of past sensualities on a non-sensual plane. The impotence is thus conceived not as a cessation of erotic energy, but as an energy in its own right, a vigor not so much diminished as gone into reverse. As if to reflect this the verse has an extraordinary thrust of jeering incandescence. "The Disabled Debauchee" must be unique among poems on this particular theme in achieving an authentically mock-heroic note. The heroic stanza which it borrows from *Gondibert* and *Annus Mirabilis* not only appropriates the grandeurs of the original it traduces, as Pope's *Dunciad* appropriates Milton's, but outdoes these originals in the energy of its witty eloquence. The theme is an old one, deriving from Ovid and Petronius, with some French and English intermediaries. "The Imperfect Enjoyment" (like Aphra Behn's "The Disappointment," attributed to Rochester in 1680) is about premature ejaculation, a recognized variant, and afflicts the speaker with a loved woman but not with whores, a matter on which Rochester is again more amusing than Freudian commentators. There's a Malamudian pathos over the languid member, "Sapless, like a wither'd *Flow'r*" (45). Flowers clearly have a more versatile existence in love poetry than literary historians recognize, and Rochester's line is prettily outdone in Behn's poem, where Cloris' hand discovers the object of her ministrations "Disarm'd ... And Cold as Flow'rs bath'd in the Morning-Dew" (113–14).

The woman's helping hand is common in such poems, beginning with Ovid (*Amores* III.vii.73ff) , and an attractive tenderness often gets into the act, displacing or softening the derision. It's especially evident in Rochester's "Song of a Young Lady. To her Ancient Lover," which belongs to yet another sub-genre (poems about old men and young girls), especially popular in the seventeenth century:

> Thy Nobler part . . .
> ....
> By Ages frozen grasp possesst,
> From his Ice shall be release:
> And, sooth'd by my reviving hand,
> In former Warmth and Vigor stand.
> All a Lover's wish can reach,
> For thy Joy my Love shall teach:
> And for thy Pleasure shall improve,
> All that Art can add to Love.
> Yet still I love thee without Art,
> *Antient Person of my Heart.*
>
> (15–26)

The woman's affectionate devotion comes over as enhanced rather than diminished by her application of technical expertise, and indeed by the sense that the man's flagging powers are part of what turns her on. There's an unforced tenderness, in Rochester's writings, for sexual configurations which others might feel impelled to scorn as bizarre or depraved: a queer geniality, which critics often miss, which erupts with an extraordinary off-beat charm in "Fair *Cloris* in a Piggsty lay," and which even suffuses the bitter little song on "Grecian Kindness" (a miniature *Troilus and Cressida* in the sense of being perhaps the shortest anti-heroic exposure of the Trojan War) with an afterglow of lazy good-nature: "While each brave *Greek* embrac'd his Punk, / Lull'd her asleep, and then grew drunk" (11–12). It is consistent with this that one of the "*Maxims* of his *Morality*," as he told Burnet, was "that he should do nothing to the hurt of any other" in gratifying his "natural Appetites." In this he differed from Sade.

These flauntings of the theme of impotence were part of the subculture of rakish coteries to which Rochester belonged: Etherege also wrote an "Imperfect Enjoyment." There was no doubt some coded self-projection, which only a gull would take for autobiographical disclosure. It is hard to recapture the exact blendings of inverse machismo or playful fabulation. Rochester was more than usually given to role-playing, in both life and letters, so the now slightly faded stand-by of the critic, the persona, doubtless needs to be wheeled in. In the poem about the Ancient Lover, it is the woman who speaks, but the man who is the focus of attention. To the extent that "persona" suggests authorial mask, it is the man who, however passively, usurps the role, his situation which is the "interesting" one. There are poems by Laforgue and by Eliot in which a woman speaks, but in which it is similarly the man's predicament (usually of erotic incapacity of some kind) which mainly comes through. It is also curious that Rochester, Laforgue, and Eliot, all wrote, while still in their twenties, portraits of men suffering or affecting an elderly sexual debility, though the refined timidities and wilting sadness of a Prufrock differ greatly from the thrusting ostentation of the Disabled Debauchee. The latter is only elderly by future projection, but even the Ancient Person of the girl's song, though wholly passive, is energized by proxy in her imagined efforts to revive his powers. He lacks identity and consciousness, and is thus spared the Prufrockian forms of *taedium vitae*, but his body is simultaneously inanimate and responsive to stimulation, like an erotic Aeolian harp.

Rochester often imagines the penis as an autonomous being, comically separate from the body's other functions and unpredictable. This is equally true whether he is writing about impotence or about irrepressible lechery. The classic example is Signior Dildo himself, who combines passivity with an inexhaustible (because mechanical) virility. In one sense, he resembles the lifeless member of the Ancient Person: ladies pick him up, manipulate and embrace him. But he's also so "Lusty a Swinger" (28; glossed by one commentator as "a very powerful person") that "passive" is hardly the right word, any more than it is for the voracious sexuality of those, both women and men, who court his penetrations, like the aforementioned Duchess, who "Has Swallow'd more Pricks, then the Ocean has Sand" (38), and who clearly rates as a very powerful person too. Henry Savile wrote to Rochester in 1671 that his presence was

> extreamly wanting heere to make friends at ye custome house where has been lately unfortunately seized a box of those leather instruments yr Lp carryed downe one of but these barbarian Farmers Prompted by ye villainous instigation of theire wives voted them prohibited goods soe that they were burnt without mercy ... Yr Lp is chosen Generall in this warr betwixt the Ballers & ye farmers. (Rochester 1980: 62)

The letter reveals that Rochester had a dildo, and was thought of as a leader of those who used them. It also records, a Restoration comedy situation, the rakes pitted against the boors at the custom-house and their starchy, and doubtless seducible, wives, but transposed to that alternative utopia of gallantry, the "real" world. As Keith Walker points out in his edition of Rochester (Rochester 1986: 273, n. 64), the poem echoes the incident, or one like it:

> Were this Signior but known to the Citizen Fopps
> He'd keep their fine Wives from the Foremen of Shops,
> But the Rascalls deserve their Horns shou'd Still grow

For Burning the Pope, and his Nephew Dildo.

(61–4)

A few lines later is an episode in which the mechanical allegory replays another familiar scenario of Restoration literature and life:

> A Rabble of Pricks, who were welcome before,
> Now finding the Porter deny'd 'em the Door,
> Maliciously waited his coming below,
> And inhumanely fell on Signior Dildo.

(81–4)

"Signior Dildo" is a delightful foolery, the product of a social Cloud-cuckoo-land that really existed in the alleys and the drawing-rooms of late seventeenth-century London. The mechanical phallus who almost turns organic as he merges in the seething mass of metropolitan lechery may look forward to some of those machines of the modernist imagination, rhapsodically celebrated as extensions of the sensuous life. Rochester lacks both the brutal sentimentality and the preening abstraction. In the humanoid comedy of Dildo and the Pricks, we witness the altogether more genial modernism of a Disney cartoon, as the Stranger flees "along the Pallmall," and "the Ballocks came wobbling after" pursuing him in "full Cry" (86, 90). Both Dildo and Pricks are *re-* rather than *de-*personalized, in no mere lifeless paradox. There is an amusing fitness in the fact that after Rochester's poem, dildoes came to be known as Signiors, as though the poem had conferred personhood on the real thing.

NOTE

1   "Reformation of Manners," *Poems on Affairs of State* (1703), 371.

6

Dryden's "Anne Killigrew": Towards a New Pindaric Political Ode

HOWARD WEINBROT

Dryden's moving ode to Anne Killigrew has been read as an excessive, even ironic panegyric rather than the ode its title and third stanza proclaim:

> And if no clust'ring Swarm of Bees
> On thy sweet Mouth distill'd their golden Dew,
> 'Twas that, such vulgar Miracles,
> Heav'n had not Leasure to renew.
> (Dryden *Works*, vol. 3: ll. 50–3)

Like others, the California editors think this an allusion to Plato in his cradle, as recorded in Cicero *De Divinatione*, 1. 36: "while Plato was an infant, asleep in his cradle, bees settled on his lips and this was interpreted to mean that he would have a rare sweetness of speech."[1] This apparent allusion, however, is twice dubious: Dryden does not claim sweetness of speech for Anne Killigrew, and Cicero does not mention distillation of honey. Pausanias in *Boetics* 9. 23, and Philostratus *Imagines* 2. 12, though, are among those who do mention that regarding Pindar. Basil Kennet relates that Pindar "was design'd by Heaven for a Divine Master in the Lyric strain," and paraphrases the well-known Pausanias as evidence: "sleeping one Day in the Fields, while a little Boy, the Bees came and fed him with their Honey: which passes for the Occasion of his first applying himself to Poetry."[2] Modern heaven, the sophisticated Dryden says, is too busy to ask the bees to signal Pindaric greatness again, but nonetheless "all the Blest Fraternity of Love / Solemniz'd there thy Birth, and kept thy Holyday above" (54–5). Dryden's allusion to Pindar both alerts us to Anne Killigrew's own putative odes and announces heavenly approbation of an earthly poet. His description of Anne's chaste love poetry as "a Lambent-flame which play'd about her Brest" (84) is another apt allusion. Cowley's Pindaric ode "Destinie" characterizes his calling as that of an obscure poet whose fated star framed his being, as "but a *Lambent Flame*" without influence in the world.[3]

Ignorance of the poem's generic groundwork allows modern commentators unwittingly to insult both Dryden and his subject. The familiar reading of the poem's irony, for example, is illogical and unhistorical. Dryden, the argument goes, is slyly satirizing Anne Killigrew; she is not even as good a poet as Katherine Philips, and does not deserve the praise lavished on her. In a recent version of this dogma, within eleven pages the poem is called *ironic* eighteen times and *satiric* ten times. Anne Killigrew herself often is a subject exposed, scorned, flawed, devalued, and inferior to Dryden (Pohli 1991).[4]

Surely, however, Dryden would have been both inhumane and imprudent to offer an introductory poem that mocks the dead, beloved daughter of a well-connected royalist family ably serving the court that he himself also serves, and with which he closely associates Anne's person and art. To diminish Anne Killigrew in such a poem would be to diminish Henry Killigrew and the Stuart court – not to mention the apparently unfeeling Dryden himself, who would be guilty of mutilating Anne Killigrew's own image. Her own epitaph reads: "When I am Dead, few Friends attend my Hearse, / And for a Monument, I leave my VERSE" (Killigrew 1967: 82).

Moreover, ironic and satiric strokes in an ode invariably are obvious, immediately perceived, and of course designed to deflate not to offer ambiguous praise to the dead. The Abbé Yart's long retrospective on the ode clarifies some of its essential functions for poet and reader. "Il faut préférer dans chaque espèce les premiers êtres aux êtres moins sensibles & moins bien faisans. . . . Une Ode doit parler à l'esprit, au jugement, aux sens, au coeur, & leur offrir. . . . les objets les plus capables de les occuper entierement." Yart later adds a point surely amenable to Dryden, Wood, and others. Though the ode includes hyperbole, that is acceptable so long as the foundation of the idea is true: "il faut permettre quelque chose à l'enthousiasme. Une hyperbole est blamable quand elle est totalement fausse."[5]

Dryden is generous to Anne Killigrew, but only supposition allows one to say he "well knew that her poetic stature was inconsiderable" (Dryden, *Poems*, 315). Like Katherine Philips, Anne Killigrew was a competent minor poet who sometimes rose to excellence. Unlike Philips, she also was distinguished as a portrait painter whose rendering of James II long was attributed to Lely.[6] Moreover, she was a beautiful, pious, and virtuous woman, a beloved daughter and sister, and a faithful servant to her sovereign. As Edward Phillips also reminds readers in 1675, her namesake was one of the remarkable "four Daughters of Sir *Anthony Cook*" praised by

John Harrington as among the most learned women in Europe (1675: 235).[7]
Anne was deservedly rewarded by heaven above and Dryden below. He
respected and perhaps ameliorated the loss within an eminent family, for
whom the poetry was more than words on paper.

The contemporary attitude towards Dryden's ode is represented in
Anthony Wood's *Athenae Oxonienses* (1697). After outlining Anne's virtues
and the family's grief, Wood adds that her posthumously published poems
include prefatory verse "wherein is nothing spoken of her, which (allowing
only for the Poetical Dress) she was not equal to, if not superior: and if
there had not been more true History in her Praises, than Compliment, her
Father would never have suffered them to pass the Press. Before them is an
Ode made to her pious Memory and Accomplishments by *John Dryden*, Poet
Laureat" (1721, 2: 1036).

Shortly thereafter, one of Dryden's funeral celebrants observes that
he "sang for *Killigrew*'s untimely fall, / And more than *Roman* made her
Funeral."[8] A few years later, Basil Kennet calls on "the Noblest Poets of
our Time" to translate the Psalms of David: "And that the Design may
want nothing of its Grace and Beauty, we may depend upon the Concur-
rence of those *English Muses*, in whom the Excellent Spirit of *Orinda*, Mrs.
Wharton, and Mrs. *Killigrew*, is reviv'd for the Glory of the Queen, and of the
Age."[9] In 1752 George Ballard hesitates before Dryden's judgment, accepts
it on Wood's authority, and adds that even "if she has failed of some of
[poetry's] excellencies, still should we have great reason to commend her for
having avoided" obscenity destructive to the art and the individual (338).
Anne Killigrew appears as well in *Poems by Eminent Ladies* (1755), as one of
those women poets who have deservedly "been approved by the greatest
writers of their times," and in her case by Dryden in presumably deserved
"lavish encomiums" (1: 3). Mary Scott affirms that judgment in 1774. Her
Female Advocate praises the "illustrious" (93) combiner of poetry and painting
to whom Dryden deservedly gave "immortal fame" (98).[10] The nature of a
Pindaric elegiac ode encourages bold embellishment – as in praise of good
poetry that reflects good genealogy. Except in obvious cases of highly drawn
satire, it does not encourage self-important irony towards its subject. Nor
does it encourage lies abhorrent to memory, to the family, to the occasion
and to the genre. None of these were perceived by contemporaries. If they
were, Samuel Johnson, who had an excellent ear for irony, could scarcely
have called "Anne Killigrew" the "noblest ode that our language ever has
produced" (1905 1: 439).[11]

We know that the genre also encourages symbolic linking of the subject
to the gods, the sovereign, the nation, and the family. However valuable
Anne is in her own right, she is yet more valuable as a hub of positive
mythic and patriotic associations. However sad her death, it can be over-

come by affirmations of continuity. However confident her poet, his resolve also can be stiffened by her superior example. His own mind in flux confronts staggering issues whose realities press upon him, require apparent digression from the apparent main topic, and finally rest upon a redefined resolution of grief. He also supplies a redefined version of a Pindaric ode, in which a young woman's pacific act, and not a young man's martial athletic act, exemplifies and preserves the state as truly as Noah preserved the race.

The first three stanzas form a virtual triad whose variously sublime tones translate Anne Killigrew's death into a privileged elevation to heaven. The first lines claim that she is "Daughter of the Skies," did not die but was promoted, did not suffer but was blessed, and lives in an immortal green paradise of tall rich palm trees. Whether her soul is "adopted to some Neighbouring Star" (6) or is otherwise in Heaven, here is bliss, the company of angels, and celestial song, which she briefly stops only to hear Dryden "In no ignoble Verse" (17). He hopes it will be like Anne Killigrew's verse itself:

> When thy first Fruits of Poesie were giv'n:
> To make thy self a welcome Inmate there:
>   While yet a young Probationer,
>   And Candidate of Heav'n.
>   (19–22)

Her poetic first fruits are like the ecclesiastical newcomer's payment of a dowry to one's superior. The reference also is part of the continuing elevation of Anne's authority, the culmination of which is the later allusion to Noah. As Cowley succinctly puts it, "The *Firstborn*, and *First-Fruits* of all things are *sacred* to God."[12] She is a "Candidate" both as one who hopes to be chosen, and as a Roman candidate for office who wears a white toga, here suggesting her moral purity. The first stanza thus links a blessed Anne to heaven that wished to select her and by which she wished to be selected.

The second stanza is equally positive, but on a lower scale – that of her birth in this world, perhaps by metempsychosis through her father, or perhaps through classical poetry whose path took her from the Greek to the English Sappho. Purged of impurities, she needs no further rebirth: "Return, to fill or mend the Quire, of thy Celestial kind" (38). Anne thus has been linked to her own family, the poetic tradition, and her specific poetic ancestor Katherine Philips, whose "Beauteous Frame" and poetry also were ended by smallpox.

Movement through mythic space is paralleled by movement through real time. Dryden's third stanza considers Anne's actual birth – a word that with "born" he repeats four times and that caused as much joy and holiday making in the celestial as in the human family.

Dryden has established the familiar odic pattern of community, of suggesting how one person or act evokes several others. He now can incorporate his first major digression, one that shows what Anne is not part of; and he can begin to characterize the nature of her poetry itself.

We see, for example, a clear distinction between how Dryden and the *we* and *our* representing "prostitute and profligate" (57) modern verse differ from "thy Heav'nly Gift of Poesy" ordained for divine love. She is a poetic secular Christ figure bearing the burdens of a fallen past. This contrast is made clear both through overt statement and through subtle contrast of *we* in the fallen world, and Anne in "thy" heavenly world: "What can we say t' excuse our Second Fall? / Let this thy *Vestal*, Heav'n, attone for all" (66–7). The digression becomes a main argument when Dryden moves from characterization of her natural art as superior in its form as it was superior in content. She might defy conventional poetic "Stores": "Such Noble Vigour did her Verse adorn, / That it seem'd borrow'd, where 'twas only born" (74–6). Her "Father was transfus'd" into her blood (26) in metempsychosis and in poetic morals: she was "By great Examples daily fed, / What in the best of Books, her Fathers Life, she read" (78–9). Even her love poetry was chaste.

At the halfway mark of the poem, Dryden moves from poetry to its sister art, and in the process has troubled his modern critics. The metaphors, perhaps unfortunately, are drawn from the hostile expansion of Louis XIV, who also stretched his sway to the next realm, also framed "A Chamber of Dependences" (95), and also justified conquest: "the Whole Fief [of painting] in right of Poetry she claim'd" (98).

This line, however, works in a complex, contradictory way. On the one hand, it suggests her regal strength that places her above the law – perhaps like Neander's description of Ben Jonson, who "invades Authors like a Monarch, and what would be theft in other Poets is onely victory in him" (*An Essay of Dramatick Poesie* [1668], *Works* 17: 57). On the other hand, the line also helps to modify Dryden's own association of Anne with hostile aggression; she claims the land, after all, on behalf of a force greater than herself. She is the good subject of a monarch who soon emerges more clearly. Moreover, she harms no one, since she is doing what lesser poets already had done; she becomes the equivalent of the Pindaric athlete, but is triumphant in pacific art. Accordingly, unlike Louis XIV she is benevolent not malevolent.

> The Country open lay without Defence:
> For, Poets frequent In-rodes there had made,

> And perfectly could represent
> The Shape, the Face, with ev'ry Lineament;
> And all the large Demains which the Dumb-sister sway'd,
> All bow'd beneath her Government,
> Receiv'd in Triumph wheresoe're she went.
>
> (99–105)

We already know that her soul and mind come from the best stock, and so Dryden evokes the inner soul as expressed by the hand: "Her Pencil drew, what e're her Soul design'd / And oft the happy Draught surpass'd the Image in her Mind" (106–7).

Dryden takes such happy triumphs from available commonplaces regarding the sister arts. In 1692, for example, Pierre Motteux reports that "the Kingdom of *Poetry* is large and well peopled, it borders on one side on that of *Painting* and on the other on that of *Music*." He later adds that there actually is a close alliance between poets and painters, as seen in "the different *Peinture* they excel in: The one, in the outward Lineaments of the Face and Body; the other in the inward Temperament and Passions of the Mind."[13] In 1706 William Harison uses the image of invasion in a positive way to describe the poet's art and the reader's response: "Each lively Image makes the Reader start, / And Poetry invades the Painter's Art."[14]

Furthermore, by briefly attributing sovereignty to Anne Killigrew, Dryden also may be playing off her own verse and its patriarchal and familial assumptions so congenial to the ode. "What is it to be monarch?" she asks in the little book Dryden's poem prefaces,

> But all th' Afflicted of a Land to take,
> And of one single Family to make?
> The Wrong'd, the Poor, th' Opprest, the Sad,
> The Ruin'd Malcontent, and Mad?
> IV
> Which a great Part of ev'ry Empire frame,
> And Interest in the common Father claime.
>
> (Killigrew 1967: 53–4)

In such a context poetry's expansion into painting is part of an understandable ongoing process; it is an act ratified by the land invaded and justified by her protective, nurturing care of those she governs.

This congenial mingling of realms is reproduced in her art itself. In rustic scenes "shallow Brooks ... flow'd so clear, / The Bottom did the Top appear" (110–11); the rivers "as in Mirrors, shew'd the Woods" (113). As she moves back in time for her subject, though, we see not only Greek and Roman ruins, emblems of their collapsed world, but lines that attribute virtually divine power to Anne. Their key allusion becomes a daring Pindaric metaphor of royal propagation that ends stanza 6 and anticipates the actions of the seminal seventh stanza:

> What Nature, Art, bold Fiction e're durst frame,
> Her forming Hand gave Feature to the Name.
>   So strange a Concourse ne're was seen before,
> But when the peopl'd Ark the whole Creation bore.
>   (123–6)

The peopled ark of course bore creation two by two, a pairing of male and female that preserves and creates a cleansed world. Dryden follows this biblical allusion with its modern but germane counterpart – Anne Killigrew's portraits of James II and Mary of Modena abstract and exemplify the Stuart court in its male and female sexual essence. He is the "bold Erected . . . Martial King" (127–8), and she is the beautiful, shapely, and heavenly form. Anne Killigrew is not merely a portrait painter; she is the modern female Noah whose art preserves God's monarch as surely as the Old Testament Noah preserved God's people.

Furthermore, as we shall see, Noah, his sons Shem and Japhet, and especially his grandson Gomer, were associated with the origin of the British race. Edward Eccleston uses what would be a long-sustained myth in his opera *Noah's Flood* (1679), loosely adapted to the Exclusion Crisis.[15] Dryden adapts it as well in Achitophel's attempt to discredit David's musty genealogy traced to Noah's Ark (*Absalom and Achitophel*, 301–2). Nicholas Amhurst plays on it in 1719, when he berates the young Pretender who "by undisputed *Right Divine*, / From STUART up to NOAH trace Your Line."[16] The venerable patriarch also is resurrected during 1745 "to prove the Succession of the *Stuarts* from the ancient Monarchical House of *Noah* . . . was never interrupted."[17] Dryden here audaciously resurrects the allusion to Noah on Anne Killigrew's behalf, the better to associate Anne with the divinely guided source of British Stuart kingship.

We recall that Dryden begins the discussion of Anne Killigrew's painterly achievements with a metaphor of conquest. He returns to that metaphor and also investigates the reality of death that combat must include. Anne's genius is like a fireball in battle that grows hotter as it is fanned during flight: "Still with a greater Blaze she shone, / And her bright Soul broke out on ev'ry side" (144–5). Only Fate can stop her conquest, and cruelly forces reality and decay upon the hitherto ebullient narrator, when Anne's death was elevation and her life sublime. Now the celebrated beauty is hidden underground; the beautiful virgin lies in a bed of dirt not love. Fate is a conqueror, and a proud, cruel, murdering, mischievous, destructive, sacrilegious felon who defaces her shrine (161) – that is, her "well-proportion'd Shape, and beauteous Face" (150) that associate her with the queen. The preserver in art has become the corrupted body ravaged by smallpox; the poet formerly equated with Katherine Philips' poetic soul, now is equated with her death and scarred body (163–4).

Indeed, the reversal extends to the martial image of Anne Killigrew as conqueror, for the cannonade is turned against her. Fate will "sweep at once her Life, and Beauty too" (156). "Sweep" surely means carry away; it also denotes artillery's lateral movement that commands and destroys specific areas in war's killing fields. Dryden thus is forced to contemplate not God's grace in raising Anne's spirit to His world, but the family's loss in contemplating a world without its beloved daughter and sister.

That probably is why Dryden's penultimate stanza uses another combination of Pindaric digression and linking, and the domestication of danger. Her then sea-captain brother Henry, as brave in his warlike way (165) as martial and warlike James (128, 131), sails home in hopes of seeing his cherished sister; he does not know that he already is "wreck'd at home" (171), and that Anne has been apotheosized as one of the navigator's guides in the seven-starred Pleiad.

This homely, familial, and utilitarian series of images takes us to a world very different from that of disembodied minds, spirits, souls, and voices in the opening stanzas. As Pindaric odist, Dryden has carefully linked his subject to her God, sovereign, nation, father, brother, art, and all of their best values; as elegist he has shown her suffering the human fate of any lesser person. That same genre, though, allows a resolution of grief: fate itself is fated to die, and "The Judging God shall close the Book of Fate; / And there the last Assizes keep" (181–2). Anne becomes a collection of "ratling Bones" requiring "Sinews o're the Skeletons ... spread." She must be "cloath'd with Flesh" (184–7), and be drawn from the tomb and soil. Dryden has moved from the superterrestrial to the subterrestrial, from Anne's initial "Celestial Song" in a heavenly quire to a humbler metamorphosis as she experiences the distant resurrection of judgment day and regains the beauty taken from her. As one of the "Sacred Poets" lightly covered (188–90) she will be

> on the Wing, [and]
> Like mounting Larkes, to the New Morning sing.
> There Thou, Sweet Saint, before the Quire shalt go,
> As Harbinger of Heav'n, the Way to show,

The Way which thou so well hast learn'd below.
(191–5)

The celebration of Anne in Heaven as part of the quire has changed to Anne celebrated for her life on earth that allows her to sing to the quire. The last word of the poem's first line is "Skies"; the last word of the poem's last line is "below." Dryden has suggested Anne's worth in heaven, and her worth here that earned her a place in heaven; he also has demonstrated the narrator's human mind in flux, celebrating the loss of a loved subject, trying bravely to accept that loss and see it as God's gain, while also realizing how deeply felt that loss must be. Her death is cruel, felonious, malicious murder – that can, nonetheless, be "accepted," in the poem at least, not through grand myths of apotheosis and transmigration of souls, but through the reduced metaphors of Anne as a guiding light to her sailor-brother and as a domestic lark singing to the new day.

That in part is what Dryden as narrator, the Killigrews as mourners, and the reader as participant have learned in this ode that uses but transmutes the familiar Pindaric conventions of community, digression, and sublime metaphors. Dryden's genius was sufficiently comprehensive to create the bombastic Almanzor and the amiable Anne Killigrew. One reason that she is the superior creation is that Dryden infuses antique received devices with a superior ethic. René Rapin defines the ode as praise of the gods and celebration of "the illustrious Actions of great Men."[18] Dryden's Anne Killigrew is a woman of modest actions; she nonetheless is illustrious in her own varied spheres and thereby helps to preserve and propagate the best of the Stuart monarchs she and her poet served.

As one could expect from an elegiac ode for young Anne, part of Dryden's achievement is gradually to mute the trumpets of praise; by listening more intently we hear more. This daughter, sister, lady in waiting, poet, and painter is indeed a lesser subject than a god; but she is valued in her own right and in her connections to the family and throne she paints and exemplifies. The monarch is reflected in and by her achievement; her presence in the court allows her to flourish and allows the court to be properly varnished and exalted in her art. As in the poem to Oldham, Dryden has subtly but clearly shifted the focus of his genre from the great and near great to promising but unfinished talent whose loss matters deeply.

He has also hinted at the distinctly nationalistic and local development of the ode in Britain. The guiding assumptions of "Anne Killigrew" are largely Christian and classical, while also planting other seeds that flourish after 1686. The poem's second stanza, for example, apparently is based on Pythagorean metempsychosis, in which Anne's soul moves up the scale of being to the best mortal home she recently inhabited. But a theory of transubstantiation was scarcely limited to Greece. Research concerning the Druids already made plain that these ancient British precursors of Christianity taught that the immortal soul moved from inferior to superior earthly roles.

This knowledge stems from Caesar's *De Bello Gallico* 6. 14, and is widely disseminated among students both of the ancient classical and ancient Celtic worlds: "the cardinal doctrine which they seek to teach is that souls do not die, but after death pass from one to another; and this belief, as the fear of death is thereby cast aside, they hold to be the greatest incentive to valour." The same passage claims that the Druids were astronomers who discuss "the stars and their movement, the size of the universe and of the earth, the order of nature, the strength and the powers of the immortal gods."[19] Since Dryden probably read Caesar as early as his days at Westminster School, his source for the gods, stars, and immortality well could have had these Celtic British as well as classical contexts. However much Caesarean, in 1685 these primitive native contexts have less emotive and emotional force than primitive Greek contexts. Though the allusion to Noah suggests that British mythic origins were useful, Dryden cannot yet be as explicit and positive as Collins could be in 1746, when he eulogizes Thomson with "In yonder grave a Druid lies" ("Ode Occasioned by the Death of Mr. Thomson," 1).

The Noah analogy, indeed, also is especially appropriate since the British version of Biblical racial history viewed Noah's grandson Gomer, son of Japhet, as the founder of the British people. As Bishop Simon Patrick says in 1695, "Our famous *Cambden* (in his Account of the first Inhabitants of *Britain*) thinks that the *Cimbri* and *Cimmerii* descended from this *Gomer*, who gave them their Name; and that the old *Britans* came from him."[20] Anne's art that recreates the generative power within Noah's ark recreates the specific generations of the British people. Praising her as "Unmixt with Forreign Filth, and undefil'd" (69) refers to her virginity, her chaste art, and her native glory. Unlike, say, John Dryden, she is protected from the French frivolity that "Made prostitute and profligate the Muse" (58). Such noble domestication of the noble ode was seminal; it waited more than a half century to flower.

NOTES

This essay is excerpted from a chapter of Weinbrot's *Britannia's Issue* (1993).

1   The California editors (3: 320) quote from the Loeb translation. So far as I

know, Eric Rotnstein is the only other commentator to avoid this misleading error (1981: 10).

2 *The Lives and Characters Of the Ancient Greek Poets* (1697), 2nd edn (London, 1735), 67. Congreve repeats the commonplace with its specific source in his *Pindarique Ode, Humbly Offer'd to the Queen ... To which is prefix'd, A Discourse on the Pindarique Ode* (London, 1706), sig. Ai^r and Ai^{r}n.

3 *The Works of Mr. Abraham Cowley*, 5th edn (London, 1678), with a separate title page for the 1667 edition of the *Pindarique Odes* (1656), 31.

4 For other earlier examples of such now persistent views, see Hope 1969; Vieth 1965; and Silber 1985. Reader response and reception critics may amuse themselves by contrasting the response to "Killigrew" by contemporaries of John Dryden, Cleanth Brooks, and Jacques Derrida.

5 Yart, *Idée de le poësie Angloise, ou traduction des meilleurs poëtes Angloises qui n'ont point encore paru dans nôtre langue* (Paris, 1749–56), 2 (1753): 228–29 (il faut préférer), 2: 295n (il faut permettre).

6 See Dryden, *Works* 3: 322, and Pohli 1991: 38 n. 8 for recognition of Anne Killigrew's artistic skills.

7 Phillips is referring to Harrington's *Orlando Furioso In English Heroical Verse* (London, 1634), praising "Lady Burlie. Lady Russell. Lady Bacon. Mistress Killygrew" (314). This ancestor of course was a namesake only.

8 Dryden, "Melpomene: *The Tragick Muse*. On the Death of John Dryden, Esq.," in *The Nine Muses, Or, Poems Written by Nine Severall Ladies Upon the Death of the late Famous John Dryden, Esq.* (London, 1700), 11.

9 *An Essay Towards a Paraphrase on the Psalms In English Verse* (London, 1706), sig. a4^v.

10 The biographical note is equally confident that Anne Killigrew "might have rivalled the greatest masters of her time" (9n).

11 Dryden's poem also appeared in its eulogistic guise in *Lucretius: A Poem Against The Fear of Death. With an Ode In Memory of The Accomplished Young Lady Mrs. Anne Killigrew, Excellent in the Two Sister Arts of Poetry and Painting* (London, 1709), 11–16.

12 Cowley, "The Plagues of Egypt," from *Works* (n. 3, above), *Pindarique Odes*, 69, n. 2 to stanza 15. Cowley adds that therefore among all ancient nations "the Priesthood belonged to the *eldest Sons*." Here, female Anne supplants her older brothers in sanctity and in paying the first fruits of priesthood.

13 *The Gentleman's Journal: Or The Monthly Miscellany* (January, 1692), 14 (kingdom), and (May, 1692), 19 (different).

14 *Woodstock Park. A Poem* (London, 1706), 4. For some readers the metaphor of conquest would have been unnecessary. See William Congreve's *Pindarique Ode* (n. 2, above): "*Poetry* ... includes painting and Musick" (sig. A2^r; italics and roman type are reversed).

15 *Noah's Flood, or The Destruction of the World. An Opera* (London, 1679), 47, for example.

16 *The Protestant Session. A Poem* (London, 1719), 21.

17 *The Speech of Mr. Kelly, The Non Juror* (Edinburgh, 1745), 11.

18 *Monsieur Rapin's Reflections on Aristotle's Treatise of Poesie*, trans. Thomas Rymer, in *The Whole Critical Works of Monsieur Rapin ... by Several Hands*, 2 vols. (London, 1706), 2: 231.

19 Caesar is quoted from the Loeb text, *The Gallic War*, trans. H. J. Edwards (Cambridge, Mass.: Harvard University Press; London: William Heinemann Ltd., 1963).

20 *A Commentary upon the Historical Books of the Old Testament*, 5th edn (London, 1738), 1: 44.

7

Ironic Monologue and "Scandalous *Ambo-Dexter* Conformity" in Defoe's *The Shortest Way with the Dissenters*

D. N. DeLuna

The story of *The Shortest Way with the Dissenters* is the stuff of familiar literary anecdote: "A certain *Author*," "Personating" High Church zeal, "strenuously pretends to prove" that the Dissenters "ought to be Destroy'd, *Hang'd, Banish'd*, and the D———l and all"; so, the Dissenters, who "never saw the *Irony of the Stile*, . . . began to look about them, to see which way they should fly to save themselves," while "*The Men of Zeal*" "*applauded the unknown Author*" and "plac'd the Book next their *Oracular Writings*." When "At last it came out" that it was written by a Dissenter, "what a clamour was rais'd at the poor Man." I quote from Defoe's own *Consolidator* of 1705, a work dense with anti-Tory invective and one of several of Defoe's works in which this version of events surrounding publication of *The Shortest Way* was first given out (207–9).

Some decades ago a number of literary critics, drawing on this account, took a special interest in Defoe's pamphlet for the questions it seemed to focus concerning the nature of irony and satire, especially in relation to the work of Swift. Is a work ironic if it employs a reductio ad absurdum strategy that would not have been clearly recognized as such by its original audience ("who never saw the *Irony of the Stile*")? Can we speak of a work of polemical attack as satiric if it is unsuccessful in clearly identifying its targets ("At last it came out")?[1] These questions remain stimulating, but, as I shall argue, when the most pertinent historical context for reading the pamphlet is identified and its verbal disguises revealed, the work proves considerably less provocative on the plane of critical theory. In *The Shortest Way*, Defoe employs an unmistakable reductio ad absurdum tactic and a series of allusions that clearly indicate ironic and satiric intent – despite what he himself seemed to claim in *The Consolidator*.

The historical context within which these maneuvers were made was the religious and political controversy surrounding the debate over occasional conformity, which first came to monopolize the attention of Dissenters and then all politically aware Englishmen at the turn of the eighteenth century. Occasional conformity, or occasional communion, refers to the post-Interregnum practice engaged in by some Dissenters of taking Anglican communion periodically, some nonconformist civic officials apparently doing so only to qualify themselves for office under the Corporation Act of 1661 and the Test Act of 1673. The practice led to heated controversy within the Dissenting community in the late 1690s, when two Dissenters became London lord mayors in succession. In 1702, the first year of Queen Anne's reign, occasional conformity became the focus of widespread partisan political debate when newly confident High Church Tories sponsored the Bill for Preventing Occasional Conformity. If passed, it would have in effect barred Dissenters from positions of public trust. *The Shortest Way* was published in December of 1702,[2] the month in which the bill was first read and debated in the Lords, a majority in the Tory-packed Commons having already passed it in November.

Some commentators have pointed up the importance of the occasional conformity debates to an understanding of *The Shortest Way*, but in each case they have suggested only indirect connections that in no way challenge its standard reading: as a univocal monologue featuring a High Church fanatic who recommends the violent suppression of dissent.[3] Closer attention to the context of the debates and to the pamphlet's concealed topical allusions reveals Defoe's mask in the work to be indeed that of a murderous High Church zealot, but one who absurdly misconstrues the bill as itself murderous. He represents it not as a measure that would outlaw occasional conformity but one that would legislate against dissent itself. In this way Defoe satirizes what he sees as the unseemly character of the High Church support of the measure. Of course he himself was not in favor of the Bill for Preventing Occasional Conformity, but he refrained from directly opposing it because he strongly disapproved of occasional conformity on moral and political grounds.[4] And indeed, in *The Shortest Way*, through innovative use of the device of the ironic monologue, he created a two-pronged satire that attacks not only the High Church support of the bill but also the practice of occasional conformity.

Because my reading of the pamphlet requires that we become aware not only of its context but also of subtle verbal manipulations that signpost and give definition to its ironic and satiric contents, the old question arises of the possible miscarriage of Defoe's intentions for the work. Would these verbal indirections have been registered by the tract's original readers? Why might Defoe have wished to provide contemporaries with misleading accounts of his pamphlet, misrepresenting its contents? With my reading in view, we are forced to pose these questions in a new way, almost in reverse. Whereas most critics have assumed miscarriage and explained that the pamphlet is an example of satiric art sacrificed to a polemical objective, I propose that we ask instead: Does *The Shortest Way* show us a Defoe who has subordinated journalistic, polemical aims to innovative, if oversubtle, satiric artistry?

II

Significant debate over occasional conformity arose within the Presbyterian community in the late years of Charles II's reign. That community, it seems, had been divided since the early 1670s, at which time the future secretary of state Sir Joseph Williamson reported a struggle between "the Presbyterians, Dons and Ducklings." The Dons, he explained, were pastors who ministered to "great men of interest," while the Duckling ministers served the "vulgars." "The first sect," he went on, "conversing more with the gentry, undervalue the second, and master it over them, and the second thinking they make it up with popularity and interest in the middling people has occasioned this schism." Williamson also drew up a division list of the leaders of each camp: "[William] Bates, [Thomas] Jacomb, [Thomas] Manton, Dons; [Samuel] Annesley, [Thomas] Vincent, [Thomas] Watson, Ducklings."[5] One modern church historian writing about this "schism" notes that in the late 1670s the so-called Dons – whose leaders were now Richard Baxter, William Bates, and John Howe – became widely known as "Reconcilers" because they were pastors who desired an accommodation of Presbyterians within the established church; while the Ducklings; whose leader was Annesley, came to be regarded as ministers who sought tolerance – indulgence rather than comprehension – because they felt that reconciliation with the Anglican Church was not workable (Thomas, 204–10).

In the 1680s these distinct agendas came to be reflected in antithetical views toward the practice of occasional conformity. The Dons took a positive view of the practice, seeing it as an act of charitable conciliation toward the Church, and Baxter was a particularly strong advocate of this position. In his *Search for the English Schismatick* of 1681, for example, he advised Dissenters to "chuse the best thou canst for thy ordinary communion. . . . But deny not occasional communion" (44). The Ducklings, on the other hand, thought of the practice as sinful intercourse with an erring church.[6]

Throughout William III's reign Dons and Ducklings continued to promote their rival agendas and views. However, in 1690 the Ducklings' goal of securing a comfortable indulgence was obtained with the passage into law of the Toleration Act of 1689 – a reconciliatory comprehension bill having died in the early months of the new reign. But the Dons remained committed to their antiseparatist aims, and throughout the 1690s they tacitly approved of the occasional conformity of their followers who had secured high public offices.[7] The Ducklings denounced these officeholders as mercenary reprobates.

Occasional conformity erupted into a subject of particularly heated controversy in 1697, when Humphrey Edwin, a Dissenter and London's current lord mayor, conformed in a provocative way: taking communion at a morning service at St. Paul's, then attending an afternoon lecture at a Dissenters' meeting hall, to which he brought his Anglican serving-boy, whom he forced to carry his symbolic sword of office. Edwin seemed to be deliberately contravening the intention of the Corporation and Test Acts, which required that all persons coming into offices of public trust receive communion in the Anglican church. Presbyterian Dissenters in particular vigorously debated Edwin's actions. To those under the persuasion of the Dons, he had displayed himself as a moderate Dissenter who, as an occasional communicant, could extend charitable latitude to his Anglican brethren. To those in the camp of the Ducklings, he had publicly prostituted his conscience for secular advancement.[8]

Defoe now entered the controversy with the first of a number of pamphlets. In *An Enquiry into the Occasional Conformity of Dissenters* (1698), he severely attacks Edwin in a preface, and in the body of the tract he condemns the practice in general. He characterizes the occasional conformer as a sinful schismatic ("*Schism* from the Church of Christ is, doubtless, a great Sin.... if I shall thus Dissent, and yet at the same time Conform; by Conforming I deny my Dissent being lawful, or by my Dissenting I damn my Conforming as sinful"; 13); and he fulminates against the practice, describing it variously as a "fast and loose game of Religion" (15), "*playing Bo-peep* with God" (17), a "Promiscuous Communion" (23), "the vilest Act of Perfidy in the World" (24), and making "the Sacred Institutions of Christ Jesus, become Pimps ... [to] Secular Interest" (24).

Defoe was, in the words of a contemporary, "an admirer and *constant Hearer*" of the Reverend Samuel Annesley.[9] And indeed, *An Enquiry into the Occasional Conformity of Dissenters* seems the spirited response of an ardent follower of that Duckling leader. In one section of the pamphlet Defoe upbraids Dissenting ministers, expressing a view very close to a Duckling's sense of authority and duty: "I have heard of some who have been said to have leave from their Ministers for this Matter [of occasional conformity]; *if so*, they have assum'd some *Dispensing Authority*, which I believe does not pertain to the Ministerial Function" (22). He goes on to suggest that Dons have been lax in their judgment of eminent Dissenting officeholders, and he prescribes these terms for readmitting an occasional-conforming "great man" back into a Dissenting assembly: "if the gay Prospect of a Great place tempt any Person beyond the Power that God's Grace is pleas'd to Assist him with, ... [he should] not be readmitted, because of his Gold Ring and Fine Apparel, without a Penitent Acknowledgment" (24).

In 1700 Defoe renewed this assault on the Dons. That year London's newly elected lord mayor, Thomas Abney, a Dissenter, qualified himself for office by conforming, and Defoe responded with a new edition of his *Enquiry into the Occasional Conformity of the Dissenters*, to which he added a preface addressed to the veteran Don, John Howe, whom he knew to be Abney's pastor. Herein Defoe challenges Howe to declare his position publicly, and he hints once again that Dons have compromised their standards in their ministrations to "great" officeholders. If a minister of Howe's learning and stature would publicly condemn occasional conformity, Defoe declares, it would go a long way toward seeing that those who have practiced it receive their "due Censure, tho' the Persons wear the Gay Cloaths and the Gold Ring."[10] Howe replied in *Some Considerations of a Preface to an Inquiry Concerning the Occasional Conformity of Dissenters* (1701), in which he assails Defoe for his narrow spirit and and judgmental attitude toward his Dissenting fellows. Defoe replied to the reply in *A Letter to Mr. Howe* (1701), in which he accuses Howe of mudslinging and of avoiding a public declaration of his position.

By 1702 Defoe had become England's most prolific and well-known critic of occasional conformity, and he had managed to bait one of London's most respected Presbyterian Dons into a pamphlet war with him. Queen Anne's accession to the throne in the spring of that year was only the first of a number of events that made many Dissenters fear the prospect of another era of persecution. Addressing Parliament in March, Anne stated, "my own principles must always keep me entirely firm to the interests and religion of the Church of England and would incline me to countenance those who had the truest zeal to support it."[11] Scores of Anglican clergymen and Tory politicians responded with public displays of affection and protective concern for the Church – perhaps the most arresting of which was the Reverend Henry Sacheverell's sermon "The Political Union," preached at the end of May. In November, the Commons passed the Bill for Preventing Occasional Conformity, and deliberations on it began in the Lords in December. Controversy over the measure and over the practice of occasional conformity raged during that winter.

Defoe published *An Enquiry into Occasional Conformity: Shewing That the Dissenters Are No Way Concern'd in It* in November. In this pamphlet he avoids expressing an opinion as to whether the bill ought to become law and instead treats the manner in which its provisions have been misrepresented – by his own account a new approach to the controversy.[12] He alleges that High Churchmen embrace the measure pretending that it legislates the violent suppression of dissent. They rally behind it "as if this Act a coming out was a Machine to blow them [the Dissenters] all up" (165). "Here comes a Bill into the House," writes Defoe, "[and] some Gentlemen ... are pleas'd to treat the Dissenters in this manner: *Well, Gentlemen, now down ye go, the Parliament are a beginning with you, and they don't use to do Business by halves.... We have got a Church Parliament now, and down ye go*" (157). In Defoe's view, opposition to the bill within the Dissenting community was split between those who had been provoked by zealous High Churchmen into believing this alarming claim and those who opposed the bill because they approved of occasional conformity. (And we may note that these reactions were not necessarily mutually exclusive, because those Dissenters who approved of occasional conformity could declare opposition to the bill on the grounds that it was intended to extirpate dissent altogether.) All those in the Dissenting community who approved of occasional conformity were, Defoe repeatedly insists, false brethren defending an indefensible practice. Occasional conformers are, we hear, "Grown Hypocrites" (160), "ill Persons" (158), and "Knaves" (164). Furthermore, "State Dissenters" who "conform for a place" (160, 162) perform "an Act Destructive of all possible Pretence for Dissenting ... [which] never was, nor never can, be defended by any Dissenter" (169). Such "Politic Dissenters," he explains, have "crept in" among sincere ones, and occasional conformity has "crept in" with them (159–60).[13] In the pamphlet's closing paragraphs he writes that "no Church of *England*-Man can think or speak worse of it [occasional conformity] than the truly Religious Dissenters have done" (171). It is, he declares, a "Corruption" that should be "Extinguished," this "Scandalous *Ambo-dexter* Conformity" (170–1).

III

The Shortest Way with the Dissenters appeared in December, just weeks after *An Enquiry into Occasional Conformity: Shewing that the Dissenters are No Way Concern'd in It*. Like this earlier and lesser-known tract, *The Shortest Way* strikes out in two directions: at the High Church advocacy of the measure and at occasional conformity itself. Unlike the earlier pamphlet, however, it uses deft satire to wage those assaults.

Modern commentators have stopped short at the recognition that Defoe wished to criticize Tory intolerance – in general or in connection with the bill – by exaggerating it through the mask of a High Churchman who would violently extirpate dissent. But in fact Defoe sought specifically to attack the High Church support of the bill, and to do so by portraying an active proponent of it who, however, mistakenly believes the legislation would directly outlaw the practice of dissent. This misconstrual is the most important signal of ironic performance, and on it depends Defoe's satiric exposure of supposed persecutorial fantasies behind the bill – secretly indulged, perhaps, by the bill's High Church supporters in Parliament, while more openly enjoyed by Church fanatics without doors. The full delineation of Defoe's mask can be disclosed through the explication of topical allusions.

To begin with, a satiric fiction entitled "The Shortest Way with the Dissenters" is projected as a piece of print propaganda in support of the measure, as its subtitle suggests: "Proposals for the Establishment of the Church" recalls the title of a High Church tract on the bill that had been published in early November, entitled *The Establishment of the Church ... Showing the Reasonableness of a Bill against Occasional Conformity.*[14] The projected author of this "Shortest Way" is a High Church pamphleteer who makes much of the fact that he is speaking at a time when a "Church of *England* Queen" (Defoe 1927–8, 13: 130) sits on the throne but who later, in his peroration, hints unmistakably at a more immediate occasion for his polemic in the current parliamentary debate over the occasional conformity bill, stating that "now the Destroyers of the Nations Peace may be overturn'd, and to this end the present Opportunity seems to be put into our Hands" (115–16). And he continues: "To this end the Face of Affairs have receiv'd such a Turn in the process of a few Months" (130). Mistaking the nature of the bill, he alludes to the means by which dissent would be directly eradicated but leaves this in the hands of the government: "I could prescribe ways and means, but I doubt not but the Government will find effectual Methods" (122); "As for the Manner, I leave it to those Hands, who have a right to execute God's Justice on the Nation's and the Church's Enemies" (126).

He does nevertheless offer some suggestions of his own for implementing the plan. One is decreeing dissent a crime punishable by hanging, with this rationale: "they that will go to Church to be chosen Sheriffs and Mayors, would go to forty Churches rather than be Hang'd." Another is punishing conventicle-goers with banishment – (now) reserving hanging sentences for active Dissenting ministers: "[Dissent would end if] one severe Law were made, and punctually executed, that who ever was found at a Conventicle, shou'd be Banished the Nation, and the Preacher be Hang'd" (128). These suggestions echo, as they absurdly distort, actual provisions of the bill. For instance, the High Churchman's mention of Dissenters who attended Church "to be chosen Sheriffs and Mayors" recalls a clause in the bill's preamble stating that the measure would inflict no new burdens on conscientious Dissenters, and that its intent was rather to restrain the practice engaged in by some Dissenters of conforming merely to qualify for public office. The proposal that anyone found at a conventicle be punished recalls a stipulation in the measure stating that once a citizen accepts public office, he will not be permitted to frequent a conventicle or meeting house during that term of office. For persistent dissent, Defoe's High Churchman recommends banishment, galleys, and the gallows, but he advises against financial punishments:

> The light foolish handling of them by Mulcts, Fines, &c; 'tis their Glory and their Advantage ... the Spirit of Martyrdom is over.... To talk of 5 *s.* a Month for not coming to the Sacrament and 1 *s. per* Week for not coming to Church is selling them a Liberty to transgress for so much Money. (127–8)

The bill contained a controversial penalties clause stating that any civic officeholder found worshipping at a conventicle will be fined £100 plus £5 for every day thereafter in which he remains in office.[15] Defoe's High Churchman works to promote extreme punishment for dissent by radically understating the actual fines proposed in the bill. But of course he misrepresents more than the amounts of the measure's financial penalties. For, as we know, he is remarking on fines that he supposes are intended not just for occasionally conforming officeholders but, rather, for all Dissenters who practice their religion publicly.

By means of the High Churchman's remarks on fining Dissenters, Defoe, using ambivalent discourse, pursues his other main target: occasional conformity. As he well knew, most Dissenters strongly objected to the bill's penalties clause. Quite contrary to what the High Churchman claims, they did not consider fines "light," "foolish," or redounding to "their Glory and their Advantage."[16] The High Churchman's reference to weekly shilling and monthly five-shilling fines not only misstates the bill's proposed fines clause; it also recalls the fines so regularly risked, and paid, by Dissenters in the recent Stuart reigns, who, if first-time violators of the First and Second Conventicle Acts, were charged up to five shillings.[17] The "Martyrdom" mentioned by the High Churchman more appropriately applies to these earlier Dissenters, who so willingly suffered financial losses because they would not compromise their religious practice. In his *Enquiry* of 1698 Defoe (more explicitly) draws an unfavorable comparison between Dissenting civic officeholders who conform "to save the Five hundred pounds and other Penalties of ... [the Test] Act" and "Primitive" Dissenters in Elizabethan and recent Stuart times who "suffered Persecution, and Loss of Estates and Liberty for the Cause" (144).

In *The Shortest Way* the suggestion that occasional conformists are mercenary is not Defoe's most serious accusation. In the following passage the High Church speaker alleges that if they are occasional conformers because of the Don-inspired belief that the Anglican and Presbyterian religions disagreed in nonessentials only, they are unjustified in their dissent and therefore odious schismatics:

> ONE of their leading Pastors ... in his Answer to a Pamphlet, entituled, An Enquiry into the Occasional Conformity, hath these Words.... Do the Religion of the Church and the Meeting-houses make two Religions? ... the Modes and Accidents are the things in which only they difer.... Now, if ... the Difference between them is only in a few Modes and Accidents, why should we expect that they will suffer ... corporeal Punishment and Banishment for these Trifles? ... if they should venture to transgress ... all the World must condemn their Obstinacy as being without ground from their own Principles.

Here the High Church pamphleteer builds a case for the indefensibility of dissent by unfairly exploiting the words of just "ONE" Dissenting spokesman, John Howe (who was debating with another – namely Daniel Defoe in his *Enquiry* of 1700 – over the issue of occasional conformity), while Defoe obliquely suggests that Howe's familiar Don's position that Anglicans and Presbyterians only disagree in "Modes and Accidents" in fact argues for the indefensibility of occasional conformity. If the practice is held to be defensible because Anglicans and Presbyterians disagree in this minimal way, then nonconformists must indeed have separated from the Church on account of "Trifles," and their failure to conform can, just as the High Churchman claims, only be "Obstinacy"; and such dissent would indeed be "without ground from their [the Dissenters'] own Principles." In his *Letter to Mr. Howe*, Defoe had stated as much: "If we differ from them in Trifles ... we have much to answer for ... in the too fatal Divisions of this Nation.... *I* know not how we shall Ward off the Blow of being guilty of Schism" (215–17). By building a double meaning into the Churchman's discourse, Defoe contends that those Don-led Dissenters who invoke the trifling nature of their separation to defend occasional conformity cannot, then, justify their dissent.

IV

In satirically presenting his speaker's recommendation of the Bill for Preventing Occasional Conformity, Defoe employs irony that relies for its detection and effects on both broadly conceptualized and highly particularized jostlings of meaning. The speaker's advocacy of the bill turns on his absurd misconstrual of it, which is detectable through subtle manipulations of allusion that disclose an attack on the High Church support of the bill. Defoe's other satiric target, occasional conformity, is struck at through an innovative handling of the device of the ironic monologue. My reading of *The Shortest Way* thus runs counter to the claims of those literary critics who have suggested that Defoe was interested in producing a work of black journalism in which ironic and satiric intentions are secondary and go unrealized.[18] Implicit in this suggestion is the view that while the pamphlet raises interesting theoretical questions about the definitional limits of irony and satire, it does not merit serious consideration as literary art. I have, I believe, shown that *The Shortest Way* in fact measures up to an ideal of literary fabulation and craftsmanship that we associate with the best ironic and satiric works of Defoe's coevals Dryden, Pope, and Swift. Another question remains, one that I raised at the outset but have not yet addressed: that of the relationship between this artistry and Defoe's polemical aims for the work.

Once the reader discovers the ironic and satiric contexts of *The Shortest Way*, Defoe's polemical points are obvious enough. But who among his contemporaries would have discerned that content? We can safely assume that a substantial, but not vast, audience of Londoners was well versed in the occasional conformity debates and the controversy over the bill in particular. Defoe may have been exaggerating when he claimed in his *Enquiry* of 1702 that "about the Bill the Press swarms with Pamphlets; [and] the Pulpit sounds with Exaltations on one Hand, and Deprecations on the other" (154);[19] but certainly the bill's introduction generated a considerable amount of news and commentary that would have been received with great interest by a public that followed current affairs. What cannot be safely assumed, I would insist, is that this public followed Defoe's treatment of the subject in *The Shortest Way*.

Among the dozen or so contemporary pamphlets and remarks answering *The Shortest Way*, there is no evidence of a reading of the work that in any way corresponds to the one I have marked out in this essay.[20] I would not, however, be willing to assume that it eluded all of Defoe's contemporaries. The contemporary climate of sub rosa Jacobite and Republican communications must have spawned readers who were adept at recognizing the ways in which political meaning was embedded in disguised form in literary and journalistic works;[21] and these readers, together with educated gentlemen skilled in literary explication, would have had a special aptitude for competently making their way through a pamphlet like this one.

If there were competent readers of *The Shortest Way*, their number would likely have grown in the months following the work's publication. Almost immediately after its appearance, government officials began to make inquiries to discover its author and printer, and Defoe then published *A Brief Explanation of a Late Pamphlet, Entitul'd, The Shortest Way with the Dissenters*, which he also appended to a second edition of *The Shortest Way* of the following February. This essay opens with his "protest" that the work did not have "the least retrospect to, or concern with the Publick Bills in Parliament"[22] – by one strategy, clearly addressed to an audience trained to read between the lines. That his pamphlet's concern with the bill was not, at least after this *Brief Explanation* appeared, lost on this audience is suggested by the fact that a complaint against the work lodged in the Commons in late February alleged it to be "full of false and scandalous Reflections upon this Parliament."[23]

But Defoe also used *A Brief Explanation* to misrepresent his pamphlet as simply the ironic impersonation of High Church bigotry in general. The work, he stresses, took "its immediate Original from the Virulent Spirits of some Men who have thought fit to express themselves to the same effect" (216). And he complains that his pamphlet had in fact been widely read as nothing less than a High Churchman's rousing and sincere call to destroy Dissenters – when "It seems Impossible that it should pass for anything but an Irony" (215).[24] Defoe followed up *A Brief Explanation* with *A Dialogue Between a Dissenter and the Observator, Concerning the Shortest Way with the Dissenters*, in which he similarly misrepresented his pamphlet and made the same claim about an unperceptive reading of it.[25] He may have feared government prosecution for the work's more particular satire; and the temptation to redouble his attack on High Churchmen by tendering the familiar satiric claim that he has all but perfectly mirrored his subject evidently proved irresistible. However, I would propose that yet another motive was paramount: by misrepresenting the ironic and satiric content of *The Shortest Way*, Defoe was working to stimulate interpretive debates over the work, which would mean additional sales and, in turn, larger numbers of readers for his far more straightforward pamphlets on occasional conformity and related topics. The literary virtuosity of the work was, by this scenario, not only no impediment to its reception but indeed a crucial and strategic part of it.

Of course, Defoe's own tactics aside, the pamphlet and its author gained tremendous notoriety on account of the government's reaction to the work – although, to be sure, this was neither solicited nor welcomed by Defoe. In mid-January he was in hiding when two notices appeared in the *London Gazette* offering a government reward for his discovery, and in late February the pamphlet was publicly burned in New Palace Yard, Westminster, an event mentioned in the *London Post* for March 1. In May two London triweeklies reported his arrest by government agents and his imprisonment in Newgate. And during these early months of 1703, at least a few answering pamphlets to *The Shortest Way* appeared (all of which subscribed to Defoe's misleading gloss on the work); John Tutchin repeatedly denounced the pamphlet in his essay journal *The Observator*; and another edition of *The Shortest Way* appeared along with other Defoe works – including his pamphlets on occasional conformity dating from 1698 – in *A Collection of the Writings of the Author of the True-Born Englishman.*[26]

More than purely circumstantial evidence tells us that Defoe was well aware of the sales and notoriety that the official action against him brought and could bring, for he had remarked in his first book, *An Essay Upon Projects* of 1697: "I *have* heard a Bookseller ... say, *That if he wou'd have a Book sell, he wou'd have it Burnt by the hand of the Common Hangman*; the Man, no doubt, valu'd his Profit above his Reputation."[27] In July of 1703 Defoe underwent public trial and endured his sentence of the pillory; and that month he capitalized on these events by publishing his *Hymn to the Pillory* and *A True Collection of the Writings of the Author of the True Born English-man.*

In subsequent years he continued to tender his usual inaccurate glosses on *The Shortest Way*, in such works as *More Reformation* (1704) and *A Second Volume of the Collected Writings of the True-Born Englishman* (1705). And he told stories about the work's enthusiastic initial reception among High Church-men, which he claimed was part of his calculated polemical effect. In the *Consolidator* (1705) he wrote, "so closely had the Author couch'd his Design" in the pamphlet that it "caus'd" High Churchmen "to caress, applaud and approve it, and thereby discover'd their real Intention, [and] so it met with Abhorrence and Detestation in all the men of *Principles, Prudence* and *Moderation*" (209). And again, later, in his *Present State of the Parties in Great Britain* of 1712, he alleged that the design of the work was "to speak in the first Person of the Party, and then, thereby, not only speak their language, but make them acknowledge it to be theirs, which they did so openly, that confounded all their Attempts afterwards to deny it."[28]

A number of lucidly written pamphlets on occasional conformity that Defoe published from 1703 to 1705, when new bills to prevent the practice were proposed in Parliament, kept the celebrity of *The Shortest Way* alive. Three did so on the title page: *More Short-Ways with the Dissenters* (1704); *The Shortest Way to Peace and Union* (1704), which uses the legend "By the Author of the Shortest-Way with the Dissenters"; and *The Experiment: Or, The Shortest Way with the Dissenters Exemplified* (1705).[29] So, too, readers of his anti-Tory pamphlets and of his periodical the *Review* were constantly put in mind of the tract. The High Church Tory journalist Charles Leslie seems to have understood the publicity technique involved when in 1706 he remarked that Defoe *"glory'd"* in *The Shortest Way* and *"Quoted* it 100 times in his after

Writings."[30] This self-publicizing is, as I have been suggesting, of a piece with Defoe's initial tendering of false glosses on the work and, perhaps more surprisingly, with his literary efforts in the work itself. If I am correct that Defoe's aim in *The Shortest Way* was the simultaneous promotion of his professional and polemical interests through the mediation of imaginative conception and verbal craftsmanship, we have in the pamphlet an extraordinary early-modern instance of the literary being put to the service of the extraliterary.

NOTES

1 See, for example, Ross 1941: 79–82; Martin Price 1953: 62–3; Paulson 1967b: 150–2; Watt 1957: 126; Booth 1961: 318–20; Novak 1966b: 402–17; and Novak 1966a: 15–23, 37–8. Novak, along with a number of more recent critics, has argued for the existence of palpable ironic pointers in the tract; see Shugrue, notes to his edition of *The Shortest Way*, 326–7; E. Anthony James 1972: 100–11; and Downie 1986: 131–6. Critics who find that there are no ironic pointers include Lerenbaum (1974) and Alkon (1976).

2 William Lee dated the pamphlet December 1 (1869: 1: xxix) but did not name the source of his information. Frank Bastian has argued that the pamphlet first appeared in late December (1981: 278). He believes, however, that the work appeared sometime around the third week of the month. Paula Backscheider claims that on December 14 Robert Harley attempted to persuade Sidney Godolphin to undertake to discover the author of *The Shortest Way* (1989: 100).

3 The connections these commentators suspect are various. James Sutherland links *The Shortest Way* to the contemporaneous parliamentary debate over the bill and asserts that the pamphlet "had the effect of increasing tension on both sides" (1971: 43). John Robert Moore entertains the possibility that Defoe was writing as a partisan insider, perhaps on the side of the bill's opponents, Harley or the Whig Lords Somers and Halifax (1958: 109–12). Benjamin Boyce, though, maintains that if the pamphlet's satire on High Churchmen was written to Harley's order, Harley secretly wanting the bill sunk, Defoe was at the same time undoing his patron's instructions, because the work contains a moment of sincere rebuke to the Dissenters, an interjection that a Dissenting audience might well have interpreted as an effort to encourage the bill's passage (1974: 58). According to J. A. Downie (1986: 131–6) and Paula Backscheider (1989: 92–4), Defoe in *The Shortest Way* expended all his energy seeking to defeat the bill because he felt that a newly emergent and popular faction of sadistic High Churchmen was behind it, and that it therefore posed a real threat to the nation's tolerance of dissent. In support of this view, Downie asserts that Defoe's primary strategy was to display a vicious High Church proposal for suppressing dissent so as to pressure the government to reject measures "which could be interpreted as unnecessarily oppressive" (136). Backscheider contends

that with this proposal Defoe attacks "the spirit that created the bill . . . rather than the bill itself" (94).

4 On Defoe's disapproval of the measure, see *A Dialogue Between a Dissenter and the Observator* (London, 1703), in *A Collection of the Writings of the True-Born Englishman* (London, 1703), 230, 231.

5 Sir Joseph Williamson, in *Calendar of State Papers – Domestic*, 1671–2: 28–9.

6 On the Ducklings' position, see Michael Watts 1978: 265.

7 In 1693 Sir William Ashurst, a Dissenter, accepted the mayoralty. In 1694 a number of eminent Dissenters – including Sir Robert Clayton, Sir Humphrey Edwin, Sir Thomas Abney, and Sir Henry Ashurst – accepted appointments as commissioners for the lieutenancy (see *Calendar of State Papers – Domestic*, 1694–5: 21). Concerning prominent occasionally conforming Dissenting parliamentarians, see N. H. Keeble 1987: 40.

8 On approving views of Edwin's behavior, see, for example, *Dialogue Betwixt Jack and Will* (London, 1697); and *A Rowland for an Oliver* (London, 1698). Disapproving views can be found in James Nichols, *Defensio Ecclesiae Anglicanae* (London, 1707–8); and *The Puritanical Justice* (London, 1697).

9 John Dunton, *The Impeachment* (London, 1714), 13. Frank Bastian was the first to rediscover this statement by Dunton (1981: 158).

10 Defoe, *An Enquiry* (1700) in *A Collection*, 134–5.

11 Quoted in William Cobbett, ed., *The Parliamentary History of England* (London, 1810), 4: 25.

12 Daniel Defoe, *An Enquiry into Occasional Conformity. Shewing That the Dissenters Are No Way Concern'd in It* (London, 1702), in *A Collection*: "The Act depending in the House of Commons about Occasional Conformity has set abundance of Heads to Work in the World; and be the House in the Right, or in the Wrong, I know my own Business, and their Temper too well to meddle with it: But I pretend to say, that all Men I have met with, who have meddled with the Argument, either in Print or otherwise, are manifestly Mistaken" (154). All quotations in the text are cited from this edition. I have in my text substituted a colon for the period appearing on the title page between the main title and subtitle.

13 Defoe's statement here about "Politic Dissenters" deliberately recalls a moment in Henry Sacheverell's *Political Union* (London, 1702): "We must Watch against These Crafty, Faithless, and Insidious Persons, who can *Creep* to Our Altars, and Partake of Our Sacraments" (61). The point of Defoe's allusion is that it is "Politic Dissenters" who deserve the kind of censure that Sacheverell has cast on the Dissenting community in general.

14 Backscheider (1989: 95–6) was, I believe, the first to call attention to this pamphlet in connection with *The Shortest Way*.

15 A text of the 1702 bill is printed in Cobbett, *Parliamentary History*, 6: 61–8.

16 The size of the proposed fines in the penalties clause was a point of controversy among parliamentarians. In December the Lords amended these proposed penalties, specifying instead a £20 penalty with no additional fines to be incurred. In early January Lords managers stated that the original clause was

"excessive." In mid-January Commons managers vigorously defended the original clause. See *Journals of the House of Lords*, 17: 76, 107, 181–3. This fines clause was also highly controversial "without doors"; on this see, for instance, the anonymous *The Case of Dissenters, as Affected by the Late Bill* (London, 1703), in *Somers Tracts*, 12: 236–40.

17   The texts of the Conventicle Acts are printed in Gould, 1862: 477–99.

18   Martin Price (1953) distinguished between "black propaganda," which merely "forge[s] statements by an enemy which might discredit him," and ironic impersonation, in which "we must know who ... [the author] pretends to be ... [and] know that he is only pretending" ("We must not only recognize the mask, we must also recognize that it is a mask" [63]). Later, Ronald Paulson described *The Shortest Way* as a work of "specifically polemical if not satiric intent"; it was – Paulson labeled it – "black journalism" (1967b: 23).

19   Defoe also writes in this *Enquiry*: "The Subject I am upon needs no Introduction, the History is in every Mans Knowledge; the Parliament are upon a Bill to prevent Occasional Conformity ... [and] every one speak their Opinions, some their Hopes, some their Fears" (154).

20   These include the pamphlets: *The Safest-Way with the Dissenters* (London, 1703); *Reflections Upon a Late Scandalous and Malicious Pamphlet Entitul'd, The Shortest Way with the Dissenters* (London, 1703); *The Shortest-Way with the Dissenters ... Consider'd* (London, 1703); *The Scribler's Doom* (London, 1703); *The Fox with his Fire-brand Unkennell'd and Insnar'd: Or, a Short Answer to Mr. Daniel Foe's Shortest Way with the Dissenters* (London, 1703); *Remarks on the Author of the Hymn to the Pillory* (London, 1703); *The New Association II* (London, 1703); *The Reformer Reform'd* (London, 1703); *A Fair Way with the Dissenters and their Patrons* (London, 1703); *The Review and Observator Review'd* (London, 1706); *A Vindication of the Earl of Nottingham* (London, 1714). Remarks were published in the newspapers: John Tutchin's *Observator*, nos. 73 (December 1702–January 1703), 75 (January 1703), 78 (January 1703); and Charles Leslie's *Rehearsal*, nos. 80 (January 1706), 94 (April 1706).

21   On the relationship between censorship and subtle literary disguise in early-modern England, see Annabel Patterson, *Censorship and Interpretation* (Madison, WI, 1984). For a discussion of how political conflict in England in the later seventeenth century led readers to become more sensitive to verbal indirections and coded language, see Richard Ashcraft, "The Language of Political Conflict in Restoration Literature," in *Politics as Reflected in Literature*, William Andrews Clark Memorial Library Seminar Papers (Los Angeles, 1989), 19–23.

22   Daniel Defoe, *A Brief Explanation of a Late Pamphlet, Entituled, The Shortest Way with the Dissenters* (London, 1703), in *A Collection*, 215.

23   *Journals of the House of Commons*, 14: 207.

24   Cf. 218: "'Tis hard ... that not one man can see it, either Churchman or Dissenter."

25   Daniel Defoe, *A Dialogue Between a Dissenter and the Observator Concerning The Shortest Way with the Dissenters* (London, 1703), in *A Collection*: "The Author of the Shortest way ... sums up all the black Things this high Party had publish'd,

into one General" (219). Compare 238: "The Author meant ... *to expose them* [the Highflyers].... all their designs [are] laid open in Minature [*sic*], and an Abridgment communicated to the World in *true Billingsgate.*" Further compare 234: "Obs[ervator]. And so you thought the *Shortest Way* was Wrote to make a beginning with you, and to set the *Dragoons of the Church* upon your Backs; did you not? *Dis*[senter]. 'Tis very true."

26 These events are recounted in detail in Bastian 1981: 279–87 and in Backscheider 1989: 100–5.
27 Defoe, *An Essay Upon Projects* (London, 1697), 173.
28 Defoe, *The Present State of the Parties in Great Britain* (London, 1712), 24.
29 Defoe also refers to *The Shortest Way* in *The Ballance* (London, 1705), 8.
30 Charles Leslie, *Rehearsal*, no. 94 (April 1706).

8

Strange Complicities: Atheism and Conspiracy in *A Tale of a Tub*[1]

ROGER D. LUND

It is one of the ironies of life in Augustan England that a society saturated by the influences of the Anglican church should have felt itself imperilled by the forces of modern atheism. Yet by the 1670s even obscure country parsons could exclaim that "Atheism that was before but a pitiful Embryo, is ... now a vaunting *Goliah*, and bids defiance (as the Giants of old) to God and Heaven, to Reason and Religion, and the whole Armies of Israel."[1] It may seem peculiar that the Church of England (buttressed by wealth, political influence, and the force of the penal code) should have portrayed itself as a mere David facing an atheistical Goliath, but such was the fear of atheism in the later seventeenth and early eighteenth centuries that even normally unflappable clerics convinced themselves that the church was in imminent danger. As John Redwood remarks, "in a world where no one would dispute the existence of God openly and in print, much less openly question the view that God had made the earth and placed man upon it ... the overruling fear [was] of a Godless, mindless world governed by random atoms and created by chance" (1976: 10).

This apprehension is clearly reflected in the works of Jonathan Swift. In one of his earliest poems, the "Ode to the Athenian Society" (1692), he berates:

> *The Wits*, I mean the Atheists of the Age,
> Who fain would rule the Pulpit, as they do the Stage,
> Wondrous *Refiners* of Philosophy,
> of Morals and Divinity,
> By the new *Modish System* of reducing all to sense.
> (Swift 1958, 1: 19, ll. 103–7)

Swift echoes charges drawn from the popular pamphleteering of his day that the stage had been depraved, that the pulpit had been compromised by heterodox opinion, and that wit had become the mark of the modern atheist. But most important, he repeats the contention, so frequently asserted as to have become an article of faith in the later seventeenth century, that the corruptions of the age might be traced to their origins in some new form of atheistical materialism.[2] The "Ode to the Athenian Society" is but the opening salvo in Swift's continuing conflict with "new *Modish System*[s] of reducing all to sense," a battle that finds its most sophisticated, at times most baffling, incarnation in *A Tale of a Tub*.

Critical emphasis on the indeterminancy of Swift's satirical identities, his personae, and his various incarnations as Dean, Drapier, Bickerstaff, or Gulliver, has often obscured the fact that above all else Swift was a stalwart churchman who never wavered in his defense of the established church, its prerogatives or its public rituals. For all that we have learned about the private affairs and psychic terrain of Jonathan Swift, the precise features of his most basic religious beliefs have remained relatively uncharted. Most of what Swift tells us of the nature of his faith concerns public conformity with the religion by law established. And while it is often difficult to pin down Swift's religious notions precisely, as Irvin Ehrenpreis remarks, certain attitudes remain constant such as "Swift's loathing for any saboteur of true religion, whether atheist, Dissenter, or quack" (1962–83, 2: 197).[3] Swift's "Apology" for the *Tale* makes the point quite clearly that, whatever else it might seem, his satire is first a defense of established religion against "those heavy, illiterate Scriblers, prostitute in their Reputations, vicious in their Lives, and ruin'd in their Fortunes, who to the shame of good Sense as well as Piety, are greedily read, meerly upon the Strength of bold, false, impious Assertions, mixt with unmannerly Reflections upon the Priesthood, and openly intended against all Religion" (5). Swift's loathing for these saboteurs of religion derived in part from their materialist denials of the immateriality of the spirit and hence the immortality of the soul, a belief central to Swift's own theology. For as his sermon "On the Trinity" makes clear, Swift held that the union of spirit and matter, body and soul was not a subject to be philosophically debated, but to be intuitively apprehended and implicitly believed (Swift, *Prose Works* 9: 159–68.) The outlines of Swift's belief in "things invisible" can be discerned not only in his religious writings, but in his political pamphlets and satirical works as well, running like a central thread through *A Tale of a Tub*.

The mere fact that Swift found it necessary to append an exculpatory "Apology" to the fifth edition of the *Tale* suggests that his pious intentions were not immediately apparent to his readers. But while his ironic defense of orthodox religion may have misfired, his statement of intention is still worth reexamining, because it tells us much about the polemical character of the *Tale* itself. Although he may arraign such generalized satiric defendants as fanaticism, reductivism, or the madness of human pretensions to reason (so often cited as the focus of Swift's concern in the *Tale*), he also trains his eye on more concrete historical targets. Indeed, as Robert M. Adams suggests, *A Tale of a Tub* is a satire growing directly out of late seventeenth-century religious controversy: "It is more a crisis book than a compromise book; and the closer we get to the immediate circumstances, the exact details surrounding the book's creation, the better our chances to see and evaluate the precise contours of the book itself" (1972: 99).

Like many of his contemporaries, Swift was particularly alarmed by the behavior of those Deists, freethinkers, and atheists previously restrained by the Licensing Act, who, after 1695, were now free to attack the church, its doctrines, practices, and priesthood. In Swift's case, moreover, the materialist threat posed by Hobbes, Lucretius, and their disciples called into play an ironic strategy analogous to that form of argumentation employed by such atheist hunters as the Cambridge Platonists, or the Boyle lecturers, who argued that all forms of heterodoxy from Epicurean materialism to doubts about the Trinity were but overt manifestations of a well-disguised atheistical conspiracy.

For those, like Swift, who had lived through the Exclusion Crisis and the Popish, Rye House, and Meal-Tub Plots, conspiracy seemed the rule, not the exception. And it seemed only natural to seek for hidden significance and hermetic correspondences in apparently unrelated events, to magnify seemingly innocent associations into villainous cabals. Hence Francis Atterbury can cry out that "there seems to be an universal Conspiracy amongst a sort of Men, under the Style of Deists, Socinians, Latitudinarians, Deniers of Mysteries . . . to undermine and overthrow the Catholick Faith."[4] William Talbot's remark that modern materialists "labour to make a Party" merely provides further evidence of the popular belief in an atheist conspiracy.[5]

For Charles Blount, who was to become one focus of this conspiratorial frenzy, there was little question that it was "not altogether safe in this Plotting Age to ask what 'tis a Clock,'"[6] a sentiment seconded by John Toland. "Such is the deplorable Condition of our Age," he writes, "that a Man dares not openly and directly own what he thinks of Divine Matters . . . if it but very slightly differs from what is receiv'd by any Party, or that is establish'd by Law; but he is either forc'd to keep perpetual Silence, or to propose his Sentiments to the World by way of Paradox under a borrow'd or fictitious Name."[7] Toland could hardly have been surprised when Peter Browne boldly asserted that no single author could ever have written *Christianity Not Mysterious*, insisting instead that it was the "*Joynt Endeavours* of a secret Club, who set themselves with a great deal of Industry to destroy all *Reveal'd Religion*."[8]

If, as Toland suggests, the unorthodox had been compelled to disguise their true opinions, then it fell to the defenders of the faith to strip away those disguises and to discover the "true meaning" and reveal the "original intentions" of these atheistical conspirators. It was work quite congenial to Swift. With his fascination for the "power of hidden intrigue upon political history" and his "habit of transforming a tendency or leaning into something absolute," Swift was uniquely suited to detect similar intrigues in the realms of learning and religion (Ehrenpreis, 2: 64, 415).[9] With a perverse prescience so typical of his age, Swift could see the oaks of atheism in the acorns of error; he could hear the roar of revolution in the whispers of dissent. In *A Tale of a Tub* Swift gives free rein to these instincts. His multivalent layerings of suggestion and innuendo produce a sustained satirical indictment of modern atheism based less on hard evidence or linear demonstration than on a relentless assertion of guilt by association.

Of those scholars who have traced the relationship between *A Tale of a Tub* and the intellectual currents of the age, Phillip Harth (1961) has provided by far the fullest account of Swift's struggle with modern atheism. Yet by stressing Swift's debt to the intellectual patterns of Anglican rationalism, Harth risks overstating the clarity and perspicuity of Swift's satire in *A Tale of a Tub*. For if one reads the *Tale* against the backdrop of contemporary anti-atheist rhetoric, it is less the rationalism of Anglican theology than the conspiratorial irrationalism of Anglican polemics that seems to govern Swift's satirical strategy. John Traugott's comment that "satire in the *Tale* seems at times to resemble the scurrilous ridicule of a host of seventeenth-century Church polemicists who had less Christianity than Thersites" (1988: 5), strikes nearer the mark and seems far more congruent with the views of such contemporary critics as Charles Gildon, who remarks that in the *Tale*, Swift has "discover'd the Shortest way with CONTROVERSY."[10]

Modern critics have often resisted the notion that *A Tale of a Tub* should first be read as a satire of contemporary ideas, arguing that "it is not ... in studies of the parochial quarrels of the Restoration that we will find a sufficient account of the evolution of the *Tale*" (Traugott 1988: 10). Perhaps not, but neither can one hope for such an account by overlooking these squabbles. "Parochial quarrels," from the battle of the Ancients and the Moderns to the anti-mercantilist objections of Irish weavers, were, after all, Swift's stock in trade, providing the spark for some of his greatest satires. To see *A Tale of a Tub* in relation to the anti-atheist polemics it so resembles is to understand Swift's satire in terms of the "crisis" to which it responds. By so doing we have a better chance of understanding the ironic hermeneutics by which Swift reveals the original intentions of the modern atheist, dramatizes the true relationships between apparently unrelated forms of error, and lays bare those strange complicities that bind all modern materialists in the same dire conspiracy.

II

One might cite any number of explanations for why such a God-intoxicated age should have felt so threatened by the specter of triumphal atheism, but a single citation from Anthony Horneck, Chaplain in Ordinary to William and Mary, may serve by way of illustration.

> Such is the degeneracy of the Age we live in that the very Fundamentals of Religion are struck at; and though Modesty was never any Quality of the Devil ... and though Practical Atheism hath been the Stratagem he hath made use of all along, yet his grand Endeavour now, and of late Years is to lead Men into Speculative: And we see it hath so far prevail'd with abundance of Men, that they are grown very Indifferent, whether they believe anything at all concerning God or Religion.[11]

Like Swift, Horneck seems less concerned with the blasphemy, drunkenness, and debauchery that characterized the "practical" atheism of the age than he is with those "new *Modish System*[s]" that lead men to "speculative" atheism.

In spite of Horneck's predictable pulpit pounding, it would be a mistake to dismiss his fears of speculative atheism too glibly. For while the Church of England had certainly faced a variety of trials in its brief history, it had never been challenged by the kind of skeptical onslaught that it faced after the Restoration. The popular influence of Hobbes's *Leviathan* (1651), Spinoza's *Tractatus* (first translated into English in 1690), Creech's translation of Lucretius (1682), Locke's *Reasonableness of Christianity* (1695), and such Deist tracts as Blount's *Oracles of Reason* (1693) and Toland's *Christianity Not Mysterious* (1696) posed a unique challenge to the defenders of orthodoxy. As if this were not trouble enough, the publication of the first fistful of Socinian pamphlets in the 1690s raised the frightening prospect of the revival of the Arian heresy within the Church of England itself.[12] The fear of speculative atheism could lead to such frantic reactions as the public burning of Arthur Bury's "Socinian" tract, the *Naked Gospel* (1690), and his summary expulsion from his place at Exeter College. Or it could inspire more reasoned responses, like the establishment of the Boyle lectures designed to prove "the Christian Religion, against notorious Infidels, *viz.*

Atheists, Theists, Pagans, Jews, Mahometans, not descending lower to any Controversies, that are among Christians themselves."[13]

Of course, it was not always clear just what modern atheism implied, and despite Boyle's warnings, the controversy inevitably involved attacks on the beliefs and practices of other Christian sects, particularly if they seemed to threaten the Church of England. Even Anglican bishops were not immune to charges of atheism, particularly if they were Latitudinarian in their sympathies.[14] As Margaret Jacob remarks, by the 1690s "epithets like deist, atheist, libertine, and finally pantheist were bandied about so much that they lost all useful meaning" (202). Unfortunately, it was all too easy to attach the label of "atheist" to one's political opponents, whatever the nature of the quarrel. And the fact that no one openly confessed to his heterodoxy meant that such tendencies had to be detected and ferreted out from beneath the mask of orthodoxy. It was often the case, as in denunciations of Thomas Hobbes (who openly declared his belief in a God), that careful readings were required to demonstrate the atheistical tendencies implicit in a writer's work. Indeed, were he to wade through *The True Intellectual System of the Universe* (1678), Cudworth's exhaustive, encyclopedic and influential inventory of error, the seventeenth-century reader might reasonably have wondered just which philosophies, ancient or modern, could be said to *escape* the taint of atheism which such close reading inevitably revealed.

Nevertheless, even a cursory review of late seventeenth-century atheist hunters reveals common elements which, to their way of thinking, link all modern "atheists" together. Certainly the popularity of modern materialism provides the most convenient focus for their pious outrage as well as an explanation for the rise of speculative atheism. Sir Charles Wolseley's *Unreasonableness of Atheism made Manifest* offers a particularly revealing specimen of this tendency to explain all modern error as an emanation of materialism. After asserting that there is no God and that the world made itself by *"meer chance ... By a casual hit of atoms one against another,"* a typical Hobbist argues for the ethical consequences that must result from such belief:

Q. Whence came the reason of mankind; and all that order and regularity we find in the world?
A. *From the meer accidental conjunction of those Atoms.*
Q. What is it that men call Religion?
A. *A politick cheat put upon the World.*
Q. Who were the first contrivers of this cheat?
A. *Some cunning men that designed to keep the world in subjection and awe ...*
Q. Is there any such thing as good and evil?
A. *No: 'tis a distinction the world hath been couzened with. ...*

Q. What becomes of a man when he dies?
A. *He returns into his first Atoms.*[15]

Quite typically, Hobbes is accused of ridiculing religion as a pious fraud, denying the immortality of the soul, and endorsing libertinism and unbridled self-love, all perversions deriving in some measure from his atheistical atomism. Because of his militant materialism, Hobbes was quite naturally tarred with an Epicurean brush, and his enemies were quick to find in both systems a common desire to free men from foolish superstitions of religion by explaining all phenomena with reference to matter and motion.[16]

Wolseley's purposeful confusion of Epicurean and Hobbist elements reveals one of the most characteristic features of late seventeenth-century opposition to all modish systems of philosophy – the conflation of error. While there were major differences between such atheist hunters as Ralph Cudworth or Sir Charles Wolseley, these philosophical distinctions often seem less significant than the common conviction that sufficient examination would reveal some form of atheistical materialism at the root of all modern heterodoxy. Swift's close friend Bishop Berkeley states the case most forcefully: "How great a friend *material substance* has been to Atheists in all ages were needless to relate." He adds:

> Impious and profane persons ... readily fall in with those systems which favour their inclinations, by deriding *immaterial substance*, and supposing the soul to be divisible, and as subject to corruption as the body; which exclude all freedom, intelligence, and design from the formation of things, and instead thereof make a self-existent, stupid unthinking substance the root and origin of all beings. (Berkeley 1965: 99–100)

Once one accepts the hypothesis that the world is nothing but matter undirected by divine Providence, then free will, intelligence, and even the immortal soul become but meaningless metaphors for the mechanical motions of material substance.

As Berkeley would later suggest in *Alciphron*, all modern materialists from Bayle to Blount belonged to the same united front (Berkeley 1871, 2: 23–57). Indeed, as John Redwood remarks, Swift's contemporaries "feared the fifth column of atheism from ancient and modern theories of the structure of matter, more than they feared the fool who forthrightly swore and atheized his thoughts," because they "could not see him" (1976: 105). And if, as Berkeley implies, materialism was but a pretext for immoral action, then the first step in the reformation of modern man must be to reveal the hidden dangers of those new materialistic systems of philosophy which encouraged wicked behavior.

We should not be surprised if *A Tale of a Tub* often seems to echo such sentiments, for this controversy over the nature of matter and spirit raged throughout the years in which Swift prepared for ordination (reading widely in works of religious controversy) and wrote the early drafts of *A Tale of a Tub*. If nothing else, Swift's recapitulation of the popular commonplaces *"That all are gone astray; That there is none that doth good, no not one; That we live in the very Dregs of Time; That Knavery and Atheism are Epidemick as the Pox..."* (51–2) reveals his vivid awareness of contemporary jeremiads. Although he pokes fun at such clichés, Swift shares the alarm they register as well as the conspiratorial predilection to detect common tendencies in a variety of errors, so characteristic of more hysterical defenders of the Anglican church. In his *Remarks Upon a Book Intitled, the Rights of the Christian Church* (1709), Swift equates the "former enemies to Christianity, such as *Socinus, Hobbes,* and *Spinosa*" with their most recent successors, *"Toland, Asgill, Coward, Gildon"* (*Prose Works* 2: 72). For all practical purposes, argues Swift, they are the same. In *Mr. Collins's Discourse of Free Thinking put into Plain English...* (1713), Swift's deliberately simple-minded exposition of Collins conflates freethinking, religious enthusiasm, Socinianism, and Epicureanism, to present "a compleat Body of Atheology" (*Prose Works* 4: 42). As such examples suggest, Swift's attacks on speculative atheism drew heavily on the polemical habits of his fellow atheist hunters, and they are habits equally evident in *A Tale of a Tub*.

The *Tale*, of course, is a satire, not a tract; for however deeply he may have been influenced by their arguments, Swift was no great admirer of the form assumed by most works of polemical theology. He remarks that "Men would be more cautious of losing their Time in such an Undertaking, if they did but consider, that to answer a Book effectually, requires more Pains and Skill, more Wit, Learning, and Judgment than were employ'd in the Writing it" (10). Neither is the pulpit the appropriate venue for learned exhortations against new modish systems. Swift would later observe that he had "been better entertained, and more informed by a Chapter in the *Pilgrim's Progress*, than by a long Discourse upon the *Will* and the *Intellect*, and *simple* or *complex Ideas*." But while he may criticize those clerics who "are fond of dilating on *Matter* and *Motion*," who "talk of the *fortuitous Concourse of Atoms*, of *Theories* and *Phoenomena*" (*Prose Works* 9: 77), Swift's advice bespeaks not a lack of interest in such matters, but rather a lively concern with the tactics of defeating the atheist threat. In *A Tale of a Tub* Swift eschews the ponderous artillery of learned disputation in favor of that mocking and ironic manner of proceeding which he locates in such works as Marvell's *Rehearsal Transpros'd* and Charles Boyle's *Dr. Bentley's Dissertations on the Epistles of Phalaris*, works that are still "read ... with pleasure, tho' the Book it answers be sunk long ago" (10). In so doing, Swift hopes to frustrate that onslaught of "answers" that might have greeted a more serious refutation of modern error.

III

John Traugott trenchantly remarks that Swift's religious vision in *A Tale of a Tub* seems born of "a judicious conjunction of punctiliousness and repression" (1988: 5). The *Tale* is nothing if not repressive, and we should not be surprised that Martin seems such a pale specimen of religious orthodoxy when we consider that the work exists not to celebrate the virtues of the blessed, a claim Swift quite disingenuously makes for it, but to enumerate the vices of the damned. Swift's choice of epigraphs to *A Tale of a Tub* suggests the strategy he means to adopt throughout his satire. The odd quotation from Irenaeus, which William Wotton translates as an invocation of "the Power of the Father, which is called Light, and Spirit, and Life, because thou has reigned in the Body" (Swift 1958b: 348), clearly points to the confusion of body and spirit that emerges as a leitmotif in the *Tale*. And as if prefiguring the vainglorious attitude of the Grub Street Hack, which tinctures every episode of the *Tale*, the citation from the first book of *De Rerum Natura* calls attention to the difficulty of the materials the poet must reveal, his pride in his originality, and his intention to "unloose the mind from the close knots of superstition."[17] While it may be the case, as Ronald Paulson has argued, that Swift's epigraphs establish the groundwork for his satire on the "Gnostic View of Man," his juxtaposition of quotations from the *Adversus Haereses* of Irenaeus, an encyclopedic catalog of heresies, and from the *De Rerum Natura* of Lucretius, perhaps the most notoriously heterodox work to be popularized during Swift's lifetime, suggests that, like Irenaeus, Swift promises his own ironic encyclopedia of error (Paulson 1960: 87–144).

Readers have often cited Section IX, the "Digression Concerning the Original, the Use, and Improvement of Madness in a Commonwealth," as the thematic fulcrum of *A Tale of a Tub*. Here, as in the "Ode to the Athenian Society," Swift arraigns *"The Establishment of New Empires by Conquest: The Advance and Progress of New Schemes in Philosophy; and the contriving, as well as the propogating of New Religions"* (162). Here as well Swift links innovations in philosophy with corruptions in religion, listing as the "great Introducers of new schemes in Philosophy. . . . *Epicurus, Diogenes, Apollonius, Lucretius, Paracelsus, DesCartes"* (166), preeminent among the usual suspects in any Augustan lineup of atheistical conspirators. It is worthwhile to consider the logic of this grouping because of its centrality in the *Tale* and because it has never been adequately explained.

As perhaps the most thoroughgoing materialist to be touted by modern philosophers, Epicurus tops Swift's list of the progenitors of new modish systems. Swift's contempt for Epicureanism is not hard to document. In his *Tritical Essay Upon the Faculties of the Mind* Swift pokes fun at the philosophical clichés of the age, including the question, "How can the *Epicureans* Opinion be true, that the Universe was formed by a fortuitous Concourse of Atoms; which I will no more believe, than that the accidental Jumbling of the Letters in the Alphabet, could fall by chance into a most ingenious and learned Treatise of Philosophy" (*Prose Works* 1: 246–7). As Ehrenpreis remarks, the fact that Swift makes fun of such cliché-mongering means neither a rejection "of the logic of the question nor the analogy in which that logic is embodied" (2: 192).[18] Swift's rejection of Epicurean atomism begins early. In his "Ode to the Athenian Society" he mocks the argument that man "Is but a Crowd of Atoms justling in a heap, / Which from Eternal Seeds begun, /Justling some thousand years till ripen'd by the Sun" (ll. 127–9). And even though Swift admired Lucretius's poetry (he claims to have read him through three times in 1696/97), he nevertheless rejected Creech's translation of *De Rerum Natura* as a "compleat System of Atheism," that had "added mightily to the Number of *Free Thinkers*" (*Prose Works*, 4: 37). While Swift may warn the young clergyman about sermons on the "fortuitous concourse of atoms," he is not above turning such a philosophical cliché to his own satirical advantage in the *Tale*. There he describes how "*Epicurus* modestly hoped, that one Time or other, a certain Fortuitous Concourse of all Mens Opinions, after perpetual Justlings, the Sharp with the Smooth, the Light and the Heavy, the Round and the Square, would by certain *Clinamina*, unite in the Notions of *Atoms* and *Void*, as these did in the Originals of all Things" (167).

With all the mock-philosophical gravity of Lucretius himself, the Hack offers a "true, natural Solution" to the problem of why the stage must be elevated so far above the crowd:

> Air being a heavy Body, and therefore (according to the System of *Epicurus*) continually descending, must needs be more so, when loaden and press'd down by Words; which are also Bodies of much Weight and Gravity, as it is manifest from those deep *Impressions* they make and leave upon us. (60)

Swift begins with the Epicurean notion that voice and sound are physical, since they strike upon the senses, and extends the metaphor to the ludicrous conclusion that such corporeal words must therefore be ingested by those in the pit who stand with mouths agape "to devour them" (61). Whenever the Hack is at a loss to explain modern phenomena of any kind, he invariably resorts to comically exaggerated Epicurean explanations, or quotes directly from his favorite text, *De Rerum Natura*. His description of the "physico-logical Scheme of Oratorical Receptacles or Machines," is but a comic specimen of that pattern of Epicurean allusion which prevails throughout the *Tale*.

As the sympathetic biographer of Epicurus and thus the popularizer of his ideas, Diogenes Laertius wins his place in Swift's indictment by innuendo. Such atheist hunters as Cudworth and Stillingfleet had cited copiously from Diogenes Laertius as an authority on Epicurean thought.[19] And while it has been suggested that Diogenes Apollonites, a disciple of Anaximenes, is the Diogenes in question here (Harth 1961: 86–7), the antimaterialist logic of Swift's grouping of "Introducers of New Schemes in Philosophy" makes it more likely that Diogenes Laertius is intended.[20]

The inclusion of Descartes among the great innovators in philosophy follows this pattern. Like Epicurus and Lucretius, Descartes had been stigmatized as a mechanist and a materialist.[21] Just as Epicurus dreamed that all men would be brought to his opinions by chance, Descartes "reckoned to see before he died, the Sentiments of all Philosophers, like so many lesser stars in his *Romantick* System, rapt and drawn within his own *Vortex*" (167). Swift gives literal form to the fears of Descartes' detractors, that his theory of vortices with its dependence upon mechanical second causes would leave no room for a God. According to Cudworth, for example, Descartes "makes God to contribute nothing more to the Fabrick of the World, than the Turning round of a *Vortex* or Whirlpool of Matter; from the fortuitous Motion of which, according to certain General Laws of Nature, must proceed all this Frame of things that now is ... without the Guidance of any Mind or Wisdom" (54).

Swift was but following the lead of those Anglican apologists and philosophers who could accept Cartesian dualism as preserving the distinction between matter and spirit, but who were made uncomfortable by the implicit materialism of other features of the Cartesian system. Swift reiterates the argument in the third voyage of *Gulliver's Travels* when the shade of Aristotle informs Gulliver that all modish systems are but temporary spasms of popular opinion, "that *Gassendi*, who had made the Doctrine of *Epicurus* as palatable as he could, and the *Vortices* of *Descartes*, were equally exploded. He predicted the same Fate of *Attraction*, whereof the present Learned are such zealous Asserters" (*Prose Works* 11: 197). Here as in the *Tale*, Swift links Descartes with the Epicureans and implies that "Systems of Nature" must invariably reduce all to sense.

By including Apollonius of Tyana, Swift makes a much wider associative leap. Samuel Butler speaks of Apollonius as the master of "Rosy Cross philosophers" and as the spiritual father of Trismegistus and Zoroaster, linking him with such hermetic philosophers as Cornelius Agrippa (*Hudibras*,

2.3.641ff). With this pedigree, Apollonius represents a significant precursor to such "dark authors" as Paracelsus and Thomas Vaughan. But for Swift, Apollonius stands for more than the mere enthusiastic foolishness of hermetic philosophy; he is a signal example of an ancient philosopher drafted into service against established religion. In this respect, as in others, Swift echoes such pious polemicists as Cudworth who attacks the first-century prophet, moralist, and magician as a heretic "assisted by the *Powers of the Kingdom of Darkness*," and who worked miracles "merely out of design, to derogate from the *Miracles* of our *Saviour Christ*" (265). The miracles of Apollonius had been cited by various modern Deists as evidence that miracles need not be the work of Divine power, that they could be naturally produced. In 1680 Charles Blount published a fragmentary translation of Philostratus's *Life of Apollonius of Tyana*, complete with footnotes praising Thomas Hobbes and ridiculing priests, Providence, and the credulity of the pious. Although he affected innocence of any mischievous motive, there can be little question that his translation of Philostratus was a deliberately provocative act. Certainly the authorities found it offensive. The book was burned by the public hangman, and Blount was generously abused for "*his profane Raillery and petty Cavils.*"[22] By including Apollonius among the other innovators in philosophy, then, Swift pointedly alludes to the religious controversy of the day and can be understood to satirize the Deists' attempts to discount miracles and deny that God works by any other means than mechanical second causes.

Swift's inclusion of Paracelsus, the most famous alchemist and occultist of the Renaissance, follows this pattern. As his focus on "dark authors" and the comic exploitation of hermetic jargon suggests, Swift was clearly fascinated by modern revivals of ancient hermetic practices and beliefs.[23] In the *Battle of the Books* Swift links Paracelsus with "*Des-cartes, Gassendi*, and *Hobbes*" (235). Indeed, Swift's treatment of Paracelsus suggests that he regarded him as a part of the modern materialistic conspiracy, a connection which provides an important clue to Swift's satire of Occultism throughout the *Tale*.

Henry More exerts a strong influence on Swift's treatment of Occult philosophers as enthusiastic madmen in the *Tale* (see Harth 1961: 60–5). But More also provides ammunition for Swift's attack on Paracelsus and his disciple Thomas Vaughan as atheistical materialists. More asks: "what Sanctuary so safe for the Atheist that derides and eludes all Religion, as such a *miraculous Influence* of the Heavens as *Paracelsus* describes in his *Scientia Astronomica*?"[24] In predictable fashion, More moves from the implicit materialism of Paracelsian astrology to the denial of the immortal soul and even of God himself: "For if the *Stars* can make such living creatures of prepared Matter that have sense and understanding, which yet have no *immortal* Souls, but wholly return into dead Matter again, why is it not so with men as well as them. And if they can contribute the power of such wonder-working wisdom as was in *Moses* and in *Christ* . . . what footsteps do there remain of proof that there is any *God* or *Spirits?*" (35). Even more alarming is the Occultists' search for the first matter of the world, which More regards as "no better than *Atheism*. For it implies that God is nothing else but the *Universal Matter* of the World" (34).[25]

More consistently attacks Occultists as materialists whose apparent descriptions of the nature of spirits are actually discussions of the behavior of matter. This strategy of confusing matter and spirit, of substituting the material for the immaterial lies at the heart of Swift's satire on new modish systems throughout the *Tale*.[26] Certainly Swift made satiric capital of the popular equation of madness and Rosicrucianism, just as he delighted in the hermetic jargon and alchemical claptrap that clogs the narrative of the *Tale*. It is not merely the arcana of Gnosticism nor the baroque silliness of Rosicrucianism that Swift burlesques in the *Tale*, however. For, like More, Swift often overlooks the Neoplatonism of modern Occultism to expose its roots in the "proto-chymistrie of the spirit," a phrase of Vaughan's that reveals the fatal paradox at the heart of modern Occultism.[27] To Swift's devout contemporaries the whole notion of "spiritual chemistry" with its confusion of body and soul, matter and spirit, would have seemed impious and would have suggested obvious links with other materialistic philosophies.

IV

Phillip Harth argues that Swift "indiscriminately mingles the names of Epicurus and Descartes with those of notorious philosophical enthusiasts," in order to denigrate Epicurus and Descartes by association (1961: 88). Certainly guilt by association is part of Swift's satiric strategy, but his choice of names is anything but indiscriminate. Rather, like those Anglican polemicists whose task it was to demonstrate the immediate threat posed by a diverse band of presumed atheists, Swift's assault on modern system builders insinuates links otherwise invisible to the unsuspecting eye. These may all be innovating madmen, Swift implies, but theirs is a methodical madness born of modern materialism. According to Swift's "Apology," the *Tale* takes as its point of departure "*the numerous and gross Corruptions in Religion and Learning*" (4) that marked the age. By insisting, however, that the religious satire of the Allegory is rigorously segregated from the satire on modern learning in the Digressions, that "the satire deals with two separate subjects, in two separate groups of sections, by means of two separate satirical methods," Harth minimizes Swift's penchant to indict by association, and his tendency to define modern abuses in learning in terms of abuses in religion, and vice versa (2–6).

Such segregation, moreover, tends to obscure the close relationship between wit and atheism which Swift first adumbrates in the "Ode to the Athenian Society" and which he develops more fully in *A Tale of a Tub*. Swift himself argues in "The Preface" to the *Tale* that "The Wits of the present Age being so very numerous and penetrating, it seems the Grandees of *Church* and *State* begin to fall under horrible Apprehensions, lest these Gentlemen ... should find leisure to pick Holes in the weak sides of Religion and Government" (39). For Swift's generation, wits were not merely a nuisance or an offense to good taste; they posed a clear and present danger to religion as well. In lines that echo popular fears of an atheist cabal, the Reverend Edward Boys, rector of Mautby in Norfolk, warns that "When God is dispoiled of his Regal Government by his Word, the very next act must be to deny his *Being*, which is now the merry employment of the *Juncto* of wits." Indeed "the *Gyants* of sin do now conceive, that to the disthroning of God, there need be no other Arms but *Scorn* and *Derision*."[28]

Indeed for Swift's contemporaries the Phrase "witty atheist" was a tautology. And in the characterization of the Hack who is at once wit, atheist, Rosicrucian, and religious fanatic, Swift incarnates that conflation of modern error which lies at the heart of his satiric strategy. However one chooses to define the voice (variously identified as Grub Street poet and critic, fellow of the Royal Society, hermetic philosopher, and fanatical Presbyterian) that we hear throughout the *Tale*, there can be little question that its mad perspective may be discerned both in the Allegory of Peter, Martin, and Jack and in the Digressions on learning. Indeed many of the Hack's religious enthusiasms derive directly from his philosophical and political interests. And whatever the particular object of reflection in the *Tale*, the voice we hear is that of a thoroughgoing materialist, "Swift's *reductio ad absurdum* of epicureanism, reducing all to sense in defiance of the Christian belief in things invisible" (Battestin 1974: 237). One has only to consult a work like Berkeley's *Alciphron*, where freethinkers are defined "in the various light of atheist, libertine, enthusiast, scorner, critic, metaphysician, fatalist and sceptic," to see how closely Swift's habits of mind resemble those of more sober-minded atheist hunters (*Works* 2: 15).

One could ask for no finer specimen of such habits than the Hack's effusion from Section V of the *Tale*:

> We ... should never have been able to compass our great Design of an everlasting Remembrance, and never-dying Fame, if our Endeavours had not

been so highly serviceable to the general Good of Mankind. This, *0 Universe*, is
the Adventurous Attempt of me thy Secretary;

—— *Quemvis perferre laborem*
Suadet, & inducit noctes vigilare serenas.
(123)

Here the Hack clearly identifies himself with the shortsighted vanity of the
modern wit and the noisy altruism of the modern projector. He also reveals
himself to be an admirer of Lucretius as well as a natural philosopher and
"Secretary" of the Universe. In this particular epithet, Swift pulls together a
number of satirical allusions to modern materialism. For example, he may
allude to Lord Clarendon's attack on Hobbes as the "Secretary of Nature."[29]
Or he may have in mind Glanvill's praise of Descartes as "the grand
Secretary of Nature," who had presented an "analytical Account of the
Universal Fabrick."[30] Since the "Digression in a Modern Kind" goes on to
burlesque a number of Occultist notions, it is also possible, as Philip Pinkus
suggests, that Swift alludes to the intellectual pretensions of various "dark
authors" (1975, 1: 104) from Paracelsus, who boasted that "the Monarchy
of all the Arts has been at length derived and conferred upon me,
Theophrastus Paracelsus, Prince of Philosophy and Medicine"[31] to Thomas
Vaughan, who had rather grandly claimed powers to elucidate "the Soul of
the World or Universal Spirit of Nature" (77–8). Above all, one hears the
echoes of Lucretius' triumphal praise of the muse who "persuades me to
undergo any labour, and entices me to spend the tranquil nights in
wakefulness, seeking by what words and what poetry at last I may be able
to display clear lights before your mind, whereby you may see into the heart
of things hidden" (15). Swift's strategy of guilt by association enables him
to suggest that not only are the Moderns consumed with a self-regarding
vanity, but also that the source of this narcissism is the atheistical materialism
of Lucretius, with analogues in the doctrines of Descartes, Paracelsus, and
Hobbes. Even the Hack's claim to be the "*freshest Modern*" (130) is cause for
concern. For as Ehrenpreis remarks, in the *Tale*, "'Modernism,' properly
defined, shows links with atheism" (1: 202).

V

Links with atheism can also be detected at the heart of those imaginary
systems – Sartorism, Aeolism, and the System of Vapors – which the Hack
advertises with such enthusiasm and which are central to the satiric mission
of the *Tale*. These systems are playfully developed and comically contrived,

but they also serve as fictional equivalents for those real materialistic systems that Swift both feared and despised.

The obvious targets of Swift's satire on Clothes-Worship are the excesses committed both by Catholic and Protestant enthusiasts down the centuries and the foppish world of modern fashion. Throughout Swift's satire on Clothes-Worship, however, the vehicle of the Hack's extended satiric metaphor implies a complex and consistent burlesque of systems of belief confusing matter with spirit and body with soul. The tailor-god himself "did daily create Men by a kind of Manufactory Operation," whose scraps are "uninformed Mass, or Substance, and sometimes whole Limbs already enlivened" (76), an account that echoes Lucretian descriptions of the formation of man from the earth by a purely accidental process. Because their god is a tailor, the members of this sect believe "the Universe to be a large *Suit of Cloaths*, which *invests* every Thing: That the Earth is *invested* by the Air; the Air is *invested* by the Stars; and the Stars are invested by the *Primum Mobile*" (77–8). Swift may allude to Thomas Vaughan's rather obscure notion that "the passive spirit is a thin aerial substance, the only immediate vestment wherein the Soul wraps herself" (79), or his equally uncertain assertion that the "magicall analyses of bodies" will reveal how life is imprisoned in the "outward and natural vestments."[32] Or he may have in mind debates about the world soul of the kind outlined in *The Oracles of Reason* where Blount describes the "*Anima Mundi*, which after our Deaths remain'd entire and separate, till it met with some other Body capable of Receiving it, and then being cloathed therewith."[33] At issue here is the belaboring of the correspondence between the macro- and micro-cosms so characteristic of Occultist rhetoric. And just as Swift reflects on the implicit materialism of astrology, so he alludes to the implicit atheism revealed by such metaphors. To many pious observers, Robert Boyle for example, the comparison of micro- and macrocosm implicitly blurred the distinction between creator and creation and even implied the kind of pantheistic hylozoism which defenders of the faith so clearly identified in the *Tractatus* of Spinoza (Colie 1963).[34] After all, to identify nature with God was in some sense to redefine Him in materialist terms.

If land is but "a fine Coat faced with green" and the sea a "Waistcoat of Water-Tabby," then by extension one might argue that the furnishings of man's mind are no less material than the haberdashery of the great globe itself: "Is not Religion a *Cloak*, Honesty a *Pair of Shoes*, worn out in the Dirt, Self-love a *Surtout*, Vanity a *Shirt*, and Conscience a *Pair of Breeches*, which, tho' a Cover for Lewdness as well as Nastiness, is easily slipt down for the service of both" (78). Here, as he does so often, Swift finds satirical material in a commonplace. Robert South had elaborated the comparison of clothing and conscience in his sermon "On the Wisdom of the World" (1676). South seemingly anticipates Swift's satirical agenda, linking the "great prevalence of that atheistical doctrine of *Leviathan*" and the rise of sectarianism. "Irreligion is accounted policy," writes South, "when it is grown even to a fashion; and passes for wit with some, as well as for wisdom with others . . . and no man is esteemed any ways considerable for policy, who wears religion otherwise than as a cloak; that is, as such a garment as may both cover and keep him warm, and yet hang loose upon him."[35] An even more telling equation of fashion with Epicurean atheism may be found in Clement Ellis's *The Vanity of Scoffing* (1674). *"Wit* changeth fashions, almost as oft as cloaths," he writes, "and one main *strain* of that *wit* which is now most modish, is with shameless *impudence*, and in *bluntest* terms, to *disclaim* against those things as idle *dreams* and lying *fables*, which all the world hath hitherto received as the most undoubted truths." Indeed "If we will calmly stand like tame fools to *their* verdict, we must all turn *Atheists* and *Epicures*" (9).[36] Swift's conclusion draws our attention to the obvious fact that for most, religion is superficial and expedient at best; but he does so in metaphors which call to mind contemporary debates over whether such spiritual virtues as honesty or conscience could ever be the product of purely mechanical causes (Bentley *Works*, 3: 35ff).

It is possible that Swift adumbrates yet another layer of conspiracy in such episodes, conflating (as he does so often) religious enthusiasts, Rosicrucians, and atheists with modern agents of political mischief. In much the same fashion Edmund Gibson, later to become bishop of London, had attacked John Toland for associating with Rosicrucians in Edinburgh. As Margaret Jacob remarks, "it is significant that of all the possible affiliations Toland might have had, Gibson tries to label him as a Rosicrucian, for by the late seventeenth century, the epithet 'Rosicrucian' had come to signify almost any social gathering of a suspicious and often secret nature" (1976: 217–18). It required only a small imaginative leap for Swift to link the Rosicrucianism of the "dark authors" with the explicit materialism of those religious sectaries and revolutionaries of the Interregnum with whom the Rosicrucians had often been associated. For Commonwealth sectaries, astrology, religious fanaticism, and pantheism had gone hand in hand with "mechanic atheism." Such enthusiasms retained their unpleasant overtones long after the Restoration, when efforts had been made to suppress them. In 1681, for example, Samuel Parker condemns those "plebians and mechanics" for having "philosophized themselves into impiety" and for reading "lectures of atheism in the streets and highways."[37] After all, the Sartorist's description of the universe as a suit of clothes is not all that dissimilar from Gerard Winstanley's assertion that "the Whole creation . . . is the clothing of God" (Jacob 1976: 27). Indeed the Levellers had openly advocated the mortalist heresy, and tracts like *Man's Mortalitie* (1643) by

Richard Overton, had denied the distinction between body and soul and had promulgated a materialist conception of the universe, becoming in the process "a lightening rod for criticism of Epicureanism" (Kargon 1966: 81). As Christopher Hill and Margaret Jacob have shown, this animistic, often materialistic hermeticism, so characteristic of the Commonwealth sectaries, maintained its attractions well into the eighteenth century and may help to account for the prominence of the "dark authors" in the *Tale* (Hill 1972: 231–8; Jacob 1986: 30–3).

In *A Tale of a Tub*, we are never far from anti-epicurean satire, and like those Bedlamite innovators in philosophy and religion arraigned in the "Digression Concerning . . . Madness," the Sartorists are enslaved by the evidence of their senses, "the Sight and the Touch" which "never examine farther than the Colour, the Shape, the Size, and whatever other Qualities dwell, or are drawn by Art upon the Outward of Bodies" (173). Theirs is the happiness of the materialist "that can with *Epicurus* content his Ideas with the *Films* and *Images* that fly off upon his Senses . . . leaving the Sower and the Dregs, for Philosophy and Reason to lap up" (174). As with Swift's satire on the cloak of religion, moreover, this episode reflects the anti-atheist rhetoric of Swift's contemporaries, in this case Bishop Burnet's description of the Epicurean principles of Lord Rochester, who on his deathbed had confessed to having been misled by "all those flights of Wit, that do feed Atheism and Irreligion: which have a false glittering in them, that dazzles some weak sighted Minds, who have not capacity enough to penetrate further than the Surfaces of things."[38] Identity is but a matter of the accidental combination of one's physical accoutrements. Thus, if one were "trimm'd up with a Gold Chain, and a red Gown, and a white Rod, and a great Horse, it is called a *Lord Mayor*; if Certain Ermins and Furs be placed in a certain position, we stile them a *Judge*, and so, an apt conjunction of Lawn and black Sattin, we intitle a *Bishop*" (79). Here it is not the fortuitous concourse of atoms but the "apt conjunction" of lawn and black satin which make up a bishop, just as ermines and furs in a "certain position" produce a judge. All can be explained by the Epicurean collision of fabric and thread. Moreover, the Hack's choice of the pronoun "it" to designate a mayor, a judge, or a bishop reveals the depth of his unexamined materialism.

The Hack also notes those "subaltern Doctrines" that attend the Sartorist "System of Religion," preeminent among them the belief that all faculties of mind, all forms of wit and imagination, are but ornaments of the body: "*Embroidery*, was *Sheer wit; Gold Fringe* was *agreeable Conversation, Gold Lace* was *Repartee*, a huge long *Periwig* was *Humor*, and a *Coat full of Powder* was very good *Raillery*" (80). This materialist literalization of spiritual qualities finally extends to the denial of the soul itself: "*That Fellow*, cries one, *has no Soul; where is his Shoulder-knot?*" (80). The Sartorists argue that if you separate the body from its clothes "you will find the Body to be only a senseless unsavory Carcass. By all which it is manifest, that the outward Dress must needs be the Soul" (80). Throughout his description of the Sartorist system, Swift subtly parodies the confusion of body and soul, spirit and matter so characteristic of various writers popularly accused of Deism or outright atheism. And like Bentley and other Boyle lecturers, Swift ironically defends the contention that matter has no inherent powers of motion or cognition, that it must be informed by divine impulse before it can move, that separated from its informing spirit, the body must indeed become "a senseless unsavory Carcass," void of thought, gross and perishable.

This is the conclusion which Swift first articulates in the "Ode to the Athenian Society":

> For when the animating Mind is fled,
> (Which Nature never can retain,
> Nor e'er call back again)
> The Body, tho' Gigantick, lyes all Cold and Dead.
>
> (288–91)

And this is the belief that motivates Swift's satiric anatomy of Sartorism, a system which, like the materialist philosophies it imitates, plays havoc with traditional distinctions between body and soul:

> Others ... held that Man was an Animal compounded of two *Dresses*, the *Natural* and the *Celestial Suit*, which were the Body and the Soul: That the Soul was the outward, and the Body the inward Clothing; that the latter was *ex traduce*; but the former of daily Creation and Circumfusion. This last they proved by *Scripture*, because *in Them we Live, and Move, and have our Being.* As likewise by Philosophy because they are *All in All, and All in every Part.* (79–80)

Tortuously allusive, this passage suggests that, like Hobbes, the Sartorists believe the soul to be corporeal, inherited from the parents *ex traduce*. The "Natural and the Celestial Suit" clearly satirizes Hobbes's notion of the materiality of the soul and may echo John Eachard's 1672 parody of Hobbes, that "some people ... have two *Men* to take care of; an *outward Man*, and an *Inward Man*. I am unable to maintain but one."[39] Swift may even have in mind Paracelsus's argument that "man is made up of two portions, that is to say of a material and spiritual body ... two bodies, an eternal and a corporeal, enclosed in one" (2: 6). Certainly the Sartorist contention that the clothes are the soul (with the implication that the soul has a specific physical location) parodies arguments of those devout apologists who had argued that the soul informs every part of the body equally, that it is "all in every part."[40]

The Sartorists buttress their argument by a willful, if witty, misinterpretation of Acts 17: 28: "in him we live, and move, and have our being," a verse which they blasphemously apply not to God but to their own clothes, in which they quite literally live and move. Swift obviously alludes to Paul's refutation of the Epicureans of Athens, but he also establishes the contemporary context of religious controversy out of which his satire arises. Opponents of Deism and modern atheism, Richard Bentley most notably, had cited Acts 17: 28 as evidence that the spirit of God is diffused through all matter and is the source of all life (Bentley *Works* 3: 27ff). Just as the Hack discusses modern writing in terms of "the infinity of matter," a catch phrase of the antimaterialist debate, here he echoes one of the most telling points of controversy between the defenders of Christianity and their Epicurean and Deistic detractors. So sensitive was Swift to the arguments and clichés of contemporary antimaterialist polemic that they naturally found their way into his satire. Indeed, Swift's parodies of those Deists and atheists he sought to discredit are often so close that his original readers can be forgiven their confusion regarding Swift's motives. It is little wonder that sober readers like William Wotton should find in the casual use of such controversial materials grounds for the charge that the anonymous author of *A Tale of a Tub* was bantering religion, in the manner of Toland, Tindal, and Blount.[41] Wotton's charges may have had their effect. Swift's "Apology" to the fifth edition of the *Tale* argues that far from ridiculing religion like the Deists and atheists of the age, he sought rather to employ wit in the defense of orthodox Christianity.

Although it has been suggested that Sartorism and Aeolism satirize different kinds of reductivism (Harth 1961: 75–7), Swift's sendup of the Aeolists links Enthusiasm, Occultism, Epicureanism, and Hobbism in the same elaborate and often recondite materialist conspiracy as his satire on Sartorism:

> The Learned *Aeolists*, maintain the Original Cause of all Things to be *Wind*, from which Principle this whole Universe was at first produced, and into which it must at last be resolved; that the same Breath which had kindled, and blew *up* the Flame of Nature should one day blow it *out*.
> *Quod procul a nobis flectat Fortuna gubernans.*
> THIS is what the Adepti understand by their *Anima Mundi*: that is to say, the *Spirit*, or *Breath*, or *Wind* of the *World*. (150–1)

As with his treatment of the Sartorists, Swift's definition of the Aeolist system turns on a line from Lucretius, "*Quod procul a nobis flectat Fortuna gubernans*," a tag taken from a larger passage in book 5 of *De Rerum Natura* where Lucretius argues that just as the world was formed by chance, in the same random fashion chance will destroy it. The Adepti are said to believe that the world was formed by accident from wind and that it will be blown out just as accidentally. While Swift may have found his model for Aeolist belief in the philosophy of Anaximenes as Harth contends, his elaboration of this imaginary system with its emphasis on random causation owes more to his contempt for modern Epicureanism (Harth 1961: 66).

If the tone is set by Lucretius, however, the basic joke is derived from Hobbes, who wreaks havoc on traditional defenses of immaterial substance and spirit with his various puns on wind, *anima*, and spirit. In *Leviathan* Hobbes remarks that "in the common language of men, *air*, and *aerial substances*, use not to be taken for *bodies*, but (as often as men are sensible of their effects) are called *wind*, or *breath*, or (because the same are called in Latin *spiritus*) *spirits*; as when they call the aerial substance, which in the body of any living creature gives it life and motion, *vital* and *animal spirits*" (Hobbes 1971: 287). There can be little question that this is the agenda reiterated by the Hack: "whether you please to call the *Forma informans* of Man, by the Name of *Spiritus, Animus, Afflatus*, or *Anima*; What are all these but several Appellations for *Wind*?" (151). Swift then compounds the implicit materialism of the system with a touch of Occultist jargon: "Since *Wind* had the Master-Share, as well as Operation in every Compound, by Consequence, those Beings must be of chief Excellence, wherein that *Primordium* appears most prominently to abound" (151). With the etymological arbitrariness of a Thomas Hobbes, the confusion of a confirmed Occultist, and the enthusiasm of a religious fanatic, the Hack yokes together a series of apparently irreconcilable assumptions. But the Hack claims nothing that Swift's contemporaries had not already asserted. By conflating what the "*Adepti* understand by their *Anima Mundi*" (150), the primordium or "prima materia," and the "*Forma Informans* of Man" with ordinary wind, the Hack exemplifies that mindless materialism condemned by Cudworth in his description of those "*Adepti* in *Atheism*" who believe in a *Conscious Intellectual Nature*," thus confusing spirit and matter (Cudworth, 136). And by equating the wind that provides the "inspiration" for Puritan preaching with the *Anima* of the Rosicrucians, Swift adopts the argument of such pious polemicists as Samuel Parker that "there is so much Affinity between Rosi-Crucianisme and Enthusiasme, that whoever entertains the one, he may upon the same Reason, embrace the other."[42] Affinities, of course, are precisely what Swift hopes to demonstrate, covert resemblances between Rosicrucians, Presbyterians, Epicureans, and Hobbists whose association might otherwise seem quite arbitrary.

Central to Swift's satiric program in the *Tale* is a technique aptly described by Maurice J. Quinlan (1967) as the "literalization of metaphor," that is "contrasting the metaphorical and the literal significance of a term, in order to reveal an ironic disparity between the two meanings." Such literalization is common in all of Swift's satires, but in the *Tale*, he gives a peculiarly materialistic emphasis to this technique, consistently substituting the most ludicrously literal equivalents for all spiritual metaphors – much in the manner of Hobbes and those Deists who had borrowed his rhetorical strategy. As Ehrenpreis observes, in the *Tale*, "the intangible is treated as tangible. This is Hobbes's sceptical method of reducing ideals to delusions; and Swift, whose flavour is remarkably close to Hobbes's, may have learned it from him" (1: 198). There can be little question that Swift found in Hobbes's ruthless literalization of metaphor in *Leviathan* an ideal rhetoric to turn back upon the pretensions of modern materialism, a rhetoric perfectly crafted to represent the "thingness" of a world seen through the eyes of one conversant only with the imagery of weight, measure, matter, and motion, one who reveals his solid poverty of mind whenever he is called upon to discuss the things of the spirit.

The antics of ranting preachers are, of course, the immediate object of Swift's contempt, but his metaphors lead us back to Hobbes who writes: "On the signification of the word *spirit*, dependeth that of the word *INSPIRATION*; which must either be taken properly; and then it is nothing but the blowing into a man some thin and subtle air or wind, in such manner as a man filleth a bladder with his breath." Therefore "We are not to understand it [inspiration] in the proper sense, as if his *Spirit* were like water, subject to effusion or infusion. . . . For the proper use of the word *infused*, in speaking of the graces of God, is an abuse of it; for those graces are virtues, not bodies to be carried hither and thither, and to be poured into men as into barrels" (1971: 295). Like Swift's, Hobbes's irony is double edged. He argues that if we use such terms as "infusion" or "inspiration" correctly, then we cannot apply them to God; yet Hobbes's insistence that spirit is but wind, a material substance, requires that if we are to speak of the actions of God's own spirit at all, we can do so only in mechanical terms.

Swift recognizes the rich comic potential in such an argument and the kind of satiric capital which can be made by describing the most "spiritual" pretenses in the metaphors of modern mechanism. Swift locates this mechanical operation of the spirit in the Presbyterian practice of delivering "their choicest *Inspiration*, fetching it with their own Hands, from the Fountain Head, in certain *Bladders*, and disploding it among the Sectaries in all Nations, who did, and do, and ever will, daily Gasp and Pant after it" (155). Swift may also have had in mind a passage from Cudworth who remarks that "[Atheists are] no better, than a kind of *Bewitched Enthusiasts* and *Blind Spiritati*, that are wholly ridden and acted by a dark, narrow and captivated Principle of Life, and, to use their own Language, *In-blown* by it.... Nay they are *Fanaticks* too, however that word seem to have a more peculiar respect to something of a Deity: All Atheists being that *Blind Goddess, Nature's, Fanaticks*" (1: 134).

Indeed there is a proverbial quality about the equation of atheism and religious fanaticism in the late seventeenth century, particularly in the High-church polemics so congenial to Swift. Charles Leslie, for example lambasts "*Atheism* and *Enthusiasm* (both which, like a Deluge, are now let loose amongst us)" and confidently asserts that "these two, tho' seemingly opposite, do naturally run into and assist one another. For *Enthusiasm*, or a False Pretence to *Revelation*, does naturally beget *Atheism*."[43] And like Leslie, Swift frequently asserts that atheists and enthusiasts pose a political threat as well. In *The Examiner* Swift attacks the Whigs for having "the whole Herd of Presbyterians, Independents, Atheists, Anabaptists, Deists, Quakers, and Socinians, openly and universally Listed under their Banners" (*Prose Works* 3: 92). Such is the logic of *A Tale of a Tub*, where the Hack is not only a Rosicrucian, a wit, a religious fanatic, and an Epicurean atheist, but is also a rabid Whig who has worn out his quill in "the Service of the State, in *Pro's* and *Con's* upon *Popish Plots*, and *Meal-Tubs*, and *Exclusion Bills*, and *Passive Obedience*..." (70). If atheists are enthusiasts, Swift implies, then enthusiasts (either political or religious) may also be seen as atheists.

This pattern of conspiratorial conflation is repeated one last time in "The Digression Concerning ... Madness" where the Hack's description of the "Redundancy of Vapor" (174) explains both the lunacy of modern religious enthusiasm and the madness of Descartes, Lucretius, and Paracelsus. After a comic description of the mad antics of Henry IV, which can only be explained with reference to Lucretius's theory of atomistic sexuality, Swift deftly satirizes the systems of Descartes and Paracelsus by suggesting that these "introducers of new schemes in philosophy" could have arrived at their individual systems only by mechanical means. "Now, I would gladly be informed," drones the Hack at his most pedantic, "how it is possible to account for such Imaginations, as these in particular Men, without Recourse to my *Phoenomenon of Vapours*, ascending from the lower Faculties to over-shadow the Brain, and thence distilling into Conceptions, for which the Narrowness of our Mother-Tongue has not yet assigned any other Name, besides that of *Madness* or *Phrenzy*" (167). Yet, because "there is something Individual in human Minds, that easily kindles at the accidental Approach and Collision of certain Circumstances, which tho' of paltry and mean Appearance, do often flame out into the greatest Emergencies of Life" (162), there results a kind of Epicurean randomness even in this theory that prevents our predicting the precise effect these vapors will have.

What is significant about the equation of madness and vapors is the way in which the Hack adopts the dogged logic of the committed materialist as he seeks to explain everything in terms of matter and mechanism. Such explanations break down, of course. For example, the question of how the motions of vapor can produce the enormous variety of madness present in the world baffles the Hack completely. For if these changes are entirely caused "either in what *Angles* it strikes and spreads over the Understanding, or upon what Species of Brain it ascends," then it is necessary to explain "how this numerical Difference in the Brain, can produce Effects of so vast a Difference from the same *Vapour*, as to be the sole Point of Individuation between *Alexander the Great, Jack of Leyden*, and Monsieur *Des Cartes*" (169–70). The hiatus in the manuscript which follows this query argues by its vacancy that an answer is impossible given the materialistic premises from which the question springs.

Unintentionally, the Hack introduces the argument which for half a century had been directed against Hobbists and Epicureans: that no mere motion of matter, no chance collision of atoms, could possibly account for the order and variety of the world or for the enormous range of differences that distinguish each individual human from every other. In his first Boyle lecture, Richard Bentley had warned of a world where "atoms can invent arts and sciences, can institute society and government, can make leagues and confederacies, can devise methods of peace and stratagems of war" (*Works*, 3: 49–50). Yet that is precisely the world Swift presents in the "Digression Concerning … Madness." The Hack also admits unwittingly that without that brand of madness caused by vapors "the World would not only be deprived of those two great Blessings, *Conquests* and *Systems*, but even all Mankind would unhappily be reduced to the same Belief in Things Invisible" (169).

It is perhaps difficult for modern readers to appreciate the panic that philosophical materialism engendered either in Swift's contemporaries or in Swift himself. Yet, if we are to understand *A Tale of a Tub* in its contemporary context, we must appreciate both the crisis of faith to which it responded and the peculiar rhetoric which that crisis inspired. The "Belief in Things Invisible" was fundamental to Swift's vocation as a priest of the Church of England. It is central to his satiric design in *A Tale of a Tub* as well. By implicating Cartesians, Epicureans, Hobbists, Rosicrucians, and religious enthusiasts in the same materialist conspiracy, Swift continues that attack on "new *Modish System*[s] of reducing all to sense" first outlined in his "Ode to the Athenian Society"; he reveals his affinities with other atheist hunters of his day; and in his own peculiar fashion he calls the mystifications of satire to the defense of Christian Mystery.

NOTES

1 *Jachin and Boaz: Or the Stedfast and Unwavering Christian* (London, 1676), 10.
2 For the most complete accounts of the fear of atheistical materialism (*c*.1670–1715), see Jacob 1976; Yolton 1983; Westfall 1958; and Redwood 1976.
3 Although their emphases differ from mine, Louis A. Landa (1954) and Kathleen Williams (1958) provide excellent treatments of Swift's religion.
4 *Letter to a Convocation-Man* (London, 1697), 6.
5 *Twelve Sermons Preached on Several Occasions* (London, 1725).
6 "Preface," *The Two First Books of Philostratus Concerning the Life of Apollonius of Tyana* (London, 1680).
7 *Christianity Not Mysterious* (London, 1696), iv–v. In *A History of Atheism in Britain* David Berman provides a detailed examination of the kinds of encoding and disguise that characterized the "esoteric" language of Deist writings.
8 *A Letter in Answer to a Book Entituled Christianity Not Mysterious* (London, 1697), 145. In his notorious tract *The Second Spira* (London, 1693), Richard Sault describes a "CLUB which within these last seven Years met together constantly, to lay down such Rules and Methods as that they might be critically wicked in every thing they could, without the Law taking hold of them" (6). On the popular charge that atheists and freethinkers met in conspiratorial cabals, see Berman 1988: 70–92.
9 Adams remarks that Swift's is a "notably agglomerative imagination" (1972: 94). For a contemporary example of this tendency to search for hidden significance and true meanings, see William Wotton's *Letter to Eusebia* (London, 1704), an answer to Toland's *Letters to Serena* (London, 1704).
10 Gildon, "To the Author of *A Tale of a Tub*," *The Golden Spy* (London, 1709).
11 *The Nature of True Christian Righteousness* (London, 1689), Sig. A3^v.
12 For a survey of the Socinian controversy, see Reedy 1985: 119–41.
13 Boyle, quoted in Jacob 1976: 144. For contemporary accounts of the cause célèbre instigated by Bury's tract, see James Harrington, *An Account of the Proceedings* ... (Oxford, 1690), Jean Le Clerc, *An Historical Vindication* ... (London, 1690), and James Parkinson, *The Fire's Continued at Oxford* ... (London, 1690).
14 See Charles Leslie, *The Charge of Socinianism Against Dr. Tillotson Considered* (London, 1695).
15 *The Unreasonableness of Atheism made Manifest*, 2nd edn (London, 1669), 197–9.
16 The publication of Thomas Creech's popular translation of *De Rerum Natura* (Oxford, 1682), merely reinforced the suspicion that Hobbes's materialism represented a modern revival of Epicurean atomism. For the best discussion of Hobbes's contemporary critics, see Samuel I. Mintz 1962; for a full account of the publishing history of Lucretius's *De Rerum Natura* in England, see Wolfgang Bernard Fleischmann 1964, esp. ch. 2. See also Mayo 1934 and Scruggs

1973–4. None of these works takes adequate account of Swift's hostility to Epicurean materialism.

17 *De Rerum Natura*, trans. W. H. D. Rouse, ed. Martin Ferguson Smith (Cambridge, Mass.: Harvard University; London: Heinemann Ltd., 1975), 76–9.

18 Confusion has always surrounded the distinction between Swift's endorsement of the moral Epicureanism of Sir William Temple and his rejection of Epicurean physics. See A. C. Elias 1982: 158 and passim.

19 Ralph Cudworth, *The True Intellectual System of the Universe* (1678; Stuttgart–Bad Connstatt: Verlag, 1964), 265–70; Stillingfleet, *Origines Sacrae*, 2 vols (1662; Oxford: Oxford University Press, 1836), 2: 462–515.

20 Diogenes Laertius continued to be seen as a disseminator of Epicurean ideas, a process encouraged by the fragmentary English translation of his *Lives of Ancient Philosophers* (London, 1702). See Fleischmann 1964: 69.

21 On responses to Descartes's presumed materialism, see Marjorie Hope Nicolson 1929: 348–66 and Sterling P. Lamprecht 1935: 181–240; see also John Edwards, *A Free Discourse Concerning Truth and Error . . .* (London, 1701).

22 M. Le Nain de Tillement, *An Account of the Life of Apollonius Tyaneus* (London, 1702), xvi.

23 Swift owned the complete works of Paracelsus; he might even have known such works as *The Atheist Unmasked* (London, 1685), in which Paracelsus is put down as a drunken atheist.

24 *Enthusiasmus Triumphatus* (1662; Los Angeles: William Andrews Clark Memorial Library, 1966), 34. Even Daniel Defoe seems to share this opinion. In *A System of Magick* (1728; Wakefield, Yorkshire: EP Publications, 1973) he remarks that astrologers, Rosicrucians, alchemists, and magicians are all enemies of true religion and the "Effluvia of Hell" (354).

25 Thomas Vaughan was so taken with the notion of extracting the first matter that he claimed he could actually "see it, handle it, and taste it" *(Works*, 398).

26 Miriam Starkman argues that Swift's satire on Occultism depends upon the "methodical muddle of spirit and matter, even as the occultists subverted the conventional dichotomy between spirit and matter" (1950: 49). See also Philip Pinkus 1960 and N. J. C. Andreasen 1963–4.

27 Quoted in Andreasen 1963–4: 411. For the fullest discussion of Swift's satire on Gnosticism, see Paulson 1960: 87–144.

28 "Epistle Dedicatory," *Sixteen Sermons* (London, 1672). Sermons of the period abound with complaints about witty atheists. For a specimen of such complaints, see Clement Ellis, *The Vanity of Scoffing* (London, 1674), and Francis Atterbury, *The Axe Laid to the Root of Christianity: or, A Specimen of the Prophaneness and Blasphemy that Abounds in some Late Writings* (London, 1706). Even the wits themselves admitted the charge. John Dunton (1969) remarks that even "Booksellers in the gross are taken for no better than a pack of Knaves and Atheists," 2: 751).

29 Edward Hyde, Earl of Clarendon, *A Brief View and Survey of the Dangerous and Pernicious Errors to Church and State, in Mr. Hobbes's Book, Entitled Leviathan* (Oxford, 1676), 39.

30 Glanvill, *The Vanity of Dogmatizing*, quoted in Starkman, pp. 67–8. Swift knew this work well and dismissed the revised version, *Scepsis Scientifica*, as a "fustian piece of abominable curious Virtuoso Stuff" (*Correspondence* 5: 30.)

31 *The Hermetic and Alchemical Writings of ... Paracelsus*, 2 vols. Trans. L. W. De Laurence, ed. A. E. Waite (Chicago: De Laurence, Scott & Co., 1910), 1: 19–20.

32 *The Magical Writings of Thomas Vaughan*, ed. and trans. A. F. Waite (London, 1888), 13.

33 *The Oracles of Reason* (1693) in *The Miscellaneous Works of Charles Blount, Esq.* (London, 1695), 119.

34 See also Andreasen 1963–4: 412.

35 "The Wisdom of This World," *Sermons Peached Upon Several Occasions*, 5 vols. (New York: Hurd & Houghton, 1866–71), 1: 183.

36 L'Estrange's *Observator*, July 12, 1681, also makes fun of the Sectarians' "Suit of Consciences."

37 *A Demonstration of the Divine Authority ...* (Oxford, 1681), iii–iv.

38 *Some Passages of the Life and Death of ... John Earl of Rochester* (London, 1680), 127.

39 *Mr. Hobbs's State of Nature Considered*, ed. Peter Ure (Liverpool: Liverpool University Press, 1958), 9.

40 Ralph Cudworth remarks that "When it is said that the *Whole Deity*, is in every Part of the World, and the *Whole Soul* in every Part of the Body, it is not to be taken in a Positive Sense, for a Whole consisting of Parts, one without the other, but in a Negative only, for ... *An Whole Undivided*; so that the meaning thereof is no more than this, that the *Deity* is not *Dividedly*, in the World, nor the Soul *Dividedly* in the *Body*" (782).

41 In his *Observations Upon The Tale of a Tub*, rpt. in the Guthkelch/Nicol-Smith edn, Wotton notes similarities to "Mr. Hobbes's banter upon in-blowing" (314), compares his treatment of Mystery with that of Toland (319), and complains frequently of the *Tale*'s "banter" on religion.

42 *A Free and Impartial Censure of the Platonick Philosophie* (Oxford, 1667), 72–3.

43 *The Snake in the Grass: or, Satan Transform'd into an Angel of Light*, 3rd edn (London, 1698), i–ii.

9

The Rape of the Lock as Miniature Epic

HELEN DEUTSCH

Heroic Commodities

To describe *The Rape of the Lock* as a miniature epic is to evoke a paradoxical vision of a perfect universe. For this tiny poem (tiny, at least, when viewed on the scale of the epics it mimics) offers a closure so complete that it seems to encompass empires. Both replete and hollow in its conflation of inner and outer, visual and verbal, spatial and temporal realms, this miniature epic embodies that genre of "multum in parvo" which Susan Stewart defines as "the miniaturization of language itself . . . a discourse which speaks to the human and cultural but not to the natural except to frame it . . . monumental, transcending any limited context of origin and at the same time neatly containing a universe" (1984: 53–4).

In *The Rape of the Lock*, Alexander Pope contains the heroic past by commodifying it. When the faithful translator of Homer pauses from his labors on the *Iliad* in order to transform Achilles' shield into Belinda's petticoat, heroic honor into drawing room chastity, what results challenges Laura Brown's characterization of this mock-epic's structure: "heroes don't own commodities" (1985: 20).[1] Brown's failure to recognize Pope's awareness (*both* in the *Rape* and in his translation of the *Iliad*) of the ways in which transcendent classical heroism bases itself on the merely material, curiously reveals less irony and more idealism about the integrity of the classics than do Pope's imitations. Much as feminist critics are right to read Belinda as a commodity, their emphasis on Pope's monolithic construction of "woman" fails to acknowledge the pervasive femininity which the poem's irony posits at the origins of epic itself. Ellen Pollak, for example, persuasively argues that the *Rape*'s incessant synecdoches conceal beneath a critique of the beau monde's sterile materialism an endorsement of a normative objectification of woman (1985: 77–107). I want to shift the focus to how Pope sees himself is compromised and objectified by a market economy, and how he uses gender to figure his own ambivalent relation to a literary market. The *Rape* itself provides the terms, terms in permanent, dazzling, and unsettling ironic play, for reading what might appear to be a binary opposition between aesthetic appreciation and satiric indignation, between heroes and commodities, as double-edged indivisibility. [2]

Such indivisibility was part of the process of composition: Pope's serious Homeric labors ran concurrently with the writing of the *Rape*, so that it becomes impossible to tell at times which poem served as the original for the other, rendering unattainable the possibility of originality. The play of mirrors between serious imitation and self-conscious parody leaves neither poem's claim to immaterial integrity intact.

The *Rape* similarly draws both on a serious epic tradition and a tradition of epic parody which by Pope's time took Homer to task for his characters' crudity and licentiousness. In both his *Iliad* and the *Rape*, Pope refines Homer both poetically and morally. As Howard Weinbrot puts it, "the more characters in *The Rape of the Lock* embrace epic values and conventions, the less pleasant they are" (1988: 30).[3] In his genealogy of epic diction in his *Life of Pope*, Samuel Johnson makes such refinement a matter of consumer demand. All successors to Homer, he argues, had to please the jaded palates of sophisticated audiences; even by Virgil's time, "the state of the world [was] so much altered, and the demands for elegance so much increased, that mere nature would be endured no longer" (*Lives* 3: 239).

Whether Homer is improved in his *Iliad*, or diminished and polished in the *Rape*, Pope achieves such refinement by a process of objectification. By a seemingly infinite repetition of a series of finite gestures whereby the ideally proper and the immediately visual are inextricably linked, Pope gives his own epic language a substantive quality not unlike that of Homeric formulae while maintaining an allusive debt to the English heroic tradition most prominently figured by Milton and Dryden. He constructs a language at once overburdened by the past and claiming access to an immediately visible world.

Pope's version of that most exemplary of heroes, Sarpedon, thus sounds pronouncedly materialistic in his famous exhortation to battle in *Iliad* XII, the set piece which began Pope's Homeric career in print:

> Why boast we, *Glaucus*, our extended Reign,
> Where *Xanthus'* streams enrich the *Lycian* Plain?
> Our num'rous Herds that range each fruitful Field,
> And Hills where Vines their Purple Harvest yield?

> Our foaming Bowls with gen'rous Nectar crown'd,
> Our Feasts enhanc'd with Musick's sprightly Sound?
> Why on those Shores are we with Joy survey'd,
> Admir'd as Heroes, and as Gods obey'd?
> Unless great Acts superior Merit prove,
> And Vindicate the bounteous Pow'rs above:
> 'Tis ours, the Dignity They give, to grace;
> The first in Valour, as the first in Place;
> That while with wondring Eyes our Martial Bands
> Behold our Deeds transcending our Commands,
> Such, they may cry, deserve the Sov'reign State,
> Whom those that Envy dare not Imitate!
> Cou'd all our Care elude the greedy Grave,
> Which claims no less the Fearful than the Brave,
> For Lust of Fame I shou'd not vainly dare
> In fighting Fields, nor urge thy Soul to War.
> But since, alas, ignoble Age must come,
> Disease, and Death's inexorable Doom;
> The Life which others pay, let Us bestow
> And give to Fame what we to Nature owe;
> Brave, tho we fall; and honour'd, if we live;
> Or let us Glory gain, or Glory give!
> (*Episode of Sarpedon* [1709]; *Works* 1: 450, ll. 27–52)

This oration exemplifies Pope's high heroic mode, and it does so, aptly enough, in miniature. Sarpedon's rhetoric, in keeping with the couplet's repetitive frame, amplifies, encloses and mirrors the original's detail. Similarly, the repetitive periphrases of heroic speech (i.e., "feathered deaths" for arrows, "fleecy care" for sheep, exemplified here by the personifications of lines 31–2) compel the reader to condense the abstract and concrete portions of each phrase into a newly imagined material whole.[4]

Sarpedon makes his plea for heroic action in a curiously static set piece. Both Pope and Homer preface the speech with a simile likening the hero to a hungry lion resolved on attack at all costs, but Pope adds a few additional lines which typically frame the speaker's words with his contemplation of a tableau:

> Resolv'd alike, Divine *Sarpedon* glows
> With gen'rous Rage, that drives him on the Foes.
> He views the Tow'rs, and meditates their Fall;
> To sure Destruction dooms the *Grecian* Wall;
> Then casting on his Friend an ardent Look,
> Fir'd with the Thirst of Glory, thus he spoke.
> (21–6)

The reader views Sarpedon's meditation on the fall of the Greek camp
through the lens of the ensuing fall of Troy's towers; modern fondness for
melancholy ruin imposes itself upon the Homeric character's dream-vision
of triumph. The speech that follows thus forecloses on narrative, offering a
heroic code enhanced by its loss. Pope elaborates on Sarpedon's first
question by rendering it as a landscape of privilege, each couplet elaborating
a visible feature of pride of place.[5] Homer's "all men look on us as if we
were immortals," escalates into the spectacle of warriors "with joy survey'd,
/ Admir'd as Heroes, and as Gods obey'd." For such a vision of superiority
to be merited, Pope's Sarpedon argues, the audience must have ocular
proof; the invisible "powers above" must become visible through "great
acts," which "grace" (or visibly adorn) social "Dignity" (or worth), itself
signified by material goods and position – "first in Place."

A hero's obligation (and here the lines are utterly Pope's invention)
becomes by such ocular proof an original image, a marvel at the top of the
hierarchy "whom those that envy dare not imitate." Pope thus rewrites the
Homeric economy of heroic glory – "let us go on and win glory for
ourselves, or yield it to others" – as a material economy of fame in which
aristocratic largesse allies itself with art in its ability to control narrative by
choosing death: "The life which others pay, let Us bestow, / And give to
Fame, what we to Nature owe."

Playing with this heroic example, Pope's mock-epic art bargains unabash-
edly with Fame by selling Nature short. While Pope's heroic couplet elevates
the concrete by linking it to the abstract, by taking the *Iliad* translation's
materialism literally, the *Rape*'s heroicomical mode persistently cuts the
abstract down to feminine scale. Sarpedon's spectacular economy metamorphoses into Clarissa's prudent reflections on the display of feminine value
in a speech which begins the *Rape*'s fifth canto, explicitly intended "to open
more clearly the MORAL of the Poem" (*Works* 2: 199, l. 7n). As Clarissa's
advice demonstrates, in the *Rape*, from the first in "Place" to the first in
"Face" is a much easier leap than it at first might have seemed.

> Say, why are Beauties prais'd and honour'd most,
> The wise Man's Passion, and the vain Man's Toast?
> Why deck'd with all that Land and Sea afford,
> Why Angels call'd, and Angel-like ador'd?
> Why round our Coaches crowd the white-glov'd Beaus,
> Why bows the Side-box from its inmost Rows?
> How vain are all these Glories, all our Pains,
> Unless good Sense preserve what Beauty gains:
> That Men may say, when we the Front-box grace,
> Behold the first in Virtue, as in Face! . . .
> But since, alas! frail Beauty must decay,

Curl'd or uncurl'd, since Locks will turn to grey,
Since painted, or not painted, all shall fade,
And she who scorns a Man, must die a Maid;
What then remains, but well our Pow'r to use,
And keep good Humour still whate'er we lose? . . .
Beauties in vain their pretty Eyes may roll;
Charms strike the Sight, but Merit wins the Soul.

(V, 9–34)

The transformation from male honor to female ornament is here complete. While Homer's Sarpedon's consciousness of death determines his choice of glory in battle, and while Pope's Sarpedon's practicality redefines heroic glory as a matter of the material display of inimitable power, knowledge of mortality in the *Rape* would seem at first glance to resign the heroine all the more completely to her status as the visible object of male desire. With Clarissa as his mouthpiece, Pope makes this speech from a precariously ironic position which both mimics and belittles the poem's resolutely feminine perspective. The ultimate distinctions in women are made between curled or uncurled, painted or not painted. The purpose of woman's prime virtue of good sense is to preserve "what Beauty gains"; while the difference between charms and merit is similarly constructed as a quantitative rather than qualitative matter of the latter's greater effectiveness in ensnaring the enemy in love's battle.[6]

But death gives Belinda choices within the object world in which she lives. The epic hero chooses between a short and glorious and a long and undistinguished life, and thereby gains the distinction of action. The bourgeois heroine chooses between the display and the use of her beauty, between the coquette's deadly charms and the wife's virtuous productivity, and thereby gains the invisible virtue of submission. Just as Pope improves upon Homer's pagan morals, so he recommends that the virtuous heroine improve upon her own estate, forfeit charms for merit, epic beauty for domestic harmony.[7] But neither Belinda nor the *Rape* can rest content with such sensible advice; Pope's heroine, like Sarpedon, wants visible glory.

Unique Curiosities

Curiosity is the place where timeless art and scientific origins, imitation and truth, ancient rules and modern progress, meet. Pope's own attempts at appropriating the classics make him both complicit with and opposed to the empirical and democratic attitude toward culture that curiosity signifies, an attitude that equates cultural value with market value, quality with quantity, an "aesthetic of selection . . . [with] that of abundance" (Benedict 1990: 75). In her study of "The 'Curious Attitude' in Eighteenth-Century Britain," Barbara Benedict defines curiosity as "culture that can be bought" (1990: 77). The ambiguities in the field of meaning which curiosity delineates in the eighteenth century signal ambivalence about such a commodification of culture. If "curiosity manifests power by means of owning and of obser- vation," its display of objects also makes such power newly and indiscrimi- nately accessible, and the ownership and exercise of such power ambiguous. Curiosity poses questions of agency and ownership which confront Pope in his epic composition: "Who shall possess curiosity and who be possessed by means of it? Who shall be 'curious' and who a 'curiosity?'" (Benedict 1990: 59).

If Homer is a kind of sublime museum of ancient vision for Pope, then *The Rape of the Lock* is his curiosity cabinet (also known as a "lady's cabinet"), his "museum of the present." Clarence Tracy's *The RAPE observ'd* (1974), which annotates the poem with period images and elaborate descriptions of the objects it represents, makes explicit for twentieth-century antiquarians what the poem had put on display for its contemporary public.[8] Like the private collections of curiosities which abounded in the eighteenth century, *The Rape of the Lock* offers the spectator a continuous game of visual connections between great and small, domestic and exotic; the pleasure of such a game consists in finding similarities within differences, China's earth in a cup of tea.[9] A miniature of the totality of foreign cultures it claims to stand for, the poem operates, like the cabinet, by collapsing the differences created by time and alterity into contiguity; objects are both brought closer, and set apart in a closed world.

From another perspective, the curiosity cabinet's display of material bases for scientific knowledge parallels the *Rape*'s disclosure of the origins of epic in objects. The *Rape* collects epic history in the form of the ornaments of empire and puts them on display. Pope gains a novel kind of cultural authority, an authority which his faithful adherence to neoclassical order would seem to belie, by creating such an ideal space within his texts, a luxury space which both exhibits his power to reorder and redefine cultural tradition, and grants a new and tenuous sort of power to the reader, particularly the female reader, who views, and by viewing defines, and by defining may devalue, such a display.

The *Rape*, in all its self-advertising triviality, in conjunction with its serious mirror-image, Pope's *Iliad*, particularly exemplifies the contentions of value to which curiosity gives rise and which lie at the heart of the commodity's mystery. Pope's appropriations of classical texts for English poetry mark him as both an example and active force in a nationalistic cultural "habit of curiosity," which "by the mid-century … had become a public activity, the show of collective cultural dominance" (Benedict 1990: 82).

Such a show, the spoils of foreign and invisible conquests, is figured in the shape of, and displayed upon, the bodies of women. When Addison attends the Royal Exchange, he sees a theater of art which is a miniature of the universe, making "this Metropolis a kind of *Emporium* for the whole Earth." Walking the floor as a "Citizen of the World," he imagines a world landscape which trade transforms into the stuff of consumption, and ultimately, of female ornament:

> Nature seems to have taken a particular Care to disseminate her Blessings among the different Regions of the World, with an Eye to this mutual Intercourse and Traffic among Mankind, that the Natives of the several Parts of the Globe might have a kind of Dependance upon one another, and be united together by their common Interest. Almost every *Degree* produces something peculiar to it. The Food often grows in one Country, and the Sauce in another. The Fruits of *Portugal* are corrected by the Products of *Barbadoes.* The Infusion of a China Plant sweetned with the Pith of an *Indian* Cane: The *Philipick* Islands give a Flavour to our *European* Bowls. The single Dress of a Woman of Quality is often the Product of an hundred Climates. The Muff and the Fan come together from the different Ends of the Earth. The Scarf is sent from the Torrid Zone, and the Tippet from beneath the Pole. The Brocade Petticoat rises out of the Mines of *Peru*, and the Diamond Necklace out of the Bowels of *Indostan*. (Addison, *Spectator* 69, 1: 292–5)[10]

From the bird's-eye view of "Nature," the aesthetic view which makes order from variety in miniature form, all the world unites in the production of luxury. From such a perspective, objects, with uncanny charm, take on lives and motion of their own, and power and labor become invisible. Petticoats rise from mines fully made, diamonds emerge from mythically embodied bowels without effort, and women exist to display, and to consume, in full regalia, the triumph of such "common interest"; the universe in miniature.

But as an individual author and appropriator, Pope makes a different sort of curious show, the flip-side, the rhyming word if you will, of curiosity's couplet. While the curious collector composes a totality out of the juxtaposition of artificial and natural, of all of history and all of nature, the curiosity itself can also, by pointing to the unique unknown, delineate the limits of the natural, and the known (Benedict 1990: 84). A writer in the *Gazette* of 1758 illustrates this well: "What entitles a thing to the epithets of rare and curious? – Certainly its being seldom to be seen; and when seen, its being possessed of some powers or properties of an uncommon and extraordinary nature. Is there then a dromedary and camel, besides those shewn at the Talbot in the Strand, in the whole island of Great Britain!"[11] Whether local or imported, "uncommon and extraordinary nature" makes a curiosity. As the young Sir Joshua Reynolds observes when he sees Pope at the art auction where images of the author are on sale to virtuosi, "Pope was seldom seen in public, so it was a great sight to see him" (Hilles 1952: 24–5). In just this way Joseph Warton's juxtaposition of two images of Pope are both curiosities and emblems of his edition of the collected works (1797) to follow. These images are curious for contradictory reasons, and as such help to illuminate how this particular poet's entry into the marketplace as a translator of epic puts the cultural oppositions inherent in the term curiosity into play.

William Hoare's full-length sketch, curious because of its elusion of "official" authorial control, offers an "Unique of this celebrated Poet."[12] Just as Warton reproduces the handwritten note on the back of the original drawing as italicized print on the facing page, so by reproducing this image he publishes that which, like Pope himself appearing at the art auction, has been deliberately kept out of circulation, rarely seen in public and thus a sight to see.

Yet the official portrait which precedes the illicit image in Warton's edition is itself a curiosity precisely because of its fitness to circulate, its distance (as a line engraving of an oil portrait after a Roman type) from any original. As such it makes the perfect curio and its original takes its fit place, in the form from which an infinite number of copies generate, in the collection of "one of the most eminent virtuosi of his day," who had converted "his large and spacious house in Great Ormond Street . . . into a Temple of Nature, and a Repository of Time," amidst "the Busts of the great Masters, the antient Greeks and Romans."[13] The curiosity collection offers both the illusion of totality and the allure of uniqueness. At once the indecipherable mark of deformity and unmistakable sign of the coherence of literary tradition, Pope's image remains in both cases a collectable object; Pope himself both subject and object of curiosity.

Pope was well aware of the synecdochal relation between collectable images and ineffable quality when he furnished his own villa at Twickenham. He covered the walls of his house with portraits of his friends and adorned his library with busts of Homer, Newton, Spenser, Shakespeare, Milton and Dryden (Mack 1969: 31–2, 251). This forum of imaginary spectators creates a material incarnation of the benign Oedipal theater he imagines in the *Essay on Criticism*:

> *You* then whose Judgment the right Course wou'd steer
> Know well each ANCIENT'S proper *Character*,
> His *Fable, Subject, Scope* in ev'ry Page,
> *Religion, Country, Genius* of his *Age*:

> Without all these at once before your Eyes,
> *Cavil* you may, but never *Criticize*.

> (118–123)

Here the critic, and as the poem goes on to demonstrate, any poet who follows Homer's poetry "Still with *It self compar'd*" (128), must collect and internalize the characters, both authorial image and text, of the ancient authorities as monitory examples. Both portrait of the author and product of his labor, such characters are to be gazed at while writing and in turn survey the writer.

All great art enters that hall of authorial portraits framed and surveyed by such a vision of limits. As Pope said in a letter (April 30, 1736) about such halls of greatness, "A Man not only shews his Taste but his Virtue, in the Choice of such Ornaments ... The History itself (if wellchosen) upon a Rich-mans Walls, is very often a better lesson than any he could teach by his Conversation" (*Correspondence* 4: 13). In great halls and ladies' cabinets, temples of nature and repositories of time, the object, both poem and portrait, speaks for itself.

Mastery At First Sight

For the eighteenth-century imitator of the classics, to put the ancients (and with them oneself) into such a museum was to cross the line not only between nature and art but also between the sexes. The imitator, who for the first time in this period was distinguished from the philologist and the scholar, civilized the classics by translating them into an elegant language accessible to proper feminine readers denied access to the originals by their lack of education in Latin and Greek (C. Thomas 1990: 1–2). Such a project thus mediates between the masculine sublime of the ancients and the beautiful refinement suitable for modern perusal and personal profit. Fidelity to the original was frowned upon not only as servile, but as impolite and ungentlemanly: the self-made classical philologist "slashing Bentley" (who in his professionalization of classical letters serves as a foil to Pope's project of making the classics widely accessible) in his uncivilized concern for textual detail, figures a kind of masculine violence not unlike that of an unrefined Homeric hero, a violence that affronts the polite reader and critic who dwell not in the study but in the drawing room of universal sentiment.

This feminization of the classics can also be played out in economic terms as feminine ornamentation of the rough, uncouth, impoverished English tongue. Empire's mirror is reversed, and the barbarousness of the ancients becomes the material of civilization. English poetry's ornamentation is the fruit of authorial plunder of classical riches: from this perspective the entrepreneurial imperialism that allows "all Arabia to breathe from yonder box" on Belinda's dressing table is also the source of both the sublime epic diction of Pope's *Iliad* and the refined and fragile neoclassical perfection of the *Rape of the Lock*'s mock epic. As Dryden argues in his "Preface to the *Aeneid*":

> If sounding Words are not of our growth and Manufacture, who shall hinder me to Import them from a Foreign Country? I carry not out the Treasure of the Nation, which is never to return; but what I bring from *Italy*, *I* spend in *England*: Here it remains, and here it circulates . . . I Trade both with the Living and the Dead, for the enrichment of our Native Language. We have enough in England to supply our necessity; but if we will have things of Magnificence and Splendour, we must get them by Commerce. (*Poems* 3: 1059)

Samuel Johnson, who said of Dryden that he saved English poetry from its "former savageness," and that in so doing he "shewed us the true bounds of a translator's liberty," makes the imperial analogy clear: "What was said of Rome, adorned by Augustus, may be applied by an easy metaphor to English poetry embellished by Dryden, 'lateritiam invenit, marmoream reliquit,' he found it brick, and he left it marble" (*Lives* 1: 469).

Bound to his classical original by a sense of republican liberty, Dryden the cultured translator is both an imperial plunderer and the civilizer of both ancient and modern tongues. If Dryden, Pope's most important predecessor as a classical imitator, can be termed the Augustus of English poetry, what epithet would do Pope justice, whose *Iliad* proved him the indisputable master and marketer of literary imitation in the eighteenth century and, Johnson admits, "added much" even to Dryden's achievements in heroic diction? "His version may be said to have tuned the English tongue, for since its appearance no writer, however deficient in other powers, has wanted melody. Such a series of lines so elaborately corrected and so sweetly modulated took possession of the publick ear; the vulgar was enamoured of the poem, and the learned wondered at the translation" (*Lives* 3: 238). While Dryden's poetic achievement is described as imperial, Pope's perfection of the heroic style is described as insinuating, a sweetness of music which takes possession of the public ear like a siren's song. If Dryden's Virgil, or the "nervous and manly" Homeric original which, Pope writes in his Preface to the *Iliad*, seizes the reader with "rapture and fire," is an experience of the masculine sublime, Pope's musicalization of epic diction, his perfect modulation of a "language of refinement" seduces the reader with the feminine beautiful.

Yet Johnson's description of Pope's civilized imitation contains its own oppositions, both blurring and creating distinctions between the lettered (masculine aristocratic and feminine middle class) sections of his audience: those ignorant of the original are enamoured by its beauty, those able to appreciate the magnitude of Pope's act of translation are struck more sublimely with wonder. Penelope Wilson (1982) has noted the way in which the ability to read Latin and Greek in the original becomes an increasingly nervously defended aristocratic male province in the eighteenth century, a mark of membership in a secret male society threatened by bluestockings such as Pope's Homeric rival Madame Dacier and Johnson's friend Elizabeth Montagu. In this sense, both Pope's *Iliad* and the *Rape* participate in a mass-marketing of culture that makes them curiosities; these texts are particularly threatening because of the way in which they make high culture accessible to women and other middle-class readers lacking in classical learning. The reader who capitalized most on the opportunity, or so Dennis and many other doubters of Pope's classical learning and gentlemanly status alleged, was Pope himself. With perhaps false modesty, Pope had written to Parnell in 1714 (the year of the publication of the expanded five-canto edition of the *Rape*), "You are a Generous Author, I a Hackney Scribler, You are a Grecian & bred at a University, I a poor Englishman of my own Educating" (*Correspondence* 1: 226).

In the *Rape*, Pope both parodies and embraces the fantasy of quick visual appropriation of privileged and painstaking literary labor, a fantasy most elaborated and most sharply derided in the aptly feminine genre of the recipe, his "Receit to make an Epick Poem":

> Another Quality required is a compleat Skill in Languages. To this I answer, that it is notorious Persons of no Genius have been oftentimes great Linguists. To instance in the *Greek*, of which there are two Sorts; the Original *Greek*, and that from which our Modern Authors translate. I should be unwilling to promise Impossibilities, but modestly speaking, this may be learned in about an Hour's time with Ease. I have known one, who became a sudden Professor of Greek, immediately upon Application of the Left-hand Page of the *Cambridge Homer* to his Eye. It is, in these Days, with Authors as with other Men, the well bred are familiarly acquainted with them at first Sight; and as it is sufficient for a good General to have *survey'd* the Ground he is to conquer, so it is enough for a good Poet to have *seen* the Author he is to be Master of. (*Guardian* 78; *Prose Works* 1: 116–17)[14]

Both the diligent Homeric translator's parody of well-bred indolence, and Johnson's description of the effects of Pope's *Iliad* on English readers, reveal the way in which this imitator's self-made and home-made authority, even when drawing on Homer's credit, guards the masculine original from, while presenting it to, a feminine audience. Such readers, as the *Rape of the*

Lock makes clear, might otherwise treat Homer's rapture and fire as mere ornament, and Pope's labor, labor which curiosity transforms into display, as child's play.

Pope's *Iliad*, then, both preserves an epic tradition and improves upon it by embodying it as an object self-consciously for sale. "A sumptuous artifact of modern polite culture," Pope's translation demonstrates the way in which refinement is both a moral and a sensual quality, allowing Pope to redefine the printed image of a classic.[15] Pope's decision in the mid-1730s to print his poems in small octavo editions, including variant readings in the footnotes, Susan Staves argues, "had the effect of making his own work look like a classic text, one fit for the new national canon of English literature that was just being established" (1988: 149).[16] The founding text of Pope's personal canon is his *Iliad*, adorned with illustrations, headpieces and tailpieces, in appropriate quarto and folio editions. When thinking of a "classic" this poet had a concrete vision of a particular form of commodity in mind.

The Rape of the Lock brings Pope's relationship with the object-world of the feminine to precarious perfection. If Pope's *Iliad* translates the idea of a classic into material form, the *Rape* has been envisioned and described by critics throughout its history as an exquisite object worthy of Belinda's dressing table. "Pope distilled as much real poetry as could be got from the drawing-room world in which the art then lived – " writes Leigh Hunt, "from the flowers and luxuries of artificial life – into that exquisite little toilet-bottle of essence, *The Rape of the Lock*."[17] Addison speaks as a delighted consumer when he calls the poem "a delicious little thing" (Johnson, *Lives* 3: 103).[18] Edmund Gosse, to whom Aubrey Beardsley dedicated his illustrated version of the *Rape*, exclaims that "the limited field of burlesque [was] never more picturesquely filled, than by this little masterpiece in Dresden china."[19] For Hazlitt the *Rape* goes beyond miniaturization to become a miracle of insubstantiality; the poem "is the most exquisite specimen of *fillagree* work ever invented. It is admirable in proportion as it is made of nothing. . . . It is made of gauze and silver spangles."[20]

The *Rape*'s triviality is its best defense against any authority but its own beautiful surface. To attempt to speak at all seriously about this poem is to be somewhat embarrassed at making such an ado about nothing. From the perspective of this miniature epic, even the ancient poets seem overly serious. Such paragons of high literary achievement, Pope writes to Arabella Fermor, "are in one respect like many modern Ladies; Let an Action be never so trivial in it self, they always make it appear of the utmost Importance" (*Works* 2: 142). What links ancient poets to modern ladies, Pope explains, is a penchant for personification, a propensity for making persons out of things, out of almost nothing. *The Rape of the Lock* lays bare not only the machinery of epic but the insubstantiality of all creations of value.

When Pope, neither ancient poet nor modern lady but ambiguously positioned between the two, looks at heroic machinery, he sees worldly machination. The sylphs in all their diaphanous insubstantiality serve to gratify the most unmentionable of physical desires: "any Mortals may enjoy the most intimate Familiarities with these gentle Spirits, upon a Condition very easie to all true *Adepts*, an inviolate Preservation of Chastity," he archly tells Arabella (*Works* 2: 143). Or as Ariel persuasively puts it in Belinda's dream in Canto I, "Whoever fair and chaste/Rejects Mankind, is by some Sylph embrac'd" (67–8). Indeed, the sylphs gratify female desires with a process that parallels the poem's perpetually synecdochal procedures. By exchanging vulnerable flesh for airy substance, chaste maidens initiate an endless sylph-run round of exchange that puts desire unendingly on the market:

> Oft when the World imagine Women stray,
> The *Sylphs* thro' mystick Mazes guide their Way,
> Thro' all the giddy Circle they pursue,
> And old Impertinence expel by new.
> What tender Maid but must a Victim fall
> To one Man's Treat, but for another's Ball?
> When *Florio* speaks, what Virgin could withstand,
> If gentle *Damon* did not squeeze her Hand?
> With varying Vanities, from ev'ry Part,
> They shift the moving Toyshop of their Heart;
> Where Wigs with Wigs, with Sword-knots Sword-knots strive,
> Beaus banish Beaus, and Coaches Coaches drive.
> This erring Mortals Levity may call,
> Oh blind to Truth! the *Sylphs* contrive it all.
>
> (I, 91–104)

The "truth" concealed from erring Mortals, the "mystick Maze" beneath the seemingly random strayings of ladies of fashion, is not an order or an end but rather an endless progression of substitutions that makes all objects of desire equally negligible.[21] Individual men have been reduced by the sylphs' and the poet's synecdochal strategies to identical wigs and swordknots, and the battle they fight within the heart's "moving Toyshop" prefigures the epic card game of Canto III and the heroic clash of actual beaus and nymphs in Canto V.[22] But the poem's own mystic maze makes it impossible to use the word "actual" seriously, or to distinguish between playing cards and persons, between the "moving Toyshop" within and that without. The human persons, as Pope observed to Arabella, are indeed as fictitious as the airy ones.

The power of the sylphs, then, is identical to that of the *Rape* itself: the power of levelling distinctions, of infinite exchange, envisioned as miniaturization. For adherents to epic's proper weight and scale, such as the irritable John Dennis, the miniaturization of Pope himself that inevitably results is dismissive:

> The *Machines* that appear in this Poem are infinitely less considerable than the *human Persons*, which is without Precedent. Nothing can be so contemptible as the *Persons*, or so foolish as the *Understandings* of these *Hobgoblins* ... these *diminutive Beings* of the intellectual World, may be said to be the *Measure* of Mr. *Pope's Capacity* and *Elevation* of Genius. They are, indeed, Beings so *diminutive*, that they bear the same Proportion to the rest of the intellectual, that Eels in Vinegar do to the rest of the material World. The latter are only to be seen thro' *Microscopes*, and the former only thro' the false Optics of a *Rosycrucian* Understanding. (Dennis *Critical Works* 2: 338–9)

As is so often the case, Dennis gets the point by missing it; in the inverted value system of the *Rape*, machines are more divine the less considerable they become. By comparing the intellectual to the material world, Dennis shows himself to be inadvertently influenced, much as Hazlitt was when he looked at the wrong end of Pope's microscope, by the rhetorical force of figuring great things by small. Seduced by that force in the same way that Hazlitt was repelled, Leigh Hunt compares Pope favorably to the more "masculine" genius of Dryden:

> Pope ... had more delicacy and fancy ... and was less confined to the region of matter of fact. Dryden never soared above earth, however nobly he walked it. The little fragile creature had wings; and he could expand them at will, and ascend, as if to no great imaginative height, yet to charming fairy circles just above those of the world about him, disclosing enchanting visions at the top of drawing rooms and enabling us to see the spirits that wait on coffee-cups and hoop-petticoats.[23]

And in an uncanny presaging of his transformation into airy substance, in a letter to Caryll (May 1, 1714), to whom the *Rape* is also dedicated, Pope announces himself a fit opponent for Homer:

> I must confess the Greek fortification does not appear so formidable as it did, upon a nearer approach; and I am almost apt to flatter myself, that Homer secretly seems inclined to correspond with me, in letting me into a good part of his designs. There are, indeed, a sort of underli[n]g auxiliars to the difficulty of the work, called commentators and criticks, who would frighten many

people by their number and bulk. These lie entrenched in the ditches, and are secure only in the dirt they have heaped about 'em with great pains in the collecting it. But I think we have found a method of coming at the main works by a more speedy and gallant way than by mining under ground; that is, by using the poetical engines, wings, and flying thither over their heads. (*Correspondence* 1: 219–20)

The original, like the reluctant heroine of a novel of seduction, is secretly inclined to correspond with a poet whose singular lack of substance charms, while pedantic critics "frighten ... by their number and bulk." Whether figured as a fun-house view at the wrong end of a telescope, the absurdity of eels in vinegar under a microscope, or the magic wand of a Pope-turned-sylph, the power of miniaturization set into motion by such "poetical engines" brings all persons, no matter how heroic their aspirations, and all personifications, no matter how divine their origin, down to size and into circulation.

NOTES

What appears here is an excerpt of the chapter so entitled in Deutsch 1996.

1 The sentence continues, "this is the primary formal configuration of the poem."
2 Deborah C. Payne (1991) does an admirable job of taking the feminist critique of the poem one step further in order to account for the poem's appeal to women readers. While Payne is right to insist on the potential unity of ideological critique and aesthetic appreciation for a reader of the *Rape*, she too suggests the necessity of an ideologically enlightened poststructuralist critic for the creation of such a unity.
3 Weinbrot's essay is particularly useful for the way in which it restores both traditional and marxist-feminist critiques of the *Rape* to a broader literary-traditional context which include the burlesquing of Homer and the deploring of Amazons.
4 This focus on the detail serves to align Pope's discourse with eighteenth-century aesthetic ideas of the feminine. See, for example, Naomi Schor 1987 and 1989: ch. 1. Both Shaftesbury's *Second Characters; or the Language of Forms* and Edmund Burke's *A Philosophical Enquiry into the Origin of Our Ideas of the Sublime and Beautiful* link attention to the detail with a vision of the feminine.
5 Homer, The *Iliad*, trans. Richmond Lattimore (Chicago: University of Chicago Press, 1951), 12.310–28. In the Lattimore translation the speech reads:

"Glaukos, why is it you and I are honored before others
With pride of place, the choice meats and the filled wine cups
in Lykia, and all men look on us as if we were immortals,

and we are appointed a great piece of land by the banks of Xanthos,
good land, orchard and vineyard, and ploughland for the planting of wheat?
Therefore it is our duty in the forefront of the Lykians
to take our stand, and bear our part of the blazing of battle,
so that a man of the close-armoured Lykians may say of us:
'Indeed, these are no ignoble men who are lords of Lykia,
these kings of ours, who feed upon the fat sheep appointed
and drink the exquisite sweet wine, since indeed there is strength
of valour in them, since they fight in the forefront of the Lykians.'
Man, supposing you and I, escaping this battle,
would be able to live on forever, ageless, immortal,
so neither would I myself go on fighting in the foremost
nor would I urge you into the fighting where men win glory.
But now, seeing that the spirits of death stand close about us
in their thousands, no man can turn aside nor escape them,
let us go on and win glory for ourselves, or yield it to others."

6   See Pollak 1985: 77–107, for the most cogent reading in this vein.
7   Here I am indebted to Weinbrot's reading. Clarissa in his view "meets the
    challenge of respecting and transcending her source, of avoiding duplicity and
    sensuality while insisting upon the obligations ... of turning noble death into
    useful life" (1988: 43–4). The key word here is "useful": just as Pope refines
    Homer, so Belinda (fruitlessly) is called upon to put potentially destructive
    beauty to productive use.
8   Tracy's style in the title makes explicit his own antiquarian impulse.
9   "Eighteenth-century curio cabinets and collections promote an aesthetic that
    relies on the eye forming connections between separate objects, finding
    similarities within differences. No longer does one object represent its class;
    rather, the spectator defines a class by comparing several – as many as possible
    – objects. Collecting thus functions as an exercise of definition by distance
    over culture and history, both one's own culture and the culture of others"
    (Benedict 1990: 77–8).
10   For two early and important essays locating Pope's construction of Belinda "as
    a consumer, the embodiment of luxury" in a cultural context of great
    ambivalence, see Louis A. Landa, 1971 and 1973. The critic to draw most
    heavily and most recently on Landa's work in her characterization of Pope's
    mercantile poetics is Laura Brown (1985); this chapter attempts to complicate
    Brown's reading in the direction of the aesthetic. See also her reading of this
    passage in *Ends of Empire*, esp. ch. 2.
11   *Gazette*, January 26, 1758, quoted in Benedict 1990: 83.
12   See Deutsch 1996, figure 4; the note next to the line drawing reads, "*This is the
    only Portrait that was ever drawn of* Mr. Pope *at full length. – It was done without his
    knowledge, as he was deeply engaged in conversation with* Mr. Allen *in the Gallery at* Prior
    Park, *by* Mr. Hoare, *who sat at the other end of the Gallery. – This drawing is therefore
    exceedingly valuable, as it is an Unique of this celebrated Poet.* Warton."

13 *Authentic Memoirs of the Life of Richard Mead, M.D.* (London, 1755), 51; quoted in Wimsatt 1965: 205–7.

14 This essay, later included in Pope's mock-Longinian treatise *Peri Bathous* (1728), was published while Pope was working on the first six books of the *Iliad* translation and revising the two-canto version of *The Rape of the Lock* (1712).

15 Susan Staves names as one of Pope's contributions to neoclassical epic the extensive critical apparatus with which the civilized English poet called visible attention to the ancient's barbarism (1988: 154). See also Mack's introduction to the Twickenham edition of Pope's *Iliad* (1967), and Weinbrot 1988.

16 See also James McLaverty (1984), who argues that "the pomp of the [*Dunciad's*] presentation is genuinely appropriate to the poem's importance." Pope himself spoke of the *Dunciad Variorum* quite seriously as an "English classick with huge Commentaries."

17 [Leigh Hunt], *Examiner*, June 1, 1817.

18 Pope took umbrage at the compliment since part of its intent was to discourage him from revising and expanding the poem.

19 Edmund Gosse to A. E. Gallatin, June 19, 1902, Princeton University Library MS; quoted in Robert Halsband 1980: 87.

20 *The Complete Works of William Hazlitt*, ed. P. P. Howe (London: J. M. Dent & Sons, 1933), 5: 72.

21 Pope's description of the endless exchange within a woman's breast is remarkable for the ways in which it parallels marxist accounts of the deceptiveness of commodity production. Just as the commodity conceals the source of its production in an appearance of randomness decked out in alluring metaphor, so coquettes appear arbitrary and appealing while concealing the contrivance of the sylphs. For the dynamic of substitution in which commodity-exchange masks the causal metonymy of its production with random and totalizing metaphor, see Terry Eagleton 1981: 30.

22 For a reading of such substitutions as part of the poem's process of refining and sublimating epic violence into display, see Weinbrot 1988: 31. For Pope's vision of himself in such a "moving Toyshop," see his *Guardian* 106, July 13, 1713 (*Prose Works* 1: 131–2). Pope's alterego, Peter Puzzle, sees himself succeed a "Lap-dog . . . a *Guiney* Pig, a Squirril and a Monky," only to witness "my Place taken up by an ill-bred awkward Puppy with a Money-bag under each Arm." Both here and in the *Rape*, for the speaker to gaze at himself from his mistress' eyes is to see himself as an object of amusement with nothing but market value.

23 Leigh Hunt, *Wit and Humour Selected from the English Poets* (1846), quoted in Bateson 1975: 220.

10

Anne Finch: Gender, Politics, and Myths of the Private Self

Carol Barash

The Publicly Private Finch and *Miscellany Poems*

Anne Finch used her training in the biblical and classical traditions, finally, to bury her sympathy to the Stuarts in myths of a private female self. In "The Introduction," the first poem in both early manuscripts of *Miscellany Poems*, the speaker describes herself not as a highly educated woman, but as one with common and primarily domestic education and responsibilities:

> They tell us, we mistake our sex, and way;
> Good breeding, fashion, dancing, dressing, play
> Are the accomplishments we shou'd desire;
> To write, or read, or think, or to enquire
> Wou'd cloud our beauty, and exhaust our time,
> And interrupt the Conquests of our prime;
> Whilst the dull mannage of a servile house
> Is held by some, our outmost art, and use.[1]

Finch calls attention to her speaker's lack of education by using archaic spellings and faulty diction to describe the way her verses will be attacked in public – the poems are "uncorrect" (4); "censures" will "their faults persue" (2). "Sure 'twas not ever thus," the speaker explains (21), going back to the Old Testament in search of models of female linguistic authority.

In the Old Testament, Finch finds both submissive women, dangerously swayed by popular opinion, and models of the poet and *femme forte*. "The Introduction" describes women rapt by the poet-prophet David, who promiscuously mingles with the crowds to win their support: "Half of the

Kingdom is already gone; / The fairest half, whose influence guides the rest / Have David's Empire o're their hearts confesst" (42–4).[2] Finch places the story of David's triumph (2 Sam. 1–6) in the context of a longer biblical narrative, which describes the return of the ark of the covenant to Jerusalem after it is stolen by the Philistines (1 Sam. 5; 1 Kings 8). In Finch's version, a chorus of "Holy Virgins" (30) – nowhere in the biblical story – accompany the ark. They "soften, and refine" the "louder notes" of the Levites, the priestly class responsible for protecting the ark, "And with alternate verse, compleat the Hymn Divine" when the ark is returned (30–2).

After a description of the people dangerously swayed by their fascination with David, Deborah rescues a nation fallen into near debauchery:

> A Woman here, leads fainting Israel on,
> She fights, she wins, she triumphs with a Song,
> Devout, majestic, for the subject fit,
> And far above her arms, exalts her wit.
> Then, to the peaceful, shady Palm withdraws,
> And rules the rescu'd Nation, with her Laws.
>
> (45–50)

Finch here describes Deborah as a *femme forte*, justly powerful as a ruler and leading her triumphant people in song. Using Deborah as her model, Finch's speaker then returns to the problem of education that opens the poem and, subtly both echoing and criticizing Milton, rails against women's lack of education:

> How are we faln, faln by mistaken rules?
> And Education's, more than Nature's Fools,
> Debarr'd from all improvements of the mind,
> And to be dull, expected, and design'd.
>
> (51–4)

Yet she is reluctant to graft her own poetic ambitions onto the model of the *femme forte*, choosing instead the retreat of the political outsider fused with the voice of nature:

> And if some one wou'd Soar above the rest,
> With warmer fancy, and ambition presst,
> So strong, the' opposing faction still appears,
> The hopes to thrive can ne'er outweigh the fears.
> Be caution'd then my Muse, and still retir'd;
> Nor be despis'd aiming to be admir'd;
> Conscious of wants, still with contracted wing
> To some few friends, and to thy sorrows sing;

> For groves of Laurel thou wert never meant;
> Be dark enough my shades, and be thou there content.
>
> (55–64)

Like Killigrew and Chudleigh, Finch takes her speaker to a place from which she might legitimately attack her critics, but then steps back, defers. Finch's manuscript poems are thus framed by a tension between the model of political and poetic authority embodied in Deborah, and the speaker's refusal to speak from that place of authority.

During Anne's reign Finch elaborates this tension, projecting her political alienation onto haunting myths of a female voice cut off from history and from others, alternately fused with the landscape, and desperately but empoweringly alone in both body and mind. We can see this process at work most clearly in "The Spleen" (where Finch calls attention to exactly what is at stake in her repeated gestures of renunciation) and in Finch's reworking of earlier manuscript poems into *Miscellany Poems, On Several Occasions* (1713).

The overlap of public and private realms in "The Spleen" begins with its subtitle, "A Pindarick Poem." While critics have most often read the poem as autobiographical,[3] even to the point of anthologizing only the central "lyric" section,[4] Finch is actually quite careful to position the self-construction of the woman poet in "The Spleen" in relation to a much larger and changing public political world. The poem's opening description of what happens to those afflicted with the spleen, begins with problems of naming and ends with the experience of political defeat:

> What art thou, *SPLEEN*, which ev'ry thing dost ape?
> Thou *Proteus* to abus'd Mankind,
> Who never yet thy real Cause cou'd find,
> Or fix thee to remain in one continued Shape.
> . . . .
> Such was the monstrous *Vision* seen,
> When *Brutus* (now beneath his Cares opprest,
> And all *Rome's* Fortunes rolling in his Breast,
> Before *Philipi's* latest Field,
> Before his Fate did to *Octavius* lead)
> Was vanquish'd by the *Spleen*.
>
> (1–4, 20–5)

Brutus, we should recall, was a regicide, the prime assassin of Julius Caesar, who killed himself after Mark Antony and Octavian defeated him at Philippi. Finch suggests in the next section of the poem that moral or spiritual failure, not "the Mortal Part" (26), should be blamed for emotional unrest:

> Falsly, the Mortal Part we blame
> Of our deprest, and pond'rous Frame,
> Which, till the first degrading Sin
> Let Thee, its dull Attendant, in.
>
> (26–9)

When the poem begins to discuss spiritual failure, the speaker blends her own voice with those who suffer from the spleen, "of *our* deprest, and pond'rous Frame" (emphasis added).

Before the fall, the speaker claims, "Man his Paradice possesst." Now, in contrast, the exotic pleasures of paradise are, paradoxically, both intoxicatingly pleasurable and overwhelming:

> Now the *Jonquille* o'ercomes the feeble Brain;
> We faint beneath the Aromatick Pain,
> Till some offensive Scent thy Pow'rs appease,
> And Pleasure we resign for short, and nauseous Ease.
>
> (40–3)

Reinforcing the poem's argument that pleasure is, ideally, whole and good, the speaker later claims that the restrictions imposed by "Religion" are the result at once of the fall and its symptom, spleen (116–22).

The fall has, at the same time, created rancorous divisions between men and women, who are depicted as feigning spleen to gain sway over one another in the next section of the poem (53–63). Spleen, however, reinforces gender hierarchy in the end, with "Lordly *Man*, born to Imperial Sway" triumphing, "And *Woman*, arm'd with *Spleen*, do's servilely Obey" (62–3). So when Finch's speaker, in the poem's most famous lines, describes the effect of spleen on her own writing, we should read that inscription of the female poetic "self" in relation to the preceding descriptions of political defeat, religious failure, and gender conflict.

Finch's speaker enters the world of the spleen through the "shade" of retirement Finch so often describes as poetic triumph, and affected by spleen she cries out against those who would limit her poetic ambitions to a lesser, female sphere:

> Because, sometimes, thou dost presume
> Into the ablest Heads to come:
> That, often, Men of Thoughts refin'd,
> . . . .
> Retiring from the Croud, are to thy Shades inclin'd.
>   O'er me alas! thou dost too much prevail:
>   I feel thy Force, whilst I against thee rail;

I feel my Verse decay, and my crampt Numbers fail.
Thro' thy black Jaundice I all Objects see,
    As Dark, and Terrible as Thee,
My Lines decry'd, and my Employment thought
An useless Folly, or presumptuous Fault:
Whilst in the *Muses* Paths I stray,
    Whilst in their Groves, and by their secret Springs
My Hand delights to trace unusual Things,
And deviates from the known, and common way;
    Nor will in fading Silks compose
    Faintly th' inimitable *Rose*,
Fill up an ill-drawn *Bird*, or paint on Glass
The *Sov'reign's* blurr'd and undistinguish'd Face,
The threatning *Angel*, and the speaking *Ass*.
                                    (78–80, 83–99)

"Spleen" is, thus, for Finch both triumph and failure. It is only once the spleen has affected the speaker that she describes her poetry as fallen, decayed failure. But, at the same time, the spleen allows her to assert that she does not wish to be a genteel woman artist, one who makes safe, insipid domestic arts or uncritically draws the monarch's "undistinguish'd Face."

"The Spleen" returns to the overlap of political, religious, and emotional failure in its closing lines with a description of Richard Lower, a physician to Charles II who supported the Whigs in the Popish Plot, sinking beneath the weight of the spleen:

    Not skilful *Lower* thy Source cou'd find,
    Or thro' the well-dissected Body trace
        The secret, the mysterious ways,
    By which thou dost surprize, and prey upon the Mind.
    Tho' in the Search, too deep for Humane Thought,
        With unsuccessful Toil he wrought,
    'Till thinking Thee to've catch'd, Himself by thee was caught,
    Retain'd thy Pris'ner, thy acknowledg'd Slave,
    And sunk beneath thy Chain to a lamented Grave.
                                    (142–50)

Whereas Jane Barker had used Lower in "A Farewell to Poetry" as an example of the moral failure of a great anatomist, suggesting that knowledge of the human body could not and should not take the place of spiritual knowledge, Finch, writing after Lower's depression and suicide, pushes the pro-Stuart implication Barker only suggested: to desert the king is, like Brutus's killing of Julius Caesar with which "The Spleen" began, akin to moral failure and regicide. But for a woman to push those meanings in this world is extremely dangerous: one is apt to be attacked as a woman, and one will experience those attacks as failure and self-doubt. So Finch's speaker retreats to the poetic "shade" of indirection, cautiously and decorously attacking her political opponents but at the same time calling attention to what is gained and lost in such a gesture of retreat.

There are similar overlaps of political, psychological, and poetic process in many of Finch's poems. The manuscript version of "To the Nightingale," for instance, includes three lines which suggest the bird is a figure of the speaker's political as well as poetic ambitions: "Hiding thus, in night, thy head, / Sure, thou'rt to some Faction Wed, / Or to false opinions bred."[5] Like the music born out of Philomel's losing her tongue, political poetry is, these deleted lines imply, maimed and debased; and yet, even though political poetry is linked to physical pain, even dismemberment, it remains an ideal. Similarly, the larger trajectory at work in "The Spleen" – calling back a poem's implicit ambitions, but also calling attention to what has been submerged and why – informs the shape of several other poems in *Miscellany Poems*, as well as the volume as a whole.

This process is most evident in the transformation of "Some occasi[o]nal Reflections Digested tho' not with great regularity into a Poeme," an unwieldy manuscript pindaric that attempts to make connections between gender and both monarchic and poetic authority, into two crisp but separate lyrics – "Glass" and "Fragment" – in *Miscellany Poems*. The first section of the manuscript poem suggests the danger of mistaking the figural for the real:

> By neer resemblance see that Bird betray'd
> Who takes the well wrought Arras for a shade
> There hopes to perch and with a chearfull Tune
> O're-passe the scortchings of the Sultry Noon.
> But soon repuls'd by the obdurate Scean
> How swift she turns but turns alas! in vain
> That piece a Grove, this shews an ambient Sky
> Where immitated Fowl their pinnions ply
> Seeming to mount in flight and aiming still more high.
> All she outstripps and with a moments pride
> Their understation silent does deride
> 'Till the dash'd Cealing strikes her to the ground
> No intercepting shrub to break the fall is found
> Recovering breath the window next she gaines
> Nor fears a stop from the transparent Panes.
>
> (Folger MS, 291–2)[6]

In this opening section of "Occasi[o]nal Reflections," just when "nature" seems to provide solace and the source of poetry – a place to "pearch …

with a chearfull Tune" – it proves a dangerous and overpowering myth, an alluring world of representations that can be neither "outstrip[pid]" nor escaped. As in Finch's other poems about birds – a finch is of course a kind of sparrow, among the most common of birds – Finch depicts her female speaker as both empowered and entrapped by her chosen solitude. This section of the poem ends with the bird – punningly a reference to the poet herself – about to bloody herself against a clear window that is nevertheless closed.

When the female bird can find no escape from the confining artifice of the aristocratic castle, the poem shifts to question the source of its own metaphors in the fourteen lines that ultimately became "Glass":

> O man what inspiration was thy guide
> Who taught thee Light and Air thus to divide
> To lett in all the usefull beames of Day
> Yett force as subtil winds without thy sash to stay
> T'extract from Embers by a strange device
> Then pollish fair these flakes of sollid Ice
> Which Silver'd o'er redouble all in place
> To give thee back thy well or ill complexion'd Face
> To Vessels blown exceed the gloomy Bowl
> Which did the Wines full excellence controul
> These shew the Body whilest you taste the Soul
> Its Colour Sparkles motion letts thee see
> Though yett th' excesse the Preacher warns to flee
> Least men att length as clearly spy through thee.
>   (Folger MS, 292; *Miscellany Poems*, 264)

"Occasi[o]nal Reflections" has three overlapping and interwoven tropes; the middle section – in some sense a mirror of the whole poem – has three images of glass: the window, the mirror, and the drinking glass, which not only reflects but also dangerously expands and conflates body and soul. In the lyric version, printed in *Miscellany Poems* with changes only in punctuation, these fourteen lines end with a warning against the pleasant blurring of boundaries caused by wine and self-reflection.

But these alluring descriptions of glass and self-empowering introspection have led the speaker away from the entrapped bird:

> But we degresse and leave th'imprison'd wretch
> Now sinking low now on a loftyer stretch
> Flutt'ring in endlesse c[i]rcles of dismay
> Till some kind hand directs the certain way
> Which through the casement an escape affoards

> And leads to ample space the only Heav'n of Birds.
>
> (Folger MS, 292)

Just as the imprisoned female bird is here freed from the confining castle, in the final section of the poem (which ultimately became "Fragment") the poem and its speaker are freed from the pleasurable prison-house of representation by using the court of James II and Mary of Modena as an archetype of heaven.

The poem titled "Fragment" is not actually a fragment (though it may refer to the longer – and in some sense more ambitious – manuscript poem from which it was shaped). In the published version, the title "Fragment" refers to what the poem's protagonist, Ardelia, has become since the banishment of James and Mary in 1688:

> So here confin'd, and but to female Clay,
> ARDELIA's Soul mistook the rightful Way:
> Whilst the soft Breeze of Pleasure's tempting Air
> Made her believe, Felicity was there;
> And basking in the warmth of early Time,
> To vain Amusements dedicate her Prime.
> Ambition next allur'd her tow'ring Eye;
> For Paradice she heard was plac'd on high,
> Then thought, the Court with all its glorious Show
> Was sure above the rest, and Paradice below.
>
> (*Miscellany Poems*, 280)

The speaker displaces her early belief in court as an earthly paradise onto the pursuit of God in heaven:

> Retirement, which the World *Moroseness* calls,
> Abandon'd Pleasures in Monastick Walls:
> These, but at distance, towards that purpose tend,
> The lowly Means to an exalted End;
> . . . .
> Pity her restless Cares, and weary Strife,
> And point some Issue to escaping Life;
> Which so dismiss'd, no Pen or Human Speech
> Th' ineffable Recess can ever teach:
> Th' Expanse, the Light, the Harmony, the Throng,
> The Bride's Attendance, and the Bridal Song,
> The numerous Mansions, and th' immortal Tree,
> No Eye, unpurg'd by Death, must ever see,
> . . . .
> Observe but here the easie Precepts given,

Then wait with chearful hope, till Heaven be known in Heaven.
(Miscellany Poems, 281–2)

In the early version – most likely written in the 1690s – the court of Mary and James remains an ideal, a type of authority that is neither confining (like the aristocratic tapestry) nor delusional (like glass), but rather a fleeting vision (a window) from this world to the next. "Occasi[o]nal Reflections" thus attempts to fuse three problems – gender and representation, the dangers of inwardness, and linguistic authority and monarchic authority – that will, for the most part, become separate domains in Finch's later work.

Female Community and Female Authority

The retreat that Finch creates for Ardelia in *Miscellany Poems* allows her protagonist not only to pursue God as both palpable and ideal, but also to recreate the ideal community once embodied for Finch in life at the Stuart court. In Finch's "The Petition for an Absolute Retreat. Inscribed to the Right Hon[ora]ble *CATHARINE* Countess of *THANET,* mention'd in the Poem under the Name of *ARMINDA*" Finch imagines an idealized place from which Ardelia can both mock the customs of the world around her, and create an alternative world shared with her aristocratic friend. Here, Finch draws on the topos of pastoral as a place of shared political alliances.[7] She seems more aware than earlier women poets of both the classical patterns of that retreat, and the English vernacular uses to which it had been put in the seventeenth century. Most important, for our purposes, Finch emphatically rethinks the pastoral topos of political retreat as a place where women's shared political sympathies can be legitimately expressed.

"The Petition" asks for simple clothes and fresh food, a place free from cumbersome rituals of entertaining that magically provides the pulp and juice of both English and oriental fruits:

> All, that did in *Eden* grow,
> All, but the *Forbidden Tree,*
> Wou'd be coveted by me;
> Grapes, with Juice so crouded up,
> As breaking thro' the native Cup;
> Figs (yet growing) candy'd o'er,
> By the Sun's attracting Pow'r;
> Cherries, with the downy Peach,
> All within my easie Reach;
> Whilst creeping near the humble Ground,

> Shou'd the Strawberry be found
> Springing whersoe'er I stray'd,
> Thro' those Windings and that Shade.
> *(Miscellany Poems*, 36)

One might say that Finch's "Petition" imagines the world from the vantagepoint of Milton's pre-lapsarian Eve, one who is an unalienated laborer (and participant) in God's lush and bountiful garden.[8] But she is also linguistically post-lapsarian in that she describes herself as "covet[ing]" the abundant and unencumbered gifts of nature and God.

In addition to "plain, and wholesome Fare" and seasonally appropriate "*Garments* [that] with the Time agree," Finch's speaker asks for an ideal "*Partner*" in paradise:

> Give me there (since Heaven has shown
> It was not Good to be alone)
> *A Partner* suited to my Mind,
> Solitary, pleas'd and kind;
> Who, partially, may something see
> Preferred to all the World in me;
> Slighting, by my humble Side,
> Fame and Splendor, Wealth and Pride.
> When but Two the Earth possest,
> 'Twas their happiest Days, and best;
> They by Bus'ness, nor by Wars,
> They by no Domestick Cares,
> From each other e'er were drawn,
> But in some Grove, or flow'ry Lawn,
> Spent the swiftly flying Time,
> Spent their own, and Nature's Prime,
> In Love; that only Passion given
> To perfect Man, whilst Friends with Heaven.
> *(Miscellany Poems*, 39–40)

Finch is here working against both the Hebrew and Christian Testaments, the description of man and woman's mutual and equal creation in Genesis 1: 27 and the Pauline injunction that "it is better to marry than to burn" (I Cor. 7: 9).[9] But in the next stanza of the poem it becomes clear that Finch imagines a female companion for Ardelia, the very same Arminda to whom the poem is addressed.

Just as the two nymphs together mourn for Mary of Modena in "On the Death of the Queen," the power of female friendship imaginatively rescues Ardelia from storms of political upheaval in "The Petition":

> Back reflecting let me say,
> So the sad *Ardelia* lay;
> Blasted by a Storm of Fate,
> Felt, thro' all the *British* State;
> . . . .
> Faded till *Arminda's* Love,
> (Guided by the Pow'rs above)
> . . . .
> With Wit, from an unmeasured Store,
> To Woman ne'er allow'd before.
>   (*Miscellany Poems*, 42–3)[10]

Whereas, in Katherine Philips's poetry, friendship was the emblem of royalist aspirations, for Finch the aristocratic woman herself becomes the emblem of those ideals. And, during the reign of Anne, grafted onto the voice of female authority associated with the female monarch, the individual aristocratic woman becomes the voice of acceptable female dissent against male prerogative. Finch achieves that triumph in and through pastoral, using her class privilege to imagine spiritual triumph, which is then deferred and displaced back onto a dark landscape that represents the negative authority of emotional retreat.

At the end of "The Petition for an Absolute Retreat," Finch's speaker soars to a vantage-point above earth and heaven, a position from which the political and religious controversies of her own time are rendered miniscule, virtually irrelevant:

> But as those, who Stars wou'd trace
> From a subterranean Place,
> Through some Engine lift their Eyes
> To the outward, glorious Skies;
> So th' immortal Spirit may,
> When descended to our Clay,
> From a rightly govern'd Frame
> View the Height, from whence she came;
> To her Paradise be caught,
> And Things unutterable taught.
> Give me then, in that Retreat,
> Give me, O indulgent Fate!
> For all Pleasures left behind,
> Contemplations of the Mind.
> Let the Fair, the Gay, the Vain
> Courtship and Applause obtain;
> Let th' Ambitious rule the Earth;
> Let the giddy Fool have Mirth;

> Give the Epicure his Dish,
> Ev'ry one their sev'ral Wish;
> Whilst my Transports I employ
> On that more extensive Joy,
> When all Heaven shall be survey'd
> From those Windings and that Shade.
> *(Miscellany Poems*, 48–9)

Finch brings out what is implicit in Philips: "retreat" and "privacy" are strategic positions, from which one can challenge dominant political and literary conventions. "The Petition" reaches inward to soar upward; in the dark, feminine "Windings" and "Shade" of her imaginary retreat, she moves to a place not only beyond this world, but beyond heaven as well. If Finch reaches the same vantage-point Chudleigh and Egerton achieve by grafting their poetic ambitions onto Queen Anne, she does so by fusing with nature and the community of other women, not with monarchic authority.

In the context of Finch's *Miscellany Poems* of 1713 – a volume which she and her husband helped to see into print[11] – "The Petition for an Absolute Retreat" becomes far less political, far more emotional than it seems in relation to Finch's use of similar tropes in elegies to James II and Mary of Modena. Throughout *Miscellany Poems*, we find Finch remaking political tropes as emotional ones. The publishing of *Miscellany Poems* in 1713 marks the single most important moment in Finch's construction of herself as a poet of emotional rather than political and religious extremity; here the ideal of the heroic woman is translated into patterns of negativity that link Finch's work to later women writers such as Emily Dickinson, Christina Rossetti, and indeed Virginia Woolf herself.[12] It is no coincidence that Finch attempted this translation when she did. In 1713 Queen Anne was quite ill, and many believed her death imminent. The Treaty of Utrecht had ended the war of the Spanish Succession and granted England control of the trans-Atlantic slave trade, but many in England believed the Treaty's other concessions too great a price to pay for peace. Supporters of the Old Pretender believed this was their moment to return the exiled Stuarts to England, and some members of Finch's family were among those preparing to assist James Francis Edward reclaim what his supporters considered his birthright. Finch and her husband, having just inherited the Winchilsea title and estate, were in this period more secure than they had been since the Glorious Revolution.

Miscellany Poems, of course, mentions none of this, but subtly and repeatedly reworks a myth of female community initiated by Katherine Philips – and most vigorously and materially enacted by Finch and other women at court with Mary of Modena – into a politically oppositional community of privately pro-Stuart women. The title-page of *Miscellany Poems*, with its factotum of two female nymphs crowning one another with palm and laurel wreaths, emphasizes women's community as a source of female poetic authority. The nymphs look rather like Amazons, their breasts hidden in shadow if not cut off. In contrast, in the factotum drawn for an early Finch manuscript, the female poet is depicted alone, surrounded by arms which have no hands, arms which cut her off from the world around her. Although she is exiled, she looks directly out at the reader – she is a fearless heroic woman, not a nymph.

The warrior woman is similarly translated into the woman poet in Finch's pseudonym Ardelia, a name which comes from Philips's poems about the Society of Friendship between Orinda and Lucasia. In Finch's early manuscripts she calls herself "Areta," suggesting a female version of Ares, Roman god of war; Arethusa, a nymph in the train of the chaste Diana, to whom Mary of Modena was often compared; as well as the Greek word for virtue. Ardelia, in contrast, is the female form of "ardelio," Latin for a meddler or busybody. If Finch's speaker burns ardently with transgressive political desires, those desires are already on the verge of being ironized as the individual woman's private emotional concerns. Whereas early appeals to aristocratic women enabled Finch, like Philips, to imagine a female community and audience for her poetry, she later used her class status to create a female poetic voice that would authorize other women to write as women. That stance required not only submerging the political origins of her early poems, but also silencing her debt to earlier, explicitly political women poets like Aphra Behn.

Finch's Female Poetic Genealogy

In Finch's "The Circuit of Apollo," Apollo surveys Kent looking for a poet he can crown with laurels. He discovers "there that Poets were not very common, / But most that pretended to Verse, were the Women" (Folger MS, 43). The poem then compares the writing of five women, beginning with Aphra Behn and ending with the speaker herself. Of Behn, the only poet to appear in her own name, Finch writes,

> He lamented for Behn o're that place of her birth,
> And said amongst Women was not on the earth
> Her superiour in Fancy, in language, or witt,
> Yet own'd that a little too loosly she writt;
> Since the art of the Muse is to stir up soft thoughts,

Yet to make all hearts beat, without blushes, or faults.

(Folger MS, 43)

Until recently this passage has attracted critical attention primarily for its biographical footnote, which claims that "Mrs. Behn was daughter to a Barber, who formerly lived in Wye, a little market Town ... in Kent."[13] In the context of the poem, however, and the Finch manuscript in which it appears, the description of Behn's writing also suggests the importance of Behn as a poetic source and model for Finch, whose works have more often been compared to those of the chaste and private Katherine Philips than to the bawdy and public Behn. Finch makes it clear in "The Circuit of Apollo" that as a poet she is working against the models of both Philips and Behn, though her debt to Behn (along with her political sympathies) must be publicly submerged. In "The Circuit of Apollo" – the first poem after "The Introduction" in the longest and most authoritative manuscript of Finch's poetry – Finch is working against a tradition in which Philips and Behn represent different models of women's public writing, an ideological construction in which appropriate women's poetry is, like the ideal bourgeois woman, sexually modest and chaste.[14]

Throughout Finch's public career as a poet, she worked within that ideological construction, and that was part of how she maintained the complicated position she had when the Romantics returned to her early in the nineteenth century as an ideal poet of nature. Wordsworth, for instance, singled out Finch, in his 1815 "Essay, Supplementary to the Preface" of *Lyrical Ballads*, as one of the few Augustan poets to use "genuine imagination" in describing "external nature."[15] Much like the truculently angelic Killigrew of Dryden's ode, Finch was for Wordsworth both ideally innocent and oddly threatening, in ways he could not fully articulate. Wordsworth knew Finch's *Miscellany Poems* of 1713 in detail, and he had a "female friend" (probably his sister Dorothy) copy out extracts from a number of them into a volume he gave to Lady Mary Lowther in 1820. In a sonnet written to accompany this manuscript volume, Wordsworth describes himself "rifl[ing] a Parnassian Cave / (But seldom trod) of mildly-gleaming ore; / And cull[ing], from sundry beds, a lucid store / of genuine crystals." Wordsworth finds in Finch's writing authentic sources, or "genuine crystals" of poetic language; and he approves of what he considers her modesty, her "mildly-gleaming ore."[16]

In her 1903 edition of Finch's writing, Myra Reynolds read Wordsworth's attention to Finch's poetry as a sign that Finch began to gain a serious audience in the nineteenth century (lxxv–lxxx). It is more the case that Wordsworth found a kindred spirit in Finch, and used her and her poetry both to create a myth of eighteenth-century poetry and to privilege his own ideal of the relationship between the poet-speaker and nature. As we have seen, Reynolds was not without critical biases of her own, and in several cases completely reworked Finch's poetry for publication. While Wordsworth seems to have been vexed by the question of whether or not Finch was what he called a "Catholic,"[17] and wished to delete Finch's complicated (and, as he dimly sensed, religiously and politically coded) references to other aristocratic women, Reynolds, ground-breaking feminist scholar that she was, was equally unable to read Finch's most ambitious and ambiguous poems, her boldly Augustan lines that often point in many conflicting directions at once.

Returning, in conclusion, to "The Circuit of Apollo," we now have a context to understand Finch's underlying allegiance to Behn in a poem that seems at first to side with Apollo and to see Behn as writing "too loosely." When Apollo compares four living women (who read him their own writing) to the dead Behn, the poem is implicitly searching – in true Augustan fashion – for someone to inherit Behn's poetic crown. After describing her own writing under the pseudonym Ardelia, Finch has Apollo end his search, and the poem breaks off. Then, in the voice of the narrator, Finch reinscribes Behn as poetic precursor and authority by reasserting the relationship between gender, desire, and poetic authority found at the end of Behn's "On Desire. A Pindarick." There Behn claimed that Helen of Troy was not raped by Paris but that she secretly loved him. Behn implies – and from her own position as a politically oppositional poet, Finch affirms – that poems which enact female sexual subjectivity would change not merely the literary conventions of romantic love, but the foundations of the epic tradition.

In Finch's poem, Apollo is about to crown Laura (Mary of Modena) for a paper (not a poem) "Wherein She Orinda ha[d] praised so high, / He own'd itt had reach'd him while yett in the sky." But just as the woman poet – Katherine Philips/Orinda – is about to fuse with the queen as the source of poetic authority, Apollo is "delight[ed]" first by the works of Valeria, then by those of Ardelia herself. While the first two writers – Alinda and Laura – have overpowered Apollo with the forces of reason (the form or "art" of Alinda's verse causes Apollo to "obey" and Laura's paper praising Philips under the name of Orinda makes Apollo "think" her the best), Valeria and Ardelia tempt him as Behn would have, by stirring up "pleasure" and "new delight." Finch claims that Ardelia writes only for her own pleasure:

> Ardelia came last as expecting least praise,
> Who writt for her pleasure and not for the Bays,
> But yett, as occasion, or fancy should sway,

> Wou'd sometimes endeavor to pass a dull day,
> In composing a song, or a Scene of a Play
> Not seeking for Fame, which so little does last,
> That e're we can taste itt, the Pleasure is Past.
> But Apollo reply'd, tho' so careless she seemd,
> Yet the Bays, if her share, would be highly esteemed.
>
> (Folger MS, 44–5)

The poem breaks off here, seeming to give Apollo the last word on Ardelia's desire for public recognition as a poet.

But Finch reinscribes the potentially sexual alliances among women writers with her veiled reference to Behn, and at the same time alludes to the authority of female desires – desires at once sexual and political, set in motion by the female monarch, palpably and even more dangerously potent without that monarch at their center. While the relationship between women's political voice and monarchic authority is displaced onto a variety of private emotional landscapes in Finch's poetry, we can nevertheless see residual tensions, gestures of self-division and self-censorship, as well as the political stakes in her movement towards the hauntingly individual lyric voice for which Wordsworth valued her.

In her repeated – almost ritualistic – gestures of muted political opposition and collective, symbolically feminine emotional inwardness, Finch creates the patterns that will dominate female lyric poetry for the next century and a half: a domestic world that opens out to and fuses with nature; female community as both a retreat from and a threat to the demands and assumptions of compulsory heterosexuality; linguistic difference – in the senses of both negativity and opposition – as an empowering but also potentially suicidal trope for the powers of a markedly female imagination.

Finch's sculpting of both individual poems, as well as the overall shape of *Miscellany Poems*, to submerge political conflict in an explicitly female lyric voice, makes her the first English woman poet in the modern sense of those words. What allows – even requires – this stance? The uncanny crossing of Finch's class status (she was the first woman to publicly sign her works "by a Lady") and her position as a political outsider, a fervent supporter of the lost Stuart cause. We might say that Finch creates both female poetry and the poetry of abjection out of this situation – or, rather more accurately, those tangled subjectivities created the abject female poet out of her.[18] It was for her fierce and loyal inwardness that the Romantics valued and imitated her, and through her dragged the bloody political entrails of women's poetry – however indirectly – back into public view. Finch's poetry, and indeed all of eighteenth-century poetry, is far richer and far more complicated for its debt to earlier, implicitly – and often explicitly – political, women poets. Finch marks both an end and a beginning, turning that political loyalty inward and making it accessible – because now primarily metaphoric – to male and female poets alike.

NOTES

This essay is excerpted from a chapter so entitled in Barash 1996.

1 "The Introduction," Folger MS, 1; line numbers from *Poems*, edited by Reynolds. Though not an adequate edition, Reynolds's is still the most widely available. I am currently completing a scholarly edition of Finch's poems and plays for Oxford University Press.

2 These lines are reminiscent of Behn's description of Monmouth lasciviously leading the dumb crowds (*A Voyage to the Isle of Love* in *Poems on Several Occasions* [London, 1684]); Finch's David is similarly both appealing and dangerous.

3 See, most recently, McGovern 1992: 159–60 and Hinnant 1994: 215–25.

4 I have elsewhere criticized Lonsdale for this truncation; see Barash 1990.

5 The lines follow l. 29 in the Folger MS.

6 In her 1903 edition, Reynolds makes these lines into "The Bird and the Arras" (51). Neither Reynolds's title nor the poem that follows in her edition has any textual authority; "The Bird and the Arras" is, in effect, Reynolds's transcription of the orts remaining from Finch's reworking of "Occasi[o]nal Reflections."

7 See Rostvig (1954) for a description of this tradition in seventeenth-century England; Hinnant describes how Finch draws on the Horatian topos (1994: 136–8); and O'Loughlin, notes that the poet's patron is the center of Horace's circle of political friendship (1978: 89–91).

8 Finch is of course working against numerous other seventeenth-century landscape poems, particularly Marvell's "The Garden."

9 This passage is also an oblique reference to the whole debate around friendship and marriage so crucial to Katherine Philips's poems from Orinda to Lucasia.

10 These lines also echo Dryden's *Killigrew Ode*.

11 Heneage Finch describes the details of publication in a letter to Thomas Brett, dated 28 Oct. 1714: "though she owns itt, to our Friends, and all the Town know her to be the Author of it yett . . . she did not allow itt to be printed with her Name in the Title page" (Bodleian Library MS Eng. Th. c. 25, fol. 99).

12 Messenger (1981) reads the pattern as a crucial strategy for surviving in a competitive market-place.

13 See Jane Jones (1990) for a description of Finch's knowledge of Behn's early life and a correction of earlier errors regarding this passage.

14 See Paula Backscheider's description of how Philips and Behn became culturally opposed "author functions" in the eighteenth century (1993: 74–80).

15 *Poems, in Two Volumes* (1807), 1: 358.

16 This manuscript miscellany was edited by Harold Littledale and published as

Poems and Extracts chosen by William Wordsworth for an album presented to Lady Mary Lowther, Christmas, 1819 (London, 1905); the poem to Lowther appears on p. 1.

17 Wordsworth to Dyce [*c.*19 Apr. 1830], *Letters of William and Dorothy Wordsworth*, ed. G. Alan Hill, 2nd edn, 8 vols (Oxford, 1979–93) 5: 239.

18 I am reading Julia Kristeva's *abject* – her sense of the symbolic identifications between the status of outsider and the feminine – as historical constructs, not ahistorical truths (*Powers of Horror: An Essay in Abjection*, trans. Leon S. Roudiez [New York: Columbia University Press, 1982]). As Judith Butler argues, abjection is a site for resistance, not a site that is already one of resistance (1989: 133–4; 1993: 70–1).

11

The Spirit of Ending in Johnson and Hume

Adam Potkay

> Oftentimes it is hard to decide what choice one should make.
>
> Aristotle, *Nichomachean Ethics*

Samuel Johnson's *Rasselas* ultimately addresses the same philosophical questions broached by the title of David Hume's essay "Of the Immortality of the Soul": what is the soul, and will it, whatever it is, outlast us? The *querelle* that surrounds this question is a familiar one, and we might expect Johnson and Hume to espouse opposing points of view. Yet their opposition is, I dare say, more distinctly apparent to the casual than to the careful reader of their texts. For despite their pat differences, Johnson and Hume's *methods* of exposition – and hence, I will argue, their underlying intentions – actually converge. That is, a similarly conceived ambiguity animates the discussion of the soul in both *Rasselas* and "Of the Immortality of the Soul." Neither text declares itself wholeheartedly for or against the prospect of immortality, much as many readers would be pleased to have them do so.

The locus of ambiguity is the same for the two texts – both avoid making an authoritative statement on the immortality of the soul by refusing to end with any air of authority. Hume's last paragraph and Johnson's final chapter would indeed both seem, *prima facie*, to deviate from or to deconstruct the preceding logic of their works: for Hume ends his attack on the immortality of the soul with a fideistic retort, while Johnson follows his defense of the soul's immortality with a conclusion that is quite adrift. I would like in this essay to reflect on the problems posed by Johnson and Hume's peculiar manner of ending their works. I will bear in mind two related questions: first, is it possible to determine to what extent Johnson or Hume is seriously committed to either confirming or subverting an orthodox faith in the immortality of the soul? And second, assuming that either author possessed even a modicum of high seriousness, how may it be reconciled with the texts' arch inconclusiveness? That is, why do both Johnson and Hume discuss our mortal end in ways that render our sense of an ending uncertain?

The middle section of *Rasselas* focuses on decidedly sublunary concerns, as the young prince Rasselas and company canvas a variety of familiar occupations and professions in search of a stable and rational happiness. What they discover, of course, is that everywhere "happiness ... [is] very much à-la-mortal, finely chequered" (Jane Austen, *Mansfield Park* [1966], 279). Unalloyed contentment is not to be found in life – unless, ironically, it may be found in a life of mortification. For the one "state of life" that Imlac praises to his young wards above all others is the "silent convent" of the monks of St. Anthony (ch. 47).

Imlac conceives the monastic life to be graced by the one expectation that (at least in this life) will not be disappointed: "Their devotion prepares them for another state, and reminds them of its approach, while it fits them for it.... There is a certain task to be performed at an appropriated hour; and their toils are cheerful, because they consider them as acts of piety, by which they are always advancing towards endless felicity." But while Imlac expounds on the virtues of monasticism with an assurance as yet unprecedented in Johnson's tale, Rasselas' attention still wanders: his thoughts are hardly riveted by, as Imlac puts it, "the state of future perfection, to which we all aspire, [where] there will be pleasure without danger, and security without restraint" (*Yale Edition* 16: 164–7). Rasselas remains intent merely on sight-seeing, and it is indeed his somewhat jaded curiosity that brings the party, in the next chapter, to the catacombs outside Cairo.

This, the penultimate chapter of *Rasselas*, is, as W. K. Wimsatt aptly remarks, "the only place [in the tale] where it may be impossible to find a smile" (1968: 129–30). In it, Imlac elaborates the so-called "metaphysical argument" for the immortality of the soul – an argument that can be traced back to the *Phaedo* and to Cicero's *De Senectute*. Imlac argues that the soul must be immortal by maintaining that "whatever perishes, is destroyed by the [dis]solution of its contexture, and separation of its parts" (172). Now the soul has no parts, just as the ideas it forms have none, but must be "indiscerptible," and hence immortal. The following quotation contains Rasselas' initial bafflement at this argument, and his eventual comprehension.

"I know not," said Rasselas, "how to conceive any thing without extension: what is extended must have parts, and you allow, that whatever has parts may be destroyed."

"Consider your own conceptions," replied Imlac, "and the difficulty will be less. You will find substance without extension. An ideal form is no less real than material bulk: yet an ideal form has no extension. It is no less certain, when you think on a pyramid, that your mind possesses the idea of a pyramid, than that the pyramid itself is standing. What space does the idea of a pyramid occupy more than the idea of a grain of corn? or how can either idea suffer laceration? As is the effect such is the cause; as thought is, such is the power that thinks; a power impassive and indiscerptible."

"But the Being," said Nekayah, "whom I fear to name, the Being which made the soul, can destroy it."

"He, surely, can destroy it," answered Imlac, "since, however unperishable, it receives from a superiour nature its power of duration. That it will not perish by any inherent cause of decay, or principle of corruption, may be shown by philosophy; but philosophy can tell no more. That it will not be annihilated by Him that made it, we must humbly learn from higher authority." (173–4)

Robert Walker, while noting Johnson's debt to earlier metaphysicians such as Clarke and Wollaston, calls Imlac's speech "perhaps the most clear and most concise version [of the metaphysical argument] that the eighteenth century produced" (1977: 60). And perhaps the most compelling: Rasselas and Nekayah, at least, are certainly convinced. Duly impressed by Imlac's rational theology, as well as his clinching appeal to "higher authority," they steadfastly determine thereafter to "think only on the choice of eternity" (*Rasselas*, 175).

But it is not only the characters within *Rasselas* who respond to Imlac's wisdom. His discourse on the soul has subsequently been applauded by a long series of readers who believe that it lies at the heart of the tale. This camp of readers tends to claim that the tale is a unified text, generically a conversion narrative or, in Walter Raleigh's phrase, a Christian "apologue."[1] Thus, in a neat symmetry, readers who would conceive of the soul as integral correspondingly choose to read the text as integral. Boswell made such a choice; for him, *Rasselas* is a unified "moral tale" that intends, "by showing the unsatisfactory nature of things temporal, to direct the hopes of man to things eternal" (*Life* 1: 342). Gwin Kolb waxes still more eloquent on the tale's moral: "The wise man ... will accept submissively the essential grimness of life, seek no more lasting felicity than is given by a quiet conscience, and live with an eye on eternity, in which he may perhaps find, through the mercy of God, the complete happiness unattainable of earth" (1951: 700).[2]

The problem with such readings, however, is that they invariably, and counter-intuitively, treat the text as if it ended with the penultimate chapter. For indeed, any reading of *Rasselas* as a religious apologue abuts against the simple fact that the "choice of eternity" isn't given the last word in the text.

In the last chapter, quite famously, "nothing is concluded": Rasselas and Nekayah maintain desires for achieving happiness in this world, however unattainable they may recognize them to be. Nekayah would "found a college of learned women, in which she would preside," and Rasselas "desired a little kingdom, in which he might administer justice in his own person ... but he could never fix the limits of his dominion, and was always adding to the number of his subjects." Similarly, Nekayah's attendant, Pekuah, "wished only to fill [the convent of St. Anthony] with pious maidens, and to be made prioress of the order." The tale ends, rather baldly: "Of these wishes that they had formed they well knew that none could be obtained. They deliberated awhile what was to be done, and resolved, when the inundation should cease, to return to Abissinia" (175–6). However inconclusive this chapter may otherwise be, it quite clearly depicts the characters' distinctly sublunary schemes of happiness.

Moreover, as Paul Fussell maintains, the final wishes of the travelers are "ironic" in that "each wish betrays the secret lust for power over others which, among decent, cultivated people like these, cloaks itself in proclaimed motives of beneficent intention" (1971: 241). Indeed, Rasselas continues to express the same earnest idealism, ethical naiveté, and self-magnifying ambition that he has evidenced all along: he has learned nothing from either Imlac's governmental realism (ch. 8), or from his own briefly sobering examination of "high stations" (chs 24 and 27).[3] The true ironic twist of the last chapter, however, lies in the quiet change of heart that separates Nekayah's promise "to think only on the choice of eternity" from her ensuing wish to administer the rules of an institution wherein one may meditate on eternity. For Nekayah – as for Pekuah – the idea of religious seclusion segues into a fantasy of dominating a place of seclusion. The "choice of eternity" seems fairly forgotten.

Are we therefore to read *Rasselas*' final chapter as undercutting Imlac's metaphysical consolations? Indeed, the tale's end would seem both to ironize the otherworldly sentiments of the penultimate chapter and to highlight their incongruity with the strong and vivid account of our world that fills out the bulk of *Rasselas*. Is Imlac's rational theology, like the similarly rarified professions of the Stoic philosopher whom Rasselas meets earlier in the tale, simply irrelevant to us mere humans? Is Imlac's other-worldliness akin to the professed apathy of the Stoic in being, finally, yet another untenable pretension of Reason? Are the technical cadences of the penultimate chapter only another instance of – to quote Rasselas on the Stoic philosopher – "the emptiness of rhetorical sound, and the inefficacy of polished periods and studied sentences" (76)? And if so, doesn't the reader of *Rasselas* who seeks an assuring moral simply rehearse Rasselas' own doomed search to find assurance? And if such a reader should then recount his own supposed enlightenment, wouldn't we, in assenting to that reading, blindly enact a *mis-en-abyme* of metaphysical error?

Christianizing readers of *Rasselas* tend to avoid these heady questions, or indeed any indications that the tale may finally be an ironic fable. And they certainly may do so without any bad faith. For as Boswell suggests, Christianizing *Rasselas* is of a piece with moralizing the biblical book of Ecclesiastes – and this latter task had, by Boswell's time, a long and familiar lineage. Indeed, when Boswell writes, "This Tale, with all the charms of oriental imagery, and all the force and beauty of which the English language is capable, leads us through the most important scenes of human life, and shews us that this stage of our being is full of 'vanity and vexation of spirit,'" he demonstrates that his sense of *Rasselas* is modeled on his understanding of Ecclesiastes (*Life* 1: 341–2). And, as Thomas R. Preston has more recently shown, the traditional patristic interpretation of Ecclesiastes holds that "the Preacher's futile quest for perfect happiness ... teaches man that he should despise and reject this world to contemplate the world to come" (1969: 274). Preston's own argument, however, is that Johnson actually abided by the "reformed" reading of Ecclesiastes, elaborated by Bishop Simon Patrick, which held that "Ecclesiastes ... is designed to show that after choosing eternity, one can and should then partake of the limited goods of this world" (280). Clearly – though Preston doesn't spell out the connection – this last point might provide a way of reconciling the worldliness of chapter 49 with the transcendent attitudes struck in the catacombs.

Other Christianizing readers have attempted more explicitly to effect this reconciliation. Earl Wasserman argues that by subverting comic closure in *Rasselas'* last chapter, "Johnson has, in effect, rescued the original Christian pattern of the Fortunate Fall from the novelistic secularized version, which he has formally repudiated ... Man does not leave Paradise Hall or the Happy Valley to repossess it securely through the acquisition of Wisdom; he acquires Heaven through the wisdom that the 'choice of eternity,' not the 'choice of life,' is essential" (1975: 25). Alternatively, Robert Walker attempts to maintain the "central" truths of Imlac's discourse by arguing that the final chapter, consisting of wishes that the travelers realize can never be satisfied on earth, effectually advances the so-called "argument from desire" – that is, the popular notion that, in William Wollaston's words, "the *great expectation*, which men have, of continuing to live in another state, *beyond the grave*, has ... been commonly admitted as one proof, that they *shall live*" (1977: 28). Walker concludes that chapter 49 "continues the argument from desire that runs throughout *Rasselas* and thus is a different path but to the same end as the chapter that precedes it" (63).

Clearly, there are grounds on which to advance a Christian reading of

Johnson's tale.[4] The success of any such reading, however, finally lies in how well it can yoke the apparently secular coda of chapter 49 to the theological context of Imlac's discourse on the integrity and imperishability of the soul. There is, of course, a second camp of readers – let us call them the secularists – who are considerably less attentive to that discourse. And, accordingly, they have fashioned a *Rasselas* very different from Boswell's. They see it as the testament of an author who was, somewhat despite himself, a religious skeptic; who possessed, for all his professions to the contrary, "the Enlightenment style."[5]

Richardson's friend Hester Mulso Chapone, who would have been happy to find an apologue in *Rasselas*, was disappointed that Johnson had published "such an ill-contrived, unfinished, unnatural, uninstructive tale" (Hilles 1965: 111). Readers closer to our own day, however, have been rather delighted than irritated with the unintegrated and, in any facilely moral sense, unprofitable nature of the tale. W. K. Wimsatt, who notes the "lumpy or bumpy," "episodic" nature of the text, goes on to praise it as a "descendental exercize" with affinities to the modern literature of the absurd. However much weight we give to its "saving [but 'exceptional'] theological clause in the Catacombs" is finally a matter of taste (115, 129–30). Joseph Wood Krutch is even less sympathetic to the wisdom of Johnson's penultimate chapter. In it, Johnson "pays to orthodoxy, as he always does, the tribute of formal profession. But these formal professions ... constitute only the formal rather than the effective moral." The effective moral is the "tragic sense of life" that accumulates from the discrete episodes of the text. Paying no heed to the episode in the catacombs, Krutch attributes no real sense of closure to *Rasselas*, but observes that the tale "does not so much end as break off"; Johnson "did not know what more to say" (176, 182–3). Paul Fussell, equally apt to ignore the tale's theological momentum, characterizes *Rasselas* as "an accumulation of shining particles," set in the "secular wasteland" (1971: 226–7).

These readings oppose Boswell's ideal of a text that coalesces in glorification of a soul without contexture. To read *Rasselas* as an essentially episodic, open-ended work is necessarily to render Imlac's discourse on the soul a merely formal tribute to orthodoxy, a mere part that can be excerpted without loss. It is as if Johnson had prefaced Imlac's metaphysics with a request to the reader to "either pass over the following chapter altogether or read the whole connectedly," for Johnson's readers seem in fact to have done one or the other. Of course, this request derives not from Johnson but from the outset of Coleridge's twelfth chapter of the *Biographia Literaria* – a chapter in which he proceeds to expound on the thorny topic of the "SUM or I AM" and its necessary relation to "the eternal I AM." As Coleridge immediately adds to his prefatory remarks, "dissevering" a part will disrupt "the organic whole": it is ambiguous if "the whole" in question is simply the chapter at hand or the entire *Biographia* – or, indeed, the self whose transcendental unity Coleridge is about to assert.[6] For in the *Biographia* as in *Rasselas*, to disrupt the organic unity of the text seems to deny the unity of the soul – and vice versa.

Of course, the reader of *Rasselas* who would treat chapter 48 as an alienable portion does not need a Coleridgean bit of advice to do so. Rather, this manner of reading corresponds to what we may call "the Enlightenment style" of writing, which is ever keen to the possibilities of aggregative rather than unified presentation. Indeed, the philosophes seem to have presupposed in much of their writing that the endings of tales or essays are indeed discerptible from the narratives or arguments that precede them. A sense of false endings is variously to be found in Voltaire's poem on the Lisbon earthquake and in *Zadig*; in Hume's "Of Miracles," "Of the Immortality of the Soul," and perhaps the last words of his *Dialogues Concerning Natural Religion*; and in the tag lines of some of Blake's *Songs of Innocence*, particularly "The Chimney Sweeper." Most of these endings are rendered suspect by abruptly evoking an authority absent until that point; in context, the author's appeal to "duty" or "higher authority" rings less like a resolving chord than a discordant note.

The example most pertinent to my discussion is Hume's essay "Of the Immortality of the Soul" (written in 1755). In the body of the essay Hume draws upon Locke and Lucretius to refute sweepingly both metaphysical and moral arguments for the soul's immortality. He quickly dismisses the type of metaphysical argument found in *Rasselas*:

> Metaphysical topics are founded on the supposition that the soul is immaterial, and that it is impossible for thought to belong to a material substance.
>
> But just metaphysics teach us, that the notion of substance is wholly confused and imperfect, and that we have no other idea of any substance than as an aggregate of particular qualities, inhering in an unknown something. Matter, therefore, and spirit are at bottom equally unknown; and we cannot determine what qualities may inhere in the one or in the other.
>
> They likewise teach us, that nothing can be decided *a priori* concerning any cause or effect; and that experience being the only source of our judgments of this nature, we cannot know from any other principle, whether matter, by its structure or arrangement, may not be the cause of thought. Abstract reasonings cannot decide any question of fact or existence. (1985: 591)

Thus, if all we know of matter is "an aggregate of particular qualities," and if the soul for all we know may be material, it follows that the soul may indeed be but an accumulation of particles. As a contexture it will dissolve with the dissolution of the body.

This initial conjecture becomes fairly conclusive in the course of Hume's essay, which presents the immortality of the soul not simply as uncertain, but as rationally untenable. Hume writes, "*physical* arguments from the analogy of nature are strong for the mortality of the soul; and these are really the only philosophical arguments, which ought to be admitted with regard to this question, or indeed any question of fact." These "physical arguments," largely derived from Book III of Lucretius, center on the reciprocity of soul and body: "The weakness of the body and that of the mind in infancy are exactly proportioned; their vigor in manhood; their sympathetic disorder in sickness; their common gradual decay in old age. The step farther seems unavoidable; their common dissolution in death" (596). Annihilation thus emerges as the unavoidable and incontestable end of Hume's logic. Indeed, his penultimate paragraph drily mocks our pretensions to rationally conceive any posthumous fate of the soul. He asks,

> By what arguments or analogies can we prove any state of existence, which no one ever saw, and which no wise resembles any that ever was seen? Who will repose such trust in any pretended philosophy, as to admit upon its testimony the reality of so marvellous a scene? Some new species of logic is requisite for that purpose; and some new faculties of the mind, which may enable us to comprehend that logic. (598)

A strict philosophical empiricism clearly can't abide the soul's immortality.

But the final twist of Hume's essay is that, after his exhaustive reasonings against immortality, he jettisons not the soul but his very method of enquiry. He offers in his final paragraph an orthodox assurance that the soul *is* indiscerptible, tersely concluding, "Nothing could set in a fuller light the infinite obligations, which mankind have to divine revelation; since we find, that no other medium could ascertain this great and important truth" (598). Hume thus appeals to a truth beyond experience. Illumination, he concedes, descends only when the light of sense goes out.

Just about no one, of course, believed that Hume meant what he said. Indeed, readers both sympathetic and antipathetic to an alleged Enlightenment program have generally concurred in not taking his fideistic professions seriously. From eighteenth-century Christian apologists such as Warburton, Hurd, and Campbell through to twentieth-century Humeans such as Norman Kemp Smith and Richard Popkin, most readers agree that Hume's codas tend to be patently ironic; that is, they pay to orthodoxy the tribute of a hollow profession.[7] One may, in effect, dismiss them.

Viewed in this light, "Of the Immortality of the Soul" becomes a particularly well-wrought essay, whose form illustrates its argument: if its fideistic ending is indeed irrelevant and discerptible, then the essay itself provides a neat metaphor for death – specifically, for death understood as what happens when parts won't coalesce. As Lucretius observes, "Death does not put an end to things by annihilating the component particles but by breaking up their conjunction."[8]

The attraction of reading Hume ironically is apparent, especially in our own skeptical age. But are we constrained to do so? Indeed, is Hume's ironic intent as obvious as is often imputed? What happens if we take him at his word? Norman Kemp Smith recognizes that Hume gives his reader the genuine option of doing so. The reader "has still the alternatives before him, either to follow Hume in his thoroughgoing scepticism, or ... to look ... for instruction only in the *via negativa* – a discipline upon which theology ... has itself found reason to insist" (Hume 1947: 75). My own concern is to suggest what might have motivated Hume to *invite*, at least optionally, a sincere fideistic reading.

Johann Georg Hamann, for one, took the Christian fideism of Hume's endings quite seriously; for him, coda is closure, and the soul's immortality secure. Hamann's *Socratic Memorabilia* (1759) evokes Hume's authority in claiming that "faith is not a work of reason and therefore cannot succumb to any attack by reason; because believing happens as little by means of reasons as tasting and seeing."[9] Years later, Hamann wrote to F. H. Jacobi, "I studied Hume just before I wrote my *Socratic Memoirs* and this is the source to which I am indebted for my doctrine of faith."[10] It is doubtful whether Hamann considered Hume a willing ally in fideistic orthodoxy, but finally the question seems not to matter. Certainly, the irrelevance of reason to faith is something Hume's philosophic style allowed Hamann to see. In a letter to Kant dated 1759, Hamann quotes the fideistic coda of Hume's "Of Miracles" at length, and joyfully proclaims, "despite all [Hume's] errors, he is like Saul among the prophets ... one can preach the truth in jest and without knowing or desiring to do so, even if one were the greatest doubter and like the serpent doubted what God said" (R. Smith 1960: 241).

As with readers of *Rasselas*, Hamann's desire to see the soul as integral is accompanied by a faith in the integrity of texts. For Hamann, Hume's essay remains whole, its last paragraph an essential part of its argument. And although we may be tempted to dismiss Hamann's reading as biased, we should first ask ourselves what a truly disinterested reading of this text might possibly be. Indeed, we only take note of Hamann's bias inasmuch as it differs from our own; and inasmuch as it does, it reveals the dubious grounds of our own assumptions concerning Hume. For Hume indeed speaks at the end of his essay like Saul among the prophets, just as Johnson's last words afford him a place among the philosophes' party.

Still, at vexing moments such as these we tend to look to some larger context for clarification; in practice, we usually turn first to biography. But, ironically, the biographies of Johnson and Hume tend to reproduce rather than resolve our dilemma. For Boswell's Johnson, as we all know, was a conservative Anglican apt to appeal on all occasions – and especially on that of his mother's death – to the consolations of a "higher authority"; but we also know, according to Murphy, that as he contemplated "his own approaching end," he was wont to chant the lines from Shakespeare's *Measure for Measure* (3.1), "Ay, but to die and go we know not where; / To lie in cold obstruction and to rot."[11] And Hume, though – as we also know from Boswell – "positive in incredulity" upon his deathbed, nevertheless is reported to have said to an Ayrshire minister, when "in the deepest affliction" for his own mother's death, "Though I threw out my speculations to entertain and employ the learned and metaphysical world, yet in other things I do not think so differently from the rest of mankind as you may imagine."[12]

Hume's biographer Ernest Campbell Mossner notes that many of Hume's Scottish friends received this remark as "the great Infidel's" bashful profession of Christian faith. That they could do so may attest less to Hume's probable intention than to his flagrant ambiguity. His remark can be interpreted in any number of boldly antithetical ways: it can mean, for example, either "I, like you, believe in the Christian testament," or "you, like me, don't really believe." (This latter sense is, incidentally, supported by Hume's deathbed comment to Boswell that no one believes in the Christian religion in the same way as he believes in the Glorious Revolution.) Still – and most importantly – the choice here remains yours, just as it does at the end of his essay on the soul, and as it does at the end of Johnson's *Rasselas*.

In short, judging from texts either by or about them, we have no better reason for reading Hume ironically than for reading Johnson integrally. In *Rasselas* and "Of the Immortality of the Soul," both Johnson and Hume authorize two opposed readings, but sanction neither: and they do so similarly, by concluding their texts twice – which may be the same thing as not concluding at all.[13] By offering two endings of equal authority, both force their readers to decide which ending to choose; any integrity (or splendid disunity) the text may have therefore depends on an act of imputation.

Indeed, both authors write in the spirit of – to use the third earl of Shaftesbury's phrase – the ancient "dialogists" (1964: 1: 129). As Norman Kemp Smith and Peter Gay variously note, Hume owes a signal debt to the type of philosophic dialogue pioneered by Cicero; and the virtue of this form, as Gay remarks, is "to defeat the claims of the absolute," to be "hospitable to the variety of experience" (1966: 172, 176).[14] Meanwhile, readers of *Rasselas* from Boswell to Saintsbury to Harold Bloom have ever been apt to compare Johnson's tale to Ecclesiastes: a work which, from the

eighteenth century onwards, has been identified as something of a philosophic dialogue. Bishop Lowth characterizes the dialectic of Ecclesiastes in
terms of "a person investigating a very difficult question, examining the
arguments on either side, and at length disengaging himself from an anxious
and doubtful disputation."[15] And thus we might just as aptly say of
Johnson's style what Dena Goodman says of Hume's: "the discourse of
Enlightenment allows precisely for the freedom of readers to come to their
own judgments because it allows (indeed, forces) them to choose between
opposing conceptions of truth" (1991–2: 188).

But why does the reader have to choose? Can't she, rather, choose not to
choose? Indeed, isn't the ground for valid choice precisely what's precluded
by the endings of *Rasselas* and "Of the Immortality of the Soul"? Paul de
Man might answer that we are left in a "state of suspended ignorance" – a
condition of uncomfortable (or only secretly delicious) ethical paralysis.[16]
This may indeed be a paralysis devoutly to be wished, merely the negative
stage of a Pyrrhonian dialectic leading to serene indifference. Hume, for
one, suggests such a scenario elsewhere in his writings: since "doubt,
uncertainty, suspence of judgment appear the only result of our most
accurate scrutiny," he suggests that we "happily make our escape into the
calm, though obscure, regions of philosophy" (*The Natural History of Religion*,
76).

But "Of the Immortality of the Soul" does not allow for any such
withdrawal. Here, not to choose *is* to choose. To leave the issue of the
soul's immortality undecided is implicitly to reject the conclusions of rational
enquiry, and thus to accept some version of the fideism entertained in the
essay's ending. *Rasselas* similarly disallows the luxury of indecision. For the
reader of *Rasselas* who would evade choosing has already been written into
the tale in the character of prince Rasselas, who seems never to choose until
the ending transforms his wavering into an apparent choice against eternity.
Thus both texts, while avoiding exhortation, require us willy-nilly to choose.
J. Hillis Miller's "ethics of reading," though offered quite categorically,
certainly holds true here: "ethical judgments ... are unwarranted but they
must follow the reading of the text," as they are "inscribed within the text as
its own failure to read itself" (53–4). In other words, *aporia* does not lead to
apatheia, but rather to an ethical engagement situated in the margins of the
text.

For both Johnson and Hume allegorize in their respective works the
distinction between positive knowledge and active belief. They do so by
giving us ample reason to believe in either (or neither) of their incompatible
endings, and by simultaneously prompting us to choose which of these
endings to endorse – asking us, in effect, which *Rasselas*, or which version
of Hume's essay, we'll ultimately choose to believe in. Thus, choosing to

believe – or (what may amount to the same thing) believing one is choosing – is shown to depend rather on the power of inclination than on any type of logical rigor.

Still, to recognize one's own inclinations for what they are is certainly different, and arguably more beneficial, than merely feeling their imperceptible force. And this, I think, is exactly the recognition that Johnson and Hume invite. For Johnson's literary practice no less than Hume's tends to abrogate the "implicit faith" and "positive bigotry" we unreflectively inherit (the terms are from Hume's *Natural History of Religion*, 60). Both possess a style that sets the dilemma – with all its dilatoriness – against the uninterrupted stream of customary assurance. Both would hinder their readers from leaping too soon to familiar conclusions. And to flounder for even a moment is already an exercise in sympathy. Indeed, inasmuch as Johnson and Hume's double vision may be said to exemplify the liberal value of tolerance, the best choice becomes that which is the most difficult to make.

In conclusion, neither *Rasselas* nor "Of the Immortality of the Soul" quite commits itself to either side of the oppositions we expect texts to conform to: integral or disintegral, religious or secularist, apologetic or critical. The texts are dialogic: they entertain a vision of contraries. Of course, the perils of balanced form are evidenced by each text's ability to accommodate the competing enthusiasms of partisan readers. For if dialogue allows for partisanship, partisanship rarely recognizes dialogue. Thus Hume, in later years, openly cautioned against the *parti pris*. In a late footnote to the *Dialogues Concerning Natural Religion*, he expressed the hope not only that dialogue might soften difference, but that some rigid philosophical oppositions might wither away altogether. He writes, "It seems evident that the dispute between skeptics and dogmatists is entirely verbal, or, at least, regards only the degrees of doubt and assurance which we ought to indulge with regard to all reasoning" (219). Rightfully understood, the dialogism of both Hume and Johnson contests the history of bifurcated readings to which it has not inevitably given rise. *Rasselas* and "Of the Immortality of the Soul" possess a spirit of generosity that appears to have been lost on their more zealous readers.

NOTES

1   That Walter Raleigh was the first critic to call *Rasselas* an "apologue" (in *The English Novel* [1894]) is noted by Edward Tomarken 1989: 13–14.

2   Kolb's recent edition of *Rasselas* (*Yale* 16) effectively suggests the centrality of chapter 48 ("Imlac Discourses on the Nature of the Soul") by weighting it with thirty-one lengthy footnotes that evoke the authority of Clarke, Wollaston,

Richard Bentley, Ralph Cudworth, Sir Thomas Browne, et al. By contrast, four notes are devoted to ch. 49 ("The Conclusion, in Which Nothing is Concluded").

3 For the gradual development of Rasselas' will-to-govern, see ch. 4 (17–18); ch. 8 (32); and, finally, ch. 44, "The Dangerous Prevalence of Imagination," where prince Rasselas confesses that his daydreams of administering "a perfect government" have led him to thoughts of parricide: "I start, when I think with how little anguish I once supposed the death of my father and brothers" (153). Recollection of this line certainly compromises the seeming innocence of Rasselas' final wish for an ever-expanding kingdom – in other words, for a kingdom that increasingly resembles the Abyssinian empire ruled by his father.

4 In an otherwise perceptive essay on *Rasselas*, Nicholas Hudson criticizes Robert Walker's Christianizing reading on the grounds that "there is little specifically Christian about *Rasselas*" (1990: 39, n. 21; and see, generally, 35–6). Certainly, however, the references to revealed religion in chapter 48 are less than cryptic: Imlac's clinching appeal to "higher authority" is prefaced by his earlier opposition between "heathenism" and "our opportunities of clearer knowledge." Moreover, in chapter 12 Imlac narrates having spent three years in Palestine, which he calls "that country whence *our* religion had its beginning" (emphasis mine). And note, finally, that while Imlac's proofs for immortality in chapter 48 are not originally Christian, Imlac offers them only as an admittedly weak supplement to the distinctly Christian devotion of the monks of St. Anthony.

5 As Peter Gay memorably remarked, "Johnson, who detested the philosophes as unprincipled infidels, accepted much of their program: he had the Enlightenment style" (1966: 21).

6 *Biographia Literaria*, ed. George Watson (London: Dent, 1975), 135.

7 Warburton and Hurd noted that Hume's writings on religion, in Ciceronian spirit, take care to avoid public censure for the infidelity they promulgate; see *Remarks on Mr. David Hume's Essay on the Natural History of Religion: Addressed to the Rev. Dr. Warburton* [1757], a new edn (London, 1777), 6–68 ("Remark XIII"). George Campbell, in "A Dissertation on Miracles" (1762), remarked of the fideistic coda of Hume's "Of Miracles," "An author is never so sure of writing unanswerably, as when he writes altogether unintelligibly"; see Hume, *Philosophical Essays, . . . to which is added Campbell's Dissertation . . .*, 2 vols (Philadelphia, 1817), 2: 615. More recently, Norman Kemp Smith, in his edition of Hume's *Dialogues Concerning Natural Religion* (1947), dubs the closing Christian turnabout of the sceptic Philo a "conventionally required proviso" (74). Richard H. Popkin, in his edition of the *Dialogues* and the two posthumously published essays, "Of Suicide" and "Of the Immortality of the Soul" (Indianapolis: Hackett, 1980), maintains more generally, "Hume sprinkled fideistic remarks throughout his writings. His opponents interpreted these remarks as insincere efforts to avoid criticism. My own suspicion is that they were intended to be ironic, to make the reader realize how silly religious belief was" (xv). Still, Popkin goes on to note Hume's unironic influence on Hamann and, through Hamann, Kierkegaard.

8   *On the Nature of the Universe*, trans. R. E. Latham (1951; rpt. Harmondsworth: Penguin, 1970), 89.

9   Ronald Gregor Smith, *J. G. Hamann, 1730–1788: A Study in Christian Existence, with Selections from his Writings* (London: Collins, 1960), 182.

10 Quoted in Terence J. German, *Hamann on Language and Religion* (Oxford: Oxford University Press, 1981), 110. For a concise account of Hamann's debt to Hume, see Philip Merlan, "From Hume to Hamann," *The Personalist 32* (Winter 1951): 11–18.

11 Boswell, of course, links the death of Johnson's mother in January 1759 with the composition of *Rasselas* (*Life*, 1: 341); Robert Walker argues more explicitly that the "death of [Johnson's] mother ... caused [him] to turn ... to the doctrine of immortality, and ... to embody it in the form of a moral apologue" (1977: 5). Arthur Murphy tells the story of Johnson's fear of annihilation in his *Essay on the Life and Genius of Samuel Johnson*; see *Johnsonian Miscellanies* 1: 439.

12 Boswell recounts Hume's deathbed incredulity in "The Account of His Last Interview with David Hume, Esq. " (*Private Papers*, 12: 227–32). Hume's remark to Patrick Boyle of Ayrshire, "at the period when David's mother died," is reproduced in Mossner 1954: 173–4.

13 In general, my sense of Johnson's prose style accords with Hazlitt's: "Dr. Johnson is ... a complete balance-master in the topics of morality ... he never elicits a truth, but he suggests some objection in answer to it" (*Selected Writings*, ed. Ronald Blythe [Harmondsworth: Penguin, 1970], 263). Similarly, for William Vesterman *Rasselas* expresses "the constant need [Johnson] feels to rebel against and unbalance settled and balanced conclusions – even his own – the need to keep from choosing one attitude to the exclusion of others," [1977: 78]). My particular notion that *Rasselas* eschews a stance of univocal authority through "concluding twice, and in opposed ways" draws upon Fredric V. Bogel's excellent reading of Johnson's *Life of Savage* (1990: 7–22).

14 See also Norman Kemp Smith's introduction to Hume's *Dialogues Concerning Natural Religion*, (Hume 1947: 40–1, 60–2).

15 Robert Lowth, *Lectures on the Sacred Poetry of the Hebrews* [1753], trans. G. Gregory, 2 vols (London, 1787), 2: 174. More recently, Elias Bickerman has written that in Ecclesiastes, the speaker's "vision transcends and embraces the opposites of his interpreters" (*Four Strange Books of the Bible* [New York: Schocken, 1967], 153).

16 *Allegories of Reading: Figural Language in Rousseau, Nietzsche, Rilke, and Proust* (New Haven: Yale University Press, 1979), 19. De Man explicitly addresses the question of ethics below: "the term *ethical* designat[es] the structural interference of two distinct value systems. In this sense, ethics has nothing to do with the will (thwarted or free) of a subject, nor *a fortiori*, with a relationship between subjects ... The passage to an ethical tonality does not result from a transcendental imperative but is the referential (and therefore unreliable) version of a linguistic confusion" (206). For an elaboration of de Man's concept of ethics, see J. Hillis Miller, "Reading Unreadability: de Man," in *The Ethics of Reading* (New York: Columbia University Press, 1987), 41–59.

12

Mary Leapor Laughs at the Fathers: Reading "Crumble-Hall"

Donna Landry

Mary Leapor's is in no sense a one-poem *oeuvre*. Although Mary Collier can be said to have written nothing so important or innovative again after *The Woman's Labour*, Mary Leapor's two volumes contain numerous poems of aesthetic interest and accomplishment. Nevertheless, there is a case to be made for her poem *Crumble-Hall* as a representative text whose literary-historical neglect has been unfortunate, if unsurprising. *Crumble-Hall* shows off Leapor's abilities as a comic and satiric writer on an ambitious scale; it represents a significant transformation of the genre of the country-house poem, so crucial in the fabrication and consequent reproduction of a propertied eighteenth-century political consensus; and it effectively condenses many of Leapor's characteristic textual maneuvers, from her strategic appropriation of poetical rhetoric recognizable as Pope's or Swift's or Gay's, to her foregrounding of class and gender as important textual determinants. *Crumble-Hall* is that rare artifact: a class-conscious plebeian country-house poem that undeniably mocks and seeks to demystify the values of the gentry, whose social power in large part depends upon the deference – and the continued exploitable subservience – of servants and laborers. Leapor's poem opens up long-closed doors and back stairways, lets light into the servants' hall, shakes things up in a literary genre that traditionally works by assuring us that the world is best organized according to ancient custom and ceremony. Pope had mocked particular country houses and their owners for failing to fulfill their pact with England's glorious agrarian past; Alastair Fowler cites earlier examples of this critical tendency in the genre (1986). But both Pope and these earlier poets nevertheless seek to preserve the country-house ideal. Leapor leaves us wondering how a literary audience could have tolerated such evidently self-serving exaggeration for so long.

Traditionally, the country-house poem serves as a panegyric to its owners and their way of life. This is as true of its first instance as of its better-known later examples. Recent feminist scholarship has proposed that the English country-house poem was invented by a woman, Aemilia Lanyer, though male poets did not follow her line with it.[1] As Raymond Williams has shown, the representation of a deceptively "natural" landscape and, less often, of a worked and working country, means a disposition of that prospect "according to a point of view," the proprietary point of view: "If we ask, finally, who the genius of the place may be, we find that he is its owner, its proprietor, its improver" (1973: 123). In *The Description of Cooke-ham* from *Salve Devs Rex Ivdaeorum*,[2] Lanyer thanks a female genius of the place, Margaret Clifford, Dowager Countess of Cumberland, "From whose desires did spring this worke of Grace" (l. 12), for commissioning this poem and supporting the poet generously during its composition. The house itself is represented as enabling divine verse – "Where princely Palace will'd me to indite, / The sacred Storie of the Soules delight" (5–6), but most of the poem is devoted to the surrounding grounds and woods, instinct with the presence of Christ and his apostles, including Margaret Clifford herself, and her daughter Anne, Countess of Dorset. This combination of panegyric and devotional verse, with its emphasis on description of the country as a spiritualized green world in which women move freely rather than of the country house, sign of aristocratic honor and legitimation of aristocratic property, tends not to be pursued by later male country-house poets, but such a green world returns emphatically at the end of *Crumble-Hall*.

The flippant tone of much of Leapor's poem, however, marks her difference from Lanyer and from the genre as a whole (with the exception of Marvell's *Upon Appleton House* and particular moments in Pope's *Epistle to Burlington*) at least until Gray's "On Lord Holland's Seat" of 1768. Leapor's *Crumble-Hall* sets out at once to mock the pretensions to grandeur of a gentry class scarcely removed from their servants and laborers in terms of education and culture, and to mock the poetic sycophancy that would write *Crumble-Hall* as a traditional panegyric in spite of these incongruities. To some extent, Leapor's ironic stance as commentator on gentry pretensions prefigures Crabbe's in *The Borough* and in the posthumous tale, *Silford Hall*. In the former, the young attorney Swallow makes crude use of traditional hospitality to stimulate profitable litigation over disputed property (1988, 1: 419–21), while in the latter, the poor schoolmaster's son, Peter Perkin, glimpses the romance of the great world when he is shown the genteel furnishings of Silford Hall – the happiest, most memorable event of his life:

> How vast that Mansion, sure for monarch plann'd,
> The rooms so many, and yet each so grand, –

> Millions of books in one large hall were found,
> And glorious pictures every room around;
> . . . .
>   He told of park and wood, of sun and shade,
> And how the lake below the lawn was made:
> He spake of feasting such as never boy,
> Taught in his school, was fated to enjoy –
> Of ladies' maids as ladies' selves who dress'd,
> And her, his friend, distinguish'd from the rest,
> By grandeur in her look and state that she possess'd.
> He pass'd not one; his grateful mind o'erflow'd
> With sense of all he felt, and they bestow'd.
>   (3: 24, ll. 720–34)

Peter's inflated sense of the happiness made possible by wealth is undercut both by his own naiveté and the kind housekeeper's comments. Like Leapor, Crabbe represents the grandeur of the country house as subtly fractured from within by class antagonisms, but his narratorial perspective remains outside and his tone, unlike Leapor's is distinctly moralizing rather than playful.

The opening of *Crumble-Hall* mockingly anatomizes the reverent traditionalism typical of the country-house poem. Crumble-Hall, we are told, has served as a repository of hospitality since Anglo-Saxon times; it has a noble past; no one has ever left it hungry. Inexorably, we are led to laugh at the sheer conventionality of country-house sentiment, designed to arouse feelings of loyalty throughout the social scale by means of the nostalgic projection of a past of shared wealth and plenty. This conventional summoning of a history of genteel largesse turns into a riot of comically conspicuous consumption that wastes resources in order to satisfy human greed:

> That *Crumble-Hall*, whose hospitable Door
> Has fed the Stranger, and reliev'd the Poor;
> Whose *Gothic* Towers, and whose rusty Spires,
> Where known of old to Knights, and hungry Squires.
> There Powder'd Beef, and Warden-Pies, were found;
> And Pudden dwelt within her spacious Bound:
> Pork, Peas, and Bacon (good old *English* Fare!),
> With tainted Ven'son, and with hunted Hare:
> With humming Beer her Vats were wont to flow,
> And ruddy *Nectar* in her Vaults to glow.
> Here came the Wights, who battled for Renown,
> The sable Frier, and the russet Clown:
> The loaded Tables sent a sav'ry Gale,

> And the brown Bowls were crown'd with simp'ring Ale;
> While the Guests ravag'd on the smoking Store,
> Till their stretch'd Girdles would contain no more.
>   Of this rude Palace might a Poet sing
> From cold *December* to returning Spring
>
>   (13–30)

Throughout the poem there is an ironical movement between the old tropes of country-house praise and less exalted disclosures: the venison is tainted, the vulnerable hare has been hunted to death to provide meat for this already groaning table, the guests gorge themselves until they are grossly bloated. Of such an establishment, the poet writes, it might be possible to sing for – at least three or four months – a bathetic deflation. But this seasonal specificity also implies that a poet might well try to seek shelter during these particularly inhospitable months by singing for supper at the gentry's table. There is something self-mocking about the very inevitability of the country-house poem in a culture in which poor poets are paid to praise their social oppressors. Thus we are alerted to the possibility of socially critical digs, jibes, and disclosures in *Crumble-Hall*.

Sometimes the limitations of a plebeian woman's education can be turned to good use, if what is generated is the very close – and critical – reading of a few inspiring texts. As with Mary Collier's intertextual relation to Stephen Duck, so also with Leapor's Popean intertextuality: the critical appropriation of a poem that seems to express some of the prejudices of the dominant culture can be radically productive. Leapor's imitation of Pope's style in the service of quite different values is particularly concentrated and effective in *Crumble-Hall*. She seizes upon the *Epistle to Burlington*, Pope's most sustained effort in the country-house mode, but goes beyond his criticism of landowning wastefulness and conspicuous consumption, for Pope confines himself to criticizing only the wealthiest and highest ranking landlords. The gentry, the middling sort, and the select few "good stewards" among the aristocracy, such as Pope's friends Burlington[3] and Bathurst, are redeemed, and the country-house ideal upheld. Leapor, while echoing Pope and frequently reminding us of his satirical outbursts in *To Burlington* against such figures of excess as Timon, forces us to reread Pope's poem through the lens of her own, and so to reread it in a different, more democratic and gender-conscious way. Whereas with Pope we must toil up Timon's monumental garden terraces to greet the host:

> My Lord advances with majestic mien,
> Smit with the mighty pleasure, to be seen:
> But soft – by regular appproach – not yet –
> First thro' the length of yon hot Terrace sweat,

> And when up ten steep slopes you've dragged your thighs,
> Just at his Study-door he'll bless your Eyes.
>
> (*Works* 3. 2; ll. 127–32)

with Leapor a sense of cramped quarters and inconvenient architecture predominates; the gentry and squierarchy appear to rule their parish and neighborhood without question, but theirs is a rule far removed from the opulence or national (perhaps prime-ministerial) significance of Timon's villa:

> Shall we proceed? – Yes, if you'll break the Wall:
> If not, return, and tread once more the Hall.
> Up ten Stone Steps now please to drag your Toes,
> And a brick Passage will succeed to those.
> Here the strong Doors were aptly fram'd to hold
> Sir *Wary's* Person, and Sir *Wary's* Gold.
>
> (84–9)

Pope's condemnation of aristocratic self-display on a Timonesque scale may now seem a limited protest, perhaps even an instance of Barthesian inoculation: attack a particularly offensive example of an accepted general practice, and the whole socio-political structure is obscurely strengthened. From Mira's perspective, even Crumble-Hall is a show place, the local center of birth, wealth, and history – figured ironically in the bulky person and fortune of that shrewd self-preservationist, Sir Wary. And Crumble-Hall should rank, in Pope's terms, with those ludicrous buildings impossible to beautify according to the tenets of Burlington's Palladianism; it is, quite literally, Pope's "some patch'd dog-hole ek'd with ends of wall" (31), an unfashionable monument to the gentry's conservatism.[4] For Mira, however, Crumble-Hall, be it ever so humble, represents the site of privilege and class exploitation.

This confrontation takes at least two forms: a critique of the gentry for failing to make use of their privileges in improving ways, and an exposure of the suppressed narratives of traditional high-literary country-house poetry – the servants' "quarter." Pope rails against Timon as a Philistine who possesses an expensive library for the sake of its commodity value; he is a connoisseur of printers and binding, not of the contents of books:

> His Study! with what Authors is it stor'd?
> In Books, not Authors, curious is my Lord;
> To all their dated Backs he turns you round,
> These Aldus printed, those Du Suëil has bound.
> Lo some are Vellom, and the rest as good

For all his Lordship knows, but they are Wood.
For Locke or Milton 'tis in vain to look,
These shelves admit not any modern book.
(133–40)

If Pope's is the sneering protest of the contemporary author who will find
no patron in this rich man, Leapor's exposure of philistinism has a more
radical edge. The issue in *Crumble-Hall* is not fine bindings versus intellectual
enlightenment, but the fact of books being possessed in the greatest quantity
by those who have plenty of leisure, but who do not read them, when there
are others too poor to own many books and without much time for study,
who nevertheless cannot get enough to read. This is the burden of over-
worked Mira's commentary on Biron's library, in which he has the audacity
to sleep. (Leapor, we should recall, possessed all of sixteen or seventeen
volumes to which she could turn in her few moments of "unprofitable
employment," though at Weston Hall there was a substantial library to
which it is most likely she enjoyed some access [Greene 1989: 13].)

> Here *Biron* sleeps, with Books encircled round;
> And him you'd guess a Student most profound.
> Not so – in Form the dusty Volumes stand:
> There's few that wear the Mark of *Biron's* Hand
> (90–3)

This vignette might pass as a not very caustic comment on genteel idleness
if we were not immediately confronted in the poem with a reminder of
Mira's situation within the text and within the social space of Crumble-Hall.
Mira's "place" is not among these neglected books, despite the overt literary
consciousness manifest in the poem "she" is producing. With the library,
we have come to the end of civilization within the house and are now to be
plunged into the servants' quarters, Mira's "proper" domain, however badly
her fingers may itch to inscribe marginalia in Biron's unmarked volumes.
Mira's proper sphere may not be quite the realm of "Old Shoes, and Sheep-
ticks bred in Stacks of Wool; / Grey *Dobbin's* Gears, and Drenching-Horns
enow; / Wheel-spokes – the Irons of a tatter'd Plough" (99–101) – the
furnishings of plebeian georgics in the manner of Duck and Collier. But
neither is she to venture freely into the beautiful prospect that can be only
glimpsed from the cramped, airless rooms at the top of the house, so often
disposed as servants quarters:

> From hence the Muse precipitant is hurl'd,
> And drags down *Mira* to the nether World.
> (107–8)

Mira's proper sphere is the site of domestic production itself within the household, the network of kitchens, pantries, sculleries, outbuildings, cottages, and kitchen gardens that supply Crumble-Hall with produce and labor. The danger in this text is that Mira might get above herself, put on airs, show too much familiarity with the beauty of leisured prospects and the freedom of the countryside: write like a traditional country-house poet, in short. From that possibility, that treacherous attraction to the aestheticizing language of pastoral, Mira's "precipitant" muse is precipitously hurled. The "precipitant" muse is getting ahead of herself, acceding to a pastoral freedom from which she is socially barred. The distinctive status of *Crumble-Hall* depends upon this exclusion, which necessitates a reversal in traditional generic procedure made explicit when Mira announces that she will represent for us the "menial Train" (110), the domestics and fieldworkers of the estate, before the gardens and groves: "Its Groves anon – its People first we sing" (111).

Crumble-Hall gives us forty-two lines of description of the lower orders that populate this "nether World," yet the chief innovation and interest of Leapor's poem do not lie in her supplying, within this self-contained section, what other country-house poems have omitted. Rather, there is a diffusion of the servant's perspective throughout the text that this temporarily exclusive focus on the servants' quarters only encapsulates. The incongruous disclosures that undermine Crumble-Hall's pretensions to awesome gentility earlier in the poem include the spider spinning high above the hall, whose web is safe because it lies beyond the reach of any broom (46–7); the "timeless" heraldic device that needs to be refurbished once a year (48–51); the mice which run safely through passages so dark that no one can see them clearly (52–5); the refusal to elaborate descriptions of the shining china bowls and tapestry that decorate the parlor, when merely noting their existence will suffice (68–71); and the observation that the subject of an historical painting looks distinctly like a member of the lower orders herself – "And, like a Milk-wench, glares the royal Maid" (79). What connects these incongruous disclosures is the perspective from which they emerge: the perspective of the female servant, responsible for cleanliness, sheen, and decorative order in the household. If Timon's Villa were possessed of spiders, mice, and artifacts that required constant tending, a male guest like Pope would not be likely to remark upon them. And more elevated members of the household at Crumble-Hall would most likely dwell not on these "menial" but material questions of domestic maintenance but on the symbolic meaning of objects compelling to gentry families, such as heraldic insignia, with its genealogical significance, and the provenance of valuable collectibles like china, wall-hangings, and oil paintings, features of the house to which Mira alludes but neglects to describe.

Mira's servant's-eye view of this establishment is particularized as a female servant's vantage-point in another way as well: in terms of a psycho-sexual dynamic that inflects the gender-specific division of labor. The entrance hall of Crumble-Hall features old and intricate wood carvings which lend a carnivalesque yet sinister air to the house's history and resonate disturbingly with Leapor's examination of patriarchal despotism in other texts. Her sparing use of the Augustan emphatic triplet, after Dryden, strikes strangely here, giving force to this image of a cruel history of gender and family relations so casually lived with as mere customary decoration:

> Strange Forms above, present themselves to View;
> Some Mouths that grin, some smile, and some that spew.
> Here a soft Maid or Infant seems to cry:
> Here stares a Tyrant, with distorted Eye:
> The Roof – no *Cyclops* e'er could reach so high.
>
> (39–43)

The text rushes breathlessly past this image of domestic tyranny, but there it is. And its significance is amplified by one of Leapor's most complex and problematical vignettes within her description of the house's "menial Train."

Ursula and Roger – a mock-georgic couple, as Margaret Doody notes (1988: 82) – occupy twenty-six vividly satirical lines and so in some sense come to stand in for their employers, who seem relatively unrepresented in the text. Thus Leapor turns the tables on the traditional country-house strategy of celebrating ownership while suppressing labor by leaving it unrepresented. The owners of Crumble-Hall remain indistinctly drawn, but two servants lay out a lower-class version of the domestic drama which we might have expected from such gentry based on Leapor's treatment of upper-class domestic relations elsewhere in her *œuvre*. Indeed Leapor pushes the nonrepresentation of proprietorship so far that Ursula herself appears to have forgotten that she has employers, or that she labors for any master other than her husband Roger. If, with Ursula, we forget the country-house framework in which this passage is embedded, the character seems to be a satire on a prosperous cottager's wife who is a slave to romance, unlike Collier's cottagers living on the verge of poverty and hunger. Ironically, however, Ursula and Roger's prosperity implicitly depends on the country house whose owners Ursula's obsessive focus on her husband occludes. Like the owners of country houses as traditionally represented, Ursula concentrates all drama and ceremony within her immediate domestic situation, to the exclusion of its relations of production. Her putative employers are as tangential to her self-representation as she would be to theirs, if this were a conventional country-house poem. Thus an ironical equivalence is established between property and labor in the country-house domain; each is represented as excluding the other symbolically while remaining materially dependent upon it. Ursula is as trapped by a domestic ideology that foregrounds romance and marriage to the exclusion of other social relations, including her own servitude, as any middle-class mistress capable of forgetting the labor of the servants who make her domestic idyll possible.

Ursula's lament exposes, from the perspective of the laboring classes, the bankruptcy of romantic gender ideology and the wretchedness of a dependent female subjectivity constructed within marriage under the sign of the "helpmate." While her exhausted husband Roger, "o'erstuff'd" with beef, cabbage, and dumplings, sleeps at the table and the dogs bark and howl, Ursula laments her fate until the kettle boils:

> "Ah! *Roger*, Ah!" the mournful Maiden cries:
> "Is wretched *Urs'la* then your Care no more,
> "That, while I sigh, thus you can sleep and snore?
> "Ingrateful *Roger*! wilt thou leave me now?
> "For you these Furrows mark my fading Brow:
> "For you my Pigs resign their Morning Due:
> "My hungry Chickens lose their Meat for you:
> "And, was it not, Ah! was it not for thee,
> "No goodly Pottage would be dress'd by me.
> "For thee these Hands wind up the whirling Jack,
> "Or place the Spit across the sloping Rack.
> "I baste the Mutton with a chearful Heart,
> "Because I know my *Roger* will have Part."
>
> Thus she – But now her Dish-kettle began
> To boil and blubber with the foaming Bran.
> The greasy Apron round her Hips she ties,
> And to each Plate the scalding Clout applies:
> The purging Bath each glowing Dish refines,
> And once again the polish'd Pewter shines.
>
> (137–55)

Ursula gives voice to an important ideological problematic whose resonances persist well into our own historical moment: the question of the "bourgeoisification" of working-class ideals about sexuality, marriage, and the family. For Ursula, domestic labor and household production have ceased to have any meaning apart from the expression of marital devotion they supposedly signify. Unlike Collier's wives, Ursula does not "work," she "sighs" while her husband sleeps, wishing he would wake up and show her some affection. At an historical moment when landed middle-class women were beginning to withdraw from production within the household economy and leaving even domestic tasks increasingly to the care of servants, when farmer's wives were beginning not to manage their stock or their dairies themselves, but to hire dairymaids, and when leisured domesticity itself was beginning to be seen as a sufficient occupation for women who could afford it, Ursula reproduces this identification with leisured domesticity at an ideological level. She thereby trivializes her work – keeping livestock, gardening, cooking, washing-up, housekeeping – by transforming these activities into mere epiphenomena of wifely devotion. The whole structure of employers and servants falls away, leaving only the heterosexual couple. One would think that the gargantuan meals Ursula prepares were destined for Roger's table alone, rather than for the gentry at Crumble-Hall, until the last line of her lament: "Because I know my *Roger* will have Part." In a household economy in which Ursula, and not her mistress, is primarily in charge of the cooking, it is possible for her to ensure that her husband will have "part" of every dish, if only after "the quality" have eaten their fill. Obsessively, Ursula invests in a conjugal romance in which Roger's labor, or his dinner, leaves him apparently too exhausted to participate. The life of physical labor minimizes the deployment of affective energies within the household, according to this satiric scheme; emotional work becomes another form of women's work, radically separated from public activity and confined within the household, only to be devalued there as "mere" domesticity, not something in which working men can be expected to engage.

Whether this domestic dysfunction is meant to be seen as confined to the workers at Crumble-Hall cannot be decided; Leapor's class-specific focus gives us the domestic drama of Ursula and Roger rather than the drama of the house's owners. This is the burden of Leapor's plebeian transformation of the country-house poem. For the gentry's marital difficulties, that more familiar tale, we have numerous other sources for citation in Leapor's work, especially *The Mistaken Lover*. There is thus no reason to assume that Leapor endorses the ideology of romantic-love-in-marriage as unproblematical for upper-class women, while satirizing only its peculiar inappropriateness for women of the laboring classes. The laboring situation of Ursula and Roger does, however, render the contradictions of romantic ideology, and its powerfully imaginary status as ideology, particularly obvious.

The disjunction between Ursula's romantic expectations and the circumstances in which she finds herself as a working man's wife and domestic laborer also dramatizes at a strikingly early historical moment what Michèle Barrett, following Mark Poster, characterizes as "a struggle between the familial ideology of the emergent bourgeoisie and the practices of other classes."[5] Barrett acknowledges Poster's argument that "the bourgeois conception of the family has become dominant – that, in fact, the imposition of the bourgeois family onto the working class is 'one of the unwritten aspects of the political success of bourgeois democracy'" (Barrett, 203–4; Poster, 196), but she maintains a useful distinction between familial ideology and actual working-class practices that Leapor's poem also articulates:

> At an ideological level the bourgeoisie has certainly secured a hegemonic definition of family life: as "naturally" based on close kinship, as properly organized through a male breadwinner with financially dependent wife and children, and as a haven of privacy beyond the public realm of commerce and industry. To a large extent this familial ideology has been accepted by the industrial working class and indeed has proved effective as motivation for male wage labour and the male "family"-wage demand. Yet there is a disjunction between the pervasiveness of this ideology (from about the mid-nineteenth century onwards) and the actual household structure of the proletariat in which it exists. Few working-class households have historically been organized around dependence on a male "breadwinning" wage and the earnings of other family members have usually been essential to maintain the household. . . . Families are enmeshed in and responsive to the ideology of "the family" as well as engaged in reproducing it. . . . The point I am emphasizing here is that we can make a distinction between the construction of gender within *families*, and the social construction of gender within an *ideology of familialism*, and we can conclude that the latter formulation is the more accurate one. (Barrett, 204–6)

Thus a good half century before industrialization makes possible the new "industrial working class," and some decades before the American and French revolutions, we find inscribed in Leapor's text the preconditions for the eventual dominance of bourgeois familial ideology. Frustrated romantic wife and exhausted, perhaps indifferent, husband who loves his creature comforts: the agrarian servants and laborers Ursula and Roger represent the soon-to-be hegemonic contradictions of gender ideology fundamental to the bourgeois family, especially the particular construction of female subjectivity effected by this cultural production. The fact that they seem to be a childless couple might then be read as accentuating the power of familial ideology to interpellate individual subjects at the deepest level of unconscious self-identification, regardless of the "real" circumstances.

These satirical characters may constitute a complex form of ideology critique, but they also exemplify Leapor's skill at appropriating high literary modes of representation. Ursula is drawn as sharply as any of Swift's or Pope's characters, and the last six lines of the passage, her kitchen rites, can stand with Pope's brilliantly squalid mock-epic games in Book II of the *Dunciad* as a parody of Augustan periphrasis in the service of "menial" contemporary materials. Most suggestively, these lines closely follow the last six lines of John Gay's "Thursday: Or, The Spell" (from *The Shepherd's Week*) which stand as an epigraph to this book's introduction. But where Gay gives us Hobnelia's swoon at Lubberkin's return as farce, the gratification of her desire through Lubberkin's willingness to "give her a green gown," to make their liaison public through pregnancy, as low comedy, Leapor represents the consequences of such romantic enthrallment as both bathetic and pathetic. The mock-heroic mode of Ursula's kitchen rites seems meant to restore us to comic stability after the absurd but painfully self-righteous masochism of her lament.

Leapor's satire thus spares neither her own class nor women as complicit with their own oppression. Is it not possible, however, that Leapor's satire here succeeds too well in displacing "responsibility" or agency for ideological interpellation onto these lower-class characters, so that the containers of ideology become the object of satire, and not the ideology itself? Or, to put it another way, does she not end up recycling traditional classist and misogynistic conventions of representation as part of her satiric apparatus? At what point does Leapor's satire cease to be critical of ideology and help perpetuate instead the very stereotypes of class – and gender-specific subjectivity that her texts also work to destabilize or render untenable? If we had some evidence of contemporary critical reception of this poem, such a determination might be easier, but the evidence is not forthcoming. I would suggest that the narrative, or rather the ideological, excess generated by Ursula's lament, in the context of *Crumble-Hall* as an anti-country-house poem, prevents any easy recuperation of this character in the service of such ideological consolidation. We would have to read Ursula and Roger entirely outside the contexts of the poem and Leapor's *oeuvre* to conclude "Servants are just like that!" or "Isn't that just like a woman!" or "How silly of the lower classes to behave in such a way!" To read the vignette out of context might be to construct such a conservatively recuperative reading, but we should remember the country-house conventions in which Ursula and Roger are embedded. As with the proprieties and proprietors of Crumble-Hall, so with its servants, who are neither outside ideology nor uncontaminated by the country-house ethos. If we also keep both class and gender in play as possible textual determinants, and refuse to read the passage outside the larger "text" of Leapor's literary production – the whole apparatus of her self-representation and her patronized presentation to the public – then the evidence for her typically critical stance and frequently demystificatory procedures may encourage us to resist a recuperative reading.

Leapor's demystification of the country household as social institution and as literary trope does not end with her satire on gender ideology, however. The poem concludes with a long-deferred escape into those pastoral groves surrounding Crumble-Hall – a briefly glimpsed alternative, even utopian, domain of leisure and freedom. But even here the landscape exists primarily as a site of conflict; the country house can no longer serve as a locus of social harmony or of harmony between human interests and a more complex ecology. The green world of the grove is no sooner escaped into than it is rent by shrieks, for like so many landlords bent on the "improvement" of an estate, Crumble-Hall's owners are felling their timber, in this case for the minor ostentation of a new parlor:[6]

> But, hark! what Scream the wond'ring Ear invades!
> The *Dryads* howling for their threaten'd Shades:
> Round the dear Grove each Nymph distracted flies
> (Tho' not discover'd but with Poet's Eyes):
> And shall those Shades, where *Philomela's* Strain
> Has oft to Slumber lull'd the hapless Swain;
> Where Turtles us'd to clasp their silken Wings;
> Whose rev'rend Oaks have known a hundred Springs;
> Shall these ignobly from their Roots be torn,
> And perish shameful, as the abject Thorn;
> While the slow Carr bears off their aged Limbs,
> To clear the way for Slopes, and modern Whims;
> Where banish'd Nature leaves a barren Gloom,
> And aukward Art supplies the vacant Room?
> Yet (or the Muse for Vengeance calls in vain)
> The injur'd Nymphs shall haunt the ravag'd Plain:
> Strange Sounds and Forms shall teaze the gloomy Green:
> And Fairy-Elves by *Urs'la* shall be seen:
> Their new-built Parlour shall with Echoes ring:
> And in their Hall shall doleful Crickets sing.
>
> (165–84)

Here Leapor's appropriation of neoclassical tropes with a sapphic tendency takes on new significance in the advocacy of a "green" politics of ecological conservation. The female pastoral idyll that offers at least a partial alternative to the miseries and confinement of marriage is enabled by the very wildness of the forest, as opposed to the worked garden or field. And the forest accommodates the exhausted swain as well; it represents not so much a separatist idyll as a realm of general liberty, of release from social constraints and relief from social oppression. With an intertextual flourish, Leapor reverses the praise that Pope had offered Burlington for his use of the forest in the service of building, commerce, and imperial exploits; for Pope, those who follow Burlington's example as improving stewards of their land are those:

> Whose rising Forests, not for pride or show,
> But future Buildings, future Navies grow:

> Let his plantations stretch from down to down,
> First shade a Country, and then raise a Town.
>   (187–90)

But for Leapor the grove represents the only site of social ventilation on the estate and should not be sacrificed for mere aggrandizement of the country house. "Improvement" and "progress" are thus subjected to ironical scrutiny at the same time that a more natural economy than the present, "improving" one and an ecological consciousness are recommended. *Crumble-Hall* is a country-house poem that advocates the containment, not the expansion, of the country house: its radical removal from the scene may be as yet unthinkable but its demystification is complete.

Of the plebeian female poets of the period, Mary Leapor possesses the most writerly *oeuvre*. Hers is also the body of work most easily assimilable to what we commonly describe today as "radical feminism," with its polemics against patriarchy, male violence, and heterosexist containments of economies of desire. Paradoxically, then, Leapor represents some of the most easily recuperable and some of the most difficult and unexpected possibilities of emergent eighteenth-century feminism. Leapor's contemporary readers would appear not to have read her as radically as some feminist readers may now wish to do. What most delights the traditional literary critic may well prevent him from recognizing what feminist readers might be most interested to discover. That Mary Leapor, a gardener's daughter and a domestic servant, should have had her work published at all, even posthumously, may still seem to us in the late twentieth century little short of miraculous. That too tells us something about the appeal of the unlikely, the curious, the peculiarly marginal, in this period of expanding literary markets. Perhaps Leapor's relative subordination of issues of class consciousness to issues of gender oppression will prove the most easily assimilable aspect of her work; it is also, I would argue, in the US context at least, the least radical, in the strict sense of constituting an uprooting of fixed assumptions, of what is historically and structurally, though differently constituted in different times and places, always already there.

Notes

This essay is excerpted from a chapter entitled "Mary Leapor Laughs at the Fathers" in Landry 1990. Citations of Leapor's verse are from *Poems upon Several Occasions*, 2 vols (London, 1748–51).

1   See *The Feminist Companion to Literature in English* (1990) and the recently begun

series from the Brown University Women Writers Project under the direction of Susanne Woods and Elaine Brennan, *Women Writers in English 1330–1830*. Lanyer does not appear in such otherwise indispensable studies of the genre as George R. Hibbard 1956 and Raymond Williams's *The Country and the City* (1973). See, for a critique of Williams and other marxist writers on the genre, Fowler 1986. See also Heather Dubrow 1979 and, in relation to Pope, Howard Erskine-Hill 1975, esp. 279–317.

2 Aemilia Lanyer, *The Description of Cooke-ham from Salve Devs Rex Invdaeorvm* (London: Printed by Valentine Simmes for Richard Bonian, 1611), Sigs H2ʳ–I1ʳ.

3 For the historical distortions involved in this view of Burlington, see Carole Fabricant 1982: 109–13.

4 The description of the rooms at Weston by Sir George Sitwell in *A Brief History of Weston Hall Northamptonshire and of the Families That Possessed It* (London: privately printed, 1927) suggests that Weston Hall may well have been Leapor's model for the house, but what Leapor satirizes, Sitwell cites as evidence "that some good architect was the designer" (13): "At the southeast corner of the house the ground falls away sharply, thus enabling kitchen and offices to be placed in a basement well lighted from the east. From the kitchen wing, a service passage at the same level led under the small paved court in front of the hall, emerging by a stairway through what is now a china cupboard close to the parlour and drawing-room. The windows, half-sunk in the ground, which light the passage, are of the 1680–90 type, and the order in which 'small beer cellar, bottle house, cellar stair door, folding doors by parlour,' follow each other in the list of 1714, indicate that this was the original planning of the house." My thanks to Richard Greene for bringing this book to my attention.

5 See Barrett 1980: 202, and Mark Poster, *Critical Theory of the Family* (London: Pluto, 1978).

6 Great alterations that sound remarkably reminiscent of Leapor's parlor-building here were made at Weston, though not until 1777, according to Sitwell: "These alterations of 1777 made the house more commodious, but ruined its beauty. A lofty Drawing- or Dining room was gained, with three airy bedchambers of the new fashion. On the other hand, the Great Parlour disappeared, the ceiling in this part being lowered to gain height for the storey above, while the hall was deprived of afternoon sun and of its view over the flower-garden," *A Brief History*, 72.

13

O Lachrymarum Fons: Tears, Poetry, and Desire in Gray

George E. Haggerty

Here rests his head upon the lap of earth
A youth to fortune and to fame unknown.
Fair Science frowned not on his humble birth,
And Melancholy marked him for her own.

Large was his bounty and his soul sincere,
Heaven did a recompence as largely send:
He gave to Misery all he had, a tear,
He gained from Heaven ('twas all he wished) a friend.
(Elegy, Gray 1969; ll. 117–24)

These epitaphic lines from Thomas Gray's "Elegy Written in a Country Churchyard" hint at a series of issues that, I will claim, Gray repeatedly explores in his letters and poetry in his attempt to define his relation to his self, his sexuality, and his relation to the world around him. Any discussion of Gray's sexuality, of course, faces insurmountable problems: although a wide range of biographers and critics have long assumed that Gray's attraction to friends such as Walpole and West and his later infatuation with other young men were erotically charged, there is no keyhole testimony to prove that Gray participated in any transgressive sexual activity.[1] Recent arguments concerning Gray's homosexuality often use "readings" of his work to *prove* the repression of his sexual desire and turn on the question of whether or not his anger and frustration are revealed in his writing.[2] Even though such readings may be irresistibly persuasive, they also raise serious doubts about how the notion of homosexuality is being used and what is being assumed about sexual identities in the eighteenth century. For late twentieth-century assumptions about "sexuality" – that it defines an individual, that it can or should be hidden, that its repression breeds anger, that it creates a subculture – hinder the clarity of many attempts to talk about eighteenth-century figures and their emotions and desires. If same-sex desire is palpable in Gray's writing, as I argue that it is, what needs to be explained is not how this reclusive eighteenth-century figure kept his sexuality hidden, but rather how he could write it so large as to make it indistinguishable from values that were celebrated in the culture at large.[3]

"He gained from Heaven ('twas all he wished) a friend": the melancholy pose that the poet adopts at the close of the elegy, the answer to the poetic dilemma that had baffled earlier attempts to finish the poem, completes the cultural transaction that Gray begins much earlier in his poems and his letters to his friends. This elegiac solution, as it were, is to constitute identity at the moment of loss and to articulate desire in the very terms of its utter inaccessibility, which in this case is represented as the poet's own gravestone.[4]

The term "sexuality" itself had no currency in the eighteenth century;[5] and most historians of sexuality now accept Foucault's much discussed observation that:

> the psychological, psychiatric, medical category of homosexuality was consti-
> tuted from the moment it was categorized – Westphal's famous article of 1870
> on "contrary sexual sensations" can stand as its date of birth – less by a type
> of sensations than by a certain quality of sexual sensibility, a certain way of
> inverting the masculine and feminine in oneself. Homosexuality appeared as
> one of the forms of sexuality when it was transposed from the practice of
> sodomy onto a kind of interior androgyny, a hermaphrodism of the soul. The
> sodomite had been a temporary aberration; the homosexual was now a
> species.[6]

Foucault claims that homosexuality was a late-nineteenth century invention that only a particular intersection of sensibility, sexology, and popular culture could have made possible. In the eighteenth century, however, the scene is not as clear as Foucault's account suggests. Sodomy was, to be sure, a practice rather than an identity, and the sodomite was by no means a fixed species. Still, as cultural historians such as Alan Bray, David Halperin, G. S. Rousseau, and Randolph Trumbach have made clear, male relations were by no means merely as practice-oriented as Foucault's comments suggest, nor did sodomy itself clearly imply any details about who might do what to whom.[7] According to Trumbach, the adult male "mollie" who was exclu-sively attracted to other males only emerged in mid-century, and even then without as clearly delineated an "identity" as some historians have suggested. Be that as it may, a certain sexual sensibility emerges in the eighteenth century that begins to have recognizable contours. When Charles-Victor de

Bonstettin, whom Gray loved with an almost reckless passion in the 1760s, described Gray many years after his death, he spoke of a man with a peculiar "sensibilité."[8] This term did have currency in the eighteenth century, of course, and it is interesting to consider the degree to which the characteristics of sensibility included the earliest conceptualization of the notion of sexuality.

In the mid to late eighteenth century, sensibility is by no means a unitary concept or a simple mode of interpreting experience. By considering the workings of desire within the concept of sensibility, as in Gray's case, it will be possible to suggest a great deal about the dynamics of subjectivity in an age of social flux. It seems to me that the culture of sensibility itself, moreover, suggests the outlines of what Foucault calls "a completely new technology of sex." I have elsewhere tried to show that there is an intimate connection between the discourse of sensibility on the one hand and the exploration and control of bodily functions on the other: how the body becomes an agent of sexual response in its very emotional organization. For the man or, in a very different way, the woman of feeling, a sigh, a tear, the touch of a pulse, or the distribution of a charitable coin can carry with it an unmistakably erotic charge, and each of them becomes, in various circumstances, the carefully articulated substitute for sexual activity itself (Haggerty 1995). To say, then, that Gray is a "man of feeling" must be only the beginning of an exploration of his position as a desiring subject in the age of sensibility. Recent cultural examinations of sensibility itself have largely neglected the question of sexuality, perhaps for the very reason that feeling seems to be an end in itself. I hope to show in this essay that feeling can function culturally to constitute the subject of male-male desire within a melancholic framework of prohibition and loss. If I argue that male-male desire is the open secret of sensibility, that is only to correct what I see as the heterosexist assumptions behind most of the work done in this field.[9] In other words, it seems to me that my attempts to queer sensibility, here and elsewhere, must be placed in this context, in which all attention to same sex desire is at best marginalized.

Foucault's description and other histories of sodomy, in any case, hardly begin to suggest the range of male-male desire before 1870. "Hermaphrodism of the soul," moreover, which Foucault quotes as a contemptible misunderstanding of sexuality, fails to acknowledge the very real process of gender codification that was going on throughout the early modern period of cultural formation, most energetically and at times virulently, of course, in the eighteenth century itself. The very notions of masculine and feminine were sites of cultural conflict throughout the century. As various feminist critics have argued, moreover, only gradually did feminine behavior become the exclusive domain of the female; even less obviously, I would argue, did notions of masculinity become the property of individual males, and not without a great deal of unresolvable conflict about what constituted masculinity and how it could function culturally most effectively.[10]

Masculinity itself, it almost goes without saying, is as much a cultural construct as femininity is. Recent theorists of masculinity, such as Kaja Silverman and Slavoj Zizek, have argued that male subjects are as thoroughly determined by Lacanian "lack" as female subjects and that male subjectivity itself is a site of the struggle of cultural determination most crucial to hegemonic control. In her attempt to read Althusser through Freud and more particularly Lacan, Silverman reopens the concept of "interpellation" to include the notion that the "state apparatus" itself, which for purposes of argument I would here call "culture," is only a "dominant fiction," rather than anything "real."[11] Male-male desire is as much a part of the "dominant fiction" of the eighteenth century as other seemingly more acceptable constructs. As theorists of homosocial desire have made clear, culture has a stake in eroticizing male relations and making women the object in a system of exchange.[12] Restoration and eighteenth-century English literature offers so many examples of male-male desire that it is reasonable to imagine that the spectacle of male love was an essential ingredient in the codification of gender difference that took place at this time.

Among various provisional masculinities that emerged throughout the century, none is more interesting than that of the man of feeling. The seeming feminization of the man of feeling has been seen by some cultural historians to have resulted in the domestication of the male and a harnessing of male aggression and male libido for the good of family life and middle-class morality.[13] The man of feeling in many ways answers the need for a new masculinity in the mid to late eighteenth century: a feminized masculinity could mystify middle-class participation in the virulent phallic aggression of emerging capitalism and hide in the tears of benevolence a preening self-satisfaction at social and intellectual superiority. This superiority, as I argue elsewhere, is often expressed in terms of sexual desire, and novelists of sensibility repeatedly equate the fine rush of feeling with the physiological manifestations of erotic excitement. The ebbs and flows of emotional eroticism might be seen as the harnessing of libertine erotic aggression in the service of an equally male-centered eroticization of the private and domestic. In any case, masculine desire, timid and tearful, becomes the basis of a new kind of middle-class hegemony that reinvests the family with erotic tension and makes social superiority itself a source of erotic self-satisfaction.[14]

An important and usually neglected counterpart of this domestication of male-female relations is an equally pervasive and culturally significant emotionalizing of male-male desire. The melancholy cast to male friendship, familiar in a range of mid-century examples but most apparent in the writings of Gray, crucially redefines the freedoms implicit in earlier codifications of masculinity and masculine prerogative.[15] What this entails can be registered most effectively perhaps by citing the locus classicus for libertine sexual behavior, these few lines from Rochester's "The Disabled *Debauchee*" (1675):

> Nor shall our *Love-fits Cloris* be forgot,
> When each the well-look'd *Link-Boy*, strove t'enjoy,
> And the best Kiss, was the deciding *Lot*,
> Whether the *Boy* fuck'd you, or I the *Boy*.
> (Poems [1984]; ll. 37–40)

The distance from this libertine model to Gray's sensibility, is more than simply temporal. It hints at a cultural shift that reorders the models for masculinity, rejecting libertine license in favor of a model of friendship that the classical tradition had already richly articulated. What Gray does, however, by working the gestures of classical literature into his private friendships is to articulate a kind of male love that challenges the culturally determined notion of "friends." Or does he? After all, Gray dramatizes emotion to give substance to his love, but he also uses that emotion to insist that his desire is (always) already frustrated. He expresses male-male desire, in other words, in terms that the culture not only allows but also requires. The erotics of friendship tie the bonds of cultural organization all the tighter.[16] Far from transgressing cultural norms or confronting an "antisodomitical" culture, I argue, Gray's world of male-male desire is a central element in the dominant fiction of the age.[17] What Gray alludes to in his poems and his letters is transgressive, to be sure. And the love he felt for his friends, if physically expressed and publicly exposed, could have been the cause for hanging. But the physical expression and the public exposure are written into Gray's poetry of feeling, where they tremble with the frustration that they must already imply. Gray's is the love that does dare speak its name, publicly and profusely, at the expense, as Gray's poems make clear, of the love itself. If Gray's poetry is a poetry of loss, then what he loses is the love he everywhere expresses. What is left of course is the feeling, and the self-satisfaction that feeling insures.

Gray and his Eton College friends were timid, intellectual boys who avoided sports and who were "poetical and romantic in temperament" (Ketton-Cremer 1955: 5).[18] They took pride in their mutual intellectual abilities, challenging one another in verse and prose, walking in the fields or sitting for hours reading Horace or Tacitus. These years also must have been full of fun and various forms of mischief. For the letters that appear

just after the boys leave Eton are ecstatically inventive and giddily intellectual. These early letters glow with the privilege that their Eton experience
imbued, and the very language in which they express their love for one
another depends for its depth and its resonances upon the shared experience
of an elitist education. The "secret society" that these boys formed, their
"Quadruple Alliance," has been likened to the "'intelligence communities'
of the mid twentieth-century Oxbridge moles," similarly emerging from the
intellectual enthusiasms of eroticized male relations within a classical tradition (William Epstein 1991: 276). But the secrets that Gray and Walpole
and West shared are the open secrets of the age of sensibility: their letters
do not so much expose as realize the rich complexity of their experience as
men of feeling. In this experience we may trace the origins of (late twentieth-
century) gay sensibility, with its open secrets, its spectacles of confession, its
giddy masquerades, and its moments of deep and painful loss.

Gray's letters to West and Walpole, it is important to remember, were
subjected to the editorial abuse of both Mason and Walpole, who combined
letters, rewrote passages, and excised entire sections that were "infantine,"
according to Walpole, and "hardly fit for schoolboys" (Gray, *Correspondence*
1: 1, n. 2). Even in the letters that do survive, however, certain passages
might cause more than an eyebrow to be raised. When Gray addresses
Walpole as "mie Nuss [nurse] att London," for instance, speaks of "your
kind promise of coming to tend me yourself," and signs himself Walpole's
"ever-dutifull & most obedient & most affectionate, loving God-daughter,
PRU"; or when he chides Walpole, "when you could give me so much
Pleasure, absent; what must you do, when with me? tho' perhaps its policy
in you to stay away so long, that you may increase my Desire of seeing
you"; it only confirms the educated speculation that these friendships are
rich in the dynamics of eroticism (*Correspondence* 1: 5–6, 8).[19] "Miss Gray,"
as his fellow pensioners called him, wrote exhilarating letters that are
effusively poetic and aggressively emotional.[20] To Walpole, he is zany and
irresistible; to West, he is thoughtful and sublime; but to both he can be an
amazingly attentive and loving friend. In his letters and in his poetry, he
celebrates them both as objects of desire and as objects, inevitably, of loss.[21]

In the terms of the Quadruple Alliance, Gray is Orozmades, the Zoroas-
trian divinity, who is mentioned in Lee's *The Rival Queens* as a "dreadful god"
who from his cave issues groans and shrieks to predict the fall of Babylon
(Gray, *Correspondence* 1: 6).[22] Walpole is usually addressed as Celadon, the
amorous shepherd in Durfé's *Astrée*. In one early letter, Gray plays with
these roles:

> From purling Streams & the Elysian Scene,
> From Groves, that smile with never-fading Green

> I reascend; in Atropos' despight
> Restored to Celadon, & upper light:
> Ye gods, that sway the Regions under ground,
> Reveal to mortal View your realms profound;
> At his command admit the eye of Day;
> When Celadon commands, what God can disobey?
>
> (*Correspondence* 1: 9; ll. 1–8)[23]

One of Gray's earliest poems, this fantasy on the power of friendship, this vision of transcendence by means of his devotion to another suggests the terms of Gray's private fantasy: here are the Edenic groves that return in the "Eton College" ode and the "upper light" of poetic imagination. But, importantly for Gray, that light is shared with a friend and is in fact impossible without the friend as an inspiration. Walpole is the light that will reveal the underground realms of the brooding Orozmades and transform the gloomy genius into a bird in flight:

> That little, naked, melancholy thing
> My Soul, when first she tryed her flight to wing;
> Began with speed new Regions to explore,
> And blunder'd thro' a narrow Postern door;
>
> (12–16)

Could Gray be alluding to a sodomitical sexual awakening here? Could his "little, naked, melancholy thing" refer to the adolescent penis that Walpole may have taught to "reascend" within the intimacy of friendship? Could the exploration of "Realms profound" that Celadon commands be a journey into the physical? It may seem speculative or even a mere insinuation to answer yes to these interpretive possibilities, but later the poem takes a turn that makes them much more likely, as the terms of the relation between the poet and his muse becomes explicit:

> Believe, that never was so faithful found
> Queen Proserpine to Pluto under ground,
> Or Cleopatra to her Marc-Antony
> As Orozmades to his Celadony.
>
> (38–41)

At another moment, after reading *The Turkish Spy*, Gray utters effusively, "When the Dew of the morning is upon me, thy Image is before mine eyes; nor, when the night overshadoweth me, dost thou depart from me.... I have beheld thee in my Slumbers, I have attempted to seize on thee, I sought for thee & behold! thou wert not there! ... thou art sweet in my thoughts as the Pine-apple of Damascus to the tast; & more refreshing, than the fragrant Breezes of Idumea.... Be thou unto me, as Mohammed to Ajesha [his wife]; as the Bowers of Admoim to those, whom the Sun hath overtaken; or as the costly Sherbets of Stamboul to the thirsty" (*Correspondence* 1:14–15).[24] The extent of the physical exuberance of this letter is unmatched and its emphasis on the promptings of desire is unmistakable. If this is not a love-letter to Walpole, it is difficult to imagine what it is. Of course, no one can assign a specific meaning to these verbal antics, as far-flung and parodic as they are. In Gray's work they represent the tantalizing possibility of fulfillment, the giddy hope that his feelings are returned, the physical assurance that desire can be realized through the senses and not just nurtured in the imagination.

After Gray's much discussed quarrel with Walpole on their Tour of Europe, this celebratory mood of friendship takes a melancholy cast. Gray's attention turns to Richard West, the Favonius (west-wind, and sometimes Zephyrille) of Eton, who may be said to have inspired this mood. West was an almost angelic presence in Gray's life, "tall and slender, thin-faced and pale-complexioned," brilliant but troubled; he was a sensitive and, as Gray later calls him, a "loving" boy who inspired some of Gray's most moving poetry (Ketton-Cremer 1955: 5).[25] In a letter Gray wrote to West in Latin (in 1738), which included an ode on West's beginning the study of law, he appended a single stanza, Lucretian in tone and form, that has been justly celebrated for its haunting beauty:

> O lachrymarum fons, tenero sacros
> Ducentium ortus ex animo; quater
>   Felix! in imo qui scatentem
>   Pectore te, pia Nympha, sensit.
> O fount of tears, that draw their sacred sources from the tender
> mind; four times happy is he who has felt you, holy Nymph,
> gushing forth from the depth of his heart.
>
>   (*Correspondence* 1: 87)[26]

With a personification as bizarre as anything in Collins, Gray articulates his attraction to his tearful friend in startling terms. The font of tears itself is sacred, springing as it does from the "tender mind," the seat of emotions of the man of feeling. This could be himself, of course, or the friend to whom he addresses the letter. The confusion of identities to a certain extent memorializes the love he is describing. The suggestion of physical intimacy in the feeling and in the happiness with which he experiences the bodily sensation of emotion is almost seductively blurred, so that the "holy Nymph" – "pia nympha" – who colors this moment of self-realization with a female presence could come to represent the emotional and physical bond between them. Happiness in a feeling that gushes forth from the heart cannot be fully divorced from the mechanics of sexual response, nor can this ecstatic address, both to himself and to his friend, suggest much less than an act of physical intimacy.[27] Desire here is constituted not only in West's poetic presence, but also in the absence that a letter implies. Like other men of feeling, Gray eroticizes emotional distance as a way of understanding the melancholy with which he knows he has been marked, and he takes pleasure in the symptom *(sinthome?)*, the tears that both commemorate and define this moment of intimacy.[28]

Another Latin poem "Ad C. Favonium Zephyrinum," sent to West from Rome, begins: "Mother of roses, for whom the gentle breezes of Favonius rise, and whose companion is pleasure-loving Venus, honoured in the dances of the Nymphs and the songs of the birds!"[29] If this is Gray's "Ode to the West-wind," it shimmers with the tactile emotions through which Gray has learned to express the complexities of his love. Roses, Venus, the dance of Nymphs, bird-song, and of course the gentle breezes of Favonius: this is Gray's erotic universe, as rich and enticing as anything in Keats or Shelley, and equally inaccessible. In the poem Gray talks about the distance between the two friends: this is now merely a physical distance, but he almost seems to understand that it will become the distance of time and memory as well. For it is finally time and memory that lock the poet in the pose that in these Latin poems he only begins to reveal: the pose of the isolated, melancholic poet of loss. When Gray finds the voice of love in this recognition of loss, his cultural transaction is complete.[30]

West's death in the late spring of 1742 affected Gray deeply. The poems he wrote that summer, both the "Ode on a Distant Prospect of Eton College" and the "Sonnet [on the Death of Richard West]," as well as the "Ode to Adversity" can all be considered testaments of his love for his friend. These poems establish Gray's position as the melancholy poet, the man isolated in his own desire at the same time that his desire is realized in melancholy itself. "Eton College," for instance, states:

> Ah, happy hills, ah, pleasing shade,
> Ah, fields beloved in vain,
> Where once my careless childhood strayed,
> A stranger yet to pain!
> I feel the gales, that from ye blow,
> A momentary bliss bestow,
> As waving fresh their gladsome wing,
> My weary soul they seem to soothe,

And, redolent of joy and youth,
To breathe a second spring.

(11–20)

This poem that so uniquely celebrates the vulnerability of childhood and
looks with forbidden desire on the world of personal memory manages, I
would argue, with its single syllable "Ah" to change the course of English
poetry.[31] The force of this monosyllable is to introduce private feeling of a
very special kind into poetry. This is the "Ah" of fond reminiscence, the
"Ah" of memory and loss, the "Ah" of friendship and youth, the "Ah" of
pure and simple emotion. But to borrow a phrase from Oscar Wilde,
emotion is never pure and rarely simple. For Gray, emotion and desire are
at times indistinguishable. "Ah," after all, can represent fulfilled as well as
frustrated desire.[32]

If friendship and youth are, like the field of Eton, "beloved in vain," they
call to mind the sonnet in which Gray lamented the loss of his emotional
companion, Richard West:

> In vain to me the smiling mornings shine,
> And reddening Phoebus lifts his golden fire:
> The birds in vain their amorous descant join,
> Or cheerful fields resume their green attire:
> These ears, alas! for other notes repine,
> A different object do these eyes require.
> My lonely anguish melts no heart but mine;
> And in my breast the imperfect joys expire.
> Yet morning smiles the busy race to cheer,
> And new-born pleasure brings to happier men:
> The fields to all their wonted tribute bear;
> To warm their little loves the birds complain.
> I fruitless mourn to him that cannot hear,
> And weep the more because I weep in vain.

These lines allude to a tradition of elegiac verse that is rich in its ability to
express loss. Loss of course is what is being expressed here: the blank and
the frustrations of loss. As Lonsdale points out, "the poet is mourning the
only friend that could have understood and shared such a grief" (*Poems*, 67).

I have elsewhere offered a reading of this poem that suggests that its
"homoplatonism" – the term is G. S. Rousseau's – works to refigure as
elegiac loss what for Gray is actual physical longing and frustrated physical
desire. As I say there, it can hardly be an accident that Gray chose as his
model a Petrarchan love sonnet or that many of his images can be traced to
a range of love poetry from Virgil and Ovid to Thomson. The octave

expresses a distinctly physical longing that is no longer available – "In vain to me the smiling mornings shine" (note that "me" is the object of loss here rather than its subject), and the sestet answers by developing this contrast. By mourning to West (rather than for him), Gray underlines the personal quality of the loss – just what it means to him – and explains the loop of grief which the last line expresses. With West finally out of reach, at the end of the poem Gray withdraws – as the man of feeling must – into the privacy of his own misery. "I . . . weep the more because I weep in vain": Gray must stop short of breaking through the language of grief to something (or someone) outside himself. "I" is the source of grief, that is, rather than "he" or "you."[33] Grief becomes the substitute for the friend and offers protection against the implications of desire. But at the same time it commemorates that desire, and perhaps its fulfillment, in conventional imagery that hides its personal intensity. Every line reveals as much as it conceals, and poetry itself, decorous and allusive, becomes the vehicle for private longing. Gray's melancholy stems from the failure of the elegy to lead him to an encounter with anything more than his own private emotion. "Friendship" involves an internal contradiction and self-confrontation that West's death now make inevitable.[34]

In "Mourning and Melancholia," Freud talks about the elaborate contours of grief and suggests that "it is really only because we know so well how to explain it that this attitude does not seem to us pathological." Gray's grief in this poem would seem pathological as well, if we did not know that the man of feeling is constituted by loss. Freud says that "melancholia is in some way related to an unconscious loss of a love-object, in contradistinction to mourning, in which there is nothing unconscious about the loss."[35] Gray is conscious of the loss he mourns but unconscious (perhaps) that in losing West he has lost himself as well. This is the basis of his melancholy, and in the poems of 1742 he discovers his poetic voice in this dynamic of despair.

This dynamic has broader cultural implications than my discussion of Gray might suggest. Other critics have begun to see the outlines of the twentieth-century closet in the literature of sensibility and have suggested that a mode of secrecy is essential to the construction of bourgeois subjectivity in the later eighteenth century.[36] Gray's melancholic pose seems to me to offer another vantage point on the shimmering edifice of twentieth-century sexual secrecy. To commemorate desire as loss is to begin the construction of a more viable closet, the one into which culture can place the man-loving-man or woman-loving-woman, whether or not he or she chooses to stay there. Eve Kosofsky Sedgwick has theorized the closet most persuasively in terms of the later nineteenth and early twentieth centuries. The history of the closet that she describes must go back to this act of accommodation that Gray and other writers of sensibility make with their culture, this act of self-realization in the lonely pose of melancholy. Sedgwick says that "same-sex desire is still structured by its distinctive public/private status, at once marginal and central, as *the* open secret."[37] Gray understands implicitly how this mechanism works, and his attempts to articulate desire in loss create a closet-like structure from which he can utter his devastating pronouncements without the risk of public exposure. Sedgwick says that "cognition itself, sexuality itself, and transgression itself have always been ready in Western culture to be magnetized into an unyielding though not an unfissured alignment with one another." Sedgwick says that in some eighteenth-century texts, "the desire that represents sexuality per se, and hence sexual knowledge and knowledge per se, is a same-sex desire. This possibility, however, was repressed with increasing energy, and hence increasing visibility, as the nineteenth-century culture of the individual proceeded to elaborate a version of knowledge/sexuality increasingly structured by its pointed cognitive *refusal* of sexuality between women, between men" (Sedgwick 1990: 73). What I am arguing here is not an eighteenth-century freedom of expression that is repressed by Victorian squeamishness at same-sex desire. Rather, I would argue, the expression of same-sex desire – in Gray, in other writers of sensibility, in Gothic fiction, in the literature of female friendship – always constitutes desire within a closet-like framework that couches desire itself in terms – melancholy, madness, sensation, platonic love – that culture provides for the purposes of naturalization and accommodation. Even in the eighteenth century, that is, there is no same-sex desire without the public/private structure of the open secret, the open secret that both celebrates the variety of same sex desire and hides its meaning within the very language with which it is expressed.

One final poem from the summer of 1742 brings Gray's position into clearer focus. As expressive and moving as either the "Sonnet" or the "Ode" is the much less discussed Latin elegy that Gray appended to his "De Principiis Cogitandi," the first Book of which was dedicated "AD FAVONIUM."[38] The thirty lines of Book 2, which I cite in their entirety because I imagine they are unfamiliar to many readers, can be translated as follows:

> So far had I, interpreter of the Muses, assiduously uncovered the secrets of Nature and first led a lucid stream from the Roman river through British fields. But now you (Tu), the inspiration and cause of so great a task, have departed in the midst of it and have hidden yourself in the eternal shadow of Death! I myself watched your breast cruelly racked by cruel suffering, a breast never slow to respond to another's pain; I watched your eyes grow dull and

your loving face grow pale, a face in which only the most exalted affection, and loyalty, and deep love of truth, and unsullied integrity were alive. Still the harshness of your lingering sickness seemed to be abating, and I hoped for the return of Health, with rosy cheeks, and you yourself with it, my dear Favonius! Foolishly trusting, alas, that we might while away the long, sunny days as before. Alas, the hopes, vainly sweet, and the futile prayers! Alas, the sunny days, now spent in mourning, which I am forced to pass without you, in weeping because you are not there, and in vain complaints![39]

It would be difficult to imagine a more poignant or a more pointed elegy. The eloquence of Gray's devotion to West – West the physical as well as the spiritual friend – and of his frustration and his desire makes even the "Sonnet" pale by comparison. The poet's desire is realized in this loss and made real in the language that echoes "the vain complaints" of the sonnet. Here, however, the poet more directly embraces his dead friend with the tears of grief and offers them in a gesture of love that is fulfilled in this moment of frustrated desire. "Alas," the term that colors so much of Gray's poetry with regret, here has a particular meaning in the loss of this friend. It is almost as if Gray finds himself in this moment of regret, realizes his own poetic capabilities in this moment of loss. Bentman says that the "picture that emerges of Gray from the letters is of a deeply passionate man who was powerfully constrained by his fear" (209). This is an attractive reading, to be sure, but it seems to me that regret is far more palpable than fear throughout Gray's work. I would argue that Gray eroticizes the regret itself in this poetry of loss, not because he is afraid of expressing his sodomitical desires, but because he knows that his love has cultural meaning only in loss.

In the second stanza, he turns to his dead friend, as he does in the sonnet, and admits, as clearly as he does anywhere, the torment of desire, not because West is a man but because he is Other – inaccessible, unrealizable, lost:

But you, blessed spirit, who do not need my grief, rejoice in the starry circuit of the heavens and the fire of pure ether whence you sprang. But, if, released from cares as you are, and no longer mortal, you should look back with pity on the labors which you yourself once suffered and have the time to acknowledge my trivial anxieties; if, by chance, you should look down from your lofty seat on the storm of human passion, the fears, the fierce promptings of desire, the joys and sorrows and the tumult of rage so huge in my heart, the furious surges of the breast; then look back on these tears, also, which stricken with love, I pour out in memory of you; this is all I can do, while my only wish is to mourn at your tomb and address these empty words to your silent ashes. (*Poems*, 328; translation [adapted], 332)

The tears that Gray pours out at the tomb of his friend are the tears of sensibility that identify love and loss in modern culture. They are the tears that open the possibility of a sexual identity that emerges from the soul (rather than from behavior). They are the tears of accommodation that culture provides to those who feel.

> O lachrymarum fons, tenero sacros
> Ducentium ortus ex animo; quater
> Felix! in imo qui scatentem
> Pectore te, pia Nympha, sensit!

"Four times happy is he who has felt you, holy Nymph, gushing forth from the depth of his heart": tears, poetry, and desire – for Gray the three are inextricable. Gray does not fear a system of cultural oppression that might expose him because he exposes himself as the melancholy figure of male-male desire. Gray does not have to create this position for himself, for culture is all too happy to provide it for him. Just as in the late twentieth century gay people have been recognized only in their mourning, so in the eighteenth century male love is recognized only in the tears of sensibility.

NOTES

1   Gray's middle-aged infatuation with Charles-Victor de Bonstettin, a young Swiss gentleman who loved Gray's poetry and found his way to Cambridge to study, is well documented. The most interesting discussion of Gray's relations with Bonstettin remains that to be found in Jean Hagstrum, "Gray's Sensibility" (1974).

2   Among the critics who have addressed Gray's sexuality are: R. W. Ketton-Cremer (1955); Hagstrum (1974); G. S. Rousseau (1985); Raymond Bentman (1992); George E. Haggerty (1992).

3   For an interesting account of the "Elegy" in eighteenth-century culture, see Guillory 1993.

4   For more about the representation of desire in the *Elegy*, see Haggerty 1992.

5   The *OED* first recorded use of the term occurs in 1800; significantly it is a poet of sensibility, Cowper, who is first cited as using the term in describing male and female qualities of plants (*OED*, s.v. "sexuality").

6   Michel Foucault, *The History of Sexuality, Volume I: An Introduction*, trans. Robert Hurley (New York: Vintage-Random House, 1980), 43; see also David M. Halperin, *One Hundred Years of Homosexuality and Other Essays on Greek Love* (New York: Routledge, 1990), esp. 26–7, and n. 52.

7   See, for instance, Alan Bray, *Homosexuality in Renaissance England* (London: Gay Men's Press, 1982), ch. 4; Halperin, *One Hundred Years of Homosexuality*, ch. 1; Rousseau 1985; Trumbach 1977, 1989. Records of sodomy trials show a very

broad legal and popular understanding of the term; see *Sodomy Trials*, ed. Randolph Trumbach (New York: Garland, 1986). For an overview of such questions, see McKeon 1995.

8   "Gray avait la gaieté dans l'ésprit et de la mélancholie dans le caractère. Mais cette mélancholie n'est qu'un besoin non-satisfait de la sensibilité," (Bonstettin, *Souvenirs* [1831], quoted in Ketton-Cremer 1955: 253); see also Hagstrum 1974: 7–11.

9   Obvious exceptions include the work of Julia Epstein, Jean Hagstrum, Robert Markley, G. S. Rousseau, and Kristina Straub.

10 See Poovey 1984; see also, Armstrong 1987; and McKeon 1995.

11 Silverman also argues, with the help of Lacan and other French theorists such as Laplanche and Pontalis, that the dominant fiction is in any case more real than any details of concrete reality. I think that it is helpful to consider how dominant fictions are created through processes that the writers of fiction, by which I include novelists, poets, and historians, implicitly understand. That is why the cultural resonances of certain fictional constructs offer a way of understanding more clearly the role of masculinity in eighteenth-century culture. (Kaja Silverman, *Male Subjectivity at the Margins* [New York: Routledge, 1992], 15–51; see also, Slavoj Zizek, *The Sublime Object of Ideology* [London: Verso, 1989], 153–200).

12 See, for instance, Eve Kosofsky Sedgwick, *Between Men: English Literature and Male Homosocial Desire* (New York: Columbia University Press, 1985).

13 See, for instance, Armstrong 1987: 48–58.

14 See Haggerty 1995, especially 140–1; other recent discussions of the man of feeling include: Barker-Benfield 1992; Frank 1989; and Mullan 1988.

15 For an account of gender difference in the late-seventeenth and early-eighteenth centuries, see McKeon 1995: 309–12.

16 "Lusit amicitiae interdum velatus amictu, / et bene composita veste fefellit Amor," Gray wrote to West translating an Italian poem into Latin: "Sometimes Love jested, concealed in the cloak of friendship, and disguised himself in seemly attire"; see *Poems* 1976: 316.

17 The phrase is from Raymond Bentman 1992: 203; although this is the best of recent articles on Gray, and inspiring in many ways, I hope to place male-male desire differently in eighteenth-century culture.

18 See also, Jacob Bryant, a contemporary of Gray's at Eton who, writing in 1798, remarks that "both Mr. Gray and his friend [Walpole] were looked upon as too delicate, upon which account they had few associates, and never engaged in any exercise, nor partook of any boyish amusement. Hence they seldom were in the fields, at least they took only a distant view of those who pursued their different diversions. Some, therefore, who were severe, treated them as feminine characters, on account of their too great delicacy, and sometimes a too fastidious behaviour" (*The Gentleman's Magazine* 25 [new Series (1846)], 140–3, quoted in *Poems*, 54–5).

19 Critics such as Hagstrum (1974), Bentman, and William Epstein, all find a dazzling array of similarly suggestive material in the letters. It is important to

remember that even in their edited form these letters were considered model in the eighteenth century. See William Epstein 1991: 278.

20   For the reference to "Miss Gray," see Sells 1980: 18.

21   The best reading of Gray's letters to West and Walpole occurs in Bentman 1992: 204–9; Bentman helpfully compares the quality of emotion in Gray's letters to West and Walpole to that in other letters between male friends. Zizek discusses Lacanian "lack" in terms that support this analysis of desire as loss: "What the object [of desire] is masking, dissimulating, by its massive, fascinating presence, is not some other positivity but *its own place*, the void, the lack that it is filling in by its presence – the lack in the Other. And what Lacan calls 'going-through the fantasy' consists precisely in the experience of such an inversion apropos of the fantasy-object: the subject must undergo the experience of how the ever-lacking object-cause of desire is in itself nothing but an objectivication, an embodiment of a certain lack; of how its fascinating presence is here just to mask the emptiness of the place it occupies, the emptiness which is exactly the lack in the Other-which makes the big Other (the symbolic order) perforated, inconsistent" (195).

22   Nathaniel Lee, *The Rival Queens. or the Death of Alexander the Great*, ed. P. F. Vernon (Lincoln: University of Nebraska Press, 1970), 38; ll. 174–85.

23   Walpole says about these lines that "One of his [Gray's] first pieces of poetry was an answer in English verse to an epistle from H. W." Lonsdale prints this as the first poem, *Poems*, 13–17.

24   For a discussion of this passage, see Hagstrum, 1974: 15; see also, Bentman 1992: 204–5; and William Epstein 1991: 278–9. Epstein notes the "epistolary ploy of Gray's assuming an alternative identity in order to write about himself."

25   For "loving," see the discussion of *De Principiis Cogitandi*, below.

26   The translation is adapted from *Poems*, 308.

27   In the "Metaphysic poem," "De Principiis Cogitandi," which Gray addressed to West in 1740 or 1741, he begins his discussion of the principles of thinking with "touch"; see *Poems*, 321–32; see also Hagstrum 1974: 13.

28   Lacan's *sinthome* is "a neologism containing a set of associations (synthetic-artificial man, synthesis between symptom and fantasy, Saint Thomas, the saint). Symptom as *sinthome* is a certain signifying formation penetrated with enjoyment: it is a signifier as a bearer of *jouis-sense*, enjoyment-in-sense." Zizek insists on "the radical ontological status of symptom: symptom, conceived as *sinthome*, is literally our only substance, the only positive support of our being, the only point that gives consistency to the subject" (Zizek, *The Sublime Object of Ideology*, 75; see Jacques Lacan, "Joyce le symptome," in *Joyce avec Lacan* [Paris, 1988]).

29   Mater rosarum, cui tenerae vigent
        Aurae Favonî, cui Venus it comes
     Lasciva, Nympharum choreis
        Et volucrum celebrata cantu!
     (*Correspondence* 1: 158; trans. Lonsdale, *Poems*, 311)

30　The best reading of this, the other Latin poems, and Gray's relation with West in general is to be found in Bentman 1992; Bentman's discussion of the *mollitudinem* with which Gray teases West in a reference to Nonius Marcellus, and its connection to the notion of "molly," is particularly suggestive (208).

31　See Linda Zionkowski (1993), who makes a similar claim for Gray's "Sonnet on the Death of Richard West"; see also Paul Oppenheimer, *The Birth of the Modern Mind: Self, Consciousness, and the Invention of the Sonnet* (New York: Oxford University Press, 1989), 184.

32　The best discussion of the poetry of sensibility is that found in John Sitter 1982.

33　The Gray *Concordance* (Cook) lists twenty uses of vain – mostly in this sense of in vain – in Gray's poetry. It is not an exaggeration to call this mood typical. See Haggerty 1992: 200–2.

34　For a similar reading of this poem, see Bentman 1992: 216–17.

35　Freud, "Mourning and Melancholia," in *General Psychological Theory*, ed. Philip Reiff (New York: Collier, 1963), 164, 166.

36　See, for instance, Andrew Elfenbein, "William Cowper and the Rise of the Domestic Man," essay delivered at the Annual Convention of the American Society of Eighteenth-Century Studies, Tucson, Arizona, 1995.

37　Eve Kosofsky Sedgwick, *Epistemology of the Closet* (Berkeley: University of California Press, 1990), 22.

38　For a reading of the emphasis on passion and fear in this elegy, see Bentman 1992: 216.

39　Hactenus haud segnis Naturae arcana retexi
　　Musarum interpres, primusque Britanna per arva
　　Romano liquidum deduxi flumine rivum.
　　　　Cum Tu opere in medio, spes tanti et causa laboris,
　　Linquis, et aeternam fati te condis in umbram!
　　Vidi egomet duro graviter concussa dolore
　　Pectora, in alterius non unquam lenta dolorem;
　　Et languere oculos vidi et pallescere amantem
　　Vultum, quo nunquam Pietas nisi rara, Fidesque,
　　Altus amor Veri, et purum spirabat Honestum.
　　Visa tamen tardi demum inclementia morbi
　　Cessare est, reducemque iterum roseo ore Salutem
　　Speravi, atque una tecum, delecte Favoni!
　　Credulus heu longos, ut quondam, fallere soles:
　　Heu spes nequicquam dulces, atque irrita vota!
　　Heu maestos soles, sine te quos dulcere flendo
　　Per desideria, et questus iam cogor inanes!
　　　　At Tu, sancta anima, et nostri non indiga luctus,
　　Stellanti templo, sincerique aetheris igne,
　　Unde orta es, fruere; atque oh si secura, nec ultra
　　Mortalis, notos olim miserata labores
　　Respectes, tenuesque vacet cognoscere curas;

Humanam si forte alta de sede procellam
Contemplere, metus stimulosque cupidinis acres,
Gaudiaque et gemitus, parvoque in corde tumultum
Irarum ingentem, et saevos sub pectore fluctus:
Respice, et has lacrimas, memori quas ictus amore
Fundo; quod possum, iuxta lugere sepulcrum
Dum iuvat, et mutae vana haec iactare favillae.
(*Poems*, 328)

14

The Culture of Travesty: Sexuality and Masquerade in Eighteenth-Century England

Terry Castle

When the eighteenth-century moralist wished to decry the cheating and whorishness of contemporary life, he found a potent image close at hand. So ubiquitous were chicanery and vice, wrote Henry Fielding in 1743 in his "Essay on the Knowledge of the Characters of Men," the world was nothing more than "a vast Masquerade," where "the greatest Part appear disguised under false Vizors and Habits" (*Miscellanies*, 1: 155). Owen Sedgewick, in the same decade, entitled a lascivious compendium of modern evils *The Universal Masquerade; or, The World Turn'd Inside Out* (1742), and later, in a *Rambler* essay describing the corruptions of wealth (No. 75), Samuel Johnson asserted that the rich and powerful "live in a perpetual masquerade, in which all about them wear borrowed characters" (*Yale Edition*, 4: 33). "The world's a masquerade!" wrote Goldsmith in his epilogue to Charlotte Lennox's *The Sister* (1762), and "the masquers, you, you, you" (*Works* 1: 53).

The rebarbative tone is ageless. The metaphor, however, places us at once in the hallucinatory lost world of eighteenth-century urban culture. For, moralism aside, each man was right in the literal sense: eighteenth-century English society was indeed a world of masqueraders and artificers, self-alienation and phantasmagoria. We are familiar of course with the many shape-shifters who inhabit the fiction and folklore of the period; Moll Flanders, Jonathan Wild, the female soldiers and masked highwaymen of contemporary balladry – these are among the archetypes of an age. But eighteenth-century culture as a whole might also be termed, without exaggeration, a culture of travesty. Especially in London, the manipulation of appearances was both a private strategy and a social institution. Readers of Boswell's journals will doubtless remember the occasions on which the future biographer adopted the guise of soldier or ruffian in order to search for clandestine sexual adventure in the London streets.[1] But travesties took place on a larger, more public scale too. Whether practiced in assembly-rooms, theatres, brothels, public gardens, or at the masquerade itself (which flourished in London from the 1720s on), collective sartorial transformation offered a cathartic escape from the self and a suggestive revision of ordinary experience. The Protean life of the city found expression in a persistent popular urge toward disguise and metamorphosis.

The historian of sexuality will find much to ponder in the exemplary diversions of the eighteenth century. For travesty, of course, is never innocent; it is often a peculiarly expressive, if paradoxical, revelation of hidden needs. In *The Masquerade* (1728), Fielding observed that to "masque the face" was "t'unmasque the mind." Likewise, Richard Steele, in *The Spectator* (No. 14), noted that contemporary masqueraders invariably dressed as what they "have a Mind to be" (1: 63). For Boswell and others, one might argue, disguise provided a much-desired emotional access to new sensual and ethical realms.

Yet travesty had an even more subversive function in eighteenth-century life. It posed an intimate challenge to the ordering patterns of culture itself. Michel Foucault speaks of the haunting power of the transvestite in the eighteenth-century imagination.[2] In fashionable *équivoque* figures like the fop and amazon, moralizing contemporaries were quick to see a profound affront to "Nature" and the order of things. "In every country," a writer in the *Universal Spectator* (December 14, 1728) observed, "Decency requires that the Sexes should be differenc'd by Dress, in order to prevent Multitudes of Irregularities which otherwise would continually be occasion'd." Nonetheless, sexual impersonation remained one of the subtle obsessions of the age. From the notorious actress Charlotte Charke, who recorded her many "mad pranks" in male garb in a famous autobiography in 1755, to the hapless Chevalier d'Éon, with his sensational attempts at transvestite espionage in the 1770s and 1780s, a host of sexual shape-shifters throughout the century parodied and charmed away the hieratic fixities of gender. Even as the eighteenth century condemned such artifices, it also found in them an intimation of a quintessential modern truth: that culture itself was an affront to "nature" – non-transcendental in origin, shaped by convention, the ultimate product of fashion. In the carnivalesque figure of the transvestite, eighteenth-century society began to explore something of its own eminently secular and artifactual nature.

In examining the role of travesty in eighteenth-century life, I shall focus here on the public masquerade – the most expansive and controversial vehicle for the shape-shifting impulse in the period. I will touch, as a matter of course, on the masquerade's contemporary association with libertinism, and its place in the history of actual sexual practices such as homosexuality.

But my main object is to present the masquerade as a representative institution – a magic lantern, as it were, in which we may see illuminated the new erotic self-consciousness of the age. For the masquerade indeed provided the eighteenth century with a novel imagery of sexual possibility. Its manifold displacements and enigmas were also heuristic – registering for the first time that ironic resistance to the purely instinctual which has increasingly come to characterize the erotic life of the West since the eighteenth century. In particular, through its stylized assault on gender boundaries, the masquerade played an interesting part in the creation of the modern "polymorphous" subject – perverse by definition, sexually ambidextrous, and potentially unlimited in the range of its desires.

The charismatic institution known as the "Midnight Masquerade" originated in England in the second decade of the eighteenth century. Similar events, to be sure, had taken place earlier; the impulse toward travesty had its historic roots in English culture. Popular religious rituals and seasonal festivities of the Middle Ages and Renaissance had often required the donning of costumes; the hobby-horse games and morris dances of rural England, in which men disguised themselves as women and animals, survived into the eighteenth century and beyond.[3] The court also had its early versions of the masquerade. Masked parties and entertainments, at times directly modelled on traditional festivals, had played an important part in the life of the English aristocracy at least since the time of Henry VIII. In the seventeenth century the masque was a lavish variation on the travesty theme: here nobility disguised themselves as gods and goddesses and acted out fantastic allegories of court life. During the Restoration period, as the Earl of Rochester's psychologically complex impersonations suggest, the court of Charles II offered a rich domain for sartorial play and self-estrangement.[4]

But only in the first decades of the century did the masquerade in the modern sense arise – as a form of large-scale commercial public entertainment, urban and non-exclusive in nature, cutting across historic lines of rank and privilege. Masquerades owed their sudden popularity in part to foreign influences; more travel abroad meant that more and more English people witnessed the traditional carnivals and fêtes of the Continent. The Venetian carnival in particular attracted large numbers of English tourists in the eighteenth century.[5] Foreign entrepreneurs, including the famous masquerade impresario John James Heidegger (the self-described "Swiss Count") and the Venetian-born Theresa Cornelys, settled in London in the first half of the century and introduced the middle-class English public to the sophisticated masked balls and ridottos of the Continent. Walpole reports that the Jubilee masquerade at Ranelagh in 1749 was advertised as being "in the Venetian manner." Masquerades throughout the century were described as "mock-carnivals."[6] Beneath the denatured trappings of urban society, however, one might also discover nostalgic longings for the popular traditions of the English rural past. Like the fairs, processions and other crowd spectacles of the city, the masquerade revivified the festive life of earlier centuries in a new capitalistic and modern form.[7]

The first important public masquerades in London were those organized by Heidegger in 1717 at the Haymarket Theatre.[8] (Heidegger, who makes a memorable appearance in *The Dunciad*, also produced the first Handel operas in England.) The new venture was an instant scandal – and an instant success. In the 1720s and 1730s, Heidegger's "Midnight Masquerades" drew between seven and eight hundred people a week. Tickets were sold at White's coffee-house and the Haymarket itself, and no one entered the theater without ticket and disguise. The event, which began at nine or ten, frequently lasted until early the next morning. In Swift's "The Progress of Marriage" (1722) an errant wife returns from a masquerade: "At five the footmen make a din, / Her ladyship is just come in" (*Complete Poems*, 245). Heidegger continued to hold masquerades at the Haymarket until his death in 1749.

The occasion had its pretensions to exclusivity: George II and the Prince of Wales are both reputed to have attended public masquerades.[9] But its real appeal lay in its heterogeneous and carnival-like atmosphere. It drew on all social ranks equally, and permitted high and low to mingle in a single "promiscuous" round. "All state and ceremony are laid aside," wrote one witness in the *Weekly Journal* (January 25, 1724), "since the Peer and the Apprentice, the Punk and the Duchess are, for so long a time, upon an equal Foot." Costume reinscribed the theme of class confusion. As Christopher Pitt wrote in "On the Masquerades" (1727):

> Valets adorned with coronets appear,
> Lacquies of state and footmen with a star,
> Sailors of quality with judges mix, –
> And chimney-sweepers drive their coach-and six.[10]

Not all observers were pleased with the masquerade's "strange Medley" of persons. "It is possible," wrote Mary Singleton (Frances Brooke) in *The Old Maid* (January 24, 1756), "the confused mixture of different ranks and conditions, which is unavoidable at a masquerade, may well be agreeable to the dregs of the people, who are fond, even at every price, of gaining admittance into a place where they may insult their superiors with impunity."

Given the liberating anonymity of the scene, collective behavior was unrestrained. Drinking, dancing, gaming, and intrigue flourished, ordinary decorum was overturned, and a spirit of saturnalia reigned. Not surprisingly, the masquerade quickly came under attack from moralists and divines. A host of anti-masquerade satires and pamphlets were published in the 1720s and continued to appear into the 1780s. Civil authorities made periodic attempts to suppress masquerades, particularly during times of social unrest, but these efforts were never very successful. For most of the century the masquerade retained a raffish and seductive hold on the public imagination. Large masquerades were held at Ranelagh Gardens and Marylebone in the 1740s and 1750s, and again at Carlisle House in Soho Square, the Pantheon and Almack's in the 1760s and 1770s. *Town and Country Magazine* for May 1770 reported a masquerade at the Pantheon attended by "near two thousand persons." Only after the French Revolution did the masquerade lose something of its subversive appeal, though occasional masquerades continued to be held in London well into the nineteenth century.[11]

Though public in nature, the masquerade had the reputation – and *frisson* – of an underground phenomenon. From the start it was felt to epitomize the clandestine sexual life of the city. This "libidinous Assembly," wrote Addison in the *Spectator* (No. 8), was perfectly contrived for the "Advancement of Cuckoldom," being nothing more than a scene of "Assignations and Intrigues" (1: 37). In his satiric *Masquerade Ticket* of 1727, William Hogarth highlighted the erotic nature of the event by depicting Haymarket masqueraders cavorting beneath statues of Venus and Priapus and two large "Lecherometers" – fanciful devices for measuring sexual excitement. Masquerade debauchery was a popular theme in eighteenth-century fiction. In the novels of Defoe, Fielding, Richardson, and Smollett, the masquerade was a conventional setting for seduction and adultery. Other writers regularly linked it with scenarios of defloration, rape, and perversion.[12] "To carry on an Intrigue with an Air of Secrecy" or "debauch a Citizen's Wife," exclaimed a character in Benjamin Griffin's *The Masquerade* (1717), "what Contrivance in the World so proper as a Masquerade?" The anonymous writer of the *Short Remarks upon the Original and Pernicious Consequences of Masquerades* of 1721 was less sanguine: the masquerade, he wrote, was nothing more than a "Congress to an unclean end."[13]

Underlying such complaints was a sense of the moral scandal implicit in costume itself. "The being in disguise," wrote the author of *Guardian* 142, "takes away the usual checks and restraints of modesty; and consequently the beaux do not blush to talk wantonly, nor the belles to listen; the one as greedily sucks in the poison, as the other industriously infuses it." Travesty eroticized the world. Not only was one freed of one's inhibitions, one might also experience, hypothetically at least, a new body and its pleasures. The exchange of garments was also an exchange of desires. The result was a flight from the "natural" – from all that was culturally preordained – into new realms of voluptuous disorder.

By all accounts, the masquerade was indeed a scene of unusual erotic stimulation. Many disguises, first of all, had an undeniably fetishistic power. Masks were considered notorious aphrodisiacs, associated with prostitutes (as in Hogarth's *Harlot's Progress*) and the perverse heightening of passion. "A Woman mask'd," Wycherley's uncouth Pinchwife had observed in *The Country Wife* (1675), "is like a cover'd Dish, gives a man a curiosity, and appetite, when, it may be, uncover'd 'twould turn his stomach" (*Complete Plays*, 293). But the mask also released its wearer from ordinary moral controls. Women, it was felt, were particularly freed from constraint. "The mask secures the Ladies from Detraction, and encourages a Liberty, the Guilt of which their Blushes would betray when barefac'd, till by Degrees they are innur'd to that which is out of their Vertue to restrain."[14] Combined with the mysterious black domino, the mask remained for the century the veritable icon of transgressive desire.

But costumes themselves were often highly suggestive and provided a rich symbolic lexicon of libidinous possibility. Granted, not every disguise of the century was meant to titillate; almost all masquerades had their requisite Turks and conjurers, Harlequins and shepherdesses, hussars and Pierrots, orange-girls and Punches. Eighteenth-century masquerade costumes were sometimes merely playful, exotic, or picturesque. Casanova himself appeared as a relatively innocuous Pierrot at an Italian masquerade.[15] But given the premium on voyeurism and self-display, visual scandal held a special place. Where else, indeed, might one find "a Nobleman [dressed] like a Cynder-Wench," or "a Lady of Quality in Dutch Trowsers, and a Woman of the Town in a Ruff and Farthingale?"[16]

Transvestite costume was perhaps the most common offense against decorum. Women strutted in jack-boots and breeches, while men primped in furbelows and flounces. Horace Walpole describes passing "for a good mask" as an old woman at a masquerade in 1742. Other male masqueraders disguised themselves as witches, bawds, nursery-maids and shepherdesses.[17] At a Richmond masquerade, *The Gentleman's Magazine* reported in April, 1776, "a gentleman appeared in woman's clothes with a head-dress four feet high, composed of greens and garden stuff, and crowned with tufts of endive nicely blanched." "The force of the ridicule," the account continued, "was felt by some of the ladies." At Almack's in 1773, one man appeared as a "procuress" and another as "Mother Cole," the matronly bawd in Cleland's *Memoirs of a Woman of Pleasure*.[18] Female masqueraders in turn metamorphosed into hussars, sailors, cardinals, or Mozartian boys. The Duchess of Bolton, Elizabeth Inchbald and Judith Milbanke, among others, appeared in male costumes at masquerades at one time or another during the century.[19] In Griffin's *The Masquerade*, the heroine attends as "a kind of Hermaphroditical Mixture; half Man, half Woman; a Coat, Wig, Hat, and Feather, with all the Ornaments requisite." Costumes representing the "Amazonian" goddess Diana (popular throughout the century) were likewise androgynous in nature.[20] The anti-masquerade writers, not surprisingly, found cross-dressing a palpable sign of masquerade depravity. The author of the *Short Remarks* complained that the confounding of garments had ever "been used by Wantons, to favour their lascivious Designs." This "artifice of the old Serpent," he wrote, was clearly intended to "regale and heighten the Temptation." Eighteenth-century masqueraders may not, indeed, have been oblivious to such imperatives. Judith Milbanke, who appeared along with her sister as "two smart Beaux" in 1778, complacently observed that she had made by far "the prettiest Fellow of the two,"[21] and the scandalous Harriette Wilson, recollecting a masquerade at which she and a female friend dressed as an "Italian or Austrian peasant-boy and girl," carefully recorded in her memoirs the various risqué comments they received from bystanders (*Memoirs* 2: 607–11).

But other costume types were also designed to inflame. The parodia sacra, or ecclesiastical parody, offered an opportunity to play upon themes of celibacy and forbidden desire. A classic vestige of carnival tradition, ecclesiastical disguises featured prominently in contemporary costume catalogues such as Thomas Jefferys' *Dresses of Different Nations* (1757) and remained fashionable throughout the century. Wayward nuns and priests, perversely amorous "Devotees," and licentious Capuchins are a staple in contemporary masquerade stories and illustrations. "I will be a Prude, a religious Prude," exclaims the flirtatious Lady Frances in Charles Johnson's *The Masquerade* (1719); "I will appear in all the gloomy inaccessible Charms of a young Devotee; there is something in this Character so sweet and forbidden" (II.ii). By a predictable symbolic inversion, prostitutes were thought particularly likely to assume pious vestments. A writer in the *Weekly Journal* (January 25, 1724) described meeting a pretty nun at a masquerade who "rapt out an Oath" and made it known "that she was of the Sisterhood, and belonged to a certain Convent, of which Mother N[eedham] is Lady Abbess." In Henry Robert Morland's painting *The Fair Nun Unmasked* (1769), a simpering mock-religieuse is shown removing her mask and suggestively exposing the jewelled crucifix on her bosom.

Still other disguises were profane from the start. Miss Chudleigh, later the Duchess of Kingston, shocked onlookers by appearing at the Jubilee masquerade in 1749 as a bare-breasted Iphigenia – "so naked," Mrs. Montagu remarked, "that the high priest might easily inspect the entrails of the victim" (Climenson 1906, 1: 264).[22] Several semi-pornographic prints commemorated her exploit. In 1755 the writer of *The Connoisseur* for February 6, described a gallant who went to a masked "Frolick" with "no breeches under his domino." In 1768 Miss Pelham appeared at a masquerade as a "blackamoor" with her legs exposed to the thighs (Ribeiro 1984: 32), and in 1770 a man went to one of Mrs. Cornelys's masquerades in Soho Square as Adam, in a flesh-colored silk body stocking complete with "an apron of fig leaves worked in it, fitting the body to the utmost nicety." The result, according to *The Gentleman's Magazine* (March 1770), was a certain "unavoidable indelicacy."

This paradoxical connection between masquerading and nakedness, it is worth noting, was a joke that recurred in various forms throughout the century. Popular wisdom held that there was a causal relation between masquerading and (subsequent) states of undress: those who "dressed up" for the masquerade would undoubtedly bare themselves later – when they retired to brothels or bagnios to consummate their secret liaisons. Such a sequence is implicit in Plate 5 of Hogarth's *Marriage à la Mode*, in which an adulterous wife and her lover have retreated to a bagnio for sex after a masquerade. At other times, less logically, the masquerade itself was associated with images of naked excess. In *Guardian* 142 (August 24, 1713), Steele linked an attack on masquerades ("the devil first addressed himself to Eve in a mask") with a parody of the "Evites," an imaginary cult of fashionable women who wore only fig-leaves. In 1755 Miss Chudleigh's scandalous appearance as Iphigenia prompted a satiric scheme for a "Naked Masquerade." At this "alfresco" event, described in *The Connoisseur* (May 1, 1755), female masqueraders were to disport themselves as "*Water-Nymphs* and *Graces*," and male masqueraders in "the half-brutal forms of *Satyres, Pans, Fauns,* and *Centaurs.*" "The *Pantheon of the Heathen Gods, Ovid's Metamorphoses,* and *Titian's Prints*," the author argued, would supply "a sufficient variety of undrest characters." In the resulting orgy, bucks might run mad with their mistresses "like the Priests and Priestesses of Bacchus celebrating the Bacchanalian mysteries."

To what extent was the Dionysian promise in masquerade spectacle fulfilled? Certainly, if all masquerades were disreputable, some were less reputable than others. Acts of outright sexual intercourse (if they occurred at all) took place, one suspects, only at the most clandestine and subfusc affairs, and certainly not at events like Heidegger's "Midnight Masquerade" or Mrs. Cornelys's public subscription balls. The sexual subculture, for instance, had its own more or less unbuttoned versions of the masquerade. In her scandalous memoirs of 1797, the courtesan Margaret Leeson described a private masquerade at which a couple performed love feats "buff to buff," and, later, another masquerade given by "Moll Hall" which degenerated into an orgy (*Memoirs* 3: 4–10). The author of the piece on the "Naked Masquerade" noted in passing that he modelled his entertainment on an actual event that had taken place the year before at Pimlico "among the lowest of the people." The participants, he observed, had been sent to

Bridewell, but "the same act, which at the *Green Lamps* or *Pimlico* appears low and criminal, may be extremely polite and commendable in the *Haymarket* or at *Ranelagh*." Similarly, in one of the numerous popular histories of Jonathan Wild, there is a description of a secret homosexual masquerade party attended by Wild, which featured a group of "He-Whores," "rigg'd in Gowns, Petticoats, Head cloths, fine lac'd Shoes, Furbelow Scarves, and Masks," all "tickling and feeling each other, as if they were a mixture of wanton Males and Females." This licentious gathering has been identified as the notorious "Sodomitish Academy" run by "Mother Clap" in Field Lane, Holborn (*Select Trials* 2: 257–8).[23]

The public masquerade was nominally more restrained, in that the shift into overt sexual behavior was seldom possible. This is not to say, however, that the masquerade's bacchanalian reputation was undeserved. The occasion was indisputably a catalyst for certain kinds of behavior, and functioned throughout the century – along with brothels, bagnios, and the London piazzas and parks – as an acknowledged public setting in which illicit sexual contacts might be made. Of course, evidence regarding actual behavior at masquerades must be primarily circumstantial; the scandal associated with the occasion meant that few participants recorded incriminating escapades directly. Often one must rely on journalistic accounts, literary descriptions, and the sometimes exaggerated comments of the masquerade's detractors. Still, eighteenth-century observers agreed (and common sense confirms) that the masquerade was indeed a "Country of Liberty" – a realm where transgressive liaisons were easily formed, precisely because they might remain anonymous.[24]

The Haymarket masquerade had its quota of prostitutes, first of all, owing in part to its location in the heart of London's prostitution district. Disguise permitted the prostitute, like the sharper, to ply her precarious trade in relative safety. The "Sisterhood of Drury" appear frequently in masquerade accounts throughout the century. On the night of a recent ball, wrote an observer in the *Weekly Journal* (January 25, 1724), "all about the Hundreds of *Drury*, there was not a *Fille de Joie* to be had that Night, for Love nor Money, being all engaged at the Masquerade; and several Men of Pleasure receiv'd Favours from Ladies who were too modest to shew their Faces, and many of them still feel the Effects of the amorous Flame which they received from the unknown Fairs." The author of *A Seasonable Apology for Mr. H—g—r* (1724), one of many anti-masquerade satires from the 1720s, ironically dedicated his work to the infamous bawd Mother Needham, whose many minions, he observed, exploited the "Mask of artificial Maidenhead" in addition to the ordinary mask of disguise. In Addison's satire in *Guardian* 154, a nun makes an assignation with a "heathen god" at a masquerade, and then agrees to meet him nearby in "the Little Piazza in Covent-garden," the famous haunt of London's "trading dames."

Few eighteenth-century commentators acknowledged the economic necessity which drove prostitutes to masquerades; the popular theme of the whore-in-disguise was used merely to underwrite the moral assault on the event itself. Yet, amid a conventional attack in *The Masquerade* ("Thus Fortune sends the gamesters luck, Venus her votary a—"), Fielding offered the following unintentionally sympathetic vignette:

> Below stairs hungry whores are picking
> The bones of wild-fowl, and of chicken;
> And into pockets some convey
> Provisions for another day.

The lines may serve as a stark reminder that prostitutes constituted, after all, the most wretchedly exploited underclass in eighteenth-century London, and that some were undoubtedly driven to the masquerade out of more than simple concupiscence.

It was not just the "Punk," however, who found a special range at masquerades. Women in general assumed unprecedented liberties. The misogynist view of the age, of course, was that any woman who attended a masquerade did so, like the harlot, in order to seek unlawful sexual pleasure. The taboo against unescorted women and girls going to masquerades remained in force throughout the century.[25] It mattered little whether a woman was a virgin or not; any woman, it was assumed, fell into sexual danger at masquerades. In a salacious story in the *Weekly Journal* (February 8, 1724) entitled "The Balls, a Tale," a wayward young woman persuades her mother to let her go to a masquerade.

> Virgins to Midnight Masques would go,
> And not a Mother durst say, No;
> She pass'd for unpolite and rude,
> And Miss would cry, Mamma's a Prude.

Needless to say, she quickly gives up her maidenhood to a sly domino named Roger. A few weeks later (April 18, 1724) the same newspaper offered the following maxim: "Fishes are caught with Hooks, Birds are ensnar'd with Nets, but Virgins with Masquerades." In turn, in married women the masquerade was thought to prompt adulterous longings. The occasion was perfect for cuckoldry, wrote Addison in *Spectator* 8, because "the Women either come by themselves or are introduced by Friends, who are obliged to quit them upon their first Entrance" (1: 37). Lady Bellaston, who seduces Tom Jones at the Haymarket while disguised as the "Queen of the Fairies," is a stereotypical eighteenth-century version of the older female masquerade libertine. In the satirical pamphlet *A Seasonable Apology for Mr. H —g—r* (1724), the comical "Countess of Clingfast" and her "Committee of Matrons" likewise relieve themselves of frigidity, green-sickness and "obstructions" by attending masquerades.

We need not mimic the pervasive misogyny of contemporary moralists (or the relentlessly anti-sexual ideology they endorsed) to recognize the element of truth in their animadversions. The critics were right to link masquerading with female sexual emancipation; the masquerade indeed provided eighteenth-century women with an unusual sense of erotic freedom. Disguise obviated a host of cultural proscriptions and taboos. A woman in masquerade might approach strangers, initiate conversation, touch and embrace those whom she did not know, speak coarsely – in short, violate all the cherished imperatives of ordinary feminine sexual decorum. Of course, only the boldest might openly acknowledge such pleasures. "I love a masquerade," wrote the brazen Harriette Wilson, "because a female can never enjoy the same liberty anywhere else" (*Memoirs* 2: 616). In an account of a Pantheon masquerade in February 1773, the *Lady's Magazine* offered similar sentiments, purportedly through the voice of an anonymous female participant: "Indeed a masquerade is one of the most entertaining diversions that ever was imported; you may hear and see, and do every thing in the world, without the least reserve – and liberty, liberty, my dear, you know, is the very joy of my heart."

Most important, masquerading granted women the essential masculine privilege of erotic object-choice. "It is delightful to me," Wilson wrote, only half-facetiously, "to be able to wander about in a crowd, making my observations, and conversing with whomsoever I please, without being liable to be stared at or remarked upon, and to speak to whom I please, and run away from them the moment I have discovered their stupidity" (*Memoirs* 2: 616). Elsewhere in her memoir, she described meeting several lovers at masquerades. It would be going too far, perhaps, to call the masquerade a feminist counterpart to the brothel; eighteenth-century culture, unremittingly patriarchal in structure, was never so Utopian in its sexual arrangements. Nonetheless, the masquerade offered contemporary women a subversive – if temporary – simulacrum of sexual autonomy. Besides obvious demi-mondaine figures like Wilson and Margaret Leeson, such distinguished women as Mary Wortley Montagu, Fanny Burney, and Elizabeth Inchbald acknowledged a fondness for masquerade privileges.[26] But unknown women too, one may assume, experienced unprecedented sensual release in the comic displacements of the night.

Likewise, homosexuals may have found a similar latitude at public masquerades. So much seems clear, at least, from contemporary attacks on the masquerade, which frequently called attention to "unnatural" liaisons struck up there. The sensational *Short Remarks upon the Original and Pernicious Consequences of Masquerades*, for example, was in large part a barely concealed assault on homosexual practices at the masquerade. Masquerade transvestism, charged its author, had led its proponents toward "Excesses, which otherwise they durst scarce have thought of" and was making the nation a veritable "Sodom for Lewdness." Citing infamous cross-dressers and bisexuals of antiquity – Sporus, Caligula, Heliogabalus and so forth – he warned that such men had been "branded in History as Monsters of Nature, the Scum, and Scandal, and Shame of Mankind." Modern masqueraders merely imitated the vice-ridden "Corybantes" and "dancing priests" of the past; the pagan "Festum Kalendarium," scene of travesty, perversion and blasphemy, was "the black Original we transcribe in our Masquerades."

Fielding adopted a somewhat less dire tone in *The Masquerade*, but likewise condemned the masquerade as a world of enveloping sexual chaos, in which any kind of wrongful connection was possible. Complaining of the effeminate men ("little apish butterflies") everywhere to be seen at the masquerade, the poet's Muse cries:

> And if the breed been't quickly mended;
> Your empire shortly will be ended:
> Breeches our brawny thighs shall grace,
> (Another Amazonian race).
> For when men women turn – why then
> May women not be chang'd to men?

That Fielding connected transvestism with active homosexuality is obvious from his later anti-lesbian satire, *The Female Husband* (1746). This semi-prurient work (based on an actual case tried by Fielding's cousin) described how a woman named Mary Hamilton disguised herself as a man and tricked several women into marriage precisely in order to satisfy "unnatural" carnal urges.[27] As if to illustrate Fielding's vision of ensuing sexual disorder, a suggestive satiric engraving from the first half of the century, "The Masquerade Dance," depicted an all-male group of masqueraders performing a wild hornpipe to the music of a piping devil.

Yet the presence of homosexuals at masquerades can be deduced in other ways too. The Haymarket, as I have mentioned, was near to Covent Garden and Spring Gardens, both important sites for male as well as female prostitution. Along with molly-clubs and similar underground sexual establishments, masquerade rooms featured in the clandestine erotic topography of the new male homosexual subculture that was gradually coming into being in eighteenth-century London.[28] Even in supposedly "decent" or nonpornographic accounts, the masquerade is an acknowledged setting for acts of real or ostensible homoerotic flirtation. At a masquerade described in *Guardian* 154, for example, the male narrator, disguised as Lucifer, is accosted by a "Presbyterian Parson" who calls him a "pretty fellow" and offers to meet him in Spring Gardens. Later in the same piece, the narrator finds himself strangely attracted to an "Indian King" who, admittedly, turns out to be a woman in disguise. Similar errors are recorded elsewhere. According to her biographer, Mrs. Inchbald, who appeared as a man at a masquerade in the 1780s, unwittingly "captivated the affections" of her own sex as a result *(Memoirs* 1: 140). The *Weekly Journal* for April 18, 1724 had an account of a man who went to the Haymarket dressed as a female Quaker, and was mistakenly almost "ravished there by a young male domino". And, in a particularly lascivious episode in Smollett's *Peregrine Pickle* (1751), a character dressed in women's clothes at a masquerade is forced, "in consequence of the Champaign he had so liberally swallowed that afternoon," to micturate in front of a group of fascinated male masqueraders. He is subsequently accosted by a Frenchman who compliments him on his "happy pisse" and fondles him, though the Frenchman later denies knowing his true sex (244–5).

But eighteenth-century pornographic writing, as one might expect, confirms the presence of outright same-sex solicitation at masquerades. In Cleland's *Memoirs of a Women of Pleasure* (1749), Fanny Hill's fellow prostitute Emily, disguised as a boy, is approached by a "handsome domino" at a public masquerade. His courtship, she finds, is "dash'd with a certain oddity," but she attributes this to the "humour" of her disguise and not to any misunderstanding about her sex. His intentions are clearly homosexual, however; he has taken her for a "smock-fac'd boy," tries to sodomize her in a nearby bagnio and, in a moment of lubricious crisis, must be redirected "down the right road" (154–6). While clearly obscene in design, the episode also points towards the underlying sociological reality; that Cleland (himself reputed to be a "sodomite" by several contemporaries) took for granted the association between the masquerade and homosexual seduction is clear, and, as with other realistic details in the novel, reflects more than mere pornographic convenience.[29]

For those hedged round by the implicit and explicit taboos of eighteenth-century sexual morality, therefore, the masquerade offered unprecedented pleasure and opportunities. Borrowing a term from the sociologist, we might call it a "backstage" area in eighteenth-century urban life – a setting in which ordinarily proscribed impulses might safely be indulged.[30] The irony was that to go "back-stage" was to go "on stage," to adopt a new self, to play a new role, through the hallucinatory derangements of costume. Throughout the century, the masquerade mediated in a paradoxical fashion between public and private spheres. Behind the mask, one preserved the essential moral and psychological privileges of privacy, while participating at the same time in the spontaneous exchanges of the group. Disguise was the crucial means towards such mediation – the gesture which at once licensed collective exchange and infused the occasion with its secretive, compelling aura.

Yet, to identify the masquerade as a privileged space for the morally unconventional does not entirely explain its powerful hold on eighteenth-century English culture. I have argued that some people may have self-consciously sought its freedoms – prostitutes, libertines, feminists, the sexual avant-garde. The masquerade had much to do, certainly, with the subterranean liberalization of erotic life in eighteenth-century London,[31] but in speaking of a "culture of travesty" I have made large claims, admittedly, for something that remained in one sense a local phenomenon. Thousands attended masquerades during the century, but what of those who never ventured to the Haymarket, Ranelagh, or Soho Square? How did the carnivalesque exploits of an urban minority impinge upon the imaginative life of society as a whole?

We cannot underestimate the power that the idea of the "Midnight Masquerade" held in eighteenth-century discourse. Indeed, we might speak of the masquerade as one of the defining topoi of eighteenth-century cultural rhetoric. The numerous literary and artistic transformations of the masquerade were at least as significant, in some sense, as the institution itself. Whether or not they attended, the majority of English people knew about the masquerades. As witnessed by a host of novels, stories, poems, pamphlets, squibs and engravings, the event remained a subject of fascination throughout the century.[32]

And, in a way, masquerade liberty was as much a common imaginative property – part of the fantasy-life of the age – as it was the privilege of the masquerade crowd. The appeal of the mask, as we have seen, was that it permitted an escape from self; internalized moral and psychological constraints disappeared – for how could one be held responsible when one was not oneself? The logic of ordinary moral agency was suspended; whatever one did, whatever ensued, might be attributed to "someone else" or assimilated to the supposedly innocent realm of "accidents." Yet similar psychological fictions operated in the masquerade fantasies of the century. In stories of masquerade seduction and adultery, the timid reader might safely identify with an "other" – seducer or victim, adulterer or adulteress – without risk, obviously, to his or her consciously held scruples. Heavy didacticism added a comfortable (if spurious) protective moral layering to these powerfully charged sexual narratives. Like the related genre of the criminal biography, the masquerade tale typically gratifies prurient or subversive interests while parading as "instructive" commentary. And just as the criminal biography, with its implicit glorification of the miscreant, reflected a growing popular revolt against traditional values (or so John Richetti has argued in *Popular Fiction before Richardson* [1969: 59]), so the sensational masquerade tale may have articulated a new subliminal collective hostility toward age-old sexual prohibitions and taboos.

One might go so far as to say that masquerade fantasy operated as a conceptual tool – a symbolic mechanism through which suppressed forms of behavior found representation. Virtually any form of perverse or proscribed sexual contact might be depicted in masquerade literature, so long as it was made to seem unintentional – an accidental function of the chaos and anonymity of the scene. The "mistake" was the crucial covering fiction. Innocent men thus couple unwittingly with prostitutes in a host of masquerade stories: in *Spectator* No. 8, for example, an unfortunate Templar mistakes "a Cloud for a Juno" and discovers his *faux pas* too late. In still other accounts, virginal young women and loyal wives are ruined as a result of tragic masquerade errors – usually when they confuse a rapist with a fiancé or husband. In a sensational tale by Eliza Haywood in *The Female Spectator* (1746), the heroine Erminia allows herself to be escorted home from the masquerade by a man she takes to be her fiancé and is forcibly undone by him. In an "Affecting Masquerade Adventure" from *The Gentleman's Magazine* of December 1754, a similar fate awaits Matilda, who is seduced after a masquerade by a mysterious domino she believes to be her husband.

Other fanciful consummations were even more lurid. I have already mentioned cases of accidental homosexuality at the masquerade; accidental incest was another popular motif. The writer of the *Short Remarks* described an unfortunate gentleman who "debauch'd his own Daughter" by mistake at a masquerade and died of horror at the discovery. In the play *The Masquerade; or, The Devil's Nursery* (1732), a "Virtuous Wife" is "an Incestuous Mother made" after another tragic masquerade mix-up. "By thee," the author of *A Seasonable Apology for Mr. H—g—r* wrote of the masquerade, "Sons aspire to the Wombs from whence they sprung; and Daughters wantonly embrace the Loyns that begot them."

While typically presented as proofs of the masquerade's diabolical nature, these narratives of accidental union also provided readers with a new and highly specific grammar of the illicit. In adumbrating their shocking tales of unwitting prostitution, adultery, homosexuality and incest, masquerade writers also gave unprecedented centrality to previously unmentionable desire – all the myriad taboo forms, in short, of non-marital, non-procreative sexuality. Their scenarios covertly dramatized new modes of intimacy, enacted outside the traditional framing institutions of marriage and the law. Like the mask, the fiction of accident was in the end, one suspects, nothing more than an enabling device, the psychological means by which subversive sexual themes found utterance. Concealed in the popular moralistic inventory of "accidental" masquerade attachments was an unprecedented imagery of transgressive pleasures.

The destabilizing power of the masquerade was expressed as much in its representations as in its own intrinsic disorders. We cannot separate the real and the fictive masquerade, for both were a part, ultimately, of a larger imaginative experiment in violation. Jean Starobinski has written that the most profound discovery of the eighteenth century was its "invention of liberty" – the intense evocation, at least in fantasy, of the freedom of the individual.[33] Granted, it would be foolish to speak of eighteenth-century western European society as sexually permissive in the modern late twentieth-century sense. But one may still speak of the general liberalizing and individualistic tendency in eighteenth-century thought. (In England, the intellectual history of feminism from Astell to Wollstonecraft lends power to such a generalization.) In the realm of sexual ideology, the movement toward individualism manifested itself variously – in a growing resistance to traditional moral authority, in self-conscious attempts to redefine the controlling institutions of marriage and the family, in the various calls for the emancipation of women, and, increasingly, in the new and controversial perception of sexual freedom as one of the privileges of civilization. For sexual radicals such as the Marquis de Sade, erotic individualism culminated, quite predictably, in an assault on the bastion of heterosexuality itself.

Western culture over the past two centuries has largely internalized (if not always officially sanctioned) this historic idealization of sexual freedom. In the twentieth century, the unconstrained nature of desire – and the need of human beings to pursue diverse objects of gratification – has become a psychological if not a political commonplace. We need not be orthodox Freudians to accept the idea of the polymorphousness of the modern subject, for whom, in theory at least, all avenues of sexual pleasure stand open. Dryden's verse, "Love variously doth various minds inspire," has been echoed most recently by Michel Foucault, who argues that through its relentless "eroticization of the body," modern Western culture has animated new objects of desire and defined forms of erotic subjectivity unknown to our forebears.[34]

Yet it is impossible to separate these important intellectual developments, finally, from the "structures of everyday life" that gave rise to them. The great theme of sexual liberty inevitably germinated in the fertile ground of eighteenth-century social practice. The real function of the masquerade may ultimately have been a heuristic one. Even while it posed as frivolity, the masquerade was also a living catalyst for reflection – a mechanism for conceptualizing, as it were, the Protean future of desire. Its "studied Devices of Pageantry and Disguise," as Benjamin Griffin called them in 1717, were also rehearsals for future transgression: theatrical experiments in the carnivalization of sexual life itself. To its voluptuous confusions, we owe – at least in part – our modern (perhaps sentimental) image of the boundlessness, freedom, and incorrigibility of Eros.

The masquerade introduced a new moral irony into sexual relations. Masquerade travesty was a mark of the profane; the inversion of sacred categories. Yet, once acknowledged, the urge toward desacralization spread outwards into society at large. In the culture of travesty, a historic new self-consciousness invaded the silent pleasure-world of the body. The flight from the "natural" had begun; the modern challenge to traditional moral and psychic structures was inaugurated. To be sure, the eighteenth-century poet of masquerade railed against the "lewd joys" of the fantastic scene:

> New ways and means to pleasure we devise,
> Since pleasure looks the lovelier in disguise.
> The stealth and frolic give a smarter gust,
> Add wit to vice, and elegance to lust.
> (Christopher Pitt, "On the Masquerades,"
> ll. 17–20)

Yet even as he turned, sardonically, from the "enormities" of the occasion, he preserved them, in the shape of an anthology – which was also a blueprint – for a universal masquerade.

NOTES

1   On Boswell's impersonations, see Max Byrd 1978: 95–7.
2   Introduction, *Herculine Barbin*, trans. Richard McDougall (New York: Pantheon, 1980), xvii.
3   E. C. Cawte, *Ritual Animal Disguise* (Cambridge: D. S. Brewer, 1978), ch. 3, esp. pp. 71 and 86.
4   On popular entertainments in the English Renaissance, see C. L. Barber, *Shakespeare's Festive Comedy: A Study of Dramatic Form and its Relation to Social Custom* (Princeton, NJ.: Princeton University Press, 1959), and Michael D. Bristol, *Carnival and Theatre: Plebian Culture and the Structure of Authority in Renaissance England* (London: Methuen, 1985). For a description of masquerading at the court of Charles II, see Gilbert Burnet 1818, 1: 292. Further anecdotal information of Resoration masquerades can be found in Sydney 1892: 367–72.
5   See Peter Burke 1978: 249; see also Joseph Spence 1975: 95.
6   See, for example, the letter condemning "mock Carnivals at Ranelagh-house" in *The Gentleman's Magazine* (May 1750).

7   On the commercialization of popular entertainment in eighteenth-century England, see Peter Burke 1978: 248–9, and Plumb 1982: 265–85.

8   See G. F. R. Barker's biographical essay, "John James Heidegger," *Dictionary of National Biography*, and Pat Rogers 1985. Public masquerades had in fact been established a few years earlier in London: there were advertisements for public masquerades at Lambeth-Wells, Spring Gardens, and elsewhere in *The Spectator* as early as 1711 (see 1: 36n.). Heidegger's Haymarket balls later in the decade, however, attracted far more public attention.

9   See "Heidegger," *DNB*, and Hogarth, *Complete Works*, 229–30.

10 *Poems and Translations* (London, 1727), reprinted in Samuel Johnson, ed., *Poets of Great Britain* (London, 1807), XLVII: 19–21.

11 Pierce Egan depicts a Regency masquerade in *Life in London* (London, 1821), Book II, ch. 3. Byron attended a masquerade at Burlington House in 1814. See Leslie A. Marchand, *Byron: A Portrait* (Chicago: University of Chicago Press, 1970), 171.

12 Suggestive masquerade scenes occur in Defoe's *Roxana* (1724); Mary Davy's *The Accomplished Rake; or The Modern Fine Gentleman* (1727): Richardson's *Pamela*, Part 2 (1741); Cleland's *Memoirs of a Woman of Pleasure* (1749); Fielding's *Amelia* (1751); Smollett's *Adventures of Peregrine Pickle* (1751), and a host of minor works of the period. A typically melodramatic shorter tale is the "Affecting Masquerade Adventure," published in *The Gentleman's Magazine* (December 1754).

13 *The Conduct of the Stage Consider'd, with Short Remarks upon the Original and Pernicious Consequences of Masquerades* (London, 1721). I refer to this work elsewhere as *Short Remarks*.

14 *Weekly Journal* (April 19, 1718).

15 See *The Memoirs of Casanova*, trans. Arthur Machen (New York: G. P. Putnam's, 1959), 4: 557. On the history of masquerade costume, see Aileen Ribeiro 1984, and Castle 1986, ch. 2.

16 Benjamin Griffin, *The Masquerade; or, An Evening's Intrigue* (London, 1717) I, i.

17 See Horace Walpole's letter to Mann, March 3, 1742 (*Correspondence*, 17: 359). *The Connoisseur* (May 1, 1755) described "one gentleman above six foot high, who came to the Masquerade drest like a child in a white frock and leading-strings, attended by another gentleman of a very low stature, who officiated as his nurse." The "two great Girls, one in a white frock, with her doll," described in *The Gentleman's Magazine* (February 1771), were also undoubtedly female impersonators.

18 *Lady's Magazine* (February 1773).

19 At a magnificent masquerade given by her husband in 1769, the Duchess of Bolton appeared first in "a Man's Black Domino," then, later in the evening, as a Persian princess. See *The Diaries of a Duchess: Extracts from the Diaries of the First Duchess of Northumberland (1716–1776)*, ed. James Greig (London: Hodder & Stoughton, 1926), 91. Elizabeth Inchbald, who had appeared as Bellario on the London stage, went to a masquerade in male dress in 1781. See *Memoirs* 1: 140–1. On Judith Milbanke's male impersonation, see *The Noels and the Milbankes, Their Letters for Twenty-Five Years*, ed. Malcolm Elwin (London:

Macdonald, 1967), 93. For other cases of eighteenth-century female cross-dressing, see Dugaw 1985; Friedli 1987; and Dekker and Lotte 1989.

20 Miss Milner, the heroine of Inchbald's *A Simple Story* (1791), is described by another character as wearing "mens cloaths" when she appears as the goddess Diana at a masquerade in that novel. Ribeiro comments on the features of the Diana costume (1984: 261–4).

21 *The Noels and the Milbankes*, 93.

22 One of the many satiric engravings commemorating Miss Chudleigh's exploit is the plate entitled "Miss Chudley in the Actual Dress as she appear'd in ye character of Iphigenia at ye Jubilee Ball or Masquerade at Ranelagh," British Museum, Print Room no. 3031.

23 Gerald Howson comments on Margaret Clap in *Thief-Taker General: The Rise and Fall of Jonathan Wild* (London: Hutchinson, 1970), 63–4.

24 James Ralph, *The Touchstone: or, a guide to all the reigning diversions* (London, 1728), 191.

25 See, for example, Eliza Haywood's warnings in *The Female Spectator*, 3rd. ed. (London, 1750), 1: 32–3. In a letter to Lady Bradshaigh, August 17, 1752, Samuel Richardson complained that "the sex is generally running into licentiousness; when home is found to be the place that is most irksome to them; when Ranelaghs, Vauxhalls, Marybones, assemblies ... and a rabble of such-like and amusements, carry them out of all domestic duty and usefulness into infinite riot and expense" (*Correspondence* 6: 25).

26 Lady Mary Wortley Montagu wrote that the Venetian custom of going about in masks led to "a universal liberty that is certainly one of the greatest *agremens* in life." She likewise believed that the amorous freedom of Turkish women was due to the "perpetual masquerade" of the veil. See Halsband 1956: 71 and 185. For Fanny Burney's description of a 1770 masquerade, see *The Early Diary of Frances Burney 1768–1778*, ed. A. R. Ellis (London, 1889), 1: 64–5. Boaden describes Inchbald's early love of "frolics" in the *Memoirs* 1: 140–1. Inchbald herself spoke nostalgically of masquerades and other "exploded fashions" in her preface to Cowley's *The Belle's Stratagem* in the *British Theatre* series (London, 1808), 19: 4–5.

27 On the historical and rhetorical dimensions of Fielding's pamphlet, see Castle 1995: ch. 5.

28 See Trumbach 1977. On the eighteenth-century molly club, see Bray 1982.

29 On Cleland's own rumored homosexuality, see Sabor's introduction to *Memoirs* (1985: xiii).

30 On the concept of the "backstage" area, see Erving Goffman, *The Presentation of Self in Everyday Life* (Garden City, NY: Anchor Books, 1959), 112–20.

31 Trumbach 1977: 23. See also Lawrence Stone's comments on the "relaxed" nature of sexual attitudes in mid-eighteenth-century London (1977: 332–5). One may dispute, of course, the extent of this tolerance; the punishments for sodomy become progressively harsher in England over the course of the century. Yet the intensifying official attack on homosexuality also suggests its growing prominence as a subcultural phenomenon.

32 On the role of the masquerade topos in eighteenth-century popular culture, see Castle 1995: ch. 7.

33 Jean Starobinski, *The Invention of Liberty*, trans. Bernard C. Swift (Geneva: Albert Skira, 1964).

34 See *The History of Sexuality: An Introduction*, trans. Robert Hurley (New York: Pantheon, 1978), for Foucault's most influential statement on the post-Enlightenment proliferation of "discourses" on sexuality. To be sure, Foucault is sometimes contradictory on the subject of whether the new descriptions of sexuality entailed new practices: in the "Preface to Transgression" in *Language, Counter-Memory, Practice: Selected Essays and Interviews*, ed. and trans. Donald F. Bouchard (Ithaca: Cornell University Press, 1977), Foucault denies that the eighteenth century proffered "any new content for our age-old acts" (30). However, in a posthumously published interview, Foucault speaks of the modern "eroticization of the body" as a concrete expansion of the "possibilities of pleasure." See Bob Gallagher and Alexander Wilson, "Michel Foucault – An Interview: Sex, Power, and the Politics of Identity," *The Advocate* (August 7, 1984), 27.

15

Theater and Counter-Theater in Burke's *Reflections on the Revolution in France*

FRANS DE BRUYN

"I shall not live to behold the unravelling of the intricate plot, which saddens and perplexes the awful drama of Providence, now acting on the moral theater of the world," wrote Edmund Burke in the opening paragraphs of the *Letters on a Regicide Peace*, his last great polemic on the French Revolution (*Writings* 9: 188). The metaphor invoked here of revolution as grand, tragic theater must be one of the most sustained leitmotivs running through the outpouring of letters, pamphlets, speeches, and treatises that the events in France provoked from Burke's prolific pen. In his earliest recorded comment on the Revolution, he wrote to Lord Charlemont on August 9, 1789 of his "astonishment at the wonderful Spectacle which is exhibited in a Neighbouring and rival Country – what Spectators, and what actors" (*Correspondence* 6: 10). The perception that all the political world's a stage is certainly not new with Burke, nor is it a point of novelty to observe, as Thomas Paine had been quick to note in 1791, that the theatrical metaphor is central to Burke's histrionic interpretation of revolutionary events. James T. Boulton voices the consensus of interpretative opinion with his argument that the theatrical references in *Reflections on the Revolution in France* are intended "to arouse the emotional fervour normally associated with serious drama and to suggest that the proper state of mind for observers of the French Revolution is that appropriate to watching a tragedy" (1963: 144).

Boulton's thesis is unexceptionable as far as it goes, but its perspective by no means exhausts the extraordinary range and complexity of Burke's theatrical allusions in his writings on the French Revolution. Taking Boulton's statement as his jumping-off point, Peter H. Melvin argues that Burke is not only advancing his own conception of the political uses of drama but also drawing attention, with characteristic insight, to the Jacobins' revolutionary political artistry, particularly their radical, totalizing conception of revolution as theater: "The whole of revolutionary society was to become a vast theater; everyone was to become an actor, a dissembler, except the Jacobins themselves" (1975: 451). As Burke himself states in the *Regicide Peace* tracts, "All sorts of shews and exhibitions calculated to inflame and vitiate the imagination, and pervert the moral sense, have been contrived" (*Writings* 9: 242).

The purpose of these public spectacles, which, Burke charged, included public rituals of denunciation – sons calling for the execution of their parents and parents denouncing their children as "royalists" or "constitutionalists" (*Writings* 9: 242) – was to purify and revolutionize French society through the coercive power of terror and mutual suspicion. Whatever their inward beliefs, citizens would be driven to enact a show of revolutionary zeal: "Anxiety which provoked mere conformity would finally produce febrile activity on behalf of the Revolution" (Melvin 1975: 451). Equally importantly, the theatrical rituals of the *ancien regime*, those public spectacles designed to enforce symbolically the authority of the existing order, were being replaced systematically by new ceremonies and observances. Thus, for a time the pomp of the Roman Catholic Church gave way to the rationalistic Cult of the Supreme Being; in Burke's horrified words, "they institute impious, blasphemous, indecent theatric rites, in honour of their vitiated, perverted reason, and erect altars to the personification of their own corrupted and bloody Republick" (*Writings* 9: 241).

Reflections on the Revolution in France was written in the opening months of the Revolution, long before the concerted theatricality of the revolutionary government became apparent. One might wish to credit Burke with a proleptic insight into the development of revolutionary ideology and behavior – by no means a frivolous or fanciful hypothesis.[1] But, another explanation can be offered for the pervasive presence of the theatrical metaphor in the *Reflections*, which is present not simply as an extended allusion embedded in the text but as an integral, architectonic element in its design. The event that occasioned the *Reflections*, Dr Richard Price's sermon at the Old Jewry commemorating the Glorious Revolution, furnishes a decisive clue. Burke's reading of Price's published sermon, *A Discourse on the Love of Our Country*, together with its appended congratulatory correspondence between the Revolution Society and the French National Assembly, alerted him suddenly to the danger the principles promulgated by the French Revolution posed to the domestic politics and social equilibrium of England. This primary concern, the risk of the revolutionary infection spreading from France to England (to borrow a favorite Burkean image), decisively influenced the shape of his argument in the *Reflections*, which, though ostensibly addressed to a French correspondent, is directed in the first instance to an English readership.

Thus, with his primary audience in mind, he is careful to address his readers in the sometimes arcane forms of eighteenth-century British political discourse. In particular, he draws attention to what might be called a "discourse of the crowd," employing emerging forms of mass political protest in late eighteenth-century England as a fundamental structural element in his treatise. Burke dwells at length on what E. P. Thompson has aptly labelled the "counter-theater" of the crowd, which countered with its own symbolism the studied theatrical style of official authority, with its coronations, levees, and Lord Mayor's days, and which opposed its own calendar of political observances to the official calendar of political celebrations and commemorations in Hanoverian England (Thompson 1974: 382–405).[2] The central dramatic plot of the *Reflections*, the October 1789 march upon Versailles, which forms the emotional climax of Burke's treatise, cannot be understood fully unless it is read in the context of the ritualized language of late eighteenth-century English insurrectionary behavior. He assimilates the novel and the unknown (the dizzying spectacle in France) to the known and familiar (civil affrays such as the Wilkite disturbances and the Gordon riots), and invokes potent English political myths dating from the Civil War and the Glorious Revolution in a violent struggle to establish the interpretative boundaries that will govern the English response to events in France. Burke finds himself locked in a conflict with the Revolution's well-wishers, both moderates and radicals, for interpretative authority: whose reading of the Revolution and whose appropriation of the symbols and rituals of English political discourse are to prevail?

In giving such vivid life to the dramatic counter-theater of the Revolution, Burke also poses some interesting questions about the official or culturally sanctioned theater of his time, which finds itself under challenge by new modes of literary consciousness and expression. In the *Reflections* a contestation of literary genres is especially apparent, as heroic tragedy finds itself being written out of the generic hierarchy. In response Burke inserts an episode of tragic sensibility into his discourse (the assualt upon the royal family), and he adds, by way of commentary on his unusual narrative procedure, a lengthy critical passage defending the authenticity of traditional tragedy and the emotional responses aroused by it. All this is in vehement rejoinder to what he regards as spurious, upstart attempts to refigure the Revolution as a lyric, comic celebration in which a new, demotic cast of protagonists treads the stage. If hierarchy could be challenged in one quarter, it could be questioned in others as well, including the hierarchical conception of literary form. The eighteenth-century model of literary genres as an interrelated system had proved flexible in accommodating new forms such as the novel, but it also made possible new ways of thinking about the relations among forms and modes of expression. Such a re-evaluation might lead to the questioning of the very premisses of hierarchy upon which the prevailing theory of genres rested. The *Reflections* witnesses to and protests the rapid process of literary innovation underway at the turn of the nineteenth century: it fuses literary and cultural criticism with political polemic in a memorable synthesis.

I

The most celebrated of the many responses to Burke's *Reflections* is Thomas Paine's *Rights of Man* (1791). That Paine's reply deserves its high reputation is evident in the incisiveness with which he defines the clash of interpretative discourses in the debate that the *Reflections* has triggered: "I cannot consider Mr Burke's book in scarcely any other light than a dramatic performance; and he must, I think, have considered it in the same light himself, by the poetical liberties he has taken of omitting some facts, distorting others, and making the whole machinery bend to produce a stage effect. Of this kind is his account of the expedition to Versailles. . . . It suits his purpose to exhibit the consequences without their causes. It is one of the arts of the drama to do so" (1969: 81–2). To Burke's tragic scenes he seeks to counterpose truth: fact opposes fiction in this passage, and life confronts art.

In a fundamental sense, Paine sees no interpretative clash at all between his and Burke's accounts of the Revolution, but only the opposition of reality to quixotic delusion. "Mr Burke should recollect that he is writing History, and not *Plays*; and that his readers will expect truth, and not the spouting rant of hightoned exclamation." Paine does not pause to reflect that historiography is as much a narrative or dramatic art as the writing of plays, an insight that Burke instinctively grasped. By assigning appropriate "facts" and "causes" to explain the "consequences" that Burke dwells upon, Paine ineluctably commits himself to his own narrative or version of events. He cannot do otherwise, for the effort to understand discrete historical events inevitably involves him in the articulation of a plot or story. Defending his sequence of explanation as more accurate and comprehensive than Burke's, Paine argues, "If the crimes of men were exhibited with their sufferings, stage effect would sometimes be lost, and the audience would be inclined to approve where it was intended they should commiserate" (72, 82). True enough, one is inclined to respond, but then the audience would be viewing a different play, as Paine intends they should.

The dramatic scenes Burke places at the center of his *Reflections* exploit a powerful double perspective, offering two simultaneous versions of the march on the king and queen at Versailles. One of these is the familiar tragic plot: the violent assault upon Marie Antoinette, followed by the *Via Dolorosa* of the royal family's forced return to Paris – Burke's "Jacobean tragedy," as Ronald Paulson terms it (1983: 76). The other is the same sequence of events with the revolutionary crowd placed in the foreground, not unlike, in a sense, the foregrounding of Satan in the opening books of *Paradise Lost.* Though he views the crowd close up, Burke is observing its behavior disapprovingly from above, very much in the manner that Alexander Pope surveys the antics of the duces in his *Dunciad.* Pope's poem invokes a generic hierarchy in which serious, elevated discourse is assimilated to the genres of tragedy and epic and is contrasted with the inferior, impure discourse of the duces, which is grotesque, burlesque, and bathetic. Pope and Burke are caught up in an elaborate rhetoric of exclusion, associating their cultural and political enemies with the grotesque, low elements of the street and carnival – an outdoor, urban culture, both repellent and fascinating, that was progressively repudiated and displaced in the eighteenth century by the more "rational" and respectable pleasures of the coffee house, salon, and spa. At the same time, the visionary force that fires them both and energizes their writing draws its power, paradoxically, from precisely those subterranean elements their impassioned discourse seeks to exorcize and exclude. As Peter Stallybrass and Allon White note with reference to Pope, "whilst Augustan poetry witnesses an unprecedented labour of transduction in which it battled against the Smithfield Muse to cleanse the cultural sphere of impure and messy semiotic matter, it also fed voraciously and incessantly from that very material."[3]

The emotional intensity and texture of authenticity that Burke communicates in his descriptions of crucial, dramatic revolutionary events – despite his having been witness to none of them – originate in his experience of the Wilkite disturbances and the Gordon Riots in London, the latter disorders a scant ten years in the past at the time of the French Revolution. Burke recalls Lord George Gordon in the *Reflections*, drawing an explicit parallel between the English "mob ... which pulled down all our prisons" and the Parisians who stormed the Bastille in July, 1789 (*Writings* 8: 135). His parliamentary speeches of the early 1790s attest repeatedly to his conviction that significant correlations existed between the two events. During the Gordon Riots of 1780, he experienced at first hand the fury of the mob, whipped up into an anti-Catholic frenzy; as an outspoken supporter of the Catholic Relief Act (1778), he had become a direct target of the rioters. Though soldiers were dispatched to protect his London house, from which books and pictures had been prudently removed, Burke himself refused to be intimidated by the crowd and went out deliberately "in the street amidst this wild assembly into whose hands I deliverd myself informing them who I was" (*Correspondence* 4: 246).

A report of the parliamentary debates following the riots (June 19 or 20, 1780) records briefly Burke's impressions of what he had seen:

> He went into a full account of the late riots; expatiated on the inhumanity of the mob; said that Mr. Langdale, with twelve children, had suffered to the amount of £50,000.... The inhumanity of fanatics, he said, was such, that after the destruction of the school near the city, a petition had been presented, desiring that the poor man, who owned it, might not have a lease of the land again to build another.... [H]e quoted, in a facetious manner, the names of several women – not being able to read and write themselves, these monsters were desirous of preventing others from receiving education.... Mr. Burke stated, in a very long speech, the means taken to bring about all the mischief; he said it had happened by the zeal of wicked and abandoned men, who had gone about industriously misleading poor, ignorant, and deluded people. (*Speeches* 2: 178–9)

Though this account offers little more than the barest summary of Burke's speech, it highlights a number of elements that were to figure prominently in his subsequent descriptions of the Parisian mob. His appeal to the emotions of his auditors through affecting personal anecdotes, his exaggerated characterization of the rioters as base, inhumane, "wicked and abandoned" fanatics and monsters, his singling out of the women participants as latter-day furies, and his recognition of a symbolic selectiveness in the crowd's choice of victims – all these elements in his analysis of the Gordon Riots recur conspicuously in the famous narrative of the march on Versailles. In that account, the Parisians invading the palace are transformed into a "band of cruel ruffians and assassins, reeking with ... blood," and they leave in their destructive wake a scene "swimming in blood, polluted by massacre, and strewed with scattered limbs and mutilated carcases." Burke's narrative continues:

> Two ... of the gentlemen of birth and family who composed the king's body guard ... with all the parade of an execution of justice, were cruelly and publickly dragged to the block, and beheaded in the great court of the palace. Their heads were stuck upon spears, and led the procession; whilst the royal captives who followed in the train were slowly moved along, amidst the horrid yells, and shrilling screams, and frantic dances, and infamous contumelies, and all the unutterable abominations of the furies of hell, in the abused shape of the vilest of women. (*Writings* 8: 121–2)

Even a cursory comparison with contemporary accounts reveals how Burke has embellished and heightened the facts; what he hoped, however, was to furnish an account that would ring imaginatively true for his audience.[4] This he accomplishes by attributing to the Parisian throng precisely those characteristics that distinguished, at least in the estimation of the English elite, the behavior of London crowds. Standing at one remove from the French Revolution, Burke offers his readers an English fiction because English political realities are his primary concern.

II

To understand fully the discourse of the crowd that informs Burke's crowded, bloody scene, one must revive imaginatively a sense of the ceremonial and theatrical splendor with which official authority clothed itself in the period – the rituals and symbolism of the courts, the Church, and the Crown. The example of Tyburn, the awful rites of public execution, conveniently illustrates both the pageantry with which government and law exercised their power and the means by which the crowd subversively undercut such awe-inspiring spectacles. In his *Enquiry into the Causes of the Late Increase of Robbers* (1751), Henry Fielding draws attention to the self-conscious theatricality of the rites by which justice was enforced: executions, he suggests, should be performed like a well-written tragedy, in which a "Murder behind the Scenes, if the Poet knows how to manage it, will affect the Audience with greater Terror than if it was acted before their Eyes" (123).[5] Fielding does not argue that executions be carried out in private but instead inveighs against the prevailing carnival atmosphere on hanging days, which often transformed malefactors into anti-heroes or even martyrs to the rigors of justice. Accordingly, he insists that an atmosphere of dramatic solemnity must be maintained – if necessary, by artifice: "The Execution should be in the highest degree solemn. It is not the Essence of the Thing itself, but the Dress and Apparatus of it, which make an Impression on the Mind, especially on the Minds of the Multitude to whom Beauty in Rags is never a desirable, nor Deformity in Embroidery disagreeable Object" (*Enquiry*, 124). As a successful dramatist, Fielding might be expected to display a keen awareness of the administration of justice as a dramatic enactment, but his analysis is none the less striking in its emphasis on the external trappings of spectacle as crucial elements in the maintenance of order and authority. Burke is of the same mind, arguing that the fomenters of the Gordon Riots should be punished with the greatest possible dramatic solemnity: "*six*, at the very utmost ... ought to be brought out and put to death, on one and the same day, in six different places, and in the most solemn manner that can be devised."[6]

The symbolism of this official theater was not lost on the crowd, which often staged its own plebian counter-theater or crowd rituals parodically mimicking the actions of its "betters." Thus, as John Brewer reports,

> on April Fool's day 1771, effigies of the Princess Dowager, Lord Bute, the Speaker of the House of Commons and the two Fox brothers were placed in two carts preceded by a hearse, and taken through the streets of London to the properly constituted execution place of all traitors, Tower Hill, where they were decapitated by a chimney-sweep who also doubled as the officiating minister; they were then ceremoniously burnt.... Here was ritual retribution on a parallel with that actually exacted during the Revolution in France. (1976: 184)[7]

The crowd's actions mimic the solemnities of a public execution: "the ritual of authority became the rites of the mob." This deliberate act of mimesis – the appropriation of the trappings of authority by a subordinate group to enact *their* conception of justice – disturbed and obsessed the authorities, as is evident in the singlemindedness with which they hunted down the standards, trophies, and symbols of the crowd during popular protests. The reason for this preoccupation with symbolic trappings is not difficult to fathom. Brewer cites the astute observation of Adam Ferguson in his *Essay on the History of Civil Society* that any civil order organized on the basis of hierarchy and subordination depends heavily on public ritual to mark subtle gradations of status and power:

> The object of every rank is precedency, and every order may display its advantages to their full extent. The sovereign himself owes great part of his authority to the sounding titles and dazzling equipage which he exhibits in public. The subordinate ranks lay claim to importance by a like exhibition, and for that purpose carry in every instant the ensigns of their birth, or the ornaments of their fortune. What else could mark out to the individual the relation in which he stands to his fellow subjects, or distinguish the numberless ranks that fill up the interval between the state of the sovereign and that of the peasant? Or what else could, in states of a great extent, preserve any appearance of order, among members disunited by ambition and interest, and destined to form a community, without the sense of any common concern?[8]

Without the official theater of state – coronations, state openings of parliament, court levees, Lord Mayor's Days – individuals would lack a collective focus, a point of cynosure, upon which to fix a sense of community and common enterprise. With the advent of an increasingly rootless, atomized, capitalist social order, "disunited by ambition and interest," these rites of state seem to Burke more crucial than ever; at the very time that subordination comes increasingly under pressure, its indispensability as an instrument of social control becomes more and more apparent. "The magistrate must have his reverence, the laws their authority," he argues. "The body of the people must not find the principles of natural subordination by art rooted out of their minds. They must respect that property of which they cannot partake" (*Writings* 8: 290). The keen consciousness of rank and forms of deference in the period ensured that parodies of official theater from below were often viewed with alarm rather than amusement. It was one thing to adopt a parodic discourse from above, as Pope does in his mock-heroic poems, but quite another to do so from the déclassé perspective of the dunces.

A similar obsession with counter-theatrical symbolism can be detected in Burke's description of the Parisian crowd at Versailles. He dwells on the throng's trophies, the two "heads ... stuck upon spears" leading the procession, which bring to mind the grisly and monitory spectacle of the traitors' heads customarily left grinning and festering on Temple Bar. The marchers on Versailles perform a consummate act of counter-theater, "all the *parade* of an execution of justice" (emphasis mine), which is all the more terrifying to Burke because it has begun to literalize what had previously been a purely symbolic discourse (as in the mock executions described above by Brewer). Though often destructive in their effects, the English rituals of political protest – "effigy burning; the hanging of a boot from a gallows; the illumination of windows (or the breaking of those without illumination); the untiling of a house" – tended to channel promiscuous violence, directing it at specific targets (Thompson 1974: 400).[9] With the French revolutionaries these rituals have taken a demonic turn, escalating crowd violence to a new level of ferocity and apparent indiscriminateness.

Burke strains for a comparison sufficently sensational to convey his sense of the monstrous indignity visited upon the royal family as they were triumphantly escorted back to Paris on October 6, 1789: "It was ... a spectacle more resembling a procession of American savages, entering into Onondaga, after some of their murders called victories, and leading into hovels hung round with scalps, their captives, overpowered with the scoffs and buffets of women as ferocious as themselves, much more than it resembled the triumphal pomp of a civilized martial nation" (*Writings* 8: 117). The contrast between theater and counter-theater is made explicit here: the "triumphal pomp of a civilized martial nation" (a phrase of exquisite, if unintentional, irony) is set against the savage spectacle of the Parisian mob, whose symbols are no longer a boot or an effigy but the bloody scalps of their victims. Burke seeks to counter the obvious symbolic force of the triumphal return to Paris by transmuting the context or discursive field within which its symbolism can become intelligible. Like Swift, who subverts Puritan claims to divine afflatus by explaining the "operation of the spirit" in the mechanical terms of pseudo-scientific discourse, conflating inspiration and libido, he undercuts the corporate and political legitimacy of the Parisian crowd's actions by reducing them to a context of anarchic savagery – that of a pre-social, Hobbesian state of nature. The protests of the crowd are thus drained of any political significance and can be read only as acts of blind, irrational violence. Burke vehemently denies any coherence or intelligibility to the crowd's counter-theatrical discourse, even as he affirms the official theater of France's "triumphal pomp," its coercive military might.[10]

III

The ritual of official theater in eighteenth-century Britain was closely tied up with calendrical observances – anniversaries of important historical events – whose commemoration had great symbolic and ideological significance. In the urbanized and increasingly politicized atmosphere of Georgian England, the time-honored dates of the agricultural year (May Day, Plough Monday, Twelfth Night, etc.) were displaced by celebrations of the nation's political landmarks: the reigning monarch's birthday; the birthday and accession of Charles II, marking the Restoration (May 29); the date of the Hanoverian succession (August 1); the birthday of William III and the occasion of his landing at Torbay, celebrated as the anniversary of the Glorious Revolution (November 4); and Guy Fawkes' Day (November 5). These holidays together constituted a Hanoverian political calendar designed, as John Brewer remarks, "to inculcate loyal values in the populace, and to emphasize and encourage the growth of a national political consensus" (1982: 247). On a number of occasions, however, particularly in the first half of the century, the calendar became a focus for ideological conflict, with Whigs and Tories, Hanoverians and Jacobites celebrating rival Hanoverian and Stuart anniversaries with processions, effigy-burnings, oaths, toasts, and commemorative sermons. Thus, for example, Jacobite attempts to burn William III in effigy on November 4, 1715 were broken up by Whig supporters, who in turn organized pope-burning processions and anniversary celebrations of their own as demonstrations of loyalty to George I.[11]

By mid-century, with the question of the royal succession no longer in dispute, the dates of the political calendar were celebrated in a spirit of general unanimity. But with the emergence of this public consensus, the calendar and its rituals of observance, like other symbols of official authority, became in their turn the targets of parody and mock-imitation. The radical movement that coalesced around John Wilkes in the 1760s created, according to Brewer, a counter-calendar of celebrations parodying the established cycle of anniversaries. "Wilkes's birthday, the anniversary of the St. George's Fields Massacre, the numerous Middlesex elections, the release of Wilkes from the King's Bench, each of these occasions was fêted not merely as a celebration but as a means of impinging upon the popular political conscience in a way that the government had employed for over a generation" (1982: 248).[12]

The demonstrations that marked these counter-celebrations were generally orchestrated by that most characteristic eighteenth-century institution, the club. The proliferation of local clubs, lodges, and societies in the period served a wide variety of purposes: economic, social, political, literary, and intellectual. Through their pooling of financial, intellectual, and organizational resources, these voluntary associations conferred a degree of independence upon their members from traditional economic and political relationships of clientage and aristocratic patronage. Radical leaders such as Wilkes found in the clubs a ready source of financial and political support which they shrewdly exploited. Unlike the loyalist societies or "mug-house" clubs of the early Hanoverian years, which were organized by the Whig gentry to inculcate loyalty to the new regime, the later associations provided an organizational foundation for independent political thought and initiative.

The symbolism and discursive activity organized around the political calendar and the clubs forms a salient, though often overlooked, constituent of the historical context within which the *Reflections* was conceived. In reviving this feature of the political culture in which Burke and the *Reflections* were immersed, I do not mean to provide a kind of scenic historic landscape or backdrop against which his work can picturesquely be situated. The aim, rather, is to "historicize" Burke's treatise: to remind ourselves, as Michael McKeon observes of literary texts in general, that the text "partakes of historical process: that it is a strenuous and exacting labor of discourse that seems thereby to detach itself from its historical medium, but that bears within its own composition the distinguishing marks of its continuity with the world it has ostensibly left behind" (1987: 37). The *Reflections* has been spectacularly successful in rising above the intellectual fray, as indicated by its status as a classic of political philosophy and of modern conservatism, but when it is resituated in the historical discourse of its time, its tone of magisterial authority gives way to one of strenuous striving and debate – a debate immersed in the contemporary, historically specific discourse symbolized by the Hanoverian calendar.

The opening pages of the *Reflections* establish the ground on which this initial battle in the propaganda war over the French Revolution is to be fought. The event Burke identifies as having occasioned his treatise, the annual meeting of the Revolution Society on November 4, 1789, does not, on the face of it, appear to pose much of a threat: "I find, upon enquiry, that on the anniversary of the Revolution in 1688, a club of dissenters, but of what denomination I know not, have long had the custom of hearing a sermon in one of their churches; and that afterwards they spent the day cheerfully, as other clubs do, at the tavern" (*Writings* 8: 56). Burke admits that there is, on the surface, "nothing" here to which he can reasonably "take exception"; he even acknowledges that he has "the honour to belong to more clubs than one, in which the constitution of this kingdom and the principles of the glorious Revolution, are held in high reverence" (56, 54). But having implicitly recognized the important role of clubs like the Revolution Society as voices and moulders of public opinion, he proceeds to repudiate and exclude what he implicitly affirms. He sets out not only to dispel any impression that the Revolution Society acts "in some sort of corporate capacity, acknowledged by the laws of this kingdom, and author-ized to speak the sense of some part of it" (57), but also to deny its legitimacy as a political voice in any capacity whatsoever, public or private.

In his vehement exclusion of the Revolution Society and its activities from the realm of legitimate political discourse, Burke betrays a profound anxiety over the power of counter-theatrical symbolism. He reiterated this anxiety on numerous occasions, including in a speech to the House of Commons on May 6, 1791, in which he links clubs and their subversive activities, anniversaries, and the specter of civil disorder:

> Were there not clubs in every quarter, who met and voted resolutions of an alarming tendency? ... Did they not preach in their pulpits doctrines that were dangerous, and celebrate at their anniversary meetings, proceedings incompat-ible with the spirit of the British constitution? ... He recurred to the events of the year 1780, and mentioned the dreadful consequences of the riots occa-sioned by Lord George Gordon. Had he at that time cautioned the House to beware of the Protestant Association, and other caballing meetings, he supposed his cautions would have been treated in the same way as those he offered now. (*Speeches* 4: 20–2)

His great fear is that the Hanoverian political calendar is about to be appropriated, or even displaced, by a revolutionary ideology with its own commemorative festivals, as he notes with dismay in *Thoughts on French Affairs* (1791):

> The appointment of festive anniversaries has ever in the sense of mankind been held the best method of keeping alive the spirit of any institution. We have one settled in London; and at the last of them, that of the 14th of July, the strong discountenance of Government, the unfavourable time of the year, and the then uncertainty of the disposition of foreign Powers, did not hinder the meeting of at least nine hundred people, with good coats on their backs,

who could afford to pay half a guinea a head to shew their zeal for the new principles. (*Writings* 8: 379–80)

Not only Bastille Day, but also October 5 and 6, commemorating the exultant return of the people of Paris with their king and queen, might well become a "festive anniversary" in a revolutionary calendar: hence, Burke's eagerness to characterize the events of those two days as a "horrid, atrocious, and afflicting spectacle" (117) rather than a triumphal progress. But try as he might to exclude this popular discourse and dismiss its proponents as outside the limits of rationality and respectability, he is none the less forced to acknowledge amongst this "rabble" the presence of many individuals with a considerable stake in their country – "with good coats on their backs" and guineas in their pockets.

Burke also fears a revival of the ideological conflict that the dates of the political calendar had occasioned in the early Hanoverian period. Dr Price's commemorative sermon sets forth a revisionist picture of the Glorious Revolution which threatens, in Burke's view, to make November 4 a celebration of political ideals that are potentially revolutionary in scope. The question at issue is what kind of narrative will be fashioned out of the facts of history; in a nation deeply imbued with the habit of defining itself in terms of its past, what version of that past, what memory, is to prevail? "In history a great volume, is unrolled for our instruction," affirms Burke, but its value depends much on *how* it is told, as he immediately warns: "It may, in the perversion, serve for a magazine, furnishing offensive and defensive weapons for parties in church and state, and supplying the means of keeping alive, or reviving dissensions and animosities, and adding fuel to civil fury" (189). This danger is evident in the revolutionary typology Price has created by juxtaposing three historical dates: the execution of Charles I, the Glorious Revolution, and the recent events in France – "confounding all the three together" (66), as Burke puts it. First, he accuses Price and his followers of turning the annual celebration of the Glorious Revolution into a subversive affirmation of radical democratic principles (thereby resituating November 4 as a ground of partisan conflict, which it had so frequently been earlier in the century, rather than as the confirmation of political consensus that it subsequently became). Second, he suspects them of transforming the anniversary of Charles's execution, January 30, from a day of solemn commemoration into one of unseemly celebration. Finally, to complete their revised political calendar, they include Bastille Day as a holiday appropriate to be observed by freedom-loving Englishmen.

In a speech before the House of Commons on May 11, 1792, Burke offers his scenario of the consequences that will follow from such observances; dissenters and radicals, he predicts, "met to commemorate the 14th of July, shall seize the Tower of London and the magazines it contains, murder the governor, and the Mayor of London, seize upon the king's person, drive out the House of Lords, occupy your gallery, and thence, as from an high tribunal, dictate to you" (*Speeches* 4: 64). Here the countertheater of the crowd, the mock-ceremonial of the street, ceases to be a symbolic gesture and threatens suddenly to become a genuine social explosion; the dream-like visions of Pope's *Dunciad*, in which the carnivalesque, populist entertainments of the Smithfield muses invade the precincts of Westminster, threaten to become a demonic, nightmarish reality. This has already happened in France, where the National Assembly has dwindled into "a profane burlesque" performing a "farce of deliberation":

> They act like the comedians of a fair before a riotous audience; they act amidst the tumultuous cries of a mixed mob of ferocious men, and of women lost to shame, who, according to their insolent fancies, direct, control, applaud, explode them; and sometimes mix and take their seats amongst them; domineering over them with a strange mixture of servile petulance and proud presumptuous authority. (*Writings* 8: 119)

The symbolic inversion alluded to in this passage – the *mundus inversus* or "world upside-down" topos in which traditional hierarchies of parent and child, husband and wife, master and servant are overturned – has burst its symbolic bounds and, in the process of literalization, has been transformed into a revolutionary action.

A central question in modern studies of the counter-theatrical and the carnivalesque has been whether such parodic behavior represents a genuine mode of subversion, or serves simply as a social "safety valve," perhaps even as a reinforcement of the existing order.[13] If Burke seemed inclined to something like the latter view in his assessments of the Gordon Riots, he swings decisively to the former in his appraisal of the events of 1789. The example of France has charged the symbolic, wish-fulfilling fantasies of counter-theater with prophetic energy: "The most wonderful things are brought about in many instances by means the most absurd and ridiculous . . . and apparently, by the most contemptible instruments" (60). Accordingly, popular demonstrations can no longer be regarded as harmless releases of energy but must be repressed as subversive enactments of radical change.

To speak of inversion or a "world upside-down" motif is to adopt the point of view of the dominant strata of society, who naturally view alternative forms of expression as culturally worthless and politically illegitimate. Thus, from Burke's perspective, the "famous sermon of the Old Jewry" can be nothing else than a farcical dramatic performance – a farrago of "Plots, massacres [and], assassinations" to satisfy a depraved, bloodthirsty audience: "A cheap, bloodless reformation, a guiltless liberty, appear flat and vapid to their taste. There must be a great change of scene; there must be a magnificent stage effect; there must be a grand spectacle to rouze the imagination, grown torpid with the lazy enjoyment of sixty years security. . . . The Preacher found them all in the French revolution" (115). Burke sounds a familiar Scriblerian note, linking political upheaval with decadence in cultural standards – a decline symbolized by the the bathetic taste of Dr Price's audience for cheap sensation and "grand spectacle." Here, as with Pope's powerful prophecy of universal darkness in *The Dunciad*, something of a conscious act of imagination is required to shake oneself free of Burke's compelling vision and to view circumstances for a moment from the dunces' perspective. Yet, that perspective is involuntarily inscribed in Burke's text, and the same events that he by turns regards as farcical or tragic assume the shape of apocalyptic comedy when they are seen through the eyes of his political opponents. The opposition between these two literary paradigms, played out in the pages of the *Reflections*, constitutes the structural core of the work: the familiar political and cultural symbolism of theater and counter-theater supply not only the content but also the fundamental form of Burke's polemic.

NOTES

The following essay is an excerpt from a chapter so named in *The Literary Genres of Edmund Burke* (Oxford: Clarendon Press, 1996).

1   In his biography of Burke, Conor Cruise O'Brien describes the tendency of undergraduate readers to jump to the conclusion "that the direst events of the Revolution – the September Massacres, the Terror, the executions of the King and Queen – had already taken place when the *Reflections* was written." All of these events, together with the eventual military despotism of Napoleon (which Burke also foresaw), lay well in the future in 1790, when his analysis was published. O'Brien argues, "Burke's astonishing capacity to see into the ways in which events were moving derived, not from any mystical intuition, but from penetrating powers of observation, judicious inference from what was observed, and thorough analysis of what was discerned by observation and inference" (1992: 403).
2   See also Ronald Paulson 1979: 26–30.
3   Peter Stallybrass and Allon White, *The Politics and Poetics of Transgression* (Ithaca: Cornell University Press, 1986), 108. On the carnivalesque and the interrelation of high and low culture, see Mikhail Bakhtin, *Rabelais and His World*, trans. Helene Iswolsky (Cambridge, MA: MIT Press, 1968); and Castle 1986.
4   Cf. the account of the attack upon Versailles in *Memoirs of Madame de La Tour*

du Pin, trans. Felice Harcourt (1969; London, 1985), 125–37. For a discussion of the social composition of the crowds participating in the Gordon Riots, see Rudé, *The Crowd in History*, 1981 [1964]. See also Marshall 1968: 236–8.

5   Douglas Hay details the elaborate spectacle and ritual that surrounded the administration of justice in eighteenth-century England (1975: 26–31). Peter Linebaugh describes the theatrical and counter-theatrical spectacle of public hangings in the period (1995: 65–9).

6   Burke, "Some Thoughts on the Approaching Executions," *The Works of the Right Honourable Edmund Burke*, Bohn's British Classics, 8 vols (London, 1854–89), 5: 516.

7   The incident was reported in *The Gentleman's Magazine* (1771: 188) and in *The Middlesex Journal* (April 2, 1771). George Rudé discusses this and similar incidents (1962: 164 et passim).

8   Adam Ferguson, *Essay on the History of Civil Society* (1767; rpt Philadelphia, 1819), 126. See also Brewer 1976: 183–4.

9   Also see Rudé 1962: 62.

10   In his essay, "The French Revolution and the Condition of England: Crowds and Power in the Early Victorian Novel," in Ceri Crossley and Ian Small, eds, *The French Revolution and British Culture* (Oxford, 1959), 113–40, David Lodge demonstrates how the memories and myths of crowd behavior in the French Revolution informed the representation of crowds and violence in the fictions of several generations of Victorian novelists. He argues that these novelists – Dickens, Gaskell, Disraeli, and Kingsley, among others – responded not only to actual history, but also to "a highly imaginative, quasi-fictional interpretation of that history" (127). Lodge acknowledges Burke's role in contributing to this "quasi-fictional interpretation," but he underestimates the extent of Burke's influence by mistakenly assuming that his depiction of the revolutionary crowd is confined to the pages of the *Reflections* and that these remarks are merely "asides in an argument that is essentially abstract – constitutional, moral, philosophical" (133). As will become apparent when we return to this subject in connection with the *Letters on a Regicide Peace* (*The Literary Genres of Edmund Burke*, ch. 5), Burke's repelled fascination with the power of the crowd in the French Revolution surfaces again and again in his writings of the 1790s. I suspect he played a larger role than Lodge estimates in shaping these Victorian attitudes and modes of representation.

11   Nicholas Rogers, "Popular Protest in Early Hanoverian London," *Past and Present*, 79 (May 1978), 77–9.

12   See also Brewer 1976: 178–9; and Rudé 1962.

13   On this point see, e.g., Fredric Jameson, *The Political Unconscious* (Ithaca: Cornell University Press, 1981), 84.

16

Cowper's Hares

DAVID PERKINS

In 1774 the poet William Cowper acquired a leveret or young hare about three months old. Its round face, snub nose, and large eyes and ears might have been perceived, consciously or unconsciously, as baby features and evoked protective emotions.[1] Moreover, it was cuddly. Its life, as Cowper doubtless knew, had to this point been one that human parents would not wish for their infant. When it was three days old, the leveret, like all English brown hares, had been placed by its mother in a shallow depression or "form," there to lie alone day and night. Its mother visited it once in twenty-four hours to nurse for three or four minutes. A shepherd's dog discovered it, and the shepherd gave it to the parish clerk, who intended it as a pet for his children. They, however, neglected it, and the compassionate clerk offered it to the poet.

At this time Cowper was emerging, still shattered, from fifteen months of insanity, and he was glad, he tells us, "of any thing that would engage my attention without fatiguing it . . . in the management of such an animal, and in the attempt to tame it, I should find just that sort of employment which my case required."[2] Soon he had two more hares. How the hares felt about being kept and managed, Cowper seems not to have worried. Young hares can sometimes be trained to be affectionate, but they cannot be domesticated. Cowper's hares were captives and would run away if they had the chance. But Cowper's conscience as a keeper of hares (and wild birds in cages) did not trouble him. He had saved the hares from being hunted.

Cowper wrote about his hares in the great epitaph for Tiny ("Epitaph on a Hare"), the Latin epitaph for Puss ("Epitaphium Alterum"), a brief prose report in the *Gentleman's Magazine* (June 1784), and occasionally in his letters. The prose piece was a favorite with children for several generations and moved an anonymous admirer (actually his cousin Theodora) to present Cowper with "a Snuff-box of tortoise-shell with a beautifull Landschape on the lid of it glazed with chrystal, having the figures of 3 hares in the fore ground" (*Letters and Prose* 2: 469). He wrote affectionately about other animals, and composed several elegies or epitaphs for pets of neighbors and friends. While the hares were with him, he also had five rabbits, two guinea pigs, a magpie, a jay, a starling, a linnet, two goldfinches, two canary birds, two dogs, and sixteen pigeons.[3] A long passage in *The Task*, his most popular poem, denounces cruelty to animals. He would not have as a friend, he says, "the man / Who needlessly sets foot upon a worm" (6: 560–3). In the language of today, Cowper was an "animal lover."

His descriptions of animals have, for my feeling, a special moral fineness. Most of us, I imagine, would like both to be understood as we really are and also to find ourselves valued – a rare experience. This is the attitude Cowper brings to animals. He avoids the idealization of animals and the mystifications about them that are often present in the poetry of the Romantic tradition. Most of the time Cowper also restrains sentimental gush. He describes animals affectionately and realistically, taking a sympathetic interest in the creatures they naturally are. His "Epitaph on a Hare," on Tiny, is an example:

> His diet was of wheaten bread,
>   And milk, and oats, and straw,
> Thistles, or lettuces instead,
>   With sand to scour his maw.
>
> On twigs of hawthorn he regal'd,
>   On pippins' russet peel;
> And, when his juicy salads fail'd,
>   Slic'd carrot pleas'd him well.
>   (*Poetical Works*, 352–3)

Keith Thomas (1983) has majestically surveyed the ideas present in Cowper's time on how animals should be treated. This essay focuses on the motivations and complexities of Cowper's attitudes to animals, viewing him both as an idiosyncratic case and also as a representative one that illuminates cultural history. One would not wish to say that either bullying in public schools or Evangelical preaching generally contributed to a growing sympathy for animals, but I think they did with Cowper. His sympathy with animals, except predatory ones, was completely sincere and (in my opinion) commendable, yet in describing persecuted animals and protesting on their behalf, he was using them as surrogates and talking also about himself. He was the victim, and in reprobating heartlessness to animals, he warred against the human (and divine) cruelty that he dreaded. The tendency to denounce human nature as cruel has of course been present in the animal protest movement from then to now.

We should ask why the victims Cowper foregrounded were animals, since slaves, prisoners, prostitutes, foundlings, and other human sufferers were available. In fact, they were championed in much humanitarian discourse of his time. Possibly the cause of animals was socially and materially less threatening than that of the human downtrodden. Also, utopian qualities of innocence and harmlessness could more readily be attributed to animals than to human beings. Sympathy for animals could obliquely express hatred of man. And, of course, animals enjoyed the enormous cachet, in Cowper's time, of representing nature. These suggestions do not sufficiently answer the question, but I shall come back to it.

No important argument has yet been adduced, on the question of right conduct toward animals, that was not already urged in the eighteenth century. The opinions of Cowper's time ranged from unapologetic assertion of human self-interest to the most conscience-stricken opposites, including recognition of animal rights. Nevertheless, there was a trend toward increased sympathy for animals and protest on their behalf. Thomas notes that with industrialization and urbanization, a significant proportion of the population had, for the first time, no direct economic dependence on farming (1983: 181–3). They could afford benevolent agitations. In conversation, Alan Richardson remarked to me that the children's literature of Cowper's time abounds in sympathetic depictions of animals.[4] Richardson speculated that in this literature animals function as introductions to human otherness. Through stories about animals, children were prepared to extend fellow feeling from its traditional centers in family, region, and class to the ethnic, social, and colonial populations on the widening horizon of eighteenth-century concern. It has also been suggested that to advocate kindness to animals was a weapon against lower-class unruliness.[5] Many of the crowd entertainments of the poor – bullbaitings, dogfights – involved cruelty to animals. In a larger generalization, the protection of animals from cruelty was part of a many-sided, civilizing campaign against the aggressive savagery of human nature. Thomas points out that pet-keeping was a direct, significant cause of increased sympathy for animals (119–20, 182).

Much modern research suggests that keeping pets is medically and psychologically beneficial to human beings. Pets amuse us by their gambols, valuably distract us by their demands, and offer companionship. They like us, seek physical contact, are not judgmental, and enhance our self-respect. They also reduce stress, lower blood pressure, and help us live longer. The difference they can make seems to be particularly important for people who feel lonely, alienated, or rejected: the handicapped, the imprisoned, the convalescent, the elderly, the insane – in fact, anyone who, for whatever reason, finds it difficult to form close relationships with other people. Pets help us to socialize not only with themselves but with our own kind. All this seems intensely relevant to Cowper, who charmed people and had a few intimate friends, but who was pathologically shy, seclusive, and anxious in ordinary social life. Hares are said to be friendly with persons they know and frantically nervous with strangers, and Cowper was no different. He was insane at times, and, even when apparently sane, he was trying hard not to become insane again. His sense of self-worth cannot have been high, since he felt that God had rejected him. During all his pet-keeping years, moreover, Cowper lived in a childless household. Since, presumably, he had normal paternal instincts, the popular and scientific belief that pets are child substitutes is undoubtedly also relevant to his case.

I do not dwell further on these considerations because they have no explanatory value for the cultural history of Cowper's time. Hardly anyone then advocated pet-keeping because of its medical benefits.[6] Cowper certainly realized that pets were therapeutic for him, but, except in his essay for the *Gentleman's Magazine*, he did not stress this personal experience in his discourse about animals.

I will for a moment dwell on various features of hares that might conceivably have strengthened Cowper's identification with them. Unlike rabbits, hares do not have bolt holes, but rely for survival on concealment and speed. Living more or less in the open, they are continually on the watch, and, though the folk belief that they never close their eyes is wrong, they are unusually anxious animals. Cowper calls them "timorous," which was the common epithet. Their behavior often seems irrational, so much so that Edward Topsell, in 1607, described them as "melancholy":

> If they hear the dogs, they raise themselves on their legs and run from them; but if fearful imagination oppress them, as they oftentimes are very sad and melancholy, supposing to hear the noise of dogs where there are none such stirring, then do they run to and fro, fearing and trembling, as if they were fallen mad.[7]

Particularly in breeding season the behavior of males or bucks has given rise to the proverb "mad as a March hare." Hares are hard to keep in zoos. A sudden fright may cause them to leap against the wire with sufficient force to kill themselves.[8] In extreme danger hares shriek, and the sound is said to resemble the scream of a terrified baby (Tegner 1969: 23). Cowper's first mental collapse was precipitated when, in order to obtain a sinecure, he was required to present himself for a pro forma examination, and with this and similar memories, he might readily have sympathized with the hare's readiness to panic.

In folk belief it was thought that male hares as well as females give birth to young. Hares change sex every year, it was said, or are hermaphroditic. There is no male hare, Topsell summed up, "that is not also female" (Evans and Thomson 1972: 24). Cowper doubtless knew better. Yet, interestingly, though his three pet hares were male, he did not give male names to Tiny, Puss, and Bess, and he also referred to them occasionally by the feminine pronoun, as is the usual custom, though no one knows the reason for it (Tegner 1969: 71). Pet-keeping was not, in itself, coded as masculine or feminine, but Cowper's preferences in pets and his attitudes toward them were not traditionally appropriate for a man. Men might make pets of horses, hunting dogs, fighting or guard dogs such as mastiffs, game-cocks, and other animals to which they attributed warlike virtues of loyalty and aggression. In his inscription for the tomb of his dog Boatswain, Byron praised the dog's beauty, strength, and courage. Women's pets, on the other hand, might be lapdogs and canaries. Moreover, the right male attitude to pets combined friendship with mastery, not the protective tenderness of Cowper that he himself thought feminine. Finding in James Hurdis another animal lover like himself, Cowper said:

> I seemed to have need of somebody to keep me in countenance . . . in my attention and attachment to animals. . . . it is well . . . that here and there a man should be found a little womanish, or perhaps a little childish in . . . kissing and coaxing, and laying them [animals] in one's bosom. (*Letters* 3: 522–3)

Cowper's sexuality is largely a mystery. He flirted a bit, in cautious, conventional ways, with some of his female friends. He lived as a housemate with Mrs. Unwin, but they seem to have had no sexual relations. Suggestions that he marry Mrs. Unwin helped to precipitate Cowper's second episode of insanity, presumably by arousing intense anxieties. Unconsciously, perhaps, she replaced the mother he had lost at the age of six. If women did not inflame Cowper, nothing suggests that men did either. It seems unlikely that Cowper was at all sexually active or even interested after his breakdown in 1763, at the age of thirty-two, for he was struggling to relieve his mind of depression and terror. There are even rumors of what his most intelligent biographer, David Cecil, calls an "intimate deformity" (1929: 21). Cecil has in mind a statement by John Newton, in a now lost letter, that Cowper once confided to Newton that he was a hermaphrodite. Most modern scholarship assumes that if Cowper said this, he did so in a fit of madness, and that the statement had no basis in fact (Ryskamp 1959: 135–44).[9] His character and way of life may suggest a more than ordinary degree of feminine identification, but, on the other hand, he performed masculine roles within the household. For example, he gardened and did carpentry, but he did not supervise the kitchen, and while Mrs. Unwin and Lady Austen knitted, he read the newspaper aloud to them. If his unaggressive, unambitious, domestically sheltered lifestyle could seem somewhat androgynous as he described it in *The Task*, it nevertheless (or all the more) appealed to many readers. Praise of a retired life in rural surroundings was a frequent theme in the poetry of the age; busy, worldly people generally enjoy imaginations of a peaceful country existence. Whatever seemed androgynous about Cowper fitted in with the sentimental culture of his moment in history. The sentimental man, represented as an ideal in much of the literature of the age, blended supposedly feminine qualities of character, such as gentleness, sensitivity, and emotional susceptibility, with supposedly masculine qualities.

Whatever else hares may have represented or been associated with, the main thing, for Cowper as for everyone else, was that they were hunted – they were "the common game of hunters," as Johnson's *Dictionary* says. Poets were usually sympathetic to hares. I have in mind the anonymous medieval poem of "The Hare, to the Hunter"; Shakespeare's famous passage on "poor Wat" in "Venus and Adonis," lines 679–708; and, among eighteenth-century poets, Book Two of William Somerville's *The Chase* (1735); Robert Burns' "On Seeing a Wounded Hare Limp By Me, which a Fellow Had Just Shot At"; and James Thomson's *The Seasons*, "Winter" (1726), lines 257–61:

> The Hare,
> Tho' timorous of Heart, and hard beset
> By Death in various Forms, dark Snares, and Dogs,
> And more unpitying Men, the Garden seeks,
> Urg'd on by fearless Want.

John Gay's "The Hare and Many Friends" (in *Fables* 1727) was a favorite with Cowper as a child. James King notes the similarities in plot between this poem and Cowper's "The Castaway"; when Gay's hare is hunted, its friends, being powerless to help, abandon it. King adds that "one of Cowper's last efforts as a poet ... was to translate three of Gay's fables, including 'The Hare,' into Latin" (1986: 9n).

In Cowper's epitaph on Tiny, the association of hares with hunting comes immediately to the fore. The poem begins:

> Here lies, whom hound did ne'er pursue,
> Nor swifter greyhound follow,

> Whose foot ne'er tainted morning dew,
> Nor ear heard huntsman's hallo.

Cowper is, of course, congratulating himself on having saved Tiny from the common fate of hares. That Tiny's "foot ne'er tainted morning dew" may suggest the pathos of captivity, but taint, in this context, means to leave a scent, to become vulnerable to the pursuing dogs. A creature leaves more scent on dewy mornings than on dry ones. Cowper perhaps remembered Alexander Pope's brilliant scene in *Windsor Forest* (ll. 101–2), where the spaniel picks up the scent on the breeze:

> But when the tainted Gales the Game betray,
> Couch'd close he lyes, and meditates the Prey.

Cowper's distinction between hound and greyhound refers to two modes of hunting. The keen noses of hounds could not easily be thrown off the trace, but these dogs were not fast enough to overtake a hare. In fact, they were bred for slowness, so that the hunt would last longer, and they persisted on the trail until the hare was exhausted and could run no further. Greyhounds, on the other hand, hunted by sight and were bred for speed. On level ground they could overtake a hare. Sometimes they were trained not to bite the hare but to toss it with their noses. Starting again to its feet, the hare would furnish longer sport. The huntsman's halloo urged the hounds on. Had Tiny been hunted and caught, he might not have been eaten. If a hare is more than a year old, its meat is strong in taste and smell. Recipes generally recommended marinades and seasonings, using wine and other ingredients that would have been expensive in the eighteenth century.[10] Hare was served in households with some wealth. They were hunted mainly for the pleasure of hunting, sometimes to protect crops, and less commonly for food.[11]

Cowper deplored hunting. In attacking it, he at times writes in a quasi-Wordsworthian way of a calm, innocent nature into which the hunter intrudes, violating and defiling it by the noise he makes and the blood he spills (*The Task* 3: 298–307). The sentimental ideal of humanity identified "pity, compassion and a reluctance to inflict pain, whether on men or beasts ... as distinctively civilized." I am quoting Keith Thomas (1983: 188), who points out that the lower classes – wagoners, coachmen, the spectators at bullbaitings and cock throwings – were often deplored as savages, persons outside the circle of civilization. Though hunters were likely to be gentry, Cowper transferred this perception to them, picturing them as boorish and uncivilized. In "The Progress of Error," a hunter who dies leaping a fence will be missed only by his dogs and his groom. In "Conversation," a hunter is smelly and noisy, fit company only for his horse and (again) his groom, neither of whom desire his company. Like most animal lovers, Cowper harbored inconsistent attitudes. At times beasts were innocent, but at other times hunters might be compared to beasts. In a letter describing a fox hunt, Cowper calls the huntsman a hound and also a fiend (*Letters* 3: 118–19). When Cowper's pet hare, Puss, escaped, it was chased through the town "by a most numerous Hunt, Consisting of Men, Women, Children, and Dogs," trying to recapture it. Cowper wanted this hunt to succeed, yet feels, as he describes it, a slight distaste for the mob uproar, which he treats as comic (*Letters* 1: 382). In a passage of *The Task* (3: 307) referred to above, he speaks of hunting as filling the scene with "riot." The hunters come into nature like a lower-class mob.

Moralists had traditionally condemned cruelty to animals, though not for the sake of the animals. Cruelty, they argued, is associated with states of mind that are dangerous to society. As Samuel Johnson remarked, one wouldn't want a vivisector for one's doctor – a "physician more dreadful than the gout or stone (*Yale Edition* 2: 55–6)."[12] Cowper cites many cruelties to animals, most of them stock examples in the protest literature of his time: the slaughterhouse, where the steer is "goaded . . . To madness, while the savage at his heels / Laughs"; the spaniel beaten "Under dissection of the knotted scourge"; the draft animals mistreated by their drivers; the horse ridden to death (*The Task* 6: 419–30). (Cowper did not ride, and reluctance to use the spur was one of the reasons.) In "The Cock-Fighter's Garland," he tells the story of a wealthy gentleman who was so enraged, when his cock retreated from a fight, that he tied the bird to the kitchen spit. He intended to roast it alive but fell dead of apoplexy. Though Cowper and Mrs. Unwin gratefully received lobsters via the mail coach, he deplored the cruelties attributable to "base gluttony" (*The Task* 6: 388). Many a person in the eighteenth century reflected that the undeserved suffering of animals seemed to impugn God's benevolence. Their uneasiness was so great that, as a way out, they sometimes argued that animals must have immortal souls. Thus God could compensate in the next world for their sufferings in this. However, nothing suggests that Cowper imagined souls in animals.

It seems likely that Cowper was peculiarly sensitive to ideas of cruelty. Though he was horrified by the slave trade and wrote a few poems against it, he was reluctant to read accounts of the sufferings of slaves, fearing that they would be hurtful to him. We know very little about the nightmares and fantasies that tormented him, sometimes night after night, for he thought them indecent and did not describe them. According to John Johnson, Cowper classified his dreams as "dreams of contempt and horror – some of shame – and some were dreams of ignominy and torture." For example, he was tortured on the rack, and he "was to be let down to the bottom of the sea with ropes and drawn up again" (King 1986: 274–5). In the most lurid instance of which we have a record, he dreamed he was taking leave of his home

> on the Evening before my Execution. I felt the tenderest regret at the separation, and look'd about for something durable to carry with me as a memorial. The iron hasp of the garden-door presenting itself, I was on the point of taking that, but recollecting that the heat of the fire in which I was going to be tormented would fuse the metal, and that it would therefore only serve to increase my insupportable misery, I left it. – I then awoke in all the horror with which the reality of such circumstances would fill me. (*Letters* 4: 374–5)

It seems at least possible that certain grim passages in his poetry echo such horrors in a displaced form. I have in mind, for example, the long passages in *The Task* on the prisoner in the Bastille (5: 379–445) and on the woe of the man who revolts from God (5: 581–610). But in such passages the personal cannot be separated with any certitude from the conventional. Whether in his mad obsession Cowper imagined himself as the torturer as well as the victim cannot be known. At times, Cowper dared to think that God had treated him cruelly. As a victim, he could strongly identify with the whipped, goaded, hunted animals. This, indeed, is the burden of his famous self-description (*The Task*, 3: 108–10):

> I was a stricken deer, that left the herd
> Long since: with many an arrow deep infixt
> My panting side was charg'd.

Animals that are not hunted or otherwise victimized by humans possess, Cowper says, an immense natural happiness: "What enjoyment they have of life!" In such perceptions, temperately though they are phrased, Cowper might seem to urge the Romantic, Wordsworthian theme that the life of nature is essentially joyful, and that animals, unalienated from nature, share this vital emotion. Like Wordsworth and other poets, Cowper interpreted gratuitous leaps and runs of animals as expressions of joy. The horse in "Charity" (171–9) gallops off when it breaks its tether, its motion conveying its delight in freedom. A similarly active horse in *The Task* "skims the spacious meadow at full speed, / Then stops and snorts," and races again (6: 331–32). "The bounding fawn ... darts across the glade ... through mere delight of heart, / And spirits buoyant with excess of glee" (327–29). (The word *darts* washes the scene with a slight sadness as it subliminally recalls hunting.) A lark flying at dawn is innocent and happy; a woodman's dog bites the snow "or ploughs it with his snout; / Then shakes his powder'd coat, and barks for joy" (5: 50–1). The squirrel that ventures forth from its bed of leaves and wool "To frisk awhile, and bask in the warm sun" is also "enjoying life" (6: 314, 325). The awkward flings of cows express an "ecstasy too big to be suppress'd" (6: 340). Despite such appreciations, Cowper feels little Romantic nostalgia for animal being. Unlike many later poets, he does not suppose that animals are happier than human beings – for example, because they lack man's psychological self-division. On the contrary, the "reasonable joy" that a good man feels in seeing a happy animal is "a far superior happiness to theirs" (6: 346–7).

When animals are happy, says Cowper, we sympathize with their state of mind and thus "augment" our own happiness (6: 132). Sympathy may mean identification, empathy, a natural response in human beings. By an imaginative reflex, we recreate in ourselves the emotions of the creatures around us. Or sympathy may mean benevolence, good will, a desire that creatures should be happy. In the latter case, sympathy may be a product of socialization. In either case, the happiness of animals is a cause of happiness in us.

One might have expected Cowper's naturalistic argument to be: animals suffer; we suffer; therefore we can sympathize with animals and strive not to increase their suffering. This, more or less, was Hardy's argument a century later. But Cowper dwells very little on the natural suffering of animals. The main exception is the powerful description in *The Task* (5: 84–95) of hungry birds in winter. In Cowper's perspective, the suffering even of wild animals is largely due to humanity. Without humans the world would be – and was intended by God to be – a place of happiness. He delights in Eden-like scenes, reminders of the world as it was before the Fall, when humans obeyed "the law of universal love" (6: 360) and the happy animals had no fear of them. In such scenes, no human being is present or there is only Cowper, a harmless man familiar to the animals. On his usual walk,

> The tim'rous [wild] hare,
> Grown so familiar with her frequent guest,
> Scarce shuns me; and the stock-dove unalarm'd
> Sits cooing in the pine-tree, nor suspends
> Her long love-ditty for my near approach.
> (6: 305–9)

Or there is a dream reported in a letter: "a beautiful Red-breast, while I sat in the open air, flew to me and perch'd on my knee. Then it stood quietly awhile to be stroak'd, and then crept into my bosom. I never in my waking hours felt a tenderer love for any thing than I felt for the little animal in my sleep" (*Letters* 4: 56). With his pet hares, dogs, kittens, and pigeons, Cowper was of course restoring, in his own garden, the innocent, trusting, and kindly relations that once existed between human and animal.

What then of the fact that Cowper was a flesh eater? His letters refer repeatedly to chickens that Mrs. Unwin was fattening for the table. Let us hope that she did not feed these foredoomed creatures by hand, as Cowper's friend Lady Throckmorton did her turkey. The letters also mention oysters, lobsters, fish, and game that disappeared down his throat, and doubtless there were also sheep and steers. That we need animal food is a consequence of Original Sin, Cowper thought, but Cowper had no doubt that we are justified in taking what we need (*The Task* 6: 456–8). His attitude to animals, however sympathetic, was still firmly hierarchical. Of course he thought that animals should be dispatched with all possible consideration; he deplored, as we noticed, the "inadvertent step" that crushed the snail on the public path (6: 564); but he approved the destruction of snails in the garden, where they endanger the plants. As for spiders in the house, snakes in the shed, and so forth, tenderness of heart shows in raising the question – is it allowable to kill destructive, noxious, unclean, or otherwise unwelcome small intruders? – but Cowper's answer lies well this side of Buddhism. So also with larger animals, such as turkeys, sheep, steers, and horses. It is not wrong to use them, but only to cause unnecessary pain by venting on them human aggression and rage.

Snails, of course, are sometimes predators – in fact, cannibals – and it is as natural to take prey as to be it. Like other nature poets of his time, Cowper rarely mentioned animal predation. The reason was not, however, that Charles Darwin had not yet alerted him. He was perfectly aware of predation; he hated wolves, tigers, and all such animals. In fact, like many persons, he demonized some animals and bestowed virtue and innocence on others, and thus, with respect to animals, his imagination inhabited a world that was morally less ambiguous than the real one. Predatory animals were both dangerous to Cowper's imaginative world and superfluous within it. They were dangerous if their existence suggested that aggression and cruelty might also be natural. They were superfluous, because everything Cowper deplored in predatory animals, everything that wolves and tigers might represent to his imagination, was more terribly present in human beings, the real objects of Cowper's fear. In fact, he liked to suggest that humankind was responsible for cruelty in animals as well as to them – for example, in the selective breeding of mastiffs.

At the age of six, in his first boarding school, Cowper was so brutally and continually bullied that he had to be removed from the school. In "Adelphi," he says that he was singled out from all the children in the school by a lad about fifteen years of age as a proper subject upon whom he might let loose the cruelty of his temper. I choose to conceal a particular recital of the many acts of barbarity with which he made it his business continually to persecute me. It will be sufficient to say that he had by his savage treatment of me imprinted such a dread of his very figure upon my mind that I well remember being afraid to lift my eyes upon him higher than his knees. (*Letters* 1: 5)

In light of present-day theories, Cowper's reported statement that he was a "hermaphrodite" raises the possibility that the bullying involved sexual abuse. The term could mean a homosexual or catamite in the eighteenth century just as it can now. Whatever happened in school, it seems likely that this experience was one source of his later attitude to dominance, aggression, and cruelty, and his identification with victims. But since our quarrels are mostly with ourselves, it is also likely that the qualities he feared were strongly represented in himself and that his suppressive energies were directed against himself as well as against others. However this may have been, his poetry – and much of *The Task* especially – represents an attempt to reprove and repress the berserk potentialities of human nature. Indeed, the whole sentimentalist movement in culture can be seen in the terms of Foucault as a disciplinary effort. The rhetorical strategy of sentimental literature was partly to erect ideals of human nature and life that would supplant the older, more combative ones. But also this literature dwelt on victims, emphasizing their helplessness, innocence, and goodness and displaying their wounds in a strong light. Thus human heartlessness and frenzy were brought before the court of conscience and condemned, though of course the descriptions of victims also titillated the sadism they were supposed to dispel.

I return now to the question raised at the start. Although many human victims were featured in the protest literature of the age, they hardly figure in Cowper's poetry. The main exception is slavery, and we have seen that Cowper was reluctant to write about it as frequently or as vehemently as his friends wished. The explanation lies, I believe, in a whirl of feelings that has played a large and growing role in cultural life since Cowper's time. Once humans are taken as the antithesis of nature, they can be represented as the aggressors, intruders, polluters, or destroyers of it. Sympathy with nature may be motivated by hatred of humans, or hatred of humans by sympathy with nature, but once this circle is in being, each emotion intensifies the other. Humans view themselves with horror, and even the victims among humankind may arouse less compassion simply because they are human. In the case of Cowper, I believe, the fear of human aggressive cruelty is fundamental. From this he flies to a protected and protective, domestic, perhaps androgynous lifestyle, and he describes this as a countercultural ideal. Edenic relations with animals are one element of this larger complex. His shame from fantasies of indecency and victimization, permeating his inner life, motivated the more strongly the counter-fantasies of innocence and lovingness that he projected on animals. But one might alternatively begin with Cowper's sympathetic identification with animals as victims, and use this to explain his hatred of human masterfulness, dominance, and brutality.

Finally, there is the question of how far Cowper blamed God, saw himself as a victim of divine power unjustly and cruelly exercised. The atrocities inflicted on slaves, he confessed to John Newton, almost made him doubt God's benevolence (*Letters* 3: 106–7). What about his own sufferings? Most modern biographers assume that Cowper imagined himself as God's victim. The paranoia that led him to hear threatening voices and imagine persecutions – for example, that Mrs. Unwin was poisoning him – might certainly color his interpretation of God's dealings with him. Moreover, the few pages of his intimate diary that have survived from June and July, 1795, offer a horrifying glimpse into Cowper's mind during a time of insanity and may represent his ordinary though secret communings with himself from 1763 on. In order to understand these jottings one must recollect that Cowper believed God had ordered him to commit suicide. This command had come as a test of his faith, and he had failed. Henceforth he had been irrevocably sentenced to damnation. He asks,

> Can any sin committed in so terrible and tempestuous a moment deserve what I must suffer? . . . Judgment was infinitely disproportion'd to Mercy. . . . Coulds't thou see me entangled as I was, and see me so entangled with such a dreadful moment approaching as must necessarily decide my fate for ever, and would most probably, nay, almost to a certainty, decide it against me, coulds't thou see and foresee all this and be merciful? Vanquist before I fell, what could I do but fall? . . . What sort of Mercy is that which a poor forlorn creature reduced to childish imbecillity through infinite distress may forfeit for ever in a moment? . . . O cruel decree! that connected such terrible consequences with the lapse of a moment. (*Letters* 4: 468–9)

"It is I who have been the hunted hare," Cowper writes, "and He who turn'd me out to be hunted has" – at this point the sentence breaks off (*Letters* 4: 468).

In a touching protest against such cruelties, Cowper depicts his parlor as a scene of innocent affection in which the animals play a leading role as both loved and loving creatures. The larger world is so dangerous, so beset with snares and hunters, that the cage figures, paradoxically, as a symbol of protective care. In his household Eden, Cowper reports in a letter to Lady

Hesketh, "Beau [the spaniel] is well as are the two cats and the 3 birds whose cages I am going to clean, and all send their love to you" (*Letters* 3: 337). One wonders, of course, whether the dog, cats, and birds send their love to each other, but Cowper could not allow himself to raise this question.

NOTES

1   See the summary of literature on the innate appeal to adults of infantile physical features in James Serpell, *In the Company of Animals: A Study of Human-Animal Relationships* (Oxford: Basil Blackwell, 1986), 61–2.
2   *The Gentleman's Magazine* (June 1784), reprinted in *Poetical Works*, 652–3.
3   This list is based on passages in Cowper's letters and on a letter from Lady Hesketh cited in Dix Harwood, *Love for Animals and How it Developed in Great Britain* (New York: n.p., 1928), 215.
4   Representative titles are: Mrs. [Sarah] Trimmer, *Fabulous Histories. Designed for the Instruction of Children, Respecting Their Treatment of Animals* (London: T. Longman, 1786); *The History of Little Goody Two-Shoes* (London: John Newbury, 1765); Thomas Day, "The History of Little Jack," in *The Children's Miscellany* (London: John Stockdale, 1788); Edward Augustus Kendall, *Keeper's Travels In Search of His Master* (London: E. Newbery, 1798); *Memoirs of Dick, The Little Poney* (London: E. Newbery, 1800). For discussion, see Pickering 1981: 12–39, 84–103.
5   Keith Tester, *Animals and Society: The Humanity of Animal Rights* (London: Routledge, 1991), 95–6.
6   One of the first attempts to use pets in the treatment of the insane took place in Cowper's time at the York Retreat, an enlightened asylum using experimental methods (Michael J. McCulloch, "Animal-Facilitated Therapy: Overview and Future Direction," in *New Perspectives on Our Lives with Companion Animals*, ed. Aron Honori Katcher and Alan M. Beck [Philadelphia: University of Pennsylvania, 1983], 411).
7   *The Historie of Four-footed Beastes* (London, 1607), quoted in George Ewart Evans and David Thomson, *The Leaping Hare* (London: Faber & Faber, 1972), 28.
8   Evans and Thomson, 28; Henry Tegner, *Wild Hares* (London: John Baker, 1969), 36–7.
9   The statement that Cowper was a hermaphrodite was made by John Newton in a letter to John Thornton. Newton's letters to Thornton were sent to Robert Southey in 1834, when Southey was writing a biography of Cowper. Southey did not publish this statement, but he referred to it in his own private correspondence, making clear that he did not believe it. Charles Greville, who had seen Newton's letters, also refers in his diary to Cowper's supposed deformity. Everyone who has written on this topic assumes that if he made the statement to Newton, Cowper meant by "hermaphrodite" a genital malformation.

10 See the recipes for roast and potted hare and for hare pie in E[liza] Smith, *The Compleat Housewife, or Accomplish'd Gentlewoman's Companion*, 15th edn (London: R. Ware, 1753), 19–20, 79, 166.

11 Tegner confirms that this is still the motivation (*Wild Hares*, 72).

12 Cf. the strong condemnation of vivisectors in Johnson's comment on Shakespeare's *Cymbeline*, I.V.23 (*Yale Edition*, 8: 881).

17

Colonizing the Breast: Sexuality and Maternity in Eighteenth-Century England

Ruth Perry

> But when mothers deign to nurse their own children, then will be a reform in morals; natural feeling will revive in every heart; there will be no lack of citizens for the state; this first step by itself will restore mutual affection.
>
> Jean-Jacques Rousseau, *Emile*

The invention of childhood, ascribed by Philippe Ariès to late seventeenth- and eighteenth-century Europe, inevitably involved a vast train of changes in the organization of the family, the politics of domestic life, the separation of public from private responsibility, and the revision of accepted conventions about human priorities.[1] If we want to know more about the effects of modern child-raising patterns on the structure of Anglo-American families and gender identities, we would do well to investigate the historical effects of this "invention of childhood." Less frequently noted, but equally momentous, was the construction in that period of bourgeois motherhood – the dimensions of which current scholarship is establishing.[2] There is overwhelming literary evidence for the centrality of representations of motherhood to eighteenth-century English culture as a newly elaborated social and sexual identity for women.[3]

I want to analyze one strand of this highly complex social phenomenon and to argue that motherhood was a colonial form – the domestic, familial counterpart to land enclosure at home and imperialism abroad. Motherhood as it was constructed in the early modern period is a production-geared phenomenon analogous to the capitalizing of agriculture, the industrializing of manufacture, and the institutionalizing of the nation state. In other words, these rearrangements in the psychological constellation of the family – the invention of childhood and the invention of motherhood – can be seen as adaptations of an existing social system to the new political and economic imperatives of an expanding English empire. The heady new belief in the rational manipulation of natural forces for greater productivity – whether in manufacture or in agriculture – can be traced in the operations of the family as well as in breeding cattle or in spinning cotton.

Eventually, as Anna Davin has argued crucially, the production of children for the nation and for the empire constituted childbearing women as a national resource.[4] Already in the eighteenth century there is some evidence of a growing demographic consciousness on the part of a nation in the process of industrializing and building an empire. More people were needed to keep up with the commercial and military interests of the state – more Englishmen were needed to man the factories, sail the ships, defend the seas, and populate the colonies. A petition presented to the House of Commons on March 10, 1756, asking for increased funds for London's Foundling Hospital shows evidence of this growing awareness. It argued that the country needed more troops for national defense, and that it was in the national interest to save the lives of these abandoned children. Drafted by members of the board of governors of the Foundling Hospital, the petition pointed out that it was more cost-effective to save this native population than to hire mercenary soldiers, as had been so recently necessary to defend against a threatened invasion from France.

This connection between England's population needs and its evolving national identity as a commercial empire is patterned in the interests of the Foundling Hospital's chief administrator in 1756, Jonas Hanway (Taylor 1979). Lifelong campaigner for the rights of abandoned children – and a member of the commercial Russia Company – Hanway made explicit the connection between England's expanding colonial power and its need for more citizens. His instrumental reason for saving the lives of English orphans was linked to his vision of the imperial destiny of England. "Increase alone," he wrote, "can make our *natural* Strength in *Men* corre-spond with our *artificial* Power in *Riches*, and both with the Grandeur and Extent of the *British Empire*."[5] Author of a history of the Caspian trade, of conduct books for women, and of treatises arguing for the Foundling Hospital, he had a financial stake in the Russia Company's brisk trade in raw silk for English wool and an emotional stake in socializing women to their proper stations, as well as in protecting abandoned children.[6] For him, national interest and morality alike urged that every effort be made to stop the appalling waste of infant life. More hands were needed to hold muskets, weave cloth, and people the empire. The "preservation of deserted children" was a patriotic duty, a cause "wherein morals, politics, and the noblest passions of the human soul, meet in a more harmonious concord."[7]

Hanway was governor of the London Foundling Hospital in 1756, on the eve of the Seven Years' War, when England was arming and anxious about having enough troops for the impending crisis. In this rising war fever, the Foundling Hospital was reconceptualized by Hanway – and by Parliament – as a national resource for replenishing a population sure to be decimated in the coming conflict. The government rallied to save the lives of English infants and voted almost unlimited appropriations to the Foundling Hospital to establish a national network of rescue and care for abandoned children. All abandoned infants of a specified age (at first two months or younger, later six months, and then twelve months) were to be admitted to the hospital for medical attention and subsequently placed in the homes of wet nurses. The Foundling Hospital paid these women for their services and set up a system of inspection to evaluate their work and its results. Thousands of women were mobilized as surrogate mothers in this way, hired to play their unique part in the war effort (Fildes, *Wet Nursing*, 174–87).

Eventually Hanway came to feel that this national effort to conserve infants for the state was ill-advised; the costs were exorbitant, and the waste of infant life was still very high. There were those, too, who felt that national revenues were being badly misspent in supporting these superfluous "bastards." In 1760, four years after the experiment had been initiated, the Foundling Hospital closed its doors to all but the foundlings of London, its mandate – and its budget – shrunk to a municipal service. According to James Stephen Taylor, "The last subsidy was paid in 1771; in sixteen years Parliament had expended over £500,000 to support some 15,000 children" (1979: 293).

The lesson learned by all concerned in this project was that commodification of motherhood on such a massive scale was too expensive. The nation simply could not – or would not – pay for maternal care on an individual basis. Even at £15 a year per woman, less than half of what a skilled (male) laborer might earn, the cost of subsidizing maternal care for unwanted children was greater than the national government was willing to pay. After a brief utopian attempt, this element of reproductive service was returned decisively to the private sphere. This episode is one chapter in the ideological appropriation of women as unpaid mothers for the nation. By the end of the century, even Mary Wollstonecraft seemed to believe that a woman's claim to citizenship depended on her willingness to "mother." Though she were faithful to her husband, Wollstonecraft wrote in 1792, the woman who "neither suckles nor educates her children, scarcely deserves the name of a wife, and has no right to that of a citizen" (*A Vindication of the Rights of Women; Works* 5: 217).

Henry Abelove, writing playfully but seriously about the population explosion in England during the late eighteenth century, has suggested that this demographic bulge was an effect of a new instrumentality characteristic of heterosexual relations – as of all other human behaviors. An increasingly utilitarian attitude toward human life and human production dictated that "nonproductive" forms of sexuality were increasingly displaced and devalued during this period, replaced by a single standard of sexual activity (1989: 125–30). That the concept of bourgeois motherhood was essential to this productive view of heterosexual relations seems to me obvious. I want to argue that motherhood, that centrally important sentimental trope of late eighteenth-century English literature, effected the colonization of women for heterosexual productive relations. Following Joan Kelly's suggestion that sexual freedom is one index of women's power in other historical periods,[8] it is important to note that motherhood functioned in this period to repress women's active sexuality. This is not to assert that women's sexuality ever was encouraged culturally, although in earlier periods it was expected. Indeed, it could be argued that the image of women as sexually active was as much a cultural construction as the subsequent image of women as pure and sexless and served in its own way the male appropriation of female sexual and reproductive services. Nonetheless, it is worth noting that in the eighteenth century, maternity came to be imagined as a counter to sexual feeling, opposing alike individual expression, desire, and agency in favor of a mother-self at the service of the family and the state. This change, represented in both physiological and psychological terms, would seem to be a paradox – the asexual mother, a contradiction in terms. Even today these categories, the "sexual" and the "maternal," function as mutually exclusive descriptive attributes, a formation that feminist intellectuals have puzzled over.[9] It is beyond the scope of this essay to establish how this shift in the social construction of women's essential nature meshed with other changes in English social identities. All I can do here is locate one dimension of this change and connect it to the observations of other literary and cultural historians.

Sexuality

Students of eighteenth-century British fiction are often struck by the difference between the women imaginatively portrayed in the fiction of the earlier part of the century and the women imagined in the fiction of the latter half of the century.[10] The rakish heroines of Restoration drama, the self-advertising amorous adventurers of the love-and-intrigue novels of Aphra Behn, Delarivière Manley, and Eliza Haywood, and the freewheeling protagonists of Daniel Defoe's *Moll Flanders* and *Roxana* stand on one side of this cultural divide, while on the other side are those latter-day paragons of virtue, Evelina, Sidney Bidulph, and Emmeline, as well as Samuel

Richardson's heroines – Pamela, Clarissa, and Harriet Byron – each one arguably more sexually repressed and sexually repressive than the one before.[11] This progressive desexualization of fictional heroines is further illustrated and amplified by an array of unrelenting plots punishing fictional women for what was rapidly becoming improper – and tragic – sexual behavior. Such characters as Sarah Fielding's adulterous Lady Dellwyn, Mrs. Inchbald's rebellious Miss Milner, Amelia Opie's convention-flouting Adeline Mowbray, or Mary Wollstonecraft's courageous and freethinking Maria are all severely punished in their respective texts for taking liberties with society's rules about female chastity.

Conduct literature, of course, since the seventeenth century had consistently counseled women against sexual flirtation – before or after marriage. I am not referring to prescriptive literature, however, but to fictional representations of women. In the earlier period, women's desire and sexual agency were portrayed in fiction with a tolerance, and even enjoyment, inconceivable in the later period. The rehabilitated prostitutes in John Dunton's series, *The Nightwalker* (1696–97),[12] or Aphra Behn's play, *The Rover* (1677), for example, have no real counterparts in the fiction of the later period.[13] After about 1740, sexually promiscuous women – or even just lusty women – are never center-stage protagonists again, although they might be part of a colorful supporting cast. As Jane Spencer says, "In the typical woman's novel in the second half of the century, there may be a seduced woman but the heroine herself remains pure" (1986: 122).

Robert Bage was one late eighteenth-century author – a feminist of sorts – who several times portrayed a woman who had had a sexual mishap of one sort or another but who, though no longer a virgin, nevertheless went on to work or marry and live respectably (see n. 13). Sir Walter Scott criticized this "dangerous tendency to slacken the reins of discipline" in an otherwise laudatory memoir of Bage. He noted that a number of respected authors – Henry Fielding and Tobias Smollett among them – "treated with great lightness those breaches of morals, which are too commonly considered as venial in the male sex." But Bage, he complained, "has extended, in some instances, that license to females, and seems at times even to sport with the ties of marriage."[14]

An anecdote in Scott's biography gives further evidence for a shift in cultural assumptions about women's sexuality in the course of the eighteenth century. To illustrate how changes in taste take place "insensibly without the parties being aware of it," Scott described the experience of his great-aunt reading Aphra Behn after an interval of sixty years. It seems that this woman, Mrs. Keith of Ravelstone, "a person of some condition" who "lived with unabated vigour of intellect to a very advanced age" and enjoyed reading "to the last of her long life," asked to borrow some novels by Aphra

Behn from her literary nephew, for she remembered being much interested in Behn in her youth. When she perused the borrowed volumes, however, she was offended by the manners and language of the work and returned them to her nephew with the cheerful suggestion that he burn them. But she remarked at the same time: "Is it not a very odd thing that I, an old woman of eighty and upwards, sitting alone, feel myself ashamed to read a book which, sixty years ago, I have heard read aloud for the amusement of large circles, consisting of the first and most creditable society in London?"[15]

Thomas Laqueur has explained this cultural reconsideration of the nature of women's sexuality as part of a process establishing women's essential biological difference from men in a revolutionary context committed to sweeping clean all *socially* determined differences among people. In the context of late eighteenth-century revolutionary claims for equality between rich and poor, aristocrats and workers, men and women, the physiological differences between male and female had to be reinvented, so to speak, to offset potentially subversive claims women might make for political equality. Thus, the reexamination of women's bodies and their sexual subject position was an attempt to establish women's biological difference from men, including the possibility that women's desire – unlike men's desire – was not biologically necessary to reproduction and not "natural."[16]

The most striking aspect of this reinterpretation of the experiences of male and female bodies was the growing certainty on the part of the medical establishment that the female orgasm – or any other manifestation of women's sexual pleasure – was irrelevant to reproduction. Since male ejaculation was known to be essential for conception, the logic of physiological analogy had indicated that a female climax was also necessary for procreation – and medical authorities had always assumed women's symmetrical physiological response whenever conception took place. One appalling consequence of this assumption had been that if a raped woman became pregnant, her assailant could be acquitted on the grounds that her pregnancy proved her pleasure and hence her consent (Browne 1987: 63). Once reproduction was recognized to be independent of women's sexual pleasure, however, the existence of women's active desire became a matter of debate.[17] Historically women had been perceived as lascivious and lustful creatures, fallen daughters of Eve, corrupting and corrupted.[18] But by the middle of the eighteenth century they were increasingly reimagined as belonging to another order of being: loving but without sexual needs, morally pure, disinterested, benevolent, and self-sacrificing.[19]

The desexualization of women was accomplished, in part, by redefining them as maternal rather than sexual beings. It is this movement I want to focus on here – this double, interlocked, mutually exclusive relationship between sexuality and maternity as it was reconstructed in the middle of the eighteenth century. For in a remarkably short span, the maternal succeeded, supplanted, and repressed the sexual definition of women, who began to be reimagined as nurturing rather than desiring, as supportive rather than appetitive.

Maternity

Motherhood has not always carried with it associations of tenderness and unstinting nurture. Nor has it always been interpreted as a woman's ultimate fulfillment. According to Linda Pollock, until 1750 or so, pregnancy was treated as if it were a disease, an abnormal condition. Expectant women, for example, were bled when they felt unwell, like any other sick person (1987: 19). The fact that women stopped menstruating during pregnancy was seen as a medical problem insofar as it left them without a regular purgative cycle; they had no outlet for "noxious humours," no way to void accumulated impurities (1990: 59). But pregnancy was not yet really of much interest to the medical establishment. The texts that created the body of opinion about pregnancy and maternity in the sixteenth and seventeenth centuries were not medical but, rather, religious and legal. This discourse was designed to provide guidance on legal questions about marriage, legitimacy, and inheritance, and women were represented as disorderly and unruly beings whose sexuality needed to be controlled so that they would bear only legitimate children (Crawford 1990: 6). Herbal recipes and medical advice about what to expect during pregnancy or lying-in were directed not toward mothers but toward midwives, nurses, and medical practitioners (Fildes 1986: 116). Nor was this medical literature privileged: parents often as not rejected the advice of printed texts in favor of family lore and local customs (Pollock 1990: 59). Few detailed suggestions about the technique of breast-feeding – how to care for breasts and nipples, how often to feed an infant, how to hold the child, or when to put it to breast – can be found in this literature at all. Women were expected to learn these things from other women in a tradition of oral advice and lore. Motherhood was not yet the object of cultural control, and women were expected to muddle through it as best they could.[20]

By the middle of the century, however, motherhood became the focus of a new kind of cultural attention. Writers began to wax sentimental about maternity, to accord it high moral stature, and to construct it as noble, strong, and self-sacrificial. Admiration for mothers – and for maternal devotion – came to be a banner under which the newly constituted middle class marched. In literature, maternal sentiment began to emerge as an emotional force capable of moving a reading public, understood as the sign of an innately moral and uniquely female sensibility. In analyzing the power and popularity of John Home's famous tragedy, *Douglas* (1756), Susan Staves has argued that its success was due to the way it handled maternity, at that time a new cultural obsession. What was original in the play, particularly noted and appreciated by contemporary audiences, she says, was Home's "attempt to articulate and dramatize what was in 1756 a new sentiment: elaborated tenderness between mothers and children" (1983: 53).

Natural but learned, instinctive but also evidence of the most exquisitely refined sensibility, motherhood was celebrated in prose and poetry while medical men set about to advise women on dress, diet, and care for their children. Both scientists and moralists suddenly had a great deal to say about how women ought to behave as mothers. A complicated print culture arose, illuminating the evolving conception of motherhood – most of it directed at the women themselves, telling them how to act and how to feel (Fildes 1986: 116). Hugh Downman's poem, *Infancy; or, The Management of Children, a Didactic Poem in Six Books* (London, 1774), is a good example of the popularity of this subject and of the way in which medical experts came to dominate the discourse. Downman himself was a physician, practicing in Exeter. His extremely popular poem, a repository in blank verse of the standard English attitudes toward motherhood in this period, went through at least seven editions by 1809. Being a doctor gave Downman special authority to pronounce on this subject, for motherhood was increasingly understood to be the province of the male medical establishment. Biologically grounded, a relationship "based in nature," motherhood was the outcome of a knowable physiological process. Maternal feeling, as the medical establishment increasingly made clear, was biologically determined; women who lacked it were abnormal. "Is there a stronger principle infix'd / In Human Nature, than the zealous warmth / A Mother t'ward her Infant feels?" asked Downman rhetorically (2: 298–300).

By contrast, recall Alexander Pope's slanderous portrait of the novelist Eliza Haywood in *The Dunciad* (1728) as a sluttish mother ("Two babes of love close clinging to her waste"), heavily and even brutishly physical ("With cow-like-udders, and with ox-like eyes" [2: 150, 156]). These images clearly belong to an earlier period, before motherhood sanctified women and removed from them the taint of sexuality. Pope's images suggest a loose and instinctive sensuality – with nothing of the moral consciousness attributed to mothers later in the century. Such bovine sexual energy as Pope represented was fast disappearing from the cultural landscape by the 1760s, repressed as a motive in fictional heroines and antiheroines alike. Newer "feminine" sentiments were being elicited and demonstrated by the novels of the age – sentiments connected with maternity, such as pity, tenderness, and benevolence. Increasingly constructed as the higher good for which a woman must be prepared to sacrifice her sexual vanity, motherhood began to carry with it the suggestion of punitive consequences for sexual activity. If fictional women characters of the previous era had mated and bred casually – like Moll Flanders – maternity was now becoming a serious duty and responsibility.

The valorization of motherhood as it played into the domestication of Englishwomen in the late eighteenth century has been treated positively for the most part by cultural historians. Nancy Armstrong, for example, has argued that the cultural discourse of novels and conduct books created a new domestic domain over which women exercised authority as they were, in turn, constructed by this discourse.[21] More than a decade ago, Lawrence Stone's *The Family, Sex, and Marriage* claimed that this period witnessed the emergence of "companionate marriage" and argued that women's new role as their husbands' companions elevated women to a higher status within society. But companionate marriage is also interpretable as a more thorough-going psychological appropriation of women to serve the emotional needs of men than ever was imagined in earlier divisions of labor by gender. Educating women to be more interesting companions for men rather than as individuals with their own economic or intellectual purposes is an ambiguous advance, not one that moves very far along the path toward equality. The bluestockings' achievement is usually represented in this light – as the ability to attract men to intellectual salons, to keep them at home in domestic space and out of the bachelor atmosphere of coffeehouses and taverns.[22] This reappropriation of female subjectivity for the sake of a new cultural discourse, which separated public from private, political from personal, and market relations from domestic relations, was a colonization of women far more thoroughgoing than any that had preceded it.

Breast-feeding

As the processes associated with childbearing became the focus for a new cultural appropriation, the maternal rather than the sexual purposes of women's bodies were increasingly foregrounded in medical literature. Medical treatises multiplied on the subject of maternal breast-feeding, urging women to nurse their own children for a variety of medical, social, and psychological reasons. This outpouring was a novel phenomenon, created both by the existence of a print culture and by a seismic shift in cultural conceptions of family. Nothing like it existed earlier. The medical establishment seemed determined to convince women to nurse their own children – for their own sakes, for the health of their children, and often for the good of the nation.[23] The tone of these treatises was admonitory, with moral exhortations mixed in among the physiological descriptions and scientific explanations. Many followed Rousseau's *Emile* (1762), castigating women as selfish, callous, and unnatural who would not give themselves the trouble to nurse or waxing sentimental and voyeuristic at descriptions of lovely mothers suckling their infants. "Let not husbands be deceived: let them not expect attachment from wives, who, in neglecting to suckle their children, rend asunder the strongest ties in nature," warned William Buchan in his 1769 *Advice to Mothers*. No woman who was not able to nurse should breed; if she could not "discharge the duties of a mother ... she has no right to become a wife" (217–18). Hugh Smith assured his women readers in 1767 that they would lose nothing by nursing. "O! That I could prevail upon my fair countrywomen to become still more lovely in the sight of men! Believe it not, when it is insinuated, that your bosoms are less charming, for having a dear little cherub at your breast" (76). Even Mary Wollstonecraft echoed this promise of domestic devotion when she recommended maternal nursing in *A Vindication of the Rights of Women*:

> Cold would be the heart of a husband, were he not rendered unnatural by early debauchery, who did not feel more delight at seeing his child suckled by its mother, than the most artful wanton tricks could ever raise; yet this natural way of cementing the matrimonial tie ... wealth leads women to spurn. To preserve their beauty, and wear the flowery crown of the day, which gives them a kind of right to reign for a short time over the sex, they neglect to stamp impressions on their husbands' hearts that would be remembered with more tenderness when the snow on the head began to chill the bosom, than even their virgin charms. (*Works* 5: 213)

Wollstonecraft reinscribes here the mutually exclusive nature of sexuality and maternity, the choice women were expected to make between trying to hold their husbands with "wanton tricks" or with the spectacle of suckling an infant – a sight to which only the most debauched of men failed to respond. Yet women of means were still choosing to hire wet nurses, choosing the ephemeral "flowery crown of the day" rather than the more "natural way of cementing the matrimonial tie." For both were not possible: either one stamped lasting impressions on a husband's heart with the image of one's maternal devotion and self-sacrifice or with one's "virgin charms," one's sexual attractions. The former was natural, appealing to all but the most degraded tastes, while the latter was "wanton" and unnaturally sexualized.

By the time Wollstonecraft wrote this passage, sentimental exhortations like hers had been appearing since the middle of the century, together with an increasing number of fictional representations of model maternal behavior and medical arguments for the "scientific" benefits of maternal breast-feeding. This discourse – in conduct books, novels, magazine essays and stories, children's books, and medical treatises – erupting as it did in the middle of the eighteenth century is testimony to the intensifying cultural significance of motherhood. The medical focus on maternal breast-feeding can be interpreted as the beginning of the physiological colonization of women's bodies corresponding to the psychological colonization of women's subjectivity in both companionate marriage and motherhood.

The locus – both symbolic and real – of this new appropriation of women's bodies for motherhood and for the state was the maternal breast. Distinctions between fathers' and mothers' parental roles, as well as male expertise about women's reproductive capacities and bodily processes, were joined here. It was as if this organ became the site of the struggle over the maternal definition of women, staged in opposition to the sexual definition of women. Increasingly, as the second half of the century unfolded, maternal breast-feeding became a moral and a medical imperative for women of all classes.

The cultural climate surrounding childbearing and breast-feeding had been noticeably different in the previous century. Not only had there been little prescriptive literature on the subject, as I have noted, but that little was directed not at mothers but at midwives and medical practitioners. Wet-nursing was so widespread in England, taken so much for granted in the seventeenth century, that aside from a few eccentric exhortations to mothers to nurse their own children, the controversy about breast-feeding focused not on who nursed the child (a wet nurse or a birth mother) but on whether or not breast-feeding was preferable to artificial feeding. According to Valerie Fildes, there was a fad during the last quarter of the seventeenth century in England among aristocrats for bypassing nursing altogether, a "radical change in ideas and practice of infant feeding among some of the wealthier classes" (1986: 288).[24] Medical experts of that period advocated raising infants "by hand" or to "dry-feeding" them, which meant eschewing breast milk altogether and feeding them water or milk gruels made with breadcrumbs, sugar, and sometimes butter or other forms of grease. This lethal practice was encouraged by James II, who, on the advice of his royal physicians in 1688, decided to dry-feed his heir in this manner. Apparently numbers of aristocrats followed suit, despite the ill success that attended this method of feeding.

This extraordinary medical advice must be understood as a backlash to what was in fact a very widespread practice of wet-nursing. For despite the peculiar desire of the wealthiest classes to raise their children "by hand," English wet-nursing was at an all-time historical high in this period.[25] Mothers from a wide spectrum of classes – the wives of merchants, farmers, scholars, lawyers, physicians, and clergymen, as well as aristocrats and gentry

– regularly hired wet nurses to breast-feed their newborns in the late seventeenth and early eighteenth centuries (Fildes 1986: 99). The aristocratic interest in raising infants "by hand" may have been motivated by a desire to distinguish their practices from those of the less wealthy classes, or by a shortage of wet nurses, or by a distaste for the lowborn women to whom they had to resort for this service. But it is noteworthy that dry-feeding had the sanction of "medical science" in this period and was considered to be the latest advance. What these phenomena demonstrate – both the enthusiasm for "dry-feeding" and the practice of hiring wet nurses – is that women's sexual identity was not yet defined, independent of class, by their willingness to give themselves to their reproductive tasks. In 1689 Walter Harris lamented that "so many *Mothers*, not only of high Rank, but even of the common Sort, can with so much Inhumanity, and more than Brutish Cruelty, desert their tender Offspring, and expose them to so many Dangers of mercenary Nurses."[26]

In 1711 Richard Steele created a cranky male reader in one of his *Spectators* (No. 246) who complained that mothers of all ranks were delegating to wet nurses the task of breast-feeding their own children. He referred to the "general Argument, that a Mother is weakened by giving suck to her Children" and observed that it was a common excuse for hiring a wet nurse. "For if a Woman does but know that her Husband can spare about three or six Shillings a Week extraordinary ... she certainly, with the Assistance of her Gossips, will soon perswade the good Man to send the Child to Nurse, and easily impose upon him, by pretending Indisposition" (2: 457–8). Steele's description conjures up a picture of wet-nursing as a widespread service in England, available to those with even a small surplus. For that segment of the population with an extra three shillings a week or more – a proportion of the population one might call the middle class – breast-feeding moved, in the course of the century, from being paid labor to being unpaid reproductive labor. That is, if there is truth in Steele's description, then women's bodily services were commodified and purchased across class lines in the early part of the eighteenth century, while in the second half of the century, those services were redefined as the unpaid labor that women owed their husbands, their families, and even the state.

By 1784, a medical treatise on childhood diseases and the "general management of infants from the birth," filled with self-congratulations to the enlightened age for "recent examples among persons of rank" of maternal nursing, observed that maternal breast-feeding had become by then a new social expectation for women. "That tyrant, Fashion," remarked the author dryly, "has prevailed over the good sense and natural feelings of many whose maternal affections can be, in no other instance, suspected" (Underwood, 173). By the 1770s and 1780s, then, breast-feeding was no longer being determined by class but by gender. "That tyrant, Fashion" had changed the way women conceived of their roles as mothers. A historian, using information in diaries, claims that 67 percent of mothers in the eighteenth century breast-fed their own infants as compared to only 43 percent in the seventeenth century, a proportion of breast-feeding mothers never equaled before or since.[27] No longer was nursing considered quite so detachable a bodily service, available for wealthier women to hire from poorer women in order to spare themselves and make their lives easier. By the end of the eighteenth century, this bodily service came to be constructed as part of all women's unpaid reproductive labor.

A comparison of Steele's discussion of breast-feeding in *The Spectator* with later discussions of the subject when it became the vogue shows how unsentimental a tone he took about motherhood and maternal nursing in the early part of the century. Females ought to nurse because it was their duty to sustain what they brought forth, as "the Earth is called the Mother of all Things, not because she produces, but because she maintains and nurses what she produces" (2: 457). Steele did not argue the naturalness of tender maternal feelings, the advantages in nursing of establishing a deep and primal bond of love between mother and child, or the peculiar suitability of women for the office of mothering; these beliefs came later. He concentrated instead on the character of the nurse and argued that mothers should not hand over their infants to "a Woman that is (ten thousand to one) neither in Health nor good Condition, neither sound in Mind nor Body, that has neither Honour nor Reputation, neither Love nor Pity for the poor Babe, but more Regard for the Money than for the whole Child" (455).

Steele's class-based objection to wet-nursing is characteristic of the earlier period: an unsuitable dependence on women of another class and a revulsion from those commonly hired to do that work – coarse country breeders or unwed mothers. With phrases that go back at least to Nicholas Culpeper's 1651 treatise on midwifery, Steele's cranky gentleman asked whether a child sent out to nurse might not "imbibe the gross Humours and Qualities of the Nurse, like a Plant in a differerent Ground, or like a Graft upon a different Stock? Do we not observe, that a Lamb sucking a Goat changes very much its Nature, nay even its Skin and Wooll into the Goat Kind?"[28] In this view, women were not all alike; their milk was not interchangeable. Class was still a more important determinant in this most intimate of matters than biological sex.[29]

Mary Astell's incidental reference to wet-nursing is another example of this class-based argument in the late seventeenth century. In her *A Serious Proposal to the Ladies* (London, 1694) she argued for maternal breast-feeding as a check on aristocratic pride rather than as a medically superior practice or an act of solidarity with working-class women. She enjoined those upper-class women to whom she always addressed herself, "how *Great* soever they are," not to "think themselves too *Good* to perform what Nature requires, nor thro' Pride and Delicacy remit the poor little one to the care of a Foster Parent. Or, if necessity enforce them to depute another to perform their Duty, they would be as choice at least in the Manners and Inclinations, as they are in the complections of their Nurses, least with their Milk they transfuse their Vices, and form in the Child such evil habits as will not easily be eradicated" (28–9). Astell's Christian asceticism, her cheerful belief in effort, and her invocation of "the natural" foreshadows later cultural attitudes about women's "duty." People should do whatever life required of them, and nursing one's own children was one of those things. Following the medical practitioners of her time, Astell understood breast milk to be a bodily fluid, like blood, that carried and transmitted one's essential nature. The class of one's wet nurse mattered, for habits, vices, manners, and inclinations might be transmitted to the child along with maternal milk.

By the middle of the eighteenth century, these ideas had changed. Mothers no longer were reproached for the class of caretakers to whom they turned over their own flesh-and-blood, but for mistakenly preferring their own independence of movement, social life, looks, or figures to the duties – and the joys – of motherhood. When William Cadogan published *An Essay upon Nursing, and the Management of Children, From Their Birth to Three Years of Age* in 1748, it was not to attack wet-nursing on the grounds of class difference. The vanity he attacked in mothers who hired wet nurses was not the vanity of class but the vanity of sexual attractiveness. He urged every woman to "prevail upon herself to give up a little of the Beauty of her Breast to feed her Offspring." From the start, his language revealed that this maternal practice was defined in opposition to female sexual vanity and was expected to contain it. The tradeoff for "beauty" was a pleasanter domestic situation to offer one's husband, a bourgeois vision of a happier home life. He pictured to men the pleasures of having their children at home rather than sent away to nurse and appealed to them to encourage rather than forbid this practice. "The Child, was it nurs'd in this way, would be always quiet, in good Humour, ever playing, laughing or sleeping. In my Opinion, a Man of Sense cannot have a prettier Rattle (for Rattles he must have of one kind or other) than such a young Child" (24). Arguing for middle-class domestic values as a substitute for decadent aristocratic pursuits, Cadogan implied that maternal nursing was the key to a quiet moral revolution.

Since this extremely influential treatise marks the beginning of medical preoccupation with maternal breast-feeding, it is worth analyzing in some detail. Written to instruct the governors of the London Foundling Hospital and adopted as its official medical guidelines, Cadogan's *Essay upon Nursing* went through at least eleven editions in French and English before the end of the century. As I have said, the class of wet nurses was not an issue for Cadogan; indeed, he took a sentimental liberal view of class: "That Mother who has only a few Rags to cover her Child loosely, and little more than her own Breast to feed it, sees it healthy and strong, and very soon able to shift for itself; while the puny Insect, the Heir and Hope of a rich Family lies languishing under a Load of Finery, that overpowers his Limbs, abhorring and rejecting the Dainties he is crammed with, till he dies a Victim to the mistaken Care and Tenderness of his fond Mother" (7).

What the enlightened doctor cared about in wet nurses was not class or morals but their condition as healthy animals. He recognized that there were cases in which it was necessary to engage wet nurses; there were families in which the birth mother was unable to nurse; moreover, wet nurses were needed to feed the hundreds of abandoned infants at the London Foundling Hospital. He advised selecting a woman who was between twenty and thirty years old and newly lactating, ideally having delivered herself within two or three months. As with valued livestock, her diet was to be supervised: she was to be fed a "proper Mixture of Flesh and Vegetables ... with a good deal of Garden Stuff, and Bread." She was to be prohibited from drinking wine or strong liquors (27).

"If we follow Nature," asserted Cadogan, "instead of leading or driving it, we cannot err." What he meant by nature in this context was "women's nature," whose "natural" characteristics consistently had revealed themselves to male physicians and not to "unlearned women" who blindly passed along the "Customs of their Great Grand-mothers" received in turn from "the Physicians of their unenlighten'd Days" (3). One by one he dismantled the standard arguments for wet-nursing and other common practices in raising infants. The assertion that nursing was debilitating to women "too weak to bear such a Drain, which would rob them of their own Nourishment," Cadogan disposed of with the observation that disease is caused not by "Want" but by "too great a Fulness and Redundancy of Humours." Therefore, since nursing was purgative for both mother and child (the colostrum was thought to have a laxative effect on the newborn), its good effect for both was assured. He inveighed against "Herbs, Roots, and Drugs," swaddling, "superstitious Practices and Ceremonies," and feeding an infant more frequently than two or three times in twenty-four hours (14, 17). He assured his readers that if his plan were followed, it would reduce the terrible mortality of children. "Half of the People that come into the World, go out of it again before they become the least Use to it, or themselves," he remonstrated. "Yet I cannot find, that any one Man of sense, and publick Spirit, has ever attended to it at all; notwithstanding the Maxim in every one's Mouth, that a Multitude of Inhabitants is the greatest

Strength and best Support of a Commonwealth" (6). It was about time that "men of sense" took an interest in this national problem.

Cadogan was convinced that women needed to be reeducated by medical men like himself to recognize where their real duty lay. The "plain natural Plan I have laid down, is never followed," he complained, "because most Mothers, of any Condition, either cannot, or will not undertake the troublesome Task of suckling their own Children" (23). He asserted the need for male control of the process in order to set it on its "natural" track. "It is with great Pleasure I see at last the Preservation of Children become the Care of Men of Sense," he wrote. "In my Opinion, this Business has been too long fatally left to the Management of Women who cannot be supposed to have proper knowledge to fit them for such a Task, notwithstanding they look upon it to be their own Province" (3). He recommended that every father have his child suckled under his own eye and that he "make use of his own Reason and Sense in superintending and directing the Management of it" (24). Although against dry-feeding in general, he believed that it was possible for a good physician to manage it properly but warned that it required "more Knowledge of Nature, and the animal Oeconomy, than the best Nurse was ever Mistress of." He was confident that in time his plan would "convince most Nurses, Aunts, Grand-mothers etc. how much they have hitherto been in the wrong" (5). Cadogan argued for the instruction of women by a male medical establishment for the sake of domestic quiet and family life. As a century earlier it was believed that women's unruly and insatiable sexuality needed to be governed by men, so now it was believed that women needed bodily instruction in matters of childbearing. "Nor to the dictates plain of candid Truth / Thy antient Nurse's doating saws prefer," warned Hugh Downman's *Infancy* (2: 108–9).[30]

Cultural Representations

Representations of the breast and of maternal breast-feeding in the fiction of Samuel Richardson and others corroborate the historical periodization of this phenomenon that I have presented here and the shift in cultural attitudes toward it. Richardson's *Clarissa* provides one of the most interesting examples of these changing attitudes about sexuality and maternity, as they crystallize in a scene in volume two. Published about the same time as Cadogan's *Essay upon Nursing*, this scene illustrates the cultural ambiguity about sexual and maternal definitions of women and clearly places the breast at the center of that ambiguity.

The relevant sequence begins at a moment when it appears that at last Lovelace will marry Clarissa and end his dangerous game. Lulling her – and us – into a false sense of security with respectful remarks about her family, sensible arrangements for obtaining a marriage license and drafts of the settlements, and repeated proposals of particular days for the happy event, he reclines his head upon her shoulder and begins to kiss her hands. "Rather bashfully than angrily reluctant," he writes to Belford, "her hands sought to be withdrawn; her shoulder avoiding my reclined cheek – apparently loath, and more loath, to quarrel with me." He then snatches away her handker-chief, and with "burning lips" he kisses "the most charming breast that ever my ravished eyes beheld." She struggles angrily out of his grasp, saying "*I see there is no keeping terms with you.* Base encroacher!" (2: 476).

Later in the letter Lovelace writes this paean to the breast – and the woman – he has tried to appropriate by stealth and force: "Let me perish, Belford, if I would not forego the brightest diadem in the world for the pleasure of seeing a twin Lovelace at each charming breast, drawing from it his first sustenance; the pious task, for physical reasons, continued for one month and no more!" (2: 477). The sexual breast briefly experienced earlier in the day is here transformed into the maternal breast, property of Lovelace the conqueror. His fantasy of possession is not a fantasy of erotic pleasure, but a fantasy of territorial claim. To discover Clarissa's sexual charms is to imagine colonizing them, domesticating them, rather than voluptuously enjoying them. He would rather own this one woman than be crowned with "the brightest diadem," he asserts. Moreover, this kingdom of one has the capacity to reproduce him – in duplicate – to create a society in his image and to nurture it singlehandedly, in an image of bountiful and even heroic nature.

The oddly medical addendum to this fantasy, the recommendation that the nursing mother continue "for one month and no more," calls our attention to the new prestige for professional medical expertise in these matters and to Richardson's own particular interest in questions of maternal breast-feeding. In the third edition of *Clarissa*, published three years later, he specifically reminds us of his earlier treatment of this subject with a footnote referring the reader to the debate in the sequel to *Pamela* published in 1741, *Pamela II*, "between Mr. B. and his Pamela, on the important subject of mothers being nurses to their own children" (2: 447).[31] There, Richardson had represented Mr. B. as forbidding Pamela to nurse their child, although she wanted to and argued with him. Whereas in most other things Mr. B. is enchanted by Pamela's unerring sense of honor and obligation, in this matter he disputes her judgment and insists that she follow his command rather than her own conscience – precisely because his rights in her sexual person are at stake. Richardson depicts their dispute and Pamela's capitu-lation in a series of letters Pamela writes to her parents from London, where she has come for her first lying-in. For Pamela and her parents in 1741, nursing was a moral duty – even a sentimental pleasure – but not yet a medical imperative. More significant, it was still seen as less urgent than a woman's duty to sexually serve her husband. Mr. B. argues that breast-feeding will engross Pamela's time in an office that was now beneath her and disturb her rest. He also objects to it on the grounds that it will interfere with his enjoyment of "her person" and the pleasing sight of her "personal graces." Her first responsibility is to his sexual satisfaction, and he is sure that nursing will interrupt his "honest pleasure" and ruin her figure. Women were not supposed to engage in sexual relations when they were nursing a baby, for it was believed it would spoil the milk – curdle it and make it sour. Physiologically, sexuality and maternity were understood to be mutually exclusive if a woman was nursing – which must account in part for the widespread use of nurses in families that could afford them.

The argument between Mr. B. and Pamela about maternal breast-feeding in the last volume of *Pamela II* is only the most prominent in a series of transactions whose effect is to separate Pamela's maternal self from her sexual self, that is, to redefine her as an ardent mother and not as Mr. B.'s sexual object. Once Pamela surrendered her long-defended chastity in legitimate marriage, Richardson had to recast the narrative conflict in the last volume as a dramatic opposition between sexuality and maternity. The emotional business of the last volume is precisely to detach motherhood from sexual desire and to reorient Mr. B.'s love accordingly. From the entertainments to which Pamela is introduced when she enters London society for the first time, to Mr. B.'s jealous competition with his infant son for Pamela's attention, to the stabilizing of their monogamous marriage through Pamela's renunciatory turn from sexual wife to chaste mother in her psychological duel with the Countess Dowager of —, the incidents of this last volume all work to clarify for us the emotions of a mother and to distinguish them from the emotions of a wife or sexual partner.[32]

The antithetical relation between nursing and sex as it was understood undoubtedly had some basis in the mild contraceptive properties of lactation, which were relatively well known.[33] It is simply less possible for a woman to conceive when she is nursing. Whether or not this commonly held opposition found both in the medical literature and in old wives' tales constituted a cultural taboo against the sexual activity of a nursing mother is a matter of dispute.[34] But Mr. B.'s refusal to share his wife's bodily services with an infant is probably typical of his historical location and his class and was an attitude that had long existed in English culture. Husbands' desire to resume sexual relations with their wives led to minimizing the maternal role – and to the general use of wet nurses. As William Gouge wrote in 1622, "Husbands for the most part are the cause that their wives nurse not their owne children,"[35] and both Linda Pollock and Valerie Fildes confirm this attitude into the early eighteenth century (1983: 50; *Wet Nursing*, 84). Even as late as 1792 Mary Wollstonecraft remarked in *A Vindication of the Rights of Women*, that there were "husbands so devoid of sense and parental affection, that during the first effervescence of voluptuous fondness they refuse to let their wives suckle their children" (*Works* 5: 142). Here Wollstonecraft emphasized the appropriation of women's sexual services as an earlier social formation than the maternal practices of her contemporary society.

The medical discourse on breast-feeding in the second half of the eighteenth century did not dwell on the biological mechanisms that made it inadvisable to nurse while engaging in sexual activity – but the opposition continued to be implied in the accusation that women were sacrificing their children to the decadent pleasures of the social whirl. It was also argued that careless wet nurses, who pretended to but did not actually abstain from sexual relations while engaged to nurse another's newborn, could ruin their milk supply and endanger their charges if they became pregnant again (Hugh Smith, 730). Even eighteenth-century medical men who explicitly denied the necessity for continence while nursing recommended waiting several hours after intercourse before nursing and encouraged general sexual moderation.[36]

The cross-cultural evidence that mothers in some societies practice sexual abstinence while nursing suggests a possible psychological or emotional basis for the strain between these two deployments of the body.[37] Feeding a newborn on demand, giving oneself over to the rhythms of the child, can be exhausting and leaves little energy for sexual play. Moreover, the erotic symbiosis between infant and mother can be so absorbing as to leave the mother uninterested in other libidinous contact. William Buchan hints at this erotic satisfaction in *Advice to Mothers* (1769): "The thrilling sensations, as before observed, that accompany the act of giving suck, can be conceived only by those who have felt them, while the mental raptures of a fond mother at such moments are far beyond the powers of description or fancy" (210). Finally, the combination of total power and selfless responsibility experienced in caring for an utterly dependent infant may be at odds with the helpless hungers of sexual desire as we know it.

The ambiguity about the function and definition of the breast as maternal or (hetero)sexual seems pivotal to me here. The locus of many a modern woman's role strain during the first year of her child's life, the breast seems to have represented for eighteenth-century women the mutually exclusive nature of motherhood and sexual desire.[38] In our own culture, the breast is defined as the quintessence of female sexuality, symbolic in its externality of both the pornographic and erogenous possibilities of female flesh. From *Playboy* bunnies to silicon implants, the culture invests the breast with great power as a sexual stimulus. For women in twentieth-century America, breasts often emblematize their femininity and their success or failure as sex objects and hence as women.[39] In eighteenth-century England, a woman who used her breasts to nurse her children literally suspended other erotic bodily practices until the child was weaned. Psychologically as well as physically, motherhood canceled a woman's (hetero)sexuality. Either a woman sent away her children to nurse (if she could afford to) and resumed her earlier social and sexual identity, or she gave herself over to the business of mothering.

Lovelace's fantasy of a domesticated Clarissa (together with Richardson's footnote to his treatment of these issues in *Pamela II*) locates this cultural ambivalence toward breasts in the middle of the eighteenth century and connects it to the new interest in maternity. The medical addendum – "for physical reasons, continued for one month and no more" – indicates how scientized these arguments had become in the years since Mr. B. worried that breast-feeding would alter Pamela's "genteel form." As if to complete the sequence of ideological conversion, Richardson wrote a third time about maternal breast-feeding in his last novel, *Sir Charles Grandison* (1753), in a manner that suggests that medical opinion about the benefits of breast-feeding for both infant and mother had by that time prevailed. Indeed, Richardson's successive treatments of maternal breast-feeding can be read as stages in an advancing belief system whose tenets included the following: that women's essential nature was to be mothers; that men's rights in women's bodies extended to their reproductive functions and, indeed, that men's ascendancy over women was based on women's "natural propensity" for motherhood; that maternal feeling was antithetic to sexual desire; and that men's heterosexual desire was an immature expression of the ultimate desire to procreate and to "have" a family. From Mr. B. who does not want his wife's reproductive labors to interfere with her sexual services, to Lovelace who fantasizes his ultimate conquest of Clarissa not as raping her but as making a mother of her, to Charlotte Grandison, Sir Charles's witty and irrepressible sister, newly softened and "feminized" by motherhood, Richardson's characters reflect the growing preoccupation with women as reproducers.

In *Sir Charles Grandison*, Charlotte Grandison is tamed by motherhood, and the scene in which she nurses her "little marmoset" celebrates her triumphal entry into true womanhood with her delighted spouse's approval and relief. This time there is no demur, whether about the optimal duration of nursing or any husbandly objection to a woman's decision to take on that office herself. The lively Charlotte Grandison is brought into line by childbearing, made to see her true nature, calmed, and fulfilled: "matronized" is Richardson's word. When she nurses her newborn infant for the first time, her husband throws himself at her feet in raptures and insists on watching, providing dramatic evidence for Hugh Smith's specular argument in *Letters to Married Women* (1767) that "though a beautiful virgin must ever kindle emotions in a man of sensibility; a chaste, and tender wife, with a little one at her breast, is certainly, to her husband, the most exquisitely enchanting object on earth."[40] In Richardson's last novel, breast-feeding brings the lively woman to heel, not the authority of her husband. Perfect Pamela may think her moral duty lies in nursing her own child, but her parents advise her that her sexual services to her husband come first, and her wifely obedience is proved by hiring a wet nurse. But by the time of *Sir Charles Grandison*, a woman's wifely obedience was guaranteed by her reproductive services, her willingness to undertake the lowly task of nursing her own child.

As fiction began to valorize maternal feeling, women's physiological needs increasingly were seen as focused in the desire for a child, and other sexual urges were interpreted as perverse. Jane Austen's *Lady Susan* records the incompatibility of these two modalities, the sexual and the maternal, insofar as its heroine is of the earlier sexual sort, caught in the moral context of the later period. A throwback to those earlier creations of Behn or Haywood, Lady Susan is as confidently sexy and verbally brilliant as a Restoration heroine. But she is out of place in the moralized and domesticated world of late eighteenth-century fiction.[41] Her incongruence in this world is detected by her insufficiently maternal behavior toward her daughter Frederika.

Other novels as well were part of the discourse that desexualized the female breast and redefined women's physiological nature for domestic life. A scene in Clara Reeve's *The Two Mentors* (London, 1783) reinscribes the husbandly adoration of maternal breast-feeding foreshadowed in *Sir Charles Grandison* and promised by a number of medical treatises and conduct manuals. Framed as a narrative about a young lord who secretly marries and impregnates a penniless gentlewoman of whom his parents disapprove, the interpolated tale tells of their interrupted flight when the young wife goes into labor. Although the best that can be done for them is done, the young woman dies tragically, soon after giving birth to a daughter. The next day Bennet, the narrator, seeking his own wife all over the house in which these events have transpired, finds her in the nursery. In his own words: "I found her – oh divine benevolence! emanation of the Divinity! first of the Christian virtues! – I found her giving her own breast to the poor little orphan child, while the tears rolled down her cheeks in compassion for it. I kneeled involuntarily to her as to a superior being. – Oh Maria! my angel wife! This action is worthy of thee, and few besides thee would have performed it." The divine Maria then asks his forgiveness for performing this office without first asking his permission, for her reproductive services are his to command. To this he replies: "Excuse you! my love . . . I adore you for it."

He then informs the new father of this turn of events, which makes possible another sentimental scene: "Tears and blessings spoke his gratitude for it" (175–6). Three times the worshipful husband bows down before his domestic madonna: when he first finds her in the nursery, when she asks his permission to continue nursing the orphan, and when he tells the bereaved husband about the angelic wet nurse of his new child. This is Mrs. Bennet's moment of glory, a moment emphasized by the text, a moment very much belonging to its particular historical context – when practices commodified earlier as services performed for wages by working-class women are remunerated ideologically (with adoration) when performed voluntarily by middle-class women.

The movement to promote breast-feeding in the latter part of the eighteenth century has always been understood as the sane light of reason penetrating the dark corners of superstitious compulsion. Randolph Trumbach has argued that breast-feeding and maternal care lowered the aristocratic death rate in the second half of the eighteenth century, and that it was "one of the finest fruits of the Enlightenment" (1978: 191). What I have been trying to suggest is that this movement involved an unprecedented cultural use of women and the appropriation of their bodies for procreation. A discourse including sentimental fiction and medical treatises functioned as a new way to colonize the female body and to designate within women's experience a new arena of male expertise, control, and instruction.

Resistance

There is at least literary evidence that the English craze for breast-feeding in the last half of the eighteenth-century, which had men kneeling to their wives, was a matter of some ambivalence to women. Maria Edgeworth's *Belinda* thematizes anxiety about the breast and its functions in a powerful narrative of loneliness and fear. Lady Delacour, an intelligent woman driven by love of admiration to extravagance and affectation, tells her history to Belinda. Like Austen's Lady Susan, she is impudent and entertaining as a character from the Restoration stage. But though all gaiety on the outside, she fears she is dying of breast cancer, the culmination of the mess she has made of domestic life. A failed mother, her first child was born dead "because I would not be kept prisoner half a year." A second starved to death at her breast: "It was the fashion in that time for fine mothers to suckle their own children. . . . There was a prodigious point made about the matter; a vast deal of sentiment and sympathy, and compliments and enquiries. But after the novelty was over, I became heartily sick of the business; and at the end of three months my poor child was sick too – I don't much like to think of it – it died."[42] Her husband, estranged by her notorious conduct, kills a man in a duel defending her honor, and the victim's grieving mother haunts her dreams. Finally, as a result of a blow on the breast during a transvestite adventure with a dueling pistol, she so injures herself that when her remaining daughter embraces her, she screams with pain and pushes her away. Thus, in stubbornly clinging to her sexual self – and refusing the responsibilities of domestic life – she does real damage to her maternal organ.

Behind a locked dressing room door, amidst the vials of ill-smelling medicines and rags, she confesses to Belinda her terror of breast cancer, from which she fears she is dying. Beth Kowaleski-Wallace has interpreted the meaning of her disease as guilt over her failure to nurse her child: "The injured breast . . . is the center of her excruciating hurt, the psychic wound which she suffers in connection with her inability to perform the mother's role" (1988: 250). But Lady Delacour's history could also be read as festering resentment at the colonization of her body, represented synecdochically by the breast that poisons her life. Her adventures and friendship with the cross-dressing Harriot Freke are attempts to escape women's domestic roles and retain an independent life. But her body is never her own, as its traumas register vividly; her desires pervert its natural functions, and its health is beyond her capacity to understand or maintain. When at last she confesses to her husband that the secret of her locked boudoir is not a lover but a diseased breast and permits a famous doctor to examine her, she finds that her injury is not mortal after all. When she accedes at last to the wisdom of male medical professionals, she is cured. But the irreducible horror of her fear and suffering remain – a record of her alienation from her female body and its vulnerability to male control. In its preoccupation with issues of women's power and domesticity, as they are contested on the site of the female breast, *Belinda* documents an extraordinary historical moment in the social construction of woman's nature.

The Memoirs of Miss Sidney Bidulph (1761), by Frances Sheridan, is another novel with an emblematic scene about breast disease. An unrelenting representation of miserable, obsessive, filial obedience, the novel has at its center an interpolated tale about a young woman with a diseased breast who lives in Sidney Bidulph's neighborhood. The circumstances that the sufferer first bruised this tender part of her anatomy while reaching for a book, that her ensuing illness interrupted her correspondence with her lover of choice, and that this lover was a physician whose skill might have prevented the disease are, in the context of the main plot of the novel, crucially symbolic. They constitute a subtext that simultaneously critiques the masochistically passive protagonist while it reinforces the message that women's bodies are vulnerable to male control and their health dependent on male knowledge. In contrast to Sidney Bidulph's suicidal docility and her obstinate obedience to her undeserving mother and husband, this young woman's firmness – her belief in her choice and judgment – saves her breast, saves her life, and most certainly saves her marriage.

The anecdote begins and ends with the wedding of the deserving young woman told by Sidney Bidulph in a letter to a friend. It seems that the bride's father had left a will stating that if she married without her brother's consent she could not inherit her fortune, but at the age of twenty-one she "had the power of bequeathing her fortune by will to whom she pleased." She falls in love with a young physician, against whose family her brother bears a grudge. It is at this juncture that she injures her breast, symbol of her jeopardized womanhood, torn between lover and brother. Her brother, angry at her refusal to marry a rich man, retains an inferior doctor who, after inflaming the infection for three months, prepares to amputate the breast. Our heroine, with a fortitude, independence, and foresight that Sidney Bidulph stood in great need of, summons her brother and her lover to the scene of her surgery to announce that, since she is now twenty-one and her life is in danger, she is willing her fortune to her lover. Whereupon this sagacious young man examines her breast and announces that her state is the result of medical bungling and that her wound can be cured and the breast spared without endangering her life. A second opinion is sought from an eminent Bath surgeon, who concurs with the physician-lover. In a simultaneous triumph of advanced urban medical knowledge and men's superior knowledge of women's reproductive bodies, the young woman perfectly recovers her health in five weeks' time (2: 266–81).

Once again, the breast is the locus of women's vulnerability to male control, the site of her sexual definition and dependence and of the struggle between men over her sexual uses. That her lover uses his superior science to save her breast – and thereby win her as his wife – seems only fair. Medicine and romantic love together construct the woman as sexual property in this sequence.

It is not merely coincidence that novels dealing with breast disease, written by women, appeared in roughly the same period as medical treatises advocating maternal breast-feeding and such sentimental scenes of maternal nursing as I have noted in the novels of Richardson and Reeve. All of these texts participated in the new cultural discourse constructing women's bodies as maternal rather than sexual, symbolized in reconceptualizing the function of the breast. Thus, the debate over the "natural" sexual or reproductive purposes of the female body found fictional representation in scenes focusing on the female breast, whether to revere it as a site of maternal self-sacrifice or to fear and loathe it as a site of inexplicable disease. If

Richardson's scenes involving breast-feeding in his successive novels illustrate the cultural appropriation of women's bodies for reproductive purposes, then the novels of Frances Sheridan and Maria Edgeworth dramatize women's resentment at this new colonization of their bodies. The scenes and images of breast disease in their novels may express how women felt victimized by their female bodies and by their new dependence on superior male medical knowledge of those bodies. These fictional representations are the other side of the new reverence for motherhood, record of a growing feeling among women that they no longer controlled their own bodies, no longer believed they could understand their own physiological processes, no longer believed in their shared medical and herbal knowledge, no longer expected to exercise independent judgment about how to deploy their bodies.

Science, national interest, "natural" feeling, and morality all concurred in the judgment that maternal practice was at the heart of real femininity. It became less and less acceptable for women to delegate their reproductive services to hired labor, to wet nurses. In other words, the effect of erasing class differences among women in this matter was to universalize the meanings and purposes of the female body and to reduce the degrees of freedom in interpreting women's sex roles. Gender – not class – increasingly defined a woman's duties. And the dimensions of gender were being redefined by medical treatises on motherhood and childcare, by conduct literature, and by the novel. Thus, the "invention" of childhood, the new sentimentality about motherhood, and the representation of the female breast in fiction of the later eighteenth century are all different aspects of the same cultural phenomenon: the reconfiguration of class and gender within English society and the colonization of the female body for domestic life.

NOTES

1   *L'Enfant et la vie familiale sous l'ancien régime* (Paris, 1960; English trans., New York, 1962), was followed by John Demos, *A Little Commonwealth: Family Life in a Plymouth Colony* (New York: Oxford University Press, 1970); Lawrence Stone 1977; and Randolph Trumbach 1978, who have claimed that until the eighteenth century, childhood was not recognized as a stage of life distinct and separable from the rest of life. Children rather were assumed to be – and were treated as – miniature adults. These social historians infer this cultural fact from the way children were depicted earlier in paintings, with adult rather than infantine physical proportions, from the way they were dressed, and from the cultural assumption in printed sources that they were miserable sinners like

their elders, rather than pure and plastic human material ready to be stamped with virtue, as John Locke thought, or guided tenderly toward their best innate moral natures, as Jean-Jacques Rousseau thought. There is no question that by the middle of the eighteenth century there was an emerging literature on the socialization of children, as well as a new market evolving for children's toys and books. But the interpretation of these facts is by no means clear. Many historians of childhood argue that the meaning of these cultural developments is that parents were now taking their children more seriously and were more attached to them, because child mortality rates were falling and they could afford to invest themselves emotionally, so to speak, in their children. Others argue that childhood socialization took on an unprecedented severity in this period as a result of the new belief that children were especially impressionable. I leave it to historians of childhood to argue about whether or not parents really loved their children in the Middle Ages and the Renaissance in the absence of literary evidence to the contrary. That maternal sentiments were being newly recorded in the eighteenth century is undeniable – and this obviously contributes to the gestalt sometimes interpreted by cultural historians as a new interest in children and in childhood in general. My own position on this question is that, of course, parents of earlier periods loved their children, despite the perpetual anxiety and painful loss incurred by illness and the deaths of half of the children before they were five. It seems to me probable that what appears to us as increased parental concern for children in the eighteenth century is simply an artifact of the penetration of print culture into domestic life, in the form of diaries, memoirs, conduct books, and children's literature. Linda A. Pollock, in her excellent assessment of this literature, remarks acutely that what seems like increased interest in the *abstract* nature of childhood and in the methods used to socialize children might simply be increased "expertise with writing as a form of communication" rather than "any significant transformations in the parent-child relationship" (1983: 269).

2 See Nussbaum 1989: ch. 9, esp. 205–12; also see Nussbaum 1991–2.

3 The construction of women *primarily* as caretaking mothers was suggested as early as 1978 by Randolph Trumbach in *The Rise of the Egalitarian Family*, although he interpreted this cultural shift as an advance for women. Ludmilla J. Jordanova in "Natural Facts: A Historical Perspective on Science and Sexuality," in *Nature, Culture, and Gender*, ed. Carol P. MacCormack and Marilyn Strathern (Cambridge: Cambridge University Press, 1980), 42–69, makes the enormously suggestive remark that "links between women, motherhood, the family and natural morality may help to explain the emphasis on the breast in much medical literature" (49). What follows in this paper is a gloss on this observation. Valerie A. Fildes has done the definitive work on the history of breast-feeding and wetnursing in England during this period. See her *Breasts, Bottles, and Babies: A History of Infant Feeding* (Edinburgh: University of Edinburgh, 1986) and *Wet Nursing: A History from Antiquity to the Present* (Oxford: Basil Blackwell, 1988). Susan Staves 1983 explained the enormous popularity of John Home's *Douglas*, first produced in 1756, as evidence of the new English

interest in motherhood in the middle of the eighteenth century. Three pioneer-
ing articles about this new ideological dimension to the social construction of
mid-eighteenth-century womanhood are Ruth Bloch, "American Feminine
Ideals in Transition: The Rise of the Moral Mother, 1785–1815," *Feminist Studies*
4 (June 1978): 101–26; Mitzi Myers 1986; and Beth Kowaleski-Wallace 1988.
Nancy Armstrong describes this social phenomenon similarly but values it
differently. She argues that this emerging definition of womanhood empowered
women insofar as it created a new domain over which they were granted
authority: "the use of leisure time, the ordinary care of the body, courtship
practices, the operations of desire, the forms of pleasure, gender differences,
and family relations" (1987: 26–7). That women were in turn defined and
constrained by this discourse seems to her an inevitable constitutive dimension
of this new power. For French materials on motherhood, breast-feeding, and
wet-nursing, see Elisabeth Badinter, *Mother Love: Myth and Reality of Motherhood:
Motherhood in Modern History* (New York: Macmillan, 1981); George D. Sussman,
Selling Mothers' Milk: The Wet-Nursing Business in France 1715–1914 (Urbana:
University of Illinois, 1982), and Mary Jacobus, "Incorruptible Milk: Breast-
feeding and the French Revolution," paper circulated at the Center for Literary
and Cultural Studies, Harvard University, Spring 1990.

4 "Imperialism and Motherhood," *History Workshop* 5 (Spring 1978): 9–65. Today,
in contemporary debates about abortion, spokespersons on both sides of the
issue – moral philosophers, legislators, and lawyers alike – refer unhesitatingly
to the "state's interest in life."

5 *Serious Considerations on the Salutary Design of the Act of Parliament for a Regular,
Uniform Register of the Parish-Poor* (London, 1762), 26; quoted in Taylor 1979:
294.

6 Hanway's *Midnight the Signal: In Sixteen Letters to a Lady of Quality* (London, 1779)
was a conduct book for gentlewomen, ostensibly the letters from a gentleman
to his ward, inveighing against the dangers of keeping late hours and other bad
habits of people of fashion. He also wrote a conduct book for servant women
called *Advice from a Farmer to His Daughter in a Series of Discourses, Calculated to
Promote the Welfare and True Interest of Servants*, 3 vols (London, 1770), printed
with a fascinating frontispiece that visually integrates the issues of gender roles,
trade, government, religion, and agriculture.

7 *Letters to the Guardians of the Infant Poor to Be Appointed by the Act of Last Session of
Parliament* (London, 1767), viii; quoted in Taylor 1979: 297.

8 "The Social Relations of the Sexes: Methodological Implications of Women's
History," in *Women, History, and Theory: The Essays of Joan Kelly* (Chicago:
University of Chicago, 1984), 1–19.

9 Contemporary feminist theorists explain the fact that the "sexual" and the
"maternal" are constituted as mutually exclusive categories as an effect of
women's exclusive care of children. See Susan Weisskopf Contratto, "Maternal
Sexuality and Asexual Motherhood," in *Women: Sex and Sexuality*, ed. Catharine
R. Stimpson and Ethel Spector Person (Chicago: University of Chicago Press,
1980), 225–40. In accounting for the complex interactions between parenting

and sexuality and how they affect the power relations between men and women, Ann Ferguson posits a system for the production and socialization of children that she calls sex/affective production, analogous to the economic production of material goods. Ann Ferguson, "On Conceiving Motherhood and Sexuality: A Feminist Approach," in *Mothering*, ed. Joyce Trebilcot (Totowa, NJ: Rowman & Allenheld, 1983), 153–82, and *Blood at the Root: Motherhood, Sexuality, and Male Dominance* (London: Pandora, 1989).

10   See Watt 1957: 161–73; Spencer 1986: esp. chs 2 and 4; and Rosalind Ballaster, "Seductive Forms: Women's Amatory Fiction 1680–1740," paper presented at Warren House Feminist Colloquium, February 24, 1989, Harvard University.

11   Evelina, Sidney Bidulph, and Emmeline are the eponymous heroines of novels by Frances Burney, Frances Sheridan, and Charlotte Smith.

12   For an argument about the positive literary construction of the women interviewed in John Dunton's *The Nightwalker*, see Shawn L. Maurer's "Reforming Men: The Construction of 'Chaste Heterosexuality' in the Early English Periodical," to be published in *Historicizing Gender*, ed. Beth Fowkes Tobin. Maurer points out that while Dunton's narrator begins by wanting to reform the nightwalking women whom he systematically ferrets out and interviews, he ends by documenting the repetitive detail of male sexual aggression and exploitation and female sexual victimization in their stories.

13   For instance, Sukey Jones in Clara Reeve's *The Two Mentors* (1783) is betrayed into one sexual adventure but quickly repents and reforms; the heroine's mother in Robert Bage's *Mount Henneth* (1781) is raped by infidels. Neither participates in illicit sexual encounters of her own volition or out of sexual desire, as do the heroines of earlier texts.

14   "Prefatory Memoir to Robert Bage," in *Ballantyne's Novelist's Library*, 10 vols (London: Hurst, Robinson & Co., 1821–24), 9: xxvii.

15   J. G. Lockhart, *Life of Sir Walter Scott* (New York: Thomas Y. Crowell & Company, 1848), 390–1.

16   Laqueur, "Orgasm, Generation, and the Politics of Reproductive Biology," *Representations* 14 (Spring 1986): 1–41.

17   Sometime around 1761, a liberal clergyman named Robert Wallace noted in his text "Of Venery" that "by a false, unnecessary, & unnaturall refinement some would deny that there is any lust in modest women & virgins." He asserted that contrary to popular opinion, "every woman during certain seasons and a certain period of life is incited to lust" (Norah Smith 1978: 419–33). That Wallace's point of view was a minority opinion by 1761, which he strenuously urged against a prevailing belief in women's "passionlessness," highlights the shift in cultural attitudes toward women's sexuality. For an analysis of "passionlessness" as it was fostered by conduct literature and by evangelical religion, see Nancy F. Cott, "Passionlessness: An Interpretation of Victorian Sexual Ideology, 1790–1850," *Signs: Journal of Women in Culture and Society* 4 (Winter 1978): 219–36. I locate the transition somewhat earlier historically than Cott, but that might reflect the difference between an American and an English context.

18   See Natalie Zemon Davis, "Women on Top," in *Society and Culture in Early Modern France* (Stanford: Stanford University Press, 1975), 124–51.

19   For an exploration of this phenomenon in the American context see Ruth H. Bloch, "The Gendered Meanings of Virtue in Revolutionary America," *Signs: Journal of Women in Culture and Society* 13 (Autumn 1987): 37–58.

20   Patricia Crawford, "'The Sucking Child': Adult Attitudes to Child Care in the First Year of Life in Seventeenth-Century England," *Continuity and Change* 1 (1986): 26–51, 30, 42; Fildes 1986: 117–18.

21   See n. 3 above. Ann Ferguson's concept of a sex/affective production system is useful here. She argues that one needs to understand the social mechanisms for the production of "key human needs – sexuality, nurturance, children – whose satisfaction is just as basic to the functioning of human society as is the satisfaction of the material needs of hunger and physical security." Using this concept, one might describe the changes in families and social relations in eighteenth-century English society as changes in women's role in the sex/affective production system – changes in the arrangements society made for the satisfaction of sexual needs, needs for nurturance, and the care and socialization of children. See Ferguson, *Blood at the Root*, 83.

22   Sylvia Harcstark Myers (1990) corrects this misapprehension definitively, documenting the achievements of bluestockings as intellectuals and writers.

23   A partial list of the treatises consulted follows: Nicholas Culpeper, *A Directory for Midwives: or, a Guide for Women, in Their Conception, Bearing, and Suckling Their Children* (London, 1651); John Maubray, *The Female Physician, Containing All the Diseases Incident to That Sex, in Virgins, Wives, and Widows* (London, 1724); William Cadogan, *An Essay upon Nursing, and the Management of Children, from Their Birth to Three Years of Age* (London, 1748); John Theobald, *A Young Wife's Guide, in the Management of Her Children* (London, 1764); Hugh Smith, *Letters to Married Women* (London, 1767); George Armstrong, *An Essay on the Diseases Most Fatal to Infants, including Rules to Be Observed in the Nursing of Children, with a Particular View to Those Who Are Brought Up by Hand* (London, 1767); William Buchan, *Advice to Mothers, on the Subject of Their Own Health, and on the Means of Promoting the Health, Strength, and Beauty, of Their Offspring* (London, 1769); William Moss, *An Essay on the Management, Nursing, and Diseases of Children, from the Birth: And on the Treatment and Diseases of Pregnant and Lying-in Women* (London, 1781); Michael Underwood, *A Treatise on the Diseases of Children, Part the Second: Containing Familiar Directions Adapted to the Nursery and the General Management of Infants from the Birth* (London, 1784).

24   For a fuller discussion of this practice among the upper classes, see also 106, 288–92. Trumbach also discusses this phenomenon (1978: 197–208).

25   Fildes, *Wet Nursing*, 79. For a contemporary satire on the aristocratic practice of bringing up a child "by hand" see Richard Steele, "On the Birth of an Heir," *The Tatler*, no. 15 (May 12, 1709).

26   *A Treatise of the Acute Diseases of Infants*, trans. J. Martyn (London, 1689), 18–19, quoted in Beth Kowaleski-Wallace, "Monster or Mother?: Eighteenth-Century Medical Discourse on Maternal Breast Feeding," paper presented at the meeting

of the American Society for Eighteenth-Century Studies, Cincinnati, April 1987. The satiric author of an early eighteenth-century medical treatise blames both the fashionable mother and the mercenary, neglectful wet nurse in the scene he imagines in the wet nurse's cottage, when the mother has been notified that her child is ill. "Down comes Madam the mother, furbulo'd, with an erect rump (crying and bellowing) and running about half mad, like a cow stung with a gad flie, and with her maid laden with pots, glasses, venice treacle, Goody Kent's powder, goat-stone, black-cherry-water, etc. And after her, easie, her husband with a coach and four, with, perhaps, a brace of doctors, or some famous child's apothecary, etc." (E. Baynard, *The History of Cold Bathing: Both Ancient and Modern, Part II* [London, 1706], 149–50, quoted in Fildes, *Wet Nursing*, 93). The cowlike attributes of this mother are meant to suggest that she ought to be nursing her own child.

27 Pollock 1983: 215. According to Susan Contratto, as recently as 1980 in the United States "fewer than 25 percent of all newborns [were] nursed, even for the five days of the usual hospital stay" (236).

28 These phrases are repeated in the 1724 treatise written by the man-midwife John Maubray (n. 23 above), 329.

29 No one save the Countess of Lincoln in the seventeenth century seemed aware of the other implication of a class-based system of wet nursing: that the child of the wet nurse might starve. "Bee not accessary to that disorder of causing *a poorer woman to banish her owne infant*, for the entertaining of *a richer womans child*," she wrote (original emphasis) (Elizabeth Clinton, Countess of Lincoln, *The Countesse of Lincolnes Nurserie* [Oxford, 1622], 19, quoted in Crawford 1990: 24. Later in the eighteenth century, this concern can also be found in Michael Underwood's treatise. In urging women to try nursing their own children before looking for a wet nurse to undertake that office, he refers to "the sacrifice that poor women make in going out to suckle other people's children, the sad consequences of which are often severely felt by their own" (174).

30 In 1781 William Moss (n. 23 above) warned against preferring the wisdom of wet nurses to the advice of physicians: "It is an opinion, very generally adopted, that the care and direction of women and children upon these occasions is most properly submitted to the management of nurses; who, from their constant practice and experience are supposed sufficiently qualified to direct it; and that it is a province in which they ought not be controlled. These arguments, which have originated in ignorance and superstition, are supported upon no other or better ground than prejudice; as daily experience proves their fallacy" (11).

31 I am grateful to Florian Stuber for calling this footnote to my attention.

32 The literary anatomizing of these two conflicting roles begins with the plays Pamela sees, the first she has ever attended: a tragedy (Ambrose Philips' *The Distressed Mother*) and a comedy (Richard Steele's *The Tender Husband; or, The Accomplished Fools*). Both plays dramatize potential dangers to matrimonial fidelity, a foreshadowing of Mr. B.'s flirtation with the Countess Dowager of ———. In *The Distressed Mother*, an adaptation of Racine's *Andromaque*, Androm-

ache must choose between saving her son by marrying Pyrrhus – thus betraying her fidelity to her dead husband, Hector – or preserving that wifely vow and sacrificing her son. The play demonstrates emblematically the double bind involved in being a wife and a mother and foreshadows the dilemma in store for Pamela. In its symbolization and its action, the narrative of this volume accentuates, explores, unsettles, but eventually ratifies Pamela's transition from being an eighteenth-century Cinderella heroine to being a model bourgeois mother and wife.

33 Dorothy McLaren, "Nature's Contraceptive: Wet Nursing and Prolonged Lactation: The Case of Chesham, Buckinghamshire 1578–1601," *Medical History* 23 (1979): 426–41; Fildes 1986: 107–8.

34 Fildes argues that by the seventeenth and eighteenth centuries, the belief that nursing mothers should abstain from sex, which goes back at least as far as Galen, was very much attenuated (1986: 104–5, 121). Linda Pollock, on the other hand, argues that "it was believed that women who were feeding should abstain from sex, on the grounds that intercourse curdled the milk, and that if the mother became pregnant her milk supply would dry up" (1987: 53–5).

35 *Of Domesticall Duties* (London, 1622), quoted in Fildes, *Wet Nursing*, 84.

36 See, for example, treatises by John Maubray (1724) and John Theobald (1764).

37 Gabrielle Palmer, *The Politics of Breastfeeding* (London: Pandora, 1988), 92–103.

38 On the role strain between maternal nursing and sexual play, see Palmer, 28–31, 92–103. For another statement of the centrality of breasts to eighteenth-century definitions of women's sexual nature, see Julia Epstein 1989: 77–9.

39 Daphna Ayalah and Isaac J. Weinstock, *Breasts: Women Speak about Their Breasts and Their Lives* (New York: Summit, 1979).

40 *Sir Charles Grandison*, 7 vols (London, 1753–4), 7: 209–13; Smith, 77.

41 For a discussion of whether *Lady Susan* was written in the 1790s or between 1800 and 1805, see B. C. Southam, *Jane Austen's Literary Manuscripts* (London: Oxford University Press, 1964), 136–48.

42 *Belinda* (London, 1801; rpt London: Pandora, 1986), 33.

18

Unparodying and Forgery: The Augustan Chatterton

Claude Rawson

Thomas Chatterton (1752–70) is famous for inventing the fifteenth-century poet Thomas Rowley, writing the latter's poems, passing them off as authentic articles, and doing all this before he died at 17. He fooled some of the people most of the time, but judges competent in the history of English language and prosody refused to be taken in, though not always as quickly as one might have expected. The enterprise was a perverse variant of the "medievalism" which produced Percy's *Reliques* (1765), as well as part of the curious mid-century flowering of pre-Romantic "forgery" whose other famous example was Macpherson's Ossian. Samuel Johnson, who rejected both, said "For Ossian there is a national pride ... for Chatterton there is nothing but the resolution to say again what has once been said," though Chatterton's Bristolian *campanilismo* can be seen as a scaled down version of Ossianic nationalism, and Chatterton wrote some Ossianic imitations of his own.

Chatterton also wrote poems in modern English from the age of 11, and by the time of his death at 17 had produced an oeuvre that fills nearly 700 pages of the big Oxford edition (1971). The modern poems, some of them highly accomplished, were in a variety of recognized eighteenth-century styles, not in the least Romantic. But it was Chatterton's "medieval" creations which captured the imagination, and their exposure as fraudulent fostered the scenario of a tender Romantic genius stifled by the hard-faced men of an eighteenth-century cultural rearguard. Chatterton's writings, including his famous sonnet to Horace Walpole, first published in Dix's *Life* (1837), contributed to the later evolution of this mythology, though their own more limited point was concerned with poverty oppressed by the arrogance of power:

> Had I the Gifts of Wealth and Lux'ry shar'd
> Not poor and Mean – Walpole! thou hadst not dared
> Thus to insult, But I shall live and Stand
> By Rowley's side – when Thou art dead and damned.

When Chatterton died at 17 of arsenical poisoning in his London attic, he became the prototype of that favorite Romantic figure, the poet slain by the critics, whose high exemplar was Keats, "snuff'd out," in Byron's jeering phrase, "by an article." Shelley placed Chatterton, "pale, his solemn agony . . . not/ Yet faded from him," first in the celestial welcoming party for the martyred Keats in *Adonais*. Henry Wallis's painting of the dead Chatterton (1856), for which George Meredith sat (or rather lay), perpetuates the tragic scene at the Tate Gallery to this day.

Long before this the paradox had established itself that it was Chatterton's "Rowleian" supporters who argued that he couldn't possibly have had the talent to write those medieval masterpieces, so that recognition of this genius actually depended on the exposure of the forgery. When Chatterton himself spoke out for wounded poets against reviewers, he did so not in accents of Romantic defiance or self-pity, but in an Augustanizing idiom crudely derived from Pope and Churchill ("Let busy Kendrick vent his little Spleen / And spit his Venom in a Magazine"), like the Byron of *English Bards*.

None of this impeded the myth of a Chatterton martyred by Augustan persecutors, promoted by nearly all Romantic poets except Byron. It is seldom noticed that even Wordsworth's "marvellous Boy" (the phrase itself an unwitting reprise of the ambivalent or contemptuous sarcasms about "that marvellous young man," "that marvellous creature," by Chatterton's arch-enemy Horace Walpole), the most memorable evocation of Chatterton as exemplar of the tragic fate of poets, is hardly a simple case:

> I thought of Chatterton, the marvellous Boy,
> The sleepless Soul that perished in his pride;
> . . . .
> We Poets in our youth begin in gladness;
> But thereof come in the end despondency and madness.

Wordsworth's *Resolution and Independence*, in which these lines appear, is known to have close links with Chatterton's late poem, the "Excelente Balade of Charitie." Its stanza (rhyme royal with a final alexandrine, as in Milton's *Nativity Ode*) was formally the same, and like Chatterton's poem it is a fable describing an encounter with a destitute old man. Its official moral contains more than a hint that the mythology of "mighty Poets in their misery dead," including Wordsworth's own investment in it in some of the poem's most memorable passages, is mere self-indulgence when compared with the misfortunes of the old leech gatherer.

The explicit tendency is thus more conventional than the lines on Chatterton might lead us to expect, and the point of real interest is that it is actually closer to Chatterton's poem by that fact. The "Excelente Balade," perhaps the last of the Rowley poems, is a Good Samaritan parable about a pauper who gets no charity from a rich abbot but is given a groat of silver and an under-cloak by a humbler priest. It's not obviously a statement about neglected genius, but may have been written close to the time of Chatterton's death and is sometimes read, as his editor Donald S. Taylor says, "as a pre-suicide statement." Taylor believes it to be somewhat earlier, and Chatterton's "suicide" is a part of the legend which has itself been questioned.

A persistent counter-scenario, promoted by several scholars and lately reactivated in Peter Ackroyd's novel *Chatterton*, has Chatterton dying of an accidental overdose of anti-venereal medication, at a period when his post-Rowleian literary career was undergoing a successful launch (exceptional for a boy of 17), and when, to judge by his letters, he seems to have been in a mood quite remote from despondency and madness. However Wordsworth read the "Balade," he is hardly likely to have designed *Resolution and Independence* as a put-down of Chatterton. He said in a letter that it describes how the leech gatherer rescued him "from my dejection and despair almost as an interposition of Providence," and Chatterton's biographer Meyerstein, with his usual preening positiveness, says the "burden" of the two poems "is the same." But in Wordsworth the broken old man is the rescuer, not the rescuee, and an inability on Wordsworth's part to register this difference would have been an extraordinary illustration of the self-absorption actually targeted in the poem itself.

The most immediately arresting thing about Chatterton's work is in fact his power and fluency in modern English and in "Augustan" literary modes. His first two poems, written in 1764, when he was 11, are in flat hard Hudibrastics with a take-it-or-leave-it sarcasm which is aggressively and extraordinarily adult. They are derivative, in part, from Swift and from Gay's *Fables*, but their brassy force has a timbre of its own. In "Apostate Will," about a Vicar of Bray character,

> He'd oft profess an hallow'd flame,
> And every where preach'd Wesley's name;
> He was a preacher and what not,
> As long as money could be got;
> He'd oft profess with holy fire,
> The labourer's worthy of his hire,

the amalgam of sanctimonious cant and slangy harshness invites comparison with the invective of Swift's later poems or with Fielding's angrier fictions.

The other poem, "unfinished" in a Swiftian way (". . . *Caetera desunt*") is "Sly Dick":

> Sharp was the Frost, the Wind was high
> And sparkling Stars bedeckt the Sky
> Sly Dick in arts of cunning skill'd,
> Whose Rapine all his pockets fill'd,
> Had laid him down to take his rest
> And soothe with sleep his anxious breast.
> 'Twas thus a dark infernal sprite
> A native of the blackest Night,
> Portending mischief to devise
> Upon Sly Dick he cast his Eyes,
> Then strait descends th'infernal sprite,
> And in his Chamber does alight:
> In visions he before him stands . . .

The dark infernal sprite, less a Gothick figure than a sharply efficient, mock-portentious property from the satiric "visions" of eighteenth-century satire (a general influence of Gay's *Fables* on Chatterton is well recognized), proposes to Sly Dick a piece of thievery which Meyerstein believes to be a schoolboy exploit by a fellow pupil at Colston school. If so, it belongs with that schoolboy world which many writers, from the Fielding of *Jonathan Wild* to W. H. Auden and Christopher Isherwood, have identified with the gangster virtues of adult criminality as well as of epic heroes.

Meyerstein, a fervent devotee of the Rowley poems, speaks of "that conversational style which he always managed with a glib gusto," but even if that's all it was, it's not in the mode with which he is normally identified: among "conversational" styles, it is that of Butler or Swift rather than Coleridge or Keats. Chatterton went on to write many poems in modern English, some in Popeian couplets which, like Byron, he managed less successfully than the low-key metres he learned from Swift and Gay.

This Augustanism extends to his "medieval" imitations. The first of these, the "Bristowe Tragedie" (1768), is more remarkable for the garrulity and repetitiousness of its narrative (which it shares with many of the "authentic" ballads of the kind it mimics, so that it testifies more to his skills as a *pasticheur* than to formal indiscipline or Romantic "freedom") than for other conversational properties, but its opening stanza

> The feather'd songster Chaunticleer
> Han wounde his bugle horne,

> And told the earlie villager
> The commynge of the morne.

announces itself as self-consciously different from some classicizing alternatives of Renaissance or Augustan tradition, as Chatterton's own note
cheekily indicates: "In my humble Opinion the foregoing Verses are far
more elegant and poetical than all the Parade of Aurora's whipping away
the Night, unbarring the Gates of the East &&." But this note, ostensibly
expressing his liberation from the "imprisoning canons" of eighteenth-
century poetry, actually evokes the parody of poetic dawns in Swift's
"Description of the Morning" and in the prose of Fielding, as well as being
a satirical footnote in a widely practiced Augustan mode.

It's a mode whose legacy is more far-reaching than is sometimes realized,
especially in the literature of romantic irony and the self-conscious modernism which derives from that, and it has left its mark in other Rowley poems
too. The boastful rant about Aurora may be compared with a non-satiric
note in the same poem: "I defy Homer, Virgil, or any of their Bardships to
produce so great a Hero as Syr Chas. Bawdyn...," which, though intended
straight, also has perceptible resemblances with the species of mock-note of
which Pope's *Dunciad* offers many examples. The elaborate authenticating
footnotes to some of Chatterton's other Rowley works, especially those
purporting to correct errors or expose textual shenanigans in his invented
authors, have an air of poker-faced mystification similarly reminiscent of
Pope's *Dunciadic* commentary, of which they may be thought to be an
underisive counterpart: "I think this Line is borrow'd from a much better
one of Rowley's ... The Reason why I think Iscam guilty of the Plagiary is
that the Songe to Ella ... was wrote when Rowley was in London...."

"Ella" is also the eponymous hero of the play *Aella*, which Chatterton
and some Chattertonians regard as a dramatic masterpiece. It's based,
anachronistically for a fifteenth-century work, on *Othello*, and has been
shown, in structure and sensibility, to resemble Restoration and eighteenth-
century adaptations of Shakespeare. The manner, as the admiring Taylor
says, is that of the heroic play: "complexities of action, character, and
situation are conflated, reduced, or eliminated; individualizing character
detail is dropped; symmetries and echoing in plot, character relationships,
and scene structure are underlined or emphatically introduced." But like the
notes to the poems, which sometimes read like a scholarly commentary
composed by Squire Western, this work of Shakespearean derivation has
absorbed the spirit of Augustan parody along with the more primary forms.
It is, as Taylor says, "operatic ... even grandiose," but the yokel ranting
("Thou are [sic] a warrioure, Hurra, thatte I kenne, / And myckle famed for
thie handie dede") is less like the grandiloquence of Dryden or Lee than the

kind of thing which parodies of the heroic play, from the *Rehearsal* to Fielding's *Tragedy of Tragedies*, perceived in the originals.

Chatterton might be said to be unparodying these parodies, in an unwitting upward reformulation of a kind to which eighteenth-century writing, especially addicted to parodic forms, had a predisposition not always adequately recognized. Better writers did it with greater control and clairvoyance, as when Pope's *Dunciad* breaks through the parody-barrier into its own stratosphere of primary heroic grandeur, whose epic stature, though disfigured, remains oddly undiminished; or when Sterne's *Tristram Shandy*, a more or less exact contemporary of Chatterton's, ostentatiously outfaced the parody of self-cherishing modernism in Swift's *Tale of a Tub* and created a generic self-mockery which wilfully escalates the Romantic egomania Swift was exposing in the first place.

Chatterton's activity is less self-aware. And his idea, at the end of a Hudibrastic satire of 1769, of switching to "a Shandeyan Stile," amounts to asking "your favor and your Smile," unpacking parody in the direction of sentimental geniality rather than of incremental convolutions of ironic self-regard. The enterprise of authenticating the Rowleian forgery entailed a parallel simplification, a non-derisive version of Augustan hoaxes of the Bickerstaff kind as well as of better-known and more transparent ironic impersonations. It is also comparable in its way to the epistolary novel's "editorial" *donnée*, which can be seen as an unparodying of the mock-editorial routines of the *Tale* or *Dunciad* (novels-in-letters were fictive "editions"); or to the editorial special effect of a post-Shandean novel like Mackenzie's *Man of Feeling*, where the device of an incomplete or mutilated manuscript is offered as something patently other than mockery of the habits of editors of ancient texts, and where even Shandean self-parody is peeled away, leaving a residue of fond unmirthful pathos.

It is here if anywhere that the shadowy presence of a "pre-Romantic" Chatterton is to be detected. And it's another of the contradictions of the Romantic myth that if Chatterton is to be considered a poet of talent (as the logic of undeceived admirers of the Rowley poems demanded), the talent not only showed itself in work outside the domain of the inspired medievalizing pasticheur whom Romantic poets admired as a precursor in the break with eighteenth-century forms, but may be seen as that of a pervasively Augustanized sensibility in the Rowley poems themselves. In this he resembles Smart, whose reputation as a visionary poet has often obstructed a proper perception of Augustan loyalism, strongly embodied in many lyric, georgic or satirical poems, but also actively proclaimed in unlikely places, including the declaration in *Jubilate Agno*, "*For I bless the Lord Jesus for the memory of GAY, POPE, and SWIFT.*" That the *Jubilate* has moments of eruptive comedy, part of the poem's strange power whether they were offered as comic or not, strengthens the resemblance, though Smart's "Let Nebai rejoice with the Wild Cucumber . . . Let Jaalah rejoice with Moly wild garlick" has a disconcerting *exalté* humor more energetic and vivid than Chatterton's often unfocused or ambivalent jests.

We are not always sure, in Chatterton, when a potential for mirth derives mainly from the gaucheness of the writing, and when it's the product of an awareness of the jokey potential of the whole enterprise of large-scale linguistic and imaginative counterfeiting. Chatterton was certianly capable of mildly libertine jokerie, as in

> There was a Broder of Orderys Blacke
> In mynster of Brystowe Cittie
> Hee layd a Damoisell onne her Backe
> So guess yee the Taile of mie Dittie,

whose street-ballad urbanity and thrust might, for all its Rowleian fancy dress, have passed Rochester's test for the "mannerly obscene," a style evidently envisaged by Rochester as more "mannerly" than Rochester's own. Chatterton fancied himself as a bit of a lad, though his bawdy, such as it is, displays the coy attenuation of Restoration raffishness which began over half a century earlier and was to culminate in the anodyne naughtiness of Tom Moore's *Poetical Works of Thomas Little* (1801), which had the power to shock Coleridge and Byron. In this stanza from a minstrel duet in *Aella*, a dialogue perhaps derived from Dryden's version of the 27th *Idyll* of Theocritus,

> I've hearde erste mie grandame saie,
> Yonge damoyselles schulde ne bee,
> In the swotie moonthe of Maie,
> Wythe yonge menne bie the grene wode tree,

we are on the way to the winking subShandean libertinage of *Under Milk Wood*. It's preferable to the callow sexual bravado Chatterton displayed in his own name, and perhaps one of the virtues of the Rowleian idiom is that it may have protected him from some unprocessed expressions of adolescent silliness.

Much attention, notably in the heavily annotated *Poems*, 1782, and in anti-Rowleian writings by Malone and Warton, is given to parallels with Dryden, Rowe, Pope and others (as well as some earlier writers, chiefly Shakespeare). These are often weak in specific resemblance, and tend not so much to establish a close textual similarity or to indicate plagiarism (i.e. from "later" writers than Rowley) as to identify the pervasiveness of linguistic usages and poetic conventions unavailable at the presumed time of writing.

The *Battle of Hastynges*, as a stanzaic epic, is laced with reminders of Pope's Homer, in later Romantic eyes an especially culpable repository of bad poetic habits. The reminders include extended similes, and also some gory special effects, frequently concerned, for example, with eyes extinguished by death or gouged out by weapons. Such items were not invented by Pope, but Chatterton was hardly likely to get them direct from Homer. The line "Before his Optics daunced a shade of nyghte," for example, has a Popeian ring, and the word "optics," as Thomas Warton pointed out, was post-Rowleian (it is used by Pope, but not in his Homer). But none of the parallels adduced in 1782 is verbally very close, the closest being from Pope's *Iliad*, 5.575, "His eyeballs darken with the shades of death." In another example,

> And from their Sockets started out his Eyes,
> And from his Mouth came out his blameless Tonge,

all the parallels cited have eyes falling out, but the detail is commonplace and specific resemblances are not close.

These special effects were routines of Homeric cruelty which Pope was usually disposed to "soften." Chatterton went to Pope mainly as an epic model, not because he shared any Popeian agenda for sanitizing ancient barbarities: it is he who added the Hitchcockian macabre humor of the extruded tongue. The adjective "blameless" (Warton says the usage is Popeian, though Pope doesn't actually use it with "tongue") is a heaving piece of sentimental overkill, and also borders on comedy. This isn't likely to be by design, but it would be rash to discount an active element of schoolboy glee, a callow exuberance in violent narrative which offers another illustration of Auden's insight into the link between what Chatterton's antagonist Walpole called (in another connection) the "mimic republic" of schoolboys, and the gangster virtues of epic and saga. Grotesque scenes of mutilation come up with a cascading frequency, a relentless flatfooted automatism, suggestive of an adolescent gusto not wholly unamused at its own power or innocent of playing to a gallery of absent schoolmates:

> Into his Bowels then his Launce he thrust:
> And drew therout a steemie drierie lode,
> Quod he these Offals are for ever curst;
> Shall serve the Coughs and Rooks and Daws for Food.
> Then on the Pleine the steamie Lode he throwde,
> Smokinge with life and dyde with crymson bloude.

Smoking and steaming gore and viscera (blood "smokde in Puddels on the dustie Pleine," "The Normans Bowels steemde upon the Feeld") are almost a Chatterton trademark, though they partly derive from Pope. In at least one place,

> The Greie Goose pinyon that thereon was set,
> Eftsoones with smokynge Crimson bloude was wet,

which seems to derive from "Chevy Chace," cited in *Poems*, 1778,

> The grey goose-wing that was thereon
> In his harts bloode was wett,

we can witness Chatterton actually superimposing the "smokynge" on a "medieval" analogue or source.

A character in Ackroyd's novel exclaims that "half the poetry of the eighteenth century is probably written by him." The literal point is that Chatterton, at one stage in the fiction, is supposed to have faked his death in 1770 in a deal with a bookseller in which he would devote his time, now that his medieval cover was blown, to forging poems by his eighteenth-century predecessors and contemporaries, including Thomson, Collins, Gray, Goldsmith and Churchill. It's a way of acknowledging Chatterton's extraordinary versatility in eighteenth-century styles, not only those evoked within the antique Rowleian mode, styles which included those of non-satiric writers as well as of Swift and Gay (and Pope, often mediated through Churchill: though Chatterton's Popeian satires – the *Consuliad*, the *Whore of Babylon* – , like Byron's, are crude by comparison with his work in lighter, less grandiloquent modes). Chatterton is made to say in Ackroyd's book, "I was a very Proteus to those who read my Works." The description also includes the boasted "Skill in the Art of Personation" which made him relate, "in their own Voices," the adventures of a man "pursewed by Bailiffs . . ., a malefactor chain'd in Newgate, . . . a young ripe Girl about to be pluck'd." This makes him sound, perhaps pointedly, like a Defoe narrator.

Parody and impersonation or "forgery" are connected. They're not the same thing, as Defoe discovered to his cost when his "final solution" pamphlet, *The Shortest Way with the Dissenters*, was taken straight. A lesson which eighteenth-century writers, including Swift, Pope and Fielding, confronted with varying mixtures of anxiety, discomfiture, or unexpected satisfaction, was that works of sustained parodic irony – an idiom which had only recently become a widely practiced mode of literary discourse – ran risks of being understood literally. When that happened, the satisfaction on offer was that of the hoax, a success, usually unlooked for, in impersonation rather than in the intended parodic mode. The corresponding cost was that if most readers missed the irony, the satirical point would be lost, which may be one reason why Swift's extermination tract, *A Modest Proposal*, unlike Defoe's, was couched in terms so outlandish that only an exceptionally obtuse minority have been disposed to take it straight.

Parody is an act of interpretation rather than impersonation, and, usually through its disposition or need to signal derision, breaches impersonation by that fact. But the readiness with which the one collapses into the other brings home the fact that parody involves an exercise in imaginative sympathy which has at some point to be stopped in its tracks. Chatterton's exercises in what I have called unparodying may be part of an instinctive resistance to this process, a kind of affirmation of the impersonating process, the impulse to imaginative sympathy, which is both contained and denied in the parodic act. That such unparodying was a strong if underrecognized feature of eighteenth-century writing suggests that a degree of self-division on these issues was cultural. A period remarkable and perhaps unique in the centrality it accorded to parodic expression, in which some of the most important works of the best writers (*A Tale of a Tub, Gulliver's Travels*, the *Dunciad, Jonathan Wild*, and in their way even *Joseph Andrews* and *Tom Jones*) were wholly or mainly parodic in structure and idiom, was drawing to a close, while an unprecedented valorization of unmediated impersonating empathy, whose application to poetry was later to be crystallized in the Keatsian notion of the "chameleon" poet, had begun to establish itself in the Richardsonian novel.

To the generation of Swift and Pope, and more ambiguously to Richardson's contemporary Fielding, the idea of the "chameleon" would have evoked the unreliably and reprehensibly changeable behavior of the hypocrite, just as Proteus the god of disguises, often disreputable in older texts, was more likely to suggest the routines of the confidence man than the powers of the artist (a long time was to elapse before those two figures could be equated, as in Thomas Mann's *Confessions of Felix Krull*). Augustan protocol, towards which Chatterton had little of the disloyalty imputed to him, shrank from full impersonation, for reasons which included gentlemanly inhibitions against self-surrender, and a residue of Platonic objections against play-acting (*hypocrite*, we are often reminded, was the Greek word for actor). The lofty disdain felt for Defoe and Richardson well into Chatterton's lifetime was an expression of class-contempt in which their character as literary impersonators of disconcerting power played an acknowledged or half-acknowledged part: "the Fellow that was *pilloryed*, I have forgot his Name," said Swift of the Defoe of *The Shortest Way* (naming him in a footnote in a later printing, without removing the bit about forgetting the name). The signposted derisions of parody in effect provided, even in the most serious works, the defense against the impersonating potential which was inherent in the mode of parody itself. Perhaps the decisive merging of the two antagonistic trends occurs in *Tristram Shandy* (1759–1767), whose publication fell wholly within Chatterton's short life and stretched over half of it.

It's within this unstable two-way traffic between parody and impersonation that it is appropriate to view the Rowley forgeries. They are an extension of the eighteenth-century styles Chatterton practiced before he invented Rowley and continued after that fiction was abandoned. In this they perhaps differ from Ossian or even Walpole's *Castle of Otranto*, being more ambivalent or uncertain in circumventing parodic survivals even as they share the new predilection for stylistic fancy dress. Walpole said it was the success of Ossian rather than his own hostility that was "the ruin of Chatterton." Chatterton himself wrote Ossianic imitations, where impersonation is sometimes more overtly compromised by parody than in the Rowley poems, though with what may have been a similar uncertainty of purpose.

The fancy dress was important too. The invention of Rowley and his milieu may or may not have been conceived as a simple "forgery," but it soon acquired considerable density and imaginative commitment in the evocation of period and place analogous to those called for by the more ambitious historical novels, and especially by those extended fictional creations whose "historical" context exists semi-independently of an individual work and is typically shared by several. It has been compared with Hardy's Wessex or Faulkner's South, for example, though these imaginative worlds did not in the same way require the factual "authentication" Chatterton felt called upon to supply. He was after all claiming a specific historical existence, not just fictional likeness, for both his "ancient" texts and their *dramatis personae*. Nevertheless, like Hardy or Faulkner, he created a Bristol based on real local knowledge as well as on a considerable exercise of invention, into which the lives and doings of his authors and the events of their narratives could be seen to fit.

To that end – on a scale which resembles the historical, topographical, linguistic and grammatical support-system compiled to sustain Tolkien's fictions, more than anything in Hardy or Faulkner – he generated in a short period a large number of pseudo-historical documents, deeds, wills, accounts, heraldic notes, catalogues of antiquities, topographical and architectural drawings and notes, accounts of Bristol, its castle and its churches, with a special emphasis on his own district of Redcliff and its church of St. Mary, genealogies, historical and biographical writings concerning the city of Bristol and its mayor Canynge, Rowley's patron, letters by both men, and so on. An enterprise on this scale is likely in its nature to transcend mere "authentication," especially when it supports and is supported by a corpus of poems and plays rooted in the material and often celebrative of it.

Chatterton's local pride acts at least as strongly as the excitations of

Tolkien's fantasy in investing his fabrications with a mythologizing radiance. The prose "Discorse on Brystowe," historical notes assembled by Rowley for Canynge, includes within itself the poem "Stay curyous Traveller and pass not bye," about St. Mary Redcliff:

> this Maystrie of a human hand
> The Pride of Bristowe and the Westerne Lande.

It is perhaps the most eloquent expression of mythologizing *campanilismo* in the whole of Chatterton, his local Bristolian version of Ossianic "national-ism," with a touch of Yeatsian elation in its conferment of a heroic glow on the place and its great man:

> Well maiest thou be astound but view it well
> Go not from hence before thou see thy fill
> And learn the Builder's Vertues and his name
> Of this tall Spyre in everye Countye telle
> And with thy Tale the lazing Rychmen shame
> Showe howe the Glorious Canynge did excelle
> How hee good Man a Friend for Kynges became.

Mythologizing isn't left to the poetry, and is in fact evident in the flattest of the "documentary" texts. Even the early series of heraldic notes, "Extracts from Craishes Herauldry," so far from being confined to mere pseudo-authenticating objectives, makes sure to invent exalted ancestries for Chatterton's friends and family. The latter gets an especially ancient Norman lineage (from "Johannes Sieur de Chateau tonne"), also a not unYeatsian touch. Such things were sometimes enlivened by *diablerie*, as when, in an extended free-standing document, Chatterton concocted a distinguished ancestry of De Berghams for a Bristol pewterer called Henry Burgum, and later derided his snobbish cravings that way: another example of the volatility of Chattertonian impersonation and its openness to satirical subversion.

The verses in which Burgum is derided are prefixed to Chatterton's "Will." This document, which is superscribed "wrote bet 11 and 2 oClock Saturday in the utmost Distress of Mind," and is sometimes taken as a prelude to Chatterton's "suicide," is in fact a satirical exercise, bequeathing "all my Vigor and Fire of Youth to Mr. George Catcott being sensible he is in most want of it" and "to Mr. Burgum all my Prosody and Grammar likewise one Moiety of my Modesty, the other moiety to any young Lady who can prove without blushing that she wants that valuable Commodity." It belongs to a well-established type of mock-will, of which the "Last Will and Testament" by Auden and Louis MacNeice in *Letters from Iceland*, and an adolescent imitation of the latter by Philip Larkin and Noel Hughes (written at about the same age as Chatterton's), are modern examples. Such a mock-will had recently appeared in the *Town and Country Magazine* (in an issue, as Meyerstein points out, to which Chatterton himself contributed), by Samuel Derrick, the poet whom Johnson refused to measure against Smart on the grounds that one couldn't settle the "precedency between a louse and a flea."

The invention of the Rowleian language is a central part of the authentication project. It differs from Spenser's because of the importance of the authentication factor, but shared Spenser's impulse to evoke a glamorized older English time, was aware of Spenser as a model, and displayed similarly rudimentary linguistic expertise. Nevertheless, Chatterton took some trouble over his invented language. It consists of about 1800 words, virtually all of which can be traced to probable sources (Bailey's *Universal Etymological English Dictionary*, supplemented by other dictionaries, including two Anglo-Saxon dictionaries, and a few authors, principally Chaucer, Spenser, Shakespeare, Camden, Percy). There are a number of Gallicisms, despite Keats's idea that Chatterton purified English of such things, though Chatterton may not have known they were French, and himself insisted on the Englishness of his medieval "authors." The rest of his vocabulary, as Taylor says, was based on a notion, evidently not restricted to him, that "fifteenth-century spelling, syntax, and word forms" were essentiually "lawless," so that he could make free with the spellings and inflections of eighteenth-century English.

The archaizing follows a few crude principles. Make as many words end in *e* or (as Tyrwhitt noted) begin with *a* as possible, change *i* to *y* at will, duplicate or otherwise add consonants freely: "Whatteverre schalle be Englysch wee wylle slea . . . Eftsoones we will retourne, and wanquished bee no moere," says Hurra the Dane in *Aella*, where both foreigner and Bristolian sometimes sound like demented "medieval" prefigurations of *Guys and Dolls* ("unmanned, uneyed, exclooded aie the lyghte," "I have a mynde wynged wythe the levyn ploome"), as though old Dan Runyounne himself had been inclooded in the Rowleian roll call. Dramatic reversals of purpose, and the pathos of heroic carnage, come over thus:

Seconde Dane

Yette I wylle synglie dare the bloddie fraie.
Botte ne; I'lle flie, and morther yn retrete . . .

Thyrde Dane

Enthoghtynge forr to scape the brondeynge foe . . .
Farr offe I spied a syghte of myckle woe . . .

The "Mynstrelles Songe" in *Aella*, "O! synge untoe mie roundelaie," elaborately and sometimes delicately derivative (from Shakespeare, Percy's *Reliques* and elsewhere), and possessed of some unusual accesses of metrical finesse, is seen off by the heroine with the words:

> Thys syngeyng haveth whatte coulde make ytte please;
> Butte mie uncourtlie shappe benymmes me of all ease.

One looks to Chatterton's schoolboy humor for a Larkinesque eruption on the lines of "And he yaf hym a sodynge gode kyk in the balles, causing him grete dole and lamentacions," alas in vain.

Nevertheless, it has at its best a claim to be taken as an artificial language, serviceable to the creation of its poetic world. Even as an exercise in learned authentication, it wasn't bad for its time, and studious efforts had to be activated to detect the fraud. An extraordinary amount of scholarship was devoted to Chatterton soon after his death, including, as Malone said, "a magnificent and accurate edition of his works," which even Shakespeare lacked. The forgery debate called for linguistic analysis of Chatterton's English, enormously in excess of the hard work Chatterton himself put into the business. Learned men like George Steevens and Thomas Tyrwhitt were stopped in their tracks, not initially certain of themselves as they embarked on heavy labors of refutation.

There is no doubt that the plan was to make money and reputation for Chatterton from the publication of ancient texts and the supply of information to William Barrett, the barber-surgeon historian of Bristol, who was largely taken in, and for the antiquarian and art-historical researches of Horace Walpole, who, after a brief hesitation, was not. But it is evident that the whole enterprise became charged with imaginative as well as imaginary elements in a way that suggests that the borders between forgery and fiction are not always clearly distinct, as Chatterton himself self-consciously noted, when, with insecure logic, he threw back at Walpole the example of his own *Castle of Otranto* in the angry poem he wrote (but did not send) in response to Walpole's rejection of his forgeries:

> Walpole! I thought not I should ever see
> So mean a Heart as thine has proved to be;
> Thou, who in Luxury nurs'd behold'st with Scorn
> The Boy, who Friendless, Penniless, Forlorn,
> Asks thy high Favour, – thou mayst call me Cheat –
> Say, didst thou ne'er indulge in such Deceit?
> Who wrote Otranto?

You might say that in Chatterton's own case the distinction between faking and fiction was not only unclear but artificial: he was quite clearly doing both. Hence everyone on all sides of the authenticity question regarded the genuineness of the material as marginal to a recognition of his abilities. Johnson, an early non-believer, said, "it is wonderful how the whelp has written such things," and Walpole himself reported, "he was a colossal genius, and might have soared I know not whither." In a sense, the forgery proved the genius of the fiction, since if the material had been genuine Chatterton's achievement would merely have been that of a lucky antiquarian find. For some of Chatterton's Romantic admirers indeed, the genius of the fiction made the fake true by fiat. Blake said, "I believe both Macpherson & Chatterton, that what they say is ancient is so ... I own myself an admirer of Ossian equally with any other poet Rowley & Chatterton also." A character in Ackroyd's novel says that he's the "greatest forger ... the greatest plagiarist in history," to be told by the hero that he's "the greatest poet in history." Chatterton himself is imagined as saying "the truest Plagiarism is the truest Poetry," and George Meredith, who modelled as Chatterton for Wallis's famous portrait, as asking the painter whether "the greatest realism is also the greatest fakery."

The example of Ossian and his forger Macpherson, also an object of devotion long after the exposure of the fraud (which took place shortly before the Chatterton affair, and the two cases are variously related) suggests the existence of cultural factors which may help to place Romantic conceptions of Chatterton's genius in a more sober perspective. Johnson's comments, and even Walpole's, suggest remarkable accomplishment for a youth in Chatterton's circumstances, perhaps in the spirit of Johnson's famous quip about women preachers: one was surprised to see it done at all. For both authors, as for the great Romantic admirers, the spuriousness of the documents hardly blocked recognition of talent, but it did not suggest the supreme imaginative gifts perceived by Coleridge or Keats. That perception was aided by a post-Rowleian mythology, of the tragic destitute youth struck down by a harsh and unfeeling establishment, which is itself one of Chatterton's imaginative achievements, most crisply expressed in the lines to Walpole. But for the fact that these were not published until 1837 in Dix's *Life*, one might say that the poem partly wrote the script of Chatterton's future reputation.

Select Bibliography

Abelove, Henry. "Some Speculations on the History of Sexual Intercourse during the Long Eighteenth Century in England." *Genders* 6 (Nov. 1989): 125–30.

Adams, Robert M. "The Mood of the Church and *A Tale of a Tub*." In *England in the Restoration and Early Eighteenth Century: Essays on Culture and Society*. Ed. H. T. Swedenberg, jnr. Berkeley: University of California Press, 1972.

Adamson, J. S. A. "The Baronial Context of the English Civil War." *Transactions of the Royal Historical Society* 40 (1990): 93–120.

Addison, Joseph. *The Spectator*. 5 vols. Ed. Donald F. Bond. Oxford: Clarendon Press, 1965.

Adorno, Theodor and Horkheimer, Max. *Dialectic of Enlightenment*. Trans. John Cummings. New York: Herder and Herder, 1972.

Alkon, Paul. "Defoe's Argument in *The Shortest Way with the Dissenters*." *Modern Philology* 73 (1976): 12–23.

Alymer, G. E. "The Meaning and Definition of 'Property' in Seventeenth-Century England." *Past and Present* 86 (1980): 87–97.

Andreasen, N. J. C. "Swift's Satire on the Occult in *A Tale of a Tub*." *Texas Studies in Literature and Language* 5 (1963–4): 410–21.

Appleby, Joyce Oldham. *Economic Thought and Ideology in Seventeenth-Century England*. Princeton: Princeton University Press, 1978.

Arendt, Hannah. *The Human Condition*. Chicago: University of Chicago Press, 1958.

Armstrong, Nancy. *Desire and Domestic Fiction: A Political History of the Novel*. New York: Oxford University Press, 1987.

Ashcraft, Richard. "The Language of Political Conflict in Restoration Literature." In *Politics as Reflected in Literature*. William Andrews Clark Memorial Library Seminar Papers. Los Angeles, 1989.

Austen, Jane. *Mansfield Park*. Ed. Tony Tanner. Harmondsworth: Penguin, 1966.

Backscheider, Paula. *Daniel Defoe: His Life*. Baltimore: Johns Hopkins University Press, 1989.

——. *Spectacular Politics: Theatrical Power and Mass Culture in Early Modern England.* Baltimore: Johns Hopkins University Press, 1993.

Ballard, George. *Memoirs of Several Ladies of Great Britain, Who Have Been Celebrated for their Writings or Skill in the Learned Languages Arts and Sciences.* Oxford, 1752.

Ballaster, Rosalind. "New Hystericism: Aphra Behn's *Oroonoko;* the Body, the Text and the Feminist Critic." In *New Feminist Discourses: Critical Essays on Theories and Texts.* Ed. Isobel Armstrong. New York: Routledge, 1992.

Barash, Carol. "Reprint Rights, Reprint Wrongs." *Women's Review of Books* (Feb. 1990).

——. *English Women's Poetry, 1649–1714: Politics, Community, and Linguistic Authority.* Oxford: Clarendon Press, 1996.

Barker, Francis. *The Tremulous Private Body: Essays in Subjection.* London: Methuen, 1984.

——. "In the Wars of Truth: Violence, True Knowledge and Power in Milton and Hobbes." In Healy and Sawday 1990: 91–109.

Barker-Benfield, G. J. *The Culture of Sensibility: Sex and Society in the Eighteenth Century.* Chicago: University of Chicago Press, 1992.

Barrett, Michèle. *Women's Oppression Today: Problems in Marxist Feminist Analysis.* London: Verso, 1980.

Barthelemy, Anthony Gerard. *Black Face, Maligned Race: The Representation of Blacks in English Drama from Shakespeare to Southerne.* Baton Rouge: Louisiana State University Press, 1987.

Bastian, Frank. *Defoe's Early Life.* London: Macmillan, 1981.

Bateson, F. W. and Joukovsky, N. A., eds. *Alexander Pope: A Critical Anthology.* Harmondsworth: Penguin, 1975.

Battestin, Martin C. *The Providence of Wit: Aspects of Form in Augustan Literature and the Arts.* Oxford: Clarendon Press, 1974.

Behn, Aphra. *Oroonoko and Other Stories.* Ed. Maureen Duffy. London: Methuen, 1986.

——. "The Epistle Dedicatory to the Right Honourable the Lord Maitland." In *Oroonoko, or The Royal Slave: A Critical Edition.* Ed. Adelaide P. Amore. Lanham, MD: University Press of America, 1987.

Bell, Maureen. "Hannah Allen and the Development of a Puritan Publishing Business, 1646–51." *Publishing History* 26 (1989): 5–66.

Benedict, Barbara. "The 'Curious Attitude' in Eighteenth-Century Britain: Observing and Owning." *Eighteenth-Century Life* 14 (1990): 59–98.

Bennett, Joan S. *Reviving Liberty: Radical Christian Humanism in Milton's Great Poems.* Cambridge, MA: Harvard University Press, 1989.

Bentley, Richard. *The Works of Richard Bentley.* Ed. Alexander Dyce. 3 vols. London, 1836–38.

Bentman, Raymond. "Thomas Gray and the Poetry of 'Hopeless Love.'" *Journal of the History of Sexuality* 3 (1992): 203–22.

Berkeley, George. *The Works of George Berkeley, D.D.* Ed. Alexander Campbell Fraser, 3 vols. Oxford: Clarendon Press, 1871.

——. *The Principles of Human Knowledge.* In *Berkeley's Philosophical Writings.* Ed. David M. Armstrong. New York: Collier, 1965.

Berman, David. *A History of Atheism in Britain.* Kent: Croom Helm, 1988.

Bernbaum, Ernest. "Mrs Behn's *Oroonoko.*" In *Anniversary Papers by Colleagues and Pupils of George Lyman Kittredge.* Boston, 1913.

Blum, Abbe. "The Author's Authority: *Areopagitica* and the Labour of Licencing." In Nyquist and Ferguson 1987: 74–96.

Bock, Gisela, Quentin Skinner, and Maurizio Viroli, eds, *Machiavelli and Republicanism.* Cambridge: Cambridge University Press, 1991.

Bogel, Fredric V. *The Dream of My Brother: An Essay on Johnson's Authority.* ELS Monograph Series, no. 47. Victoria: University of Victoria Press, 1990.

Booth, Wayne. *The Rhetoric of Fiction.* Chicago: University of Chicago Press, 1961.

Boswell, James. *The Private Papers of James Boswell from Malahide Castle.* Ed. Geoffrey Scott and Frederick A. Pottle. 18 vols. New York, 1928–34.

——. *Life of Johnson.* Ed. R. W. Chapman. Introduction by Pat Rogers. Oxford: Oxford University Press, 1980.

Boulton, James T. *The Language of Politics in the Age of Wilkes and Burke.* London: Routledge, 1963.

Boyce, Benjamin. "*The Shortest Way:* Characteristic Defoe Fiction." In *Quick Springs of Sense.* Ed. Larry Champion. Athens, GA: University of Georgia Press, 1974.

Bray, Alan. *Homosexuality in Renaissance England.* London: Gay Men's Press, 1982.

Brewer, John. *Party Ideology and Popular Politics at the Accession of George III.* Cambridge: Cambridge University Press, 1976.

——. "Commercialization and Politics." In McKendrick 1982.

Brooks, Cleanth. "The Case of Miss Arabella Fermor." In *Essential Articles for the Study of Alexander Pope.* Ed. Maynard Mack. Hamden, CT: Archon Press, 1964.

Brown, Laura. *Alexander Pope.* London: Basil Blackwell, 1985.

——. "The Romance of Empire: *Oroonoko* and the Trade in Slaves." In Nussbaum and Brown 1987.

——. *Ends of Empire: Women and Ideology in Eighteenth-Century English Literature.* Ithaca: Cornell University Press, 1993.

Browne, Alice. *The Eighteenth-Century Feminist Mind.* Brighton: Harvester, 1987.

Brownley, Martine Watson. "The Narrator in *Oroonoko.*" *Essays in Literature* 4 (1977), 174–81.

Burke, Edmund. *The Speeches of the Right Honourable Edmund Burke, in the House of Commons, and in Westminster-Hall.* London, 1816.

——. *A Philosophical Enquiry into the Origin of Our Ideas of the Sublime and Beautiful.* Ed. James T. Boulton. South Bend, IN: Notre Dame University Press, 1968.

——. *The Correspondence of Edmund Burke.* Ed. Thomas W. Copeland. 10 vols. Cambridge: Cambridge University Press, 1958–78.

——. *The Writings and Speeches of Edmund Burke.* Ed. P. J. Marshell. Oxford: Clarendon Press, 1981–.

Burke, Peter. *Popular Culture in Early Modern Europe.* New York: Harper & Row, 1978.

Burnet, Gilbert. *History of His Own Times.* Ed. Thomas Burnet. 6 vols. London, 1818.

Burnet. *Some Passages of the Life and Death of . . . John Earl of Rochester.* London, 1680.

Butler, Judith. *Gender Trouble: Feminism and the Subversion of Identity.* New York: Routledge, 1989.

——. *Bodies That Matter: on the Discursive Limits of "Sex."* New York: Routledge, 1993.

Byrd, Max. *London Transformed: Images of the City in the Eighteenth Century.* New Haven: Yale University Press, 1978.

Castle, Terry. *Masquerade and Civilization: The Carnivalesque in Eighteenth-Century English Culture and Fiction.* Stanford, CA: Stanford University Press, 1986.

Cecil, David. *The Stricken Deer: The Life of Cowper.* London: Constable, 1929.

Chatterton, Thomas. *The Complete Works of Thomas Chatterton.* Ed. Donald S. Taylor in association with Benjamin B. Hoover. 2 vols. Oxford: Clarendon Press, 1971.

Cirillo, Albert R. "Noon-Midnight and the Temporal Structure of *Paradise Lost.*" *English Literary History* 29 (1962): 210–33.

Cleland, John. *Memoirs of a Woman of Pleasure.* Ed. Peter Sabor. Oxford: Oxford University Press, 1985.

Climenson, E. J., ed. *Elizabeth Montagu, The Queen of the Blue-Stockings.* 2 vols. London: John Murray, 1906.

Cobbett, William, ed., *The Parliamentary History of England.* London, 1810.

Colie, Rosalie. "Spinoza in England." *Proceedings of the American Philosophical Society* 107.3 (1963): 183–219.

——. *"My Ecchoing Song." Andrew Marvell's Poetry of Criticism.* Princeton: Princeton University Press, 1970.

Collins, William. *The Poems of Thomas Gray, William Collins, and Oliver Goldsmith.* Ed. Roger Lonsdale. London: Longman, 1972.

Cotton, Anthony. "London Newsbooks in the Civil War: Their Political Attitudes and Sources of Information." Ph.D. thesis, Oxford, 1971.

Cowper, William. *The Poetical Works of William Cowper.* Ed. H. S. Milford. 4th edn London: Oxford University Press, 1934.

——. *The Letters and Prose Writings of William Cowper.* Ed. James King and Charles Ryskamp. 5 vols, Oxford; Clarendon Press, 1979–86.

Crabbe, George. *The Complete Poetical Works.* Ed. Norma Dalrymple-Champneys and Arthur Pollard. 3 vols. Oxford: Clarendon Press, 1988.

Crawford, Patricia. " 'The Sucking Child': Adult Attitudes to Child Care in the First Year of Life in Seventeenth-Century England." *Continuity and Change* 1 (1986): 26–51.

Cust, Richard, and Ann Hughes, eds. *Conflict in Early Stuart England: Studies in Religion and Politics 1603–1642.* London: Longman, 1989.

Defoe, Daniel. *The Shortest Way with the Dissenters.* In *Novels and Selected Writings of Daniel Defoe.* Oxford, 1927–28.

Dekker, Rudolf M. and Lotte C. Van de Pol. *The Tradition of Female Transvestism in Early Modern Europe.* New York: St. Martin's Press, 1989.

Dennis, John. *The Critical Works of John Dennis.* Ed. Edward Niles Hooker. 2 vols. Baltimore: Johns Hopkins University Press, 1939–43.

Deutsch, Helen. *Resemblance and Disgrace: Alexander Pope and the Deformation of Culture.* Cambridge, MA: Harvard University Press, 1996.

Dews, Peter, ed., *Habermas: Autonomy and Solidarity: Interviews with Jürgen Habermas.* London: Verso, 1986.

Dix, John Ross. *The Life of Thomas Chatterton* (1837). London: Routledge, 1993.

Donaldson, Ian. *The World Upside-Down: Comedy from Jonson to Fielding.* Oxford: Clarendon Press, 1970.

Doody, Margaret Anne. "Swift among the Women." *Yearbook of English Studies* 18 (1988): 68–92.

Dowling, Paul M. "*Areopagitica* and *Areopagiticus.* The Significance of the Isocratic Precedent," *Milton Studies* 21 (1985): 49–69.

Downie, J. A. "Defoe's *Shortest Way with the Dissenters.*" *Prose Studies* 9 (1986): 131–6.

Dryden, John. *The Works of John Dryden.* Ed. H. T. Swedenberg et al. University of California Press, 1956–.

——. *The Poems of John Dryden.* Ed. James Kinsley. 4 vols. Oxford: Clarendon Press, 1958.

Dubrow, Heather. "The Country-House Poem: A Study in Generic Development." *Genre* 12 (Summer 1979): 153–79.

Dugaw, Dianne. "Balladry's Female Warriors: Women, Warfare, and Disguise in the Eighteenth Century." *Eighteenth-Century Life* 9, n.s. 2. (1985): 1–20.

Dunton, John. *The Life and Errors of John Dunton,* 1705; New York: Burt Franklin, 1969.

Eachard, John. *Mr. Hobbs's State of Nature Considered.* Ed. Peter Ure Liverpool: Liverpool University Press, 1958.

Eagleton, Terry. *Walter Benjamin, or Towards a Revolutionary Criticism.* London: Verso, 1981.

Ehrenpreis, Irvin. *Swift: The Man, His Works, and the Age.* 3 vols. Cambridge, MA: Harvard University Press, 1962–83.

Eisenstein, Elizabeth L. *The Printing Revolution in Early Modern Europe.* Cambridge: Cambridge University Press, 1983.

Elias, A. C. *Swift at Moor Park: Problems in Biography and Criticism.* Philadelphia: University of Pennsylvania Press, 1982.

Engell, James. *Forming the Critical Mind: Dryden to Coleridge.* Cambridge, MA: Harvard University Press, 1989.

Enzminger, Robert L. "Michael's Options and Milton's Poetry," *English Literary Renaissance* 8 (1978): 208.

Epstein, Julia. *The Iron Pen: Frances Burney and the Politics of Women's Writing.* Madison: University of Wisconsin Press, 1989.

Epstein, William H. "Assumed Identities: Gray's Correspondence and the 'Intelligence Communities' of Eighteenth-Century Studies." *The Eighteenth Century: Theory and Interpretation* 32 (1991): 274–88.

Erskine-Hill, Howard. *The Social Milieu of Alexander Pope: Lives, Example, and the Poetic Response.* New Haven: Yale University Press, 1975.

Fabricant, Carole. *Swift's Landscape.* Baltimore and London: The Johns Hopkins University Press, 1982.

Fallon, Stephen M. "Milton's Sin and Death: The Ontology of Allegory in *Paradise Lost.*" *English Literary Renaissance* 17 (1987): 329–50.

The Feminist Companion to Literature in English: Women Writers from the Middle Ages to the Present. Ed. Virginia Blain, Patricia Clements, and Isobel Grundy. New Haven: Yale University Press, 1990.

Ferguson, Margaret W. "Juggling the Categories of Race, Class, and Gender: Aphra Behn's *Oroonoko.*" *Women's Studies* 19 (1991): 159–81.

Ferry, Anne Davidson. *Milton's Epic Voice: The Narrator in "Paradise Lost."* Cambridge: Cambridge University Press, 1963.

Fielding, Henry. *The Female Husband and Other Writings* [including *The Masquerade*]. Ed. Claude E. Jones. Liverpool: Liverpool University Press, 1960.

——. "An Essay on the Knowledge of the Characters of Men." In *Miscellanies.* Ed. Henry Knight Miller. Oxford: Clarendon Press, 1972.

Fildes, Valerie. *Breasts, Bottles, and Babies: A History of Infant Feeding.* Edinburgh: University of Edinburgh, 1986.

Filmer, Robert. *Patriarcha, or the Natural Power of Kings Asserted* (1680). Ed. Peter Laslett. Oxford: Blackwell, 1949.

Finch, Anne. *Poems of Anne Finch, Countess of Winchilsea.* Ed. Myra Reynolds. Chicago: University of Chicago Press, 1903.

——. *Miscellany Poems, on Several Occasions.* London, 1713.

Fish, Stanley. *Surprised by Sin: The Reader in Paradise Lost.* New York: St. Martin's Press, 1967.

——. "Driving from the Letter: Truth and Indeterminacy in Milton's *Areopagitica.*" In Nyquist and Ferguson 1987: 234–54.

Fleischmann, Wolfgang Bernard. *Lucretius and English Literature 1680–1740.* Paris: A. G. Nizet, 1964.

Fowler, Alastair. "Country House Poems: The Politics of a Genre." *The Seventeenth Century* 1 (1986): 1–14.

Frank, Joseph. *Hobbled Pegasus: A Descriptive Bibliography of Minor English Poetry, 1641–1660.* Albuquerque: University of New Mexico Press, 1968.

Frank, Judith. "'A Man Who Laughs Is Never Dangerous': Character and Class in Stern's *A Sentimental Journey.*" *ELH* 56 (1989): 97–124.

French, Milton J., ed. *The Life Records of John Milton.* 5 vols. New Brunswick: Rutgers University Press, 1950.

Friedli, Lynn. "'Passing Women' – A Study of Gender Boundaries in the Eighteenth Century." In *Sexual Underworlds of the Enlightenment.* Ed. G. S. Rousseau and Roy Porter. Manchester: Manchester University Press, 1987: 234–60.

Frye, Northrop. *Anatomy of Criticism.* Princeton: Princeton University Press, 1957.

Fussell, Paul. *Samuel Johnson and the Life of Writing.* New York: Harcourt Brace Jovanovich, 1971.

Gallagher, Catherine. *Nobody's Story: The Vanishing Acts of Women Writers in the Marketplace, 1670–1820.* Berkeley: University of California Press, 1994.

Gay, Peter. *The Enlightenment: An Interpretation.* Vol. 1, *The Rise of Modern Paganism.* New York: Knopf, 1966.

Goldsmith, Oliver. *Works.* Ed. Peter Cunningham. New York: G. P. Putnam's, 1908.

Goodman, Dena. "The Hume-Rousseau Affair: From Private *Querelle* to Public *Procès.*" *Eighteenth-Century Studies* 25 (Winter 1991–92): 171–201.

Gould, George. ed., *Documents Relating to the Settlement of the Church of England.* London, 1862.

Gray, Thomas. *Correspondence of Thomas Gray.* Ed. Paget Toynbee and Leonard Whibley. 3 vols. Oxford: Clarendon Press, 1935.

Greene, Richard. "Mary Leapor: A Problem of Literary History." Unpublished Ph.D. thesis. Oxford University, 1989.

Guffey, George. "Aphra Behn's *Oroonoko*: Occasion and Accomplishment." In *Two English Novelists.* Los Angeles: William Andrews Clark Memorial Library, 1975, 3–41.

Guillory, John. "Mute Inglorious Miltons: Gray, Wordsworth, and the Vernacular Canon." In *Cultural Capital: The Problem of Literary Canon Formation.* Chicago: University of Chicago Press, 1993.

Gunn, J. A. W. *Politics and the Public Interest in the Seventeenth Century.* London: Routledge and Toronto: University of Toronto Press, 1969.

Guss, Donald L. "Enlightenment as Process: Milton and Habermas." *PMLA* 106 (1991): 1156–69.

Habermas, Jürgen. *The Structural Transformation of the Public Sphere: An Inquiry into a Category of Bourgeois Society.* Trans. Thomas Burger with Frederick Lawrence. Cambridge, MA: MIT Press, 1989.

Haggerty, George E. "'The Voice of Nature' in Gray's *Elegy.*" In *Homosexuality in Renaissance and Enlightenment England: Literary Representations in Historical Context.* Ed. Claude J. Summers. New York: Haworth Press, 1992, 199–214.

——. "Amelia's Nose; or Sensibility and Its Symptoms." *The Eighteenth Century: Theory and Interpretation* 36 (1995): 139–56.

Hagstrum, Jean. "Gray's Sensibility." In *Fearful Joy: Papers from the Thomas Gray Bicentenary Conference at Carleton University.* Ed. J. Downey and B. Jones. Montreal: McGill–Queen's University Press, 1974, 6–19.

Halperin, David M. *One Hundred Years of Homosexuality and Other Essays on Greek Love.* New York: Routledge, 1990.

Halsband, Robert. *The Life of Lady Mary Wortley Montagu.* Oxford: Clarendon Press, 1956.

——. *The Rape and Its Illustrations.* Oxford: Clarendon Press, 1980.

Harrington, James. *Oceana.* In *The Political Works of James Harrington.* Ed. J. G. A. Pocock. Cambridge: Cambridge University Press, 1977.

Harth, Phillip. *Swift and Anglican Rationalism: The Religious Background of A Tale of a Tub.* Chicago: University of Chicago Press, 1961.

Hay, Douglas. "Property, Authority, and the Criminal Law." In *Albion's Fatal Tree: Crime and Society in Eighteenth-Century England.* Ed. D. Hay et al. New York: Pantheon Books, 1975.

Healy, Thomas and Sawday, Jonathan, eds. *Literature and the English Civil War.* Cambridge: Cambridge University Press, 1990.

Heffernan, James. "Ekphrasis and Representation." *New Literary History* 22 (Spring 1991): 297–316.

Heidegger, Martin. *Lettre sur l'humanisme.* Ed. and trans. Roger Munier. Paris: Aubier, 1957.

Hibbard, George R. "The Country-house Poem of the Seventeenth Century." *Journal of the Warburg and Courtauld Institutes* 19 (1956): 159–74.

Hill, Christopher. *Milton and the English Revolution.* New York: Viking, 1977.

——. "Milton and Marvell." In *Approaches to Marvell: The York Tercentenary Lectures.* Ed. C. A. Patrides. London: Routledge, 1978, 1–30.

——. *The World Turned Upside Down: Radical Ideas during the English Revolution.* New York: Viking, 1972.

Hilles, Frederick, ed. *Portraits by Sir Joshua Reynolds.* New York: McGraw Hill, 1952.

——. "*Rasselas,* an 'Uninstructive Tale'." In *Johnson, Boswell and Their Circle: Essays Presented to Laurence Fitzroy Powell.* Oxford: Clarendon, 1965, 111–21.

Hinnant, Charles H. *The Poetry of Anne Finch: An Essay in Interpretation.* Newark, DE: University of Delaware Press, 1994.

Hobbes, Thomas. *Leviathan.* Ed. Michael Oakeshott. New York: Collier, 1971.

——. *De Cive: The English Version.* Ed. Howard Warrender. Oxford: Clarendon Press, 1983.

Hogarth, William. *Hogarth's Complete Works.* Ed. J. Ireland and John Nichols. Edinburgh, 1883.

Hope, A. D. "Anne Killigrew, or The Art of Modulating." *Southern Review* 1 (1963): 4–14. Rpt. in *Dryden's Mind and Art.* Ed. Bruce King. Edinburgh: Oliver and Boyd, 1969.

Hopkins, Robert H. "The Personation of Hobbism in Swift's *Tale of a Tub* and *Mechanical Operation of the Spirit.*" *Philological Quarterly* 45 (1966): 372–8.

Howson, Gerald. *Thief-Taker General: The Rise and Fall of Jonathan Wild.* London: Hutchinson, 1970.

Hudson, Nicholas. "Three Steps to Perfection: *Rasselas* and the Philosophy of Richard Hooker." *Eighteenth-Century Life* 14 (Nov. 1990): 29–39.

Hume, David. *Dialogues Concerning Natural Religion.* Ed. Norman Kemp Smith. London: Thomas Nelson & Sons, 1947.

——. *Essays Moral, Political, and Literary.* Ed. Eugene F. Miller. Indianapolis: Liberty Classics, 1985.

——. *The Natural History of Religion.* Ed. H. E. Root. Stanford: Stanford University Press, 1957.

Hunter, William B. "The Provenance of the *Christian Doctrine.*" *Studies in English Literature* 32, no. 1 (Winter 1992): 129–42, 163–6.

Inchbald, Elizabeth. *Memoirs of Mrs. Inchbald.* Ed. James Boaden. London, 1833.

Ingrassia, Catherine. "Women Writing/Writing Women: Pope, Dulness, and 'Feminization' in the *Dunciad.*" *Eighteenth-Century Life* 14 (Nov. 1990): 40–58.

Jacob, Margaret C. *The Newtonians and the English Revolution, 1689–1720.* Ithaca: Cornell University Press, 1976.

——. *The Radical Enlightenment: Pantheists, Freemasons, and Republicans.* London: Allen & Unwin, 1986.

James, E. Anthony. *Defoe's Many Voices.* Amsterdam: Radopi N.V., 1972.

Johnson, Samuel. *The Yale Edition of the Works of Samuel Johnson.* Yale University Press, 1958–. 1: *Diaries, Prayers and Annals.* Ed. E. L. MacAdam, Jnr., with Donald and Mary Hyde. 2: *The Idler and The Adventurer.* Ed. Walter J. Bate, John M. Bullitt, and L. F. Powell. 3–5: *The Rambler*. Ed. J. Bate and Albrecht B. Strauss. 6: *Poems*. Ed. E. L. MacAdam, Jnr., with George Milne. 7–8: *Johnson on Shakespeare*. Ed. Arthur Sherbo with an introduction by Bertrand Bronson. 9: *A Journey to the Western Islands of Scotland*. Ed. Mary Lascelles. 10: *Political Writings*. Ed. Donald J. Greene. 14: *Sermons*. Ed. Jean H. Hagstrum and James Gray, 15: *A Voyage to Abyssinia*, Ed. Joel J. Gold. 16: *Rasselas and other tales*. Ed. Gwin J. Kolb.

——. *Lives of the English Poets*. Ed. George Birkbeck Hill. 3 vols. Oxford: Clarendon Press, 1905.

——. *Johnsonian Miscellanies*. Ed. George Birkbeck Hill. 1897. 2 vols. Rpt. New York: Barnes & Noble, 1967.

Jones, Jane. "New Light on the Background and Early Life of Aphra Behn." *Notes & Queries* n.s. 37 (1990): 288–93.

Kantorowicz, Ernst. *The King's Two Bodies*. Princeton: Princeton University Press, 1957.

Kargon, Robert Hugh. *Atomism in England from Hariot to Newton*. Oxford: Clarendon Press, 1966.

Keeble, N. H. *The Literary Culture of Nonconformity*. Leicester: Leicester University Press, 1987.

Kelley, Maurice and Samuel D. Atkins. "Milton's Annotations of Euripides."*Journal of English and Germanic Philology* 60 (1961): 680–7.

Kendrick, Christopher. *Milton: A Study in Ideology and Form*. New York and London: Methuen, 1986.

Kermode, Frank, and Keith Walker, eds. *Andrew Marvell*. New York: Oxford University Press, 1990.

Ketton-Cremer, R. W. *Thomas Gray: A Biography*. Cambridge: Cambridge University Press, 1955.

Killigrew, Anne. *Poems (1686) by Mrs. Anne Killigrew*. A Facsimile Reproduction with an Introduction by Richard Morten. Gainsville, FL: Scholars' Facsimile and Reprints, 1967.

——. *William Cowper: A Biography*. Durham: Duke University Press, 1986.

Kolb, Gwin. "The Structure of *Rasselas*." *PMLA* 66 (1951): 698–717.

Kolbrener, William. " 'Plainly Partial': The Liberal *Areopagitica*." *ELH* 60 (1993): 57–78.

Kowaleski-Wallace, Beth. "Home Economics: Domestic Ideology in Maria Edgeworth's *Belinda*." *The Eighteenth Century: Theory and Interpretation* 29 (1988): 242–62.

Krutch, Joseph Wood. *Samuel Johnson*. New York: Henry Holt, 1944.

Lambert, Sheila. "The Printers and the Government, 1604–1637." In *Aspects of Printing from 1600*. Ed. Robin Myers and Michael Harris. Oxford: Oxford Polytechnic Press, 1987, 1–29.

——. "Richard Montagu, Arminianism and Censorship." *Past and Present* 124 (1989): 36–68

Lamprecht, Sterling P. "The Role of Descartes in Seventeenth-Century England." *Studies in the History of Ideas* 3 (1935): 181–240.

Landa, Louis A. *Swift and the Church of Ireland*. Oxford: Clarendon Press, 1954.

——. "Pope's Belinda, The General Emporie of the World, and the Wondrous Worm." *South Atlantic Quarterly* 70 (Spring 1971): 215–35.

——. "Of Silkworms, Farthingales and the Will of God." *Studies in the Eighteenth Century*. Ed. R. F. Brissenden. Vol. 2. Toronto: University of Toronto Press, 1973, 259–77.

Landry, Donna. *The Muses of Resistance: Laboring-Class Women's Poetry in Britain, 1939–1996*. Cambridge: Cambridge University Press, 1990.

Lee, Nathaniel. *The Rival Queens, or the Death of Alexander the Great*. Ed. P. F. Vernon. Lincoln: University of Nebraska Press, 1970.

Lee, William. *Daniel Defoe*. London, 1869.

Leeson, Margaret. *Memoirs of Margaret Leeson, Written by Herself*. 3 vols. Dublin, 1797.

Lerenbaum, Miriam. "'An Irony Not Unusual': Defoe's *The Shortest Way with the Dissenters*." *Huntington Library Quarterly* 37 (1974): 227–50.

Lewalski, Barbara K. "Structure and Symbolism of Vision in Michael's Prophesy, *Paradise Lost*, Books XI–XII." *Philological Quarterly* 42 (1963): 25–35.

——. *Paradise Lost and the Rhetoric of Literary Forms*. Princeton: Princeton University Press, 1985.

——. "Forum: Milton's *Christian Doctrine*." *Studies in English Literature* 32, no. 1 (Winter 1992): 143–54.

Lindenbaum, Peter. "John Milton and the Republican Mode of Literary Production." *Yearbook of English Studies* 21 (1991): 121–36.

Lindenberger, Herbert. *Historical Drama: The Relation of Literature and Reality*. Chicago: University of Chicago Press, 1975.

Linebaugh, Peter. "The Tyburn Riot against the Surgeons." In *Albion's Fatal Tree: Crime and Society in Eighteenth-Century England*. Ed. D. Hay et al. New York: Pantheon Books, 1975.

Littledale, Harold, ed. *Poems and Extracts chosen by William Wordsworth for an album presented to Lady Mary Lowther, Christmas, 1819*. London, 1905.

Locke, John. *Two Treatises of Government: A Critical Edition*. Ed. Peter Laslett. Cambridge: Cambridge University Press, 1960.

Lodge, David. "The French Revolution and the Condition of England: Crowds and Power in the Early Victorian Novel." In *The French Revolution and British Culture*. Ed. Ceri Crossley and Ian Small. New York: Oxford University Press, 1959.

Loewenstein, David. *Milton and the Drama of History: Historical Vision, Iconoclasm and the Literary Imagination*. Cambridge: Cambridge University Press, 1990.

—— and James Grantham Turner, eds. *Politics, Poetics, and Hermeneutics in Milton's Prose*. Cambridge: Cambridge University Press, 1990.

Lonsdale, Roger, ed. *The Poems of Gray, Collins, and Goldsmith*. London: Longman (1969).

Mack, Maynard. *The Garden and the City*. Toronto: University of Toronto Press, 1969.

Madsen, William G. *From Shadowy Types to Truth: Studies in Milton's Symbolism*. New Haven: Yale University Press, 1968.

Marchand, Leslie A. *Byron: A Portrait*. Chicago: University of Chicago Press, 1970.

Marcus, Leah. *The Politics of Mirth. Jonson, Herrick, Milton, Marvell, and the Defense of Old Holiday Pastimes*. Chicago: University of Chicago Press, 1986.

Marshall, Dorothy. *Dr Johnson's London*. New York: Wiley, 1968.

Marvell, Andrew. *The Rehearsal Transpros'd*. Ed. D. I. B. Smith. Oxford: Clarendon Press, 1971.

——. *The Poems and Letters of Andrew Marvell*. Ed. H. M. Margoliouth. (Rev. by Pierre Legouis with E. E. Duncan-Jones.) 2 vols. 3rd edn Oxford: Clarendon Press, 1972.

Mason, H. A. *To Homer through Pope: An Introduction to Homer's* Iliad *and Pope's Translation*. London: Chatto & Windus, 1972.

Masson, David. *Life of Milton*. 7 vols. Cambridge and London: Macmillan, 1859–94.

Mayo, Thomas Franklin. *Epicurus in England 1650–1725*. Dallas, TX: Southwest Press, 1934.

McGovern, Barbara. *Anne Finch and her Poetry*. Athens, GA: University of Georgia Press, 1992.

McKendrick, Neil, John Brewer, and J. H. Plumb. *The Birth of a Consumer Society: The Commercialization of Eighteenth-Century England*. Bloomington: Indiana University Press, 1982.

McKeon, Michael. "Historicizing *Absalom and Achitophel*." In Nussbaum and Brown 1987: 23–40.

——. "Historicizing Patriarchy: The Emergence of Gender Difference in England, 1660–1760." *Eighteenth-Century Studies* 28 (1995): 295–322.

McLaverty, James. "The Mode of Existence of Literary Works of Art: The Case of the *Dunciad Variorum*." *Studies in Bibliography* 37 (1984): 82–105.

Meehan, Michael. *Liberty and Poetics in Eighteenth-Century England*. London: Croom Helm, 1986.

Melvin, Peter H. "Burke on Theatricality and Revolution." *Journal of the History of Ideas* 36 (1975), 447–68.

Messenger, Ann. "Publishing Without Perishing: Lady Winchilsea's *Miscellany Poems* of 1713." *Restoration* 5 (1981): 27–37.

Meyerstein, Edward Harry William. *A Life of Thomas Chatterton*. New York, Russell & Russell, 1972.

Milton, John. *The Complete Prose Works of John Milton*. Ed. Don M. Wolfe et al. 8 vols. New Haven: Yale University Press, 1953–82.

——. *John Milton: Complete Poems and Major Prose*. Ed. Merrit Y. Hughes. Indianapolis: Bobbs-Merrill, 1957.

Mintz, Samuel I. *The Hunting of Leviathan: Seventeenth-Century Reactions to the Materialism and Moral Philosophy of Thomas Hobbes*. Cambridge: Cambridge University, 1962.

Moore, John Robert. *Daniel Defoe: Citizen of the Modern World*. Chicago: Chicago University Press, 1958.

Mossner, Ernest Campbell. *Life of David Hume*. Austin: University of Texas Press, 1954.

Mullan, John. *Sentiment and Sociability: The Language of Feeling in the Eighteenth Century*. Oxford: Clarendon Press, 1988.

Murrin, Michael. *The Allegorical Epic: Essays in Its Rise and Decline*. Chicago: University of Chicago Press, 1980.

Myers, Mitzi. "Impeccable Governesses, Rational Dames, and Moral Mothers: Mary

Wollstonecraft and the Female Tradition in Georgian Children's Books." *Children's Literature* 14 (1986): 31–59.

Myers, Sylvia Harcstark. *The Bluestocking Circle: Women, Friendship, and the Life of the Mind in Eighteenth-Century England.* Oxford: Clarendon Press, 1990.

Nardo, Anna K. *Milton's Sonnets and the Ideal Community.* Lincoln, NE: University of Nebraska Press, 1979.

Nedham, Marchamont. *The Case of the Commonwealth of England, Stated.* Ed. Philip A. Knachel. Charlottesville: University of Virginia Press, 1969.

Nicolson, Marjorie Hope. "The Early Stage of Cartesianism in England." *Studies in Philosophy* 26 (1929): 348–66.

Norbrook, David. "Marvell's 'Horatian Ode' and the Politics of Genre." In Healy and Sawday 1990: 147–69.

Novak, Maximillian. "Defoe's Use of Irony." In *Irony in Defoe and Swift.* Los Angeles: William Andrews Clark Memorial Library, 1966a.

——. "Defoe's *Shortest way with the Dissenters*: Hoax, Parody, Paradox, Fiction, Irony, and Satire." *Modern Language Quarterly* 27 (1966b): 402–17.

Nussbaum, Felicity. *The Autobiographical Subject: Gender and Ideology in Eighteenth-Century England.* Baltimore: Johns Hopkins University Press, 1989.

——. "'Savage' Mothers: Narratives of Maternity in the Mid-Eighteenth Century." *Cultural Critique* (Winter 1991–92): 123–51.

—— and Brown, Laura, eds. *The New Eighteenth Century: Theory, Politics, English Literature.* New York: Methuen, 1987.

Nyquist, Mary and Ferguson, Margaret W. *Re-Membering Milton: Essays on the Texts and Traditions,* London and New York: Methuen, 1987.

O'Brien, Conor Cruise. *The Great Melody.* Chicago: University of Chicago Press, 1992.

O'Loughlin, Michael. *The Garlands of Repose: The Literary Celebration of Civic and Retired Leisure.* Chicago: University of Chicago press, 1978.

Paine, Thomas. *Rights of Man.* Ed. Henry Collins. Harmondsworth: Penguin, 1969.

Parker, William Riley. *Milton: A Biography.* 2 vols. Oxford: Oxford University Press, 1968.

Pateman, Carole. *The Sexual Contract.* Oxford: Polity, 1988.

Patterson, Annabel. *Censorship and Interpretation: The Conditions of Writing and Reading in Early Modern England.* Madison: University of Wisconsin Press, 1984.

Patterson, Lyman Ray. *Copyright in Historical Perspective.* Nashville, TN: Vanderbilt University Press, 1968.

Paulson, Ronald. *Theme and Structure in Swift's Tale of a Tub.* New Haven: Yale University Press, 1960.

——. *Satire and the Novel.* New Haven, 1967a.

——. *Fictions of Satire.* Baltimore, 1967b.

——. *Popular and Polite Art in the Age of Hogarth and Fielding.* Notre Dame, IN: University of Notre Dame Press, 1979.

——. *Representations of Revolution (1789–1820).* New Haven: Yale University Press, 1983.

Payne, Deborah C. "Pope and the War Against Coquettes; or, Feminism and *The*

Rape of the Lock Reconsidered – Yet Again." *The Eighteenth Century: Theory and Interpretation* 32 (1991): 3–24.

Pearl, Valerie. *London and the Outbreak of the Puritan Revolution: City Government and National Politics,* 1625–43. Oxford: Oxford University Press, 1961.

Pearson, Jacqueline. "Gender and narrative in the fiction of Aphra Behn" I and II. *Review of English Studies,* 42 (1991), 40–56; 179–90.

Phillips, Edward. *Theorum Poetarum, or a Compleat Collection of the Poets, Especially the Most Eminent of all Ages.* London, 1675.

Pickering, Samuel F., jnr. *John Locke and Children's Books in Eighteenth-Century England.* Knoxville: University of Tennessee, 1981.

Pinkus, Philip. "*A Tale of a Tub* and the Rosy Cross." *Journal of English and Germanic Philology* 59 (1960): 669–79.

——. *Swift's Vision of Evil.* 2 vols. Nos 3–4. Victoria, B.C.: English Literary Monograph Series, 1975.

Plumb, J. H. "Commercialisation and Society." In McKendrick 1982.

Pocock, J. G. A. *The Machiavellian Moment: Florentine Humanism and the Atlantic Republican Tradition.* Princeton, NJ: Princeton University Press, 1975.

——. *Virtue, Commerce, and History.* Cambridge: Cambridge University Press, 1985.

Pohli, Carol Virginia. "Formal and Informal Space in Dryden's Ode 'To the Pious Memory of . . . Anne Killigrew'." *Restoration* 15 (1991): 27–40.

Pollak, Ellen. *The Poetics of Sexual Myth: Gender and Ideology in the Verse of Swift and Pope.* Chicago: University of Chicago Press, 1985.

Pollock, Linda. *Forgotten Children: Parent-Child Relations from 1500 to 1900.* Cambridge: Cambridge University Press, 1983.

——. *A Lasting Relationship: Parents and Children over the Centuries.* Hanover, N.H. & London: University Press of New England, 1987.

——. "Embarking on a Rough Passage: The Experience of Pregnancy in Early-Modern Society." In *Women As Mothers in Pre-Industrial England.* Ed. Valerie Fildes. London: Routledge, 1990, 39–68.

Poovey, Mary. *The Proper Lady and the Woman Writer: Ideology as Style in the Works of Mary Wollstonecraft, Mary Shelley, and Jane Austen.* Chicago: University of Chicago Press, 1984.

Pope, Alexander. *The Prose Works of Alexander Pope.* Vol. 1. Ed. Norman Ault. Oxford: Basil Blackwell, 1936.

——. *The Twickenham Edition of the Works of Alexander Pope.* General ed. John Butt, Methuen. 1: *Pastoral Poetry and An Essay on Criticism.* Ed. E. Audra and Aubrey Williams 1961. 2: *The Rape of the Lock.* Ed. Geoffrey Tillotson, 3rd edn 1962. 3.1: *An Essay on Man.* Ed. Maynard Mack 1950. 3.2: *Epistles to Several Persons.* Ed. F. W. Bateson, 2nd edn 1961. 4: *Imitations of Horace.* Ed. John Butt, 2nd edn 1953. 5: *The Dunciad.* Ed. James R. Sutherland, 3rd edn 1963. 6: *Minor Poems.* Ed. Norman Ault 1954. 7–8: *The Iliad.* Ed. Maynard Mack 1967. 9–10: *The Odyssey.* Ed. Maynard Mack 1967. *Index.* Ed. Maynard Mack 1969.

Potter, Lois. *Secret Rites and Secret Writing: Royalist Literature, 1641–1660.* Cambridge: Cambridge University Press, 1989.

Preston, Thomas R. "The Biblical Context of Johnson's *Rasselas.*" *PMLA* 84 (1969): 274–81.

Price, Martin. *Swift's Rhetorical Art.* New Haven: Yale University Press, 1953.

Price, Richard. *Political Writings.* Ed. D. O. Thomas. Cambridge: Cambridge University Press, 1991.

Quilligan, Maureen. *Milton's Spenser: The Politics of Reading.* Ithaca: Cornell University Press, 1983.

Quinlan, Maurice J. "Swift's Use of Literalization as a Rhetorical Device." *PMLA* 82 (1967): 516–21.

Radzinowicz, Mary Ann. "'Man as Probationer of Immortality': *Paradise Lost*, XI–XII." In *Approaches to "Paradise Lost."* Ed. C. A. Patrides. Toronto: University of Toronto Press, 1968.

———. *Toward "Samson Agonistes": The Growth of Milton's Mind.* Princeton: Princeton University Press, 1978.

———. "'To Make the People Fittest to Chuse': How Milton Personified His Program for Poetry." *CEA Critic* 48, no. 8 (1986): 3–23.

Rapaport, Herman. *Milton and the Postmodern.* Lincoln: University of Nebraska Press, 1983.

Raylor, Timothy. "New Light on Milton and Hartlib." *Milton Quarterly* 27 (1993): 19–31.

Raymond, Joad, ed. *Making the News: An Anthology of the Newsbooks of Revolutionary England 1641–1660.* Moreton-in-Marsh, Gloucestershire: Windrush, 1993.

Redwood, John. *Reason, Ridicule and Religion: The Age of Enlightenment in England, 1660–1750.* Cambridge, MA: Harvard University Press, 1976.

Reedy, Gerard. *The Bible and Reason: Anglicans and Scripture in Late Seventeenth-Century England.* Philadelphia: University of Pennsylvania Press, 1985.

Ribeiro, Aileen. *The Dress Worn at Masquerades in England, 1730 to 1790, and its Relation to Fancy Dress in Portraiture.* New York: Garland, 1984.

Richardson, Samuel. *The Correspondence of Samuel Richardson.* Ed. Ann Barbauld. 6 vols. London, 1806.

———. *Clarissa; or, The History of a Young Lady* (1747–8). 4 vols. New York: Dutton, 1962.

Richetti, John. *Popular Fiction Before Richardson: Narrative Patterns 1700–1739.* Oxford: Clarendon Press, 1969.

Ridgley-Clark, David. "Landscape Painting Effects in Pope's Homer." *The Journal of Aesthetics and Art Criticism* 22 (Fall 1963).

Rochester, John Wilmot, Second Earl of. *The Letters of John Wilmot, Earl of Rochester.* Ed. Jeremy Treglown. Oxford: Clarendon Press, 1980.

———. *The Poems of John Wilmot, Earl of Rochester.* Ed. Keith Walker. Oxford: Blackwell, 1984.

Rogers, Katherine M. "Fact and Fiction in Aphra Behn's *Oroonoko.*" *Studies in the Novel* 20 (1988), 1–15.

Rogers, Pat. "Masquerades and Operas: Hogarth, Heidegger and Others." In *Literature and Popular Culture in Eighteenth Century England.* Brighton: Harvester, 1985, 40–70.

Ross, John. *Swift and Defoe.* Berkeley: University of California Press, 1941.

Rostvig, Maren-Sofie. *The Happy Man: Studies in the Metamorphoses of a Classical Ideal 1600–1700.* 2 vols. Oslo, 1954.

Rotnstein, Eric. *The Routledge History of English Poetry.* Vol. 3, *Restoration and Eighteenth-Century Poetry 1660–1780.* London: Routledge, 1981.

Rousseau, G. S. "The Pursuit of Homosexuality in the Eighteenth Century: 'Utterly Confused Category' and/or Rich Repository." *Eighteenth-Century Life* 9 (1985): 132–68.

Rudé, George. *Wilkes and Liberty: A Social Study,* 1962 [Rpt. London, 1983].

——. *The Crowd in History: A Study of Popular Disturbances in France and England 1730–1848.* London: Lawrence and Wishart, 1981.

Ryan, Alan. *Property and Political Theory.* Oxford: Clarendon Press, 1984.

Ryskamp, Charles. *William Cowper of the Inner Temple, Esq.* Cambridge: Cambridge University Press, 1959.

Saccamano, Neil. "The Consolations of Ambivalence: Habermas and the Public Sphere." *Modern Language Notes* 106 (1991): 685–98.

Sasek, Lawrence A. "The Drama of *Paradise Lost,* Books XI and XII." In *Studies in English Renaissance Literature.* Ed. Waldo F. McNair. Baton Rouge, LA: Louisiana State University, 1962, 181–96.

Schiffhorst, Gerald J. "Patience and the Education of Adam in *Paradise Lost.*" *South Atlantic Review* 49, no. 4 (1984): 55–63.

Schor, Naomi. *Reading in Detail: Aesthetics and the Feminine.* London: Methuen, 1987 (rpt. Routledge, 1989).

Schwartz, Regina. "From Shadowy Types to Shadowy Types: The Unendings of "*Paradise Lost.*" *Milton Studies* 24 (1988): 123–39.

Scott, Jonathan. *Algernon Sidney and the Restoration Crisis, 1677–1683.* Cambridge Cambridge University Press, 1992.

Scruggs, Charles. "Swift's Use of Lucretius in *A Tale of a Tub.*" *Texas Studies in Literature and Language* 15 (1973–4): 39–49.

Sedgwick, Eve Kosofsky. *Between Men: English Literature and Male Homosocial Desire.* New York: Columbia University Press, 1985.

——. *Epistemology of the Closet.* Berkeley: University of California Press, 1990.

Select Trials for Murderers, Robberies, Rapes, Sodomy, Coining, Frauds, and Other Offences at the Sessions-House in the Old Bailey. 2 vols. London, 1742.

Sells, A. L. Lytton. *Thomas Gray: His Life and Works.* London: Allen and Unwyn, 1980.

Shaftesbury, Cooper, Anthony Ashley, third Earl of. *Characteristics of Men, Manners, Opinions, Times.* Ed. John M. Robertson. Indianapolis, Bobbs-Merrill, 1964.

——. *Second Characters; or the Language of Forms.* Ed. Benjamin Rand. Cambridge: Cambridge University Press, 1914.

Shawcross, John T. "Forum: Milton's *Christian Doctrine.*" *Studies in English Literature* 32, no. 1 (Winter 1992): 155–62.

Sherman, Sandra. "Printing the Mind: The Economics of Authorship in *Areopagitica.*" *ELH* 60 (1993): 323–47.

Shugrue, Michael, ed. *Selected Poetry and Prose of Daniel Defoe*. New York: Holt, Rinehart and Winston

Sidney, Algernon. *Discourses Concerning Government*. 3rd edn, London, 1751.

Silber, C. Anderson "Nymphs and Satyrs: Poets, Readers, and Irony in Dryden's Ode to Anne Killigrew." *Studies in Eighteenth-Century Culture* 14 (1985): 193–222.

Sitter, John. *Literary Loneliness in Eighteenth-Century England*. Ithaca: Cornell University Press, 1982.

Smith, Bruce James. *Politics and Remembrance: Republican Themes in Machiavelli, Burke, and Tocqueville*. Princeton: Princeton University Press, 1985.

Smith, Nigel. "*Areopagitica*: Voicing Contexts, 1643–5." In Loewenstein and Turner 1990: 103–22.

Smith, Norah. "Sexual Mores in the Eighteenth Century: Robert Wallace's 'Of Venery.'" *Journal of the History of Ideas* 39 (July–Sept. 1978): 419–33.

Smith, Ronald Gregor. *J. G. Hamann, 1730–1788: A Study in Christian Existence, with Selections from his Writings*. London: Collins, 1960.

Smollet, Tobias. *The Adventures of Peregrine Pickle*. Ed. James L. Clifford. Rev. Paul-Gabriel Boucé. Oxford: Oxford University Press, 1983.

Spadafora, David. *The Idea of Progress in Eighteenth-Century Britain*. New Haven: Yale University Press, 1990.

Spence, Jospeh. *Letters from the Grand Tour*. Ed. Slava Klima. Montreal: McGill–Queens University Press, 1975.

Spencer, Jane. *The Rise of the Woman Novelist: From Aphra Behn to Jane Austen*. Oxford: Basil Blackwell, 1986.

Stafford, Barbara. *Body Criticism: Imaging the Unseen in Enlightenment Art and Medicine*. Cambridge, MA: MIT Press, 1991.

Starkman, Miriam. *Swift's Satire on Learning in "A Tale of a Tub."* Princeton: Princeton University Press, 1950.

Starr, G. A. "Aphra Behn and the Genealogy of the Man of Feeling." *Modern Philology* 87 (1990): 362–72.

Staves, Susan. "Douglas's Mother." In *Brandeis Essays in Literature*. Ed. John Hazel Smith. Waltham, MA: Brandeis University Press, 1983.

——. "Pope's Refinement." *The Eighteenth Century: Theory and Interpretation* 29 (1988): 145–63.

Stearns, Raymond Phineas. *The Strenuous Puritan*. Urbana, IL: University of Illinois Press, 1954.

Steele, Richard. *The Guardian*. In *British Essayists*. New York: E. Sergeant, 1810. vols. 16–18.

Stein, Arnold. "The Paradise Within and the Paradise Without." *Modern Language Quarterly 26* (1965): 586–600.

Stewart, Susan. *On Longing: Narratives of the Miniature, the Gigantic, the Souvenir, the Collection*. Baltimore: Johns Hopkins University Press, 1984.

Stone, Lawrence. *The Family, Sex and Marriage in England 1500–1800*. New York: Harper & Row, 1977.

Stopes, Charlotte Carmichael. *British Freewomen: Their Historical Privileges* 3rd edn London: Swan Sonnenschein, 1907.

Sutherland, James. *Daniel Defoe: A Critical Study.* Cambridge, MA: Harvard University Press, 1971.

Swift, Jonathan. *The Prose Works of Jonathan Swift.* Ed. Herbert Davis. 16 vols. Oxford: Blackwell, 1939–75.

——. *The Poems of Jonathan Swift.* Ed. Harold Williams. 2nd edn, 3 vols. Oxford: Clarendon Press, 1958a.

——. *A Tale of a Tub To Which is Added The Battle of the Books and the Mechanical Operation of the Spirit.* Ed. A. C. Guthkelch and D. Nichol Smith. 2nd edn Oxford: Clarendon Press, 1958b.

——. *The Complete Poems.* Ed. Pat Rogers. New Haven: Yale University Press, 1983.

Sydney, William Connor. *Social Life in England from the Restoration to the Revolution.* New York: Macmilllan, 1892.

Taylor, James Stephen. "Philanthropy and Empire: Jonas Hanway and the Infant Poor of London." *Eighteenth-Century Studies* 12 (Spring 1979): 285–305.

Teskey, Gordon. "From Allegory to Dialectic: Imagining Error in Spenser and Milton." *PMLA* 101 (1986): 9–23.

Thomas, Claudia. "Pope's Iliad and the Contemporary Context of his 'Appeals to the Ladies.'" *Eighteenth-Century Life* 14 (1990): 1–17.

Thomas, Keith. *Man and the Natural World: Changing Attitudes in England 1500–1800.* London: Allen Lane, 1983.

Thomas, Roger. "Comprehension and Indulgence." In *From Uniformity to Union.* Ed. Geoffrey Nuttall and Owen Chadwick. London, 1962, 191–253.

Thompson, E. P. "Patrician Society, Plebeian Culture." *Journal of Social History* 7 (1974): 382–405.

Thomson, James. *The Seasons.* Ed. James Sambrook. Oxford: Clarendon, 1981.

Tillotson, Geoffrey. *On the Poetry of Pope.* Oxford: Clarendon Press, 1950.

Tomarken, Edward. *Johnson, "Rasselas," and the Choice of Criticism.* Lexington: University of Kentucky, 1989.

Tracy, Clarence. *The RAPE observ'd: an edition of Alexander Pope's poem The rape of the lock, illustrated by means of numerous pictures, from contemporary sources, of the people, places, and things mentioned, with an introduction and notes by Clarence Tracy.* Toronto: University of Toronto Press, 1974.

Traugott, John. "*A Tale of a Tub.*" In *Modern Essays on Eighteenth-Century Literature.* Ed. Leopold Damrosch, jnr. New York: Oxford University Press, 1988.

Trumbach, Randolph. "London's Sodomites: Homosexual Behavior and Western Culture in the Eighteenth Century." *Journal of Social History* 2 (1977): 1–33.

——. *The Rise of the Egalitarian Family: Aristocratic Kinship and Domestic Relations in Eighteenth-Century England.* New York: Academic Press, 1978.

——. "Sodomitical Assaults, Gender Role, and Sexual Development in Eighteenth-Century London." In *The Pursuit of Sodomy: Male Homosexuality in Renaissance and Enlightenment Europe.* Ed. Kent Gerard and Gert Hekma. New York: Harrington Park Press, 1989.

Tully, James. "The Framework of Natural Rights in Locke's Analysis of Property: A Contextual Reconstruction." *Theories of Property: Aristotle to the Present.* Ed. Anthony Parel and Thomas Flanagan. Calgary, 1979.

Turner, James Grantham. "Pope's Libertine Self-Fashioning." *The Eighteenth Century: Theory and Interpretation* 29 (1988): 123–44.

Vaughan, Thomas. *The Complete Works of Thomas Vaughan.* Ed. A. E. Waite. New York: University Books, 1968.

Vesterman, William. *The Stylistic Life of Samuel Johnson.* New Brunswick: Rutgers University Press, 1977.

Vieth, David M. "Irony in Dryden's Ode to Anne Killigrew." *Studies in Philology* 62 (1965): 91–100.

von Maltzahn, Nicholas. *Milton's "History of Britain": Republican Historiography in the English Revolution.* Oxford: Clarendon Press, 1991.

Walker, Robert. *Eighteenth-Century Arguments for Immortality and Johnson's "Rasselas."* ELS Monograph Series. Victoria: University of Victoria, 1977.

Wallace, John M. *Destiny his Choice: The Loyalism of Andrew Marvell.* Cambridge: Cambridge University Press, 1968.

Walpole, Horace. *Horace Walpole's Correspondence.* Ed. W. S. Lewis et al. 48 vols. New Haven: Yale University Press, 1939–83.

Wasserman, Earl. "Johnson's *Rasselas*: Implicit Contexts." *Journal of English and Germanic Philology* 74 (1975): 1–25.

Watt, Ian. *The Rise of the Novel: Studies in Defoe, Richardson and Fielding.* Berkeley: University of California Press, 1957.

Watts, Michael. *The Dissenters.* Oxford: Clarendon Press, 1978.

Webster, Charles. *The Great Instauration: Science, Medicine and Reform 1626–1660.* London: Duckworth, 1975.

Wedgwood, C. V. *The Trial of Charles I.* London: Collins, 1964.

Weinbrot, Howard D. "*The Rape of the Lock* and the contexts of warfare." In *The Enduring Legacy: Alexander Pope tercentary essays.* Ed. G. S. Rousseau and Pat Rogers. Cambridge: Cambridge University Press, 1988.

——. *Britannia's Issue: The Rise of British Literature From Dryden to Ossian.* Cambridge: Cambridge University Press, 1993.

Westfall, Richard S. *Science and Religion in Seventeenth-Century England.* New Haven and London: Yale University Press, 1958.

Weston, "The Noble Primitive as Bourgeois Subject," *Literature and History* 10 (1984): 59–71.

Wilding, Michael, "Milton's *Areopagitica*: Liberty for the Sects," *Prose Studies* 9 (1986): 7–38.

——. *Dragon's Teeth: Literature in the English Revolution.* Oxford: Clarendon Press, 1987.

Williams, Harold, ed. *The Correspondence of Jonathan Swift.* 5 vols. Oxford: Clarendon Press, 1965.

Williams, Kathleen. *Jonathan Swift and the Age of Compromise.* Lawrence: University of Kansas Press, 1958.

Williams, Raymond. *Keywords: A Vocabulary of Culture and Society.* New York: Oxford University Press, 1983.

——. *The Country and the City.* New York: Oxford University Press, 1973.

Williamson, George "The Education of Adam." In *Milton: Modern Essays in Criticism*. Ed. Arthur E. Barker. New York: Oxford University Press, 1965.

Wilson, Harriette. *The Memoirs of Harriette Wilson Written by Herself*. 2 vols. London: The Navarre Society, 1924.

Wilson, Penelope. "Classical Poetry and the Eighteenth-Century Reader." In *Books and Their Readers in Eighteenth-Century England*. Ed. Isabel Rivers. New York: St. Martin's Press, 1982, 69–96.

Wimsatt, William K. *The Portraits of Alexander Pope*. New Haven: Yale University Press, 1965.

——. "In Praise of *Rasselas*: Four Notes (Converging)." In *Imagined Worlds: Essays on Some English Novels and Novelists in Honour of John Butt*, ed. Maynard Mack and Ian Gregor. London: Methuen, 1968.

Wittreich, Joseph Anthony. "Milton's *Areopagitica*: Its Isocratic and Ironic Contexts." *Milton Studies* 4 (1972): 101–15.

Wolfe, Don M. *Milton in the Puritan Revolution*. New York: Thomas Nelson and Sons, 1941.

Wollstonecraft, Mary. *The Works of Mary Wollstonecraft*. Ed. Janet Todd and Marilyn Butler. New York: New York University Press, 1989.

Women Writers in English 1330–1830. Ed. Susanne Woods and Elaine Brennan. Brown University Women Writers Project. Oxford University Press: 1993–.

Wood, Anthony. *Athenae Oxonienses. An Exact History of all the Writers and Bishops Who have had their Education in the most Antient and Famous University of Oxford*. 2nd edn. London, 1721.

Woolrych, Austin. "Milton and the Good Old Cause." In *Ringing the Bell Backward: The Proceedings of the First International Milton Symposium*. Ed. Ronald G. Shafer. Indiana, PA: Indiana University of Pennsylvania Press, 1982.

——. "The Date of the Digression in Milton's *History of Britain*." In *For Veronica Wedgwood These: Studies in Seventeenth-Century History*. Ed. Richard Ollard and Pamela Tudor-Craig. London: Collins, 1986.

Worden, Blair. "Literature and Censorship in Early Modern England." In *Too Mighty to Be Free Censorship and the Press In Britain and the Netherlands*. Ed. A. C. Duke and C. A. Tamse. Zutphen: De Walburg Pers, 1988, 45–62.

Wordsworth, William. "Essay, Supplementary to the Preface [of Lyrical Ballads]." In *Poems and Extracts chosen by William Wordsworth for an album presented to Lady Mary Lowther, Christmas, 1819*. London, 1905.

—— and Wordsworth, Dorothy. *The Letters of William and Dorothy Wordsworth*. Ed. G. Alan Hill. 2nd edn. 8 vols. Oxford: Oxford University Press, 1979–93.

Wycherley, William. *The Complete Plays of William Wycherley*. Ed. Gerald Weales. New York: Norton, 1966.

Yolton, John W. *Thinking Matter: Materialism in Eighteenth-Century Britain*. Minneapolis: University of Minnesota, 1983.

Zionkowski, Linda. "Gray, Marketplace, and the Masculine Poet." *Criticism* 35 (1993): 589–608.

Index

Ackroyd, Peter, 335, 341, 347
Addison, Joseph, 175, 255, 259–60
Arendt, Hannah, 17–18
Astell, Mary, 314–15
Austen, Jane, 322

Bage, Robert, 306
Ballard, George, 116
Barrett, Michele, 227–8
Baxter, Richard, 128
Behn Aphra, 198–9, 200–1, 305; "On
    Desire. A Pindarick," 200; "The
    Disappointment," 110; *The Lucky
    Chance*, 98; *Oroonoko*, 86–7, 88–101;
    The Rover, 306; "The Unfortunate
    Bride; Or, The Blind Lady a Beauty,"
    87–8
Benedict, Barbara, 174, 175
Berkeley, George, Bishop, 148, 155
Blount, Charles, 144, 146, 153
Boswell, James, 206, 208, 209
Buchan, William, 311, 320
Burke, Edmund, 278–80; *Correspondence*,
    271, 272; *A Discourse on the Love of
    Our Country*, 272; "Letters on a
    Regicide Peace," 271, 272; *Reflections
    on the Revolution in France*, 271, 272–7,
    281–5; "Some Thoughts on the
Approaching Executions," 277;
    Speeches, 276, 282, 284; *Thoughts on
    French Affairs*, 282–3

Cadogen, William, 315–17
Charles II, 17
Chatterton, Thomas, 333–5, 342–3, 345;
    Aella, 337–8, 339, 345–6; "Apostate
    Will," 335–6; *Battle of Hastynges*,
    340–1; "Bristowe Tragedie," 336–7;
    Consuliade, 341; "Discorse on
    Brystowe, 344; "The Excelente
    Balade," 335; "Extracts from
    Craishes Herauldry," 344; *Poems*, 339;
    "Sly Pick," 336; "Stay curyous
    Traveller and pass not bye," 344;
    Whore of Babylon, 341; "Will," 344
Cleland, John, 263
Coleridge, Samuel Taylor, 209–10
Cowley, Abraham, 115, 117
Cowper, William, 287, 289, 290–2,
    298–300; "The Castaway," 292;
    "Charity," 295;" "The Cock-Fighter's
    Garland," 294; "Conversation,"
    293–4; "Epitaph on a Hare," 287,
    288, 292–3; "Epitaphium Alterum,"
    287; *Letters*, 291, 294, 295, 297, 298,
    299, 300; "The Progress of Error,"

293; *Task*, 288, 292, 293, 294, 295–7, 298
Crabbe, George; *The Borough*, 219; *Silford Hall*, 219–20
Cromwell, Oliver, 17
Cudworth Ralph, 147, 148, 152
Culpeper, Cheney, 19–20

Defoe, Daniel, 106; *A Brief Explanation of a Late Pamphlet*, 136; *A Collection of Writings by the Author of the True-Born Englishman*, 137; *The Consolidator*, 126, 137; *A Dialogue Between a Dissenter and the Observator*, 136; *An Enquiry into the Occasional Conformity of Dissenters* (1698), 129–30, 133; *An Enquiry into Occasional Conformity* (1702), 130, 131, 135; *An Essay Upon Projects*, 137; *The Experiment: Or, The Shortest Way with the Dissenters Exemplified*, 137; *Hymn to the Pillory*, 137; *A Letter to Mr. Howe*, 130, 134; *Moll Flanders*, 305; *More Reformation*, 137; *More Short-Ways with the Dissenters*, 137; *Present State of the Parties in Great Britain*, 137; *Roxanna*, 305; *The Shortest Way to Peace and Union*, 137; *The Shortest Way with the Dissenters*, 126–8, 131–8, 341
Dennis, John, 182
Downman, Hugh, 309, 317
Dryden, John, 266; *Absalom and Achitophel*, 120; *An Essay of Dramatick Poesie*, 118; "Ode to Anne Killigrew," 114–23; "Preface to the *Aeneid*," 178
Dunton, John, 306

Edgeworth, Maria, 323–4, 326
Ellis, Clement, 158
Euripides, 32–3; *Electra*, 25; *Phoenissae*, 25; *The Suppliant Women*, 24–5

Fielding, Henry, 106, 107, 251, 255, 337; *Enquiry into the Causes of the Late Increase of Robbers*, 277; *The Female Husband*, 262; *The Masquerade*, 252,

260, 262; *Tom Jones*, 260–1; *Tragedy of Tragedies*, 338
Fielding, Sarah, 306
Filmer, Robert, 96–7
Finch, Anne, Countess of Winchelsea; "The Circuit of Apollo," 198–9, 200; "Fragment," 191, 193–4; "Glass," 191, 192; "The Introduction," 186; *Miscellany Poems*, 186, 188, 191, 194, 197–8, 201–2; "To the Nightingale," 191; "The Petition," 194–7; "Some occasi[o]nal Reflections," 191–3; "The Spleen," 188–91
Foucault, Michel, 28, 234–6, 252, 266, 270 n.34, 298
Freud, Sigmund, 80–1, 243

Gay, John, 228–9, 292
Gray, Thomas, 234–5, 237–8, 243–4; "Ad C. Favonium Zephyrinum," 241; *Correspondence*, 238–9, 240; "De Principiis Cogitandi," 244–6; "Elegy Written in a Country Churchyard," 233, 234; "On Lord Holland's Seat," 219; "Ode on a Distant Prospect of Eaton College," 239, 241–2; "Ode to Adversity," 241; "Sonnet [on the Death of Richard West]," 241, 242–3
Griffin, Benjamin, 255, 256–7, 266–7

Habermas, Jurgen, 14–18, 31, 32
Hall, John, 19, 20, 21
Hamann, Johann Georg, 212
Hanway, Jonas, 303–4
Harrington, James, 50–1
Harris, Walter, 313
Hartlib, Samuel, 19–20
Haywood, Eliza, 265, 305
Heidegger, John James, 253, 254
Heidegger, Martin, 15, 17
Hobbes, Thomas, 24, 144, 146, 148, 162, 163
Hogarth, William, 255, 258
Howe, John, 128, 130

Hume, David; *Dialogues Concerning Natural Religion*, 210, 215; "Of the Immortality of the Soul," 204, 210–12, 213–15; "Of Miracles," 210; *The Natural History of Religion*, 214, 215
Hunt, Leigh, 180, 182

Inchbald, Elizabeth, 256, 261, 263, 306

James II, 312
Johnson, Charles, 257
Johnson, Samuel, 116, 294; *Life of Dryden*, 178; *Life of Pope*, 170, 178; *Rambler*, 251; *Rasselas*, 204–10, 213–15

Lanyer, Aemilia, 219
Leapor, Mary; *Crumble-Hall*, 218–19, 220–31; "The Mistaken Lover," 227
Lévi-Strauss, Claude, 73–4, 82
Livy, 77
Locke, John, 97, 146
Lucretius, 144, 146, 150, 151, 161, 212

Macpherson, James, 333, 347
Marvell, Andrew, 40, 105; "Upon Appleton House," 69–74, 219; "The Garden," 72–3; "An Horatian Ode upon Cromwell's Return from Ireland," 69, 74–84;" "On Paradise Lost," 54–5
Milton, John, 15, 16, 18, 20; *Areopagitica*, 13–14, 19, 20, 22, 23–32, 44–5, 47, 48, 56; *Character of the Long Parliament*, 47; *Christian Doctrine*, 49, 51, 52; *Of Education*, 27; *Eikonoklastes*, 48; *First Defense of the English People*, 26; *History of Britain*, 47, 48, 49–50, 57; "On the New Forcers of Conscience under the Long Parliament," 46; *Paradise Lost*, 30, 40–4, 51–2, 53–4, 55–66, 275; *Paradise Regained*, 51; *The Reason of Church Government*, 48; *The Redie and Easie Way*, 42; *Second Defense*, 46; *Tetrachordon*, 32

Montagu, Mary Wortley, 257, 261
More Henry, 153–4

Nedham, Marchamont, 20, 27

Opie, Amelia, 306

Paine, Thomas, 274
Percy, Thomas, 333
Philips, Katherine, 115, 117, 196, 197, 199
Pitt, Christopher, 254, 267
Pope, Alexander, 105–6, 218; *Correspondence*, 177, 179, 182–3; *Dunciad*, 228, 275, 284, 309, 337, 338; "Epistle to Burlington," 219, 221–3, 230–1; *Essay on Criticism*, 176–7; *Iliad*, 169, 170–3, 174, 178–80, 340; "Preface to the *Iliad*," 178; *Rape of the Lock*, 169–70, 172–5, 178–83; "Receit to make an Epick Poem," 179; *Windsor Forest*, 293

Reeve, Clara, 322–3
Richardson, Samuel, 305–6, 325–6; *Clarissa*, 317–18, 321; *Pamela II*, 218–19, 321; *Sir Charles Grandison*, 321–3
Rochester, John Wilmot, Second Earl of, 105–6, 253, 339; "Allusion to Horace," 105; "From Artemiza to Chloe," 105; "By all *Loves* soft, yet mighty *Pow'rs*," 108, 109; "The Disabled Debauchee," 106, 109–10, 112–13, 237; "The Imperfect Enjoyment," 110; "On Mistress Willis," 107, 108; "A Ramble in Saint James's Parke," 106; "Signior Dildo," 106, 107, 112; "Song of a Young Lady. To her Ancient Lover," 110–11
Rousseau, Jean-Jacques, 302, 311

Savile, Henry, 112
Scott, Mary, 116

Scott, Walter, 306
Shelly, Percy Bysshe, 334
Sheridan, Francis, 324–5, 326
Singleton, Mary (Francis Brooke), 254
Smart Christopher, 338–9
Smith, Hugh, 311, 320, 322
Smollett, Tobias, 255, 263
South, Robert, 157–8
Steele, Richard, 252, 313, 314
Sterne, Laurence, 338, 343
Stevens, Wallace, 72
Swift, Jonathan, 105, 107–8, 342; *Battle of the Books*, 153; "Description of Morning," 337; *Gulliver's Travels*, 152; *Mr. Collins' Discourse*, 149; *A Modest Proposal*, 342; "Ode to the Athenian Society," 142–3, 150, 151, 155, 160, 165; *The Progress of Marriage*, 254; *Remarks Upon a Book*, 149; *A Tale of a Tub*, 143–4, 145–6, 149–65, 338;

"On the Trinity," 143; *Tritical Essay Upon the Faculties of the Mind*, 151

Thomas, Keith, 288, 289, 293
Thomson, James, 292
Toland, John, 144, 146
Topsell, Edward, 290, 291

Walpole, Horace, 238, 239–40, 253–4, 256, 333, 334, 346, 347; *Castle of Otranto*, 343
West, Richard, 238, 240, 241
Wild, Jonathan, 259
Wilson, Harriette, 257, 261
Wolseley, Sir Charles, 147–8
Woods Anthony, 116
Wollstonecraft, Mary, 304, 306, 311–12, 320
Wordsworth, William, 199–200, 334–5
Wycherley, William, 256